# SWAHILI GRAMMAR
## (INCLUDING INTONATION)

# SWAHILI GRAMMAR

## (INCLUDING INTONATION)

By

## E. O. ASHTON

Sometime Senior Lecturer in Swahili at the
School of Oriental and African Studies
University of London

LONGMAN

LONGMAN GROUP LIMITED
London
*Associated companies, branches and representatives
throughout the world*

© Longman Group Ltd
(formerly Longmans, Green and Co Ltd) 1944

*First Published 1944*
*Second Edition 1947*
*This Impression 1980*

ISBN 0 582 62701 X

Printed in Singapore by
Ban Wah Press

# ACKNOWLEDGMENTS

I AM greatly indebted to my colleague Dr. A. N. Tucker, who has unstintingly helped me to give form to the matter in this book. Without his aid and co-operation the Section on Intonation could not have been included. Also for the time and care he has given to the reading of the proofs I am most grateful.

My thanks are also due to Miss M. A. Bryan for reading through the manuscript and for many helpful suggestions and reminders, and to Mr. M. H. Barwani of the Zanzibar Education Department for most of the additional passages for reading and translation.

A set of five double-sided records has been prepared by the Linguaphone Institute, which should be invaluable to students of Swahili.

They have been recorded by Swahili speakers, under the supervision of Mrs. Ashton.

Full particulars can be obtained from the Linguaphone Institute, 207/209 Regent Street, London, W.1.

# BIBLIOGRAPHY

| | | |
|---|---|---|
| "Baraza": | Weekly Newspaper | E. A. Standard, Nairobi. |
| A. R. Barlow: | *Tentative Studies in Kikuyu Grammar and Idiom* | Edinburgh, 1911. |
| H. Binns: | *Swahili–English Dictionary* | S.P.C.K., 1925. |
| Mrs. F. Burt: | *Swahili Grammar and Vocabulary*, 2nd edition | S.P.C.K., 1917. |
| C. M. Doke: | *Bantu Linguistic Terminology* | Longmans, 1935. |
| | *A Text-book of Zulu Grammar* | Longmans, 1931. |
| F. Johnson: | *Standard English–Swahili Dictionary* | Oxford University Press, 1939. |
| | *Standard Swahili–English Dictionary* | Oxford University Press, 1939. |
| L. Krapf: | *Swahili–English Dictionary* | Trubner & Co., 1882. |
| H.T.Kayamba: | *Tulivyoona na Tulivyofanya Uingereza* | Sheldon Press, 1932. |
| A. C. Madan: | *English–Swahili Dictionary* | Oxford University Press, 1902. |
| | *Swahili–English Dictionary* | Oxford University Press, 1903. |
| "Mambo Leo": | A monthly publication | Government Press, Dar-es-salam. |
| F. Marconnes: | *A Grammar of Central Karanga* | Witwatersrand University Press 1931. |
| "Mazungumzo ya Walimu wa Unguja": | A monthly publication | U.M.C.A. Press, Zanzibar. |
| J. Mbotela: | *Uhuru wa Watumwa* | Sheldon Press, 1934. |
| C. Meinhof,trans. N.J.van Warmelo: | *Introduction to the Phonology of the Bantu Languages* | Berlin, 1932. |
| J. O'Neil: | *A Shona Grammar* | Longmans, 1935. |
| A. B. S. Ranger: | *Chinsenga Handbook* | Sheldon Press, 1928. |
| E. Steere: | *Swahili Exercises* | S.P.C.K., 1919. |
| | *Swahili Exercises* (revised by Canon Hellier) | Sheldon Press, 1933. |
| W. E. Taylor: | *African Aphorisms* | S.P.C.K., 1891. |
| A. Werner: | *Introductory Sketch of the Bantu Languages* | Kegan Paul, 1919. |
| A. & M. Werner: | *A First Swahili Book* | Sheldon Press. |
| Collections of Stories: | | |
| | *Hekaya za Abunawas* | Macmillan & Co., 1927. |
| | *Masomo ya Pili* | Sheldon Press, 1931. |
| | *Mfalme wa Nyoka* | Sheldon Press, 1930. |
| *New Testament:* | Zanzibar and Mombasa versions | B.F.B.S. |

# CONTENTS

A*                              ix

# CONTENTS

## FOLDING REFERENCE TABLE B

# PART ONE

## CHAPTER I

### EXPLANATORY

THIS book embodies the results of many years' practical experience in teaching, and seeks to put into more detailed and permanent form the linguistic principles set forth in the author's "Idea Approach to Swahili"—*S.O.A.S. Bulletin*, 1935, vol. VII, part 4. It is divided into two parts.

Part I takes the form of progressive lessons with exercises. These exercises have been compiled from everyday conversational phrases, and also include extracts from representative vernacular literature.

In Part II the student is regarded as sufficiently advanced to study each remaining topic exhaustively. Only a few exercises are given here, but vernacular literature has been much drawn upon to illustrate the correct use of grammatical forms, particularly in the case of derivative verbs and the compound tenses of the verb, which often express fine shades of meaning. Part II also includes final remarks on Part I topics, which were not needed in the early stages of learning the language.

The inclusion of a number of "Aphorisms" has a twofold purpose—to illustrate grammatical points and at the same time to give the student an insight into Swahili thought. In the early stages of learning the language, the student should only attempt to memorize one or two out of each section. They have been taken from Taylor's *African Aphorisms* (now out of print), and the spelling has been altered so as to bring it into line with the standardized spelling advocated by the Interterritorial Language Committee.

The introduction of Intonation and its bearing upon syntax is a new feature in the writing of Bantu grammars. Only the rudiments of the Swahili Intonation system have been discussed here, and emphatic speech in particular has been

1

but lightly touched on. It is hoped that enough examples have
been given to enable the student to put into practice the principles laid down. Where possible the help of an African speaker
should be enlisted.[1] Students who desire merely to gain a
knowledge of written Swahili may omit the passages concerned
and ignore the intonation instructions given in the exercises.

The book is intended to serve also as a work of reference
for those already acquainted with a Bantu language. To
facilitate its use as such, summaries of salient points have
been added with references to the text itself. These summaries should also help the beginner to see how any particular section under discussion fits into the structure of the
language as a whole.

It should be particularly noted that the Vocabularies only
contain the words used in the exercises and in the lists of
nouns given in the text. The meaning of these words should
not be limited to that given, for Swahili words often cover a
wide range of English words. Frequent reference to the
*Standard Swahili-English Dictionary* is therefore essential, so
that by the understanding of the root idea of any word, the
student may be enabled to use it in its wider application. In
this way he will recognize the flexibility of a Bantu language
and realize the necessity to express the idea behind words,
rather than to equate Bantu words with English words.

On the other hand as the student becomes more closely
acquainted with Swahili he should note its preciseness. Examples of this may be seen in the many derivative forms of
the verb, its numerous tenses to express particular shades of
meaning, the use of the object prefix and the -O of Reference
to direct attention to a particular word—to quote but a few.

The grammatical terminology used has as far as possible
been brought into agreement with that employed in Standard
Swahili works. The introduction of a few new terms such as
the -O of Reference, and the -A of Relationship, etc., has,
however, been found necessary.

[1] For the intonation study in this book the speech of Mr. Barwani
has been taken as a type. A certain amount of variety within the Tone
Patterns is naturally to be expected between one speaker and another.
The speech described here is, for the most part, moderately slow and
deliberate.

# CHAPTER II

## SPELLING AND PRONUNCIATION[1]

SWAHILI spelling follows fairly closely the normal convention for African languages: "Vowel letters with Continental values, consonant letters with English values." There are, however, certain important points to be observed, and the reader is recommended to enlist the help of a Swahili speaker in practising the examples given in this chapter.

### VOWELS

There are five main vowel sounds in Swahili, represented by the letters:

A not so far back in the mouth, as in English "father",
           e.g. **kata** (cut)
E often as in English "better",   e.g. **embe** (mango)
 (not as in English "play")
I as in English "see",     e.g. **kiti** (chair)
O a centralized vowel somewhat
 closer than in English "law"  e.g. **moto** (fire)
 (not as in English "go")
U as in English "too",     e.g. **lulu** (pearl)

|  | Bi-labial | Labio-dental | Den-tal | Alveo-lar | Post-alveo-lar | Pala-tal | Velar | Glot-tal |
|---|---|---|---|---|---|---|---|---|
| Explosive | p |  |  | t | ch |  | k |  |
| Implosive | b | f v |  | d |  | j | g |  |
| Fricative |  | f v | th dh | s z | sh |  | kh gh | h |
| Nasal | m |  |  | n |  | ny | ng' |  |
| Liquid, etc. | w |  |  | r l |  | y |  |  |
| Nasal compound | mb | mv |  | nd nz | nj |  | ng |  |

Note the following points:

*Explosive.*

P, T, CH, K are normally pronounced as in English, but with

[1] For a detailed discussion see "Swahili Phonetics" by A. N. Tucker and E. O. Ashton (*African Studies*, vol. i, nos. 2 and 3—also published separately).

3

little aspiration. Where, however, they begin words in the N-Class and in certain other cases, they are usually pronounced with strong aspiration. Compare the pronunciation of **paa** (roof) and **paa** (gazelle), **tembo** (palm wine) and **tembo** (elephant), **uchafu** (dirt) and **chachu** (yeast), **kaa** (charcoal and **kaa** (land crab). See also p. 83.

*Implosive.*

B, D, J, G are normally pronounced implosively, and the J is very palatal. In the nasal compounds MB, ND, NJ, NG, however, they are pronounced explosively as in English *lumber*, *thunder*, *danger* and *anger*, while the J element is post-alveolar. Compare the pronunciation of **buzi** (large goat) and **mbuzi** (goat), **dege** (large bird) and **ndege** (bird), **kijia** (small path) and **njia** (path), **kigoma** (small drum) and **ngoma** (drum).

*Fricative.*

TH and DH are pronounced as in English *thick* and *this* respectively. They occur in words of Arabic origin, e.g.: **thelatha** (three), **dhambi** (crime).

In some words these sounds are accompanied by velarization (a kind of "throatiness") by speakers who know Arabic, e.g. **tafadhali** (please).

KH is pronounced as in Scottish *loch*, German *Dach*, Dutch *gaan*, but most Swahili speakers use H for it. e.g. **subalkheri** (good morning); cp. **kwa heri** (good-bye).

GH is the voiced counterpart of KH, e.g. **ghali** (scarce).

*Nasal.*

NY is pronounced like the gn of French *baigner*. NG' is pronounced like the ng of English *singer*, e.g. **nyanya** (grandmother), **ng'ombe** (cattle).

M and N are often syllabic, e.g. **m-tu** (person), **m-paji** (donor), **m-bwa** (dog), **n-ta** (wax), **n-cha** (point).

*Liquid.*

R is trilled as in Scottish, e.g. **raha** (rest).

The other consonants are pronounced as in English.

### Syllabic Division, Stress, Intonation

Swahili, unlike most Bantu languages, is not a "tone" language. Intonation here, as in English, is largely governed by stress, though the stress-tone patterns of Swahili naturally differ from those of English. These patterns will be explained in detail in later chapters, but the following introductory remarks are appropriate here:

The Swahili syllable is an open one, i.e. it normally ends in a vowel, e.g.:

**Ne-nda.** Go. **Ni-ta-ku-pi-ga.** I shall hit you.

The nasal prefix, when found, has also syllabic value.

**m-pa-ji** giver, **n-ne** four. **Ni-li-m-pi-ga.** I hit him.

Stress, accompanied by length and a falling tone, lies normally on the penultimate syllable of a word or phrase, e.g.:

**ne'nda, mpa'ji, nitakupi'ga, nilimpi'ga.**

Compare: **ji'ko** kitchen, **jiko'ni** in the kitchen.

Note how syllabic nasal consonants, when occurring in this position, may themselves bear the stress.

**m'bwa** dog, **m'to** pillow **n'ge** scorpion.

There are certain cases in which the stress does not fall on the penultimate syllable:

(*a*) A few trisyllabic words, borrowed from Arabic, usually have the stress on the first syllable, e.g.:

**nu'sura** almost. **ra'tili** pound. **thu'muni** an eighth.

(*b*) At the end of a question requiring "yes" or "no" as an answer the stress and falling tone lie on the last syllable, e.g.:

**Ulimpiga'?** Did you hit him?

# CHAPTER III

## ROOTS, STEMS AND AFFIXES

WORDS which consist of a root[1] only are rare in Swahili. The majority are composed of a root with one or more affixes. Thus -tu is a root. The addition of a prefix gives it the status of a word, m-tu person.

A change in prefix modifies its meaning:—wa-tu persons, people; ji-tu giant; ma-ji-tu giants; u-tu manhood; ki-tu thing; vi-tu things.

Roots are numerous. Affixes are few and limited in number, nevertheless a realization of the part they play in relation to the root is essential.

Roots vary in character:

(i) Some are basically nominal, as for instance -tu already mentioned or -ti giving rise to m-ti tree; ki-ti native stool; ki-ji-ti stick; ji-ti large tree; u-ji-ti tall slender tree; and their respective plural forms mi-ti, vi-ti, vi-ji-ti, n-ji-ti.

In addition some nominal roots have a common form with adjectives: m-ke wife; -ke female.

(ii) Other roots give rise to verbs and nouns, or to verbs, nouns and adjectives:— shind-a \ conquer; m-shind-i or m-shinda-ji a conqueror; m-shind-e one who is conquered.

iv-a get ripe, ripen; u-biv-u ripeness; -biv-u ripe.

Some of these roots are themselves probably derived from ideophones.[2] Thus:

| | | | |
|---|---|---|---|
| mwagika mwa | rush out like water | mwaga | pour out |
| bweka bwe | bark | mbwa | dog |

(iii) A third group appear to be basically pronominal, but some of these roots when given an adverbial prefix function as adverbs. Each root in this group expresses an individual

[1] Root. The irreducible element of a word; the primitive radical form without prefix, suffix, or other inflexion, and not admitting of analysis.

Stem. That part of a word depleted of all prefixal inflexions. Doke, *Bantu Linguistic Terminology*, pp. 192, 200.

In this book roots and stems are usually discussed together.

[2] See page 313

6

or particular concept, viz. a demonstrative, possessive, enumerative or interrogative concept. To take but two examples:[1]

**-le** expresses a demonstrative concept of non-proximity.
**-pi** expresses an interrogative concept.

Thus:

| | | | |
|---|---|---|---|
| **yu-le** | that one, i.e. person | **ku-le** | that direction = there |
| **yu-pi?** | which one? i.e. person | **wa-pi?** | which direction? = where? |

These three main groups of roots and stems with a few numeral roots and the -A of Relationship[2] together with appropriate affixes constitute the foundation on which Swahili grammatical construction is based. The first step, therefore, to understanding the structure of the Swahili language is to recognize: (a) that both roots and affixes express a particular concept; (b) that affixes differ in function; and (c) that if two or more affixes are added to one root, the meaning of each contributes to the meaning of the word as a whole. For example:

| | |
|---|---|
| end-**a** | Verb expresses an idea of motion—go. |
| **mw**-end-**o** | A journey. **mw-** and **-o** give the root nominal function. |
| end-**elea** | **-elea** adds a concept of repetition or continuity to verb end-**a**, which in English is expressed by a different word—progress (verb). |
| **ma**-end-**eleo** | **ma-** and **-o** give nominal function to verb **endelea** to express progress (noun). |

It is impracticable to attempt to give a list of roots under (i) and (ii), but a full list of pronominal roots and stems (iii) is given on the next page.

A full list of affixes is given on p. 9. As only a few are necessary in the early stages of learning Swahili, discussion of

---

[1] These and others are discussed fully in a later chapter.
[2] The -A of Relationship is a particle on which most of the prepositions and conjunctions are formed except those borrowed from Arabic.

## PRONOMINAL ROOTS AND STEMS

| Personal | Possessive | Demonstrative | Interrogative | Reference | Enumerative | State |
|---|---|---|---|---|---|---|
| I, me; we, us; etc., etc. | My, mine; our, ours; etc., etc. | That | Who? What? Where? When? etc. | | All | "having" |
| mi-mi we-we ye-ye si-si ni-nyi wa-o | -a-ngu -a-ko -a-ke -e-tu -e-nu -a-o | -le | -ni? -pi? | -o | -ote | -enye |

others is postponed until the need arises. As each affix comes under discussion, its place in the table should be noted *in relation to its function*, for in a Bantu language function is more important than form, and one affix often has more than one function. In fact "One form, many functions" is a formula which explains many constructions. Thus:

Kucheza **ki**-toto.    To play in a childish way. **ki-** is here an adverbial prefix to **-toto**.

**Ki**-toto kizuri.    A fine infant. **ki-** is here a diminutive nominal prefix to **-toto**.

Sound change plays an important part in all Bantu languages, and Swahili is no exception to the rule. Both prefixes and suffixes are subject to the rules of sound change. These changes are set out in the text and also summarized in tables. They follow well-defined lines and affect both vowels and consonants.

Swahili has been enriched by many borrowings from other languages, especially from Arabic. Many of these borrowings take Swahili suffixes and obey the rules of sound change, but others do not conform to any of the rules governing inflexion in a Bantu language.

# REFERENCE TABLE OF AFFIXES
### (Some are subject to sound change)

| | Prefixes | | | Suffixes |
|---|---|---|---|---|
| Class Prefixes . ⎫ | M- | WA-; M- | MI-; | |
| Adjectival Concords ⎬ | KI- | VI-; JI- | MA-; | -I -JI -U -O -E -A |
| Noun Formatives ⎭ | N- | N-; U- | PA-[1] | |
| Feminine Noun Formative . . . | | | | -KAZI[2] |
| Pronominal Concords | YU- | WA-; U- | I-; | |
| | KI- | VI-; LI- | YA-; | |
| | I- | ZI-; U- | PA- | |
| **Personal Prefixes:** | | | | |
| Subject of Verbs . | NI- | U- A- | (YU-) | |
| | TU- | M- WA- | | |
| Object of Verbs . | NI- | KU- M- | | |
| | TU- | WA- WA- | | |
| Reflexive Prefix . | JI- | | | |
| **Adverbial Formatives:** | | | | |
| Time and Place | KU- PA- MU- | | | -NI |
| Manner . . | VI- | | | |
| Likeness . . | KI- | | | |
| State . . | U- | | | |
| Verbal Derivatives . | | | | -IA -ILIA; |
| | | | | -WA -IWA; |
| | | | | -IKA -IKANA; |
| | | | | -YA -FYA -VYA |
| | | | | -SA -SHA -ZA |
| | | | | -ISHA -IZA; |
| | | | | -MA; -TA; |
| | | | | -UA -UKA; |
| | | | | -PA; -NA |
| **Conjugational Affixes:** | | | | |
| Mood . . . | | | | -A -E |
| Tense . . . | -LI- -TA- -NA- -A- | | | |
| | -ME- HU- -KA- -KI- | | | |
| | -NGA- -JAPO- | | | |
| | -NGE- -NGALI- | | | |
| Negation . . . | HA- -SI- | | | -I |
| Number . . . | | | | -NI |

[1] Adjectival Concord only.

[2] mjakazi female slave; kijakazi young girl slave.

9

# CHAPTER IV

## (1) NOUN CLASSES AND CONCORDIAL PREFIXES

Nouns in Swahili fall into classes distinguished by Nominal Prefixes. These are termed Class Prefixes. With two exceptions, the prefix in the plural Class differs from that of the singular Class. Thus:

| | | | |
|---|---|---|---|
| **m**-tu | a person | **wa**-tu | persons, people |
| **m**-ti | a tree | **mi**-ti | trees |
| **ki**-tu | a thing | **vi**-tu | things |
| **ji**-cho | an eye | **ma**-cho | eyes |
| **n**-jia | a path | **n**-jia | paths |
| **u**-limi | a tongue | **n**-dimi | tongues |
| **ku**-cheza | to play, playing | | |
| Mahali | a place | Mahali | places |

Each class is associated with one or more underlying ideas. Thus Nouns with M- WA- as the distinguishing prefixes for singular and plural respectively express the names of human beings. **m**-tu person, pl. **wa**-tu. Words in other classes are associated with more than one underlying idea. These will be mentioned as each class comes under discussion. It must not, however, be imagined that nouns are marshalled into their classes strictly in accordance with these ideas. Consequently in all classes, nouns will be found which do not conform to the general tendency of the class concerned. This is especially true of nouns derived from verbs.

The Noun dominates the sentence. Words relating to it are brought into concordial relationship with it by affixes termed *concords*.

Each Noun has two sets of Concords.

(i) *Pronominal Concords* (P.C.). These are used with pronominal roots (see list, p. 8) and with the -A of Relationship. Except in the Living Class they also function as the subject and object prefixes of the verb. Thus:

10

**m**-ti **u**-le **u**-mekufa.  Lit. Tree that-one it is dead.  That tree is dead.

**m**-ti.        Singular Noun of the M- MI- Classes.

**u**-le.        P.C. **u** brings demonstrative root **-le** into concordial relationship with **m**-ti.

**u**-mekufa.  P.C. **u** functions as subject prefix to verb, **-mekufa** (is dead), and brings it into concordial relationship with **m**-ti.

(ii) *Adjectival Concords* (A.C.).  These concords are the same in form as the Class Prefixes (except in one instance), and are required with roots or stems used as adjectives.

**m**-ti **m**-zuri.  Tree fine one, i.e. A fine tree.  **m**- brings root **-zuri** into concordial relationship with **m**-ti.

## (2) INTONATION PATTERNS

There are four main intonation patterns in Swahili, classified here according to the pattern of the last two syllables of the word, phrase or sentence.  Within each of these patterns variations of tone occur, but the distinguishing characteristics of each pattern remain constant.

| Tone Pattern | Penultimate Syllable | Final Syllable | Typical Example |
|---|---|---|---|
| I | Stressed | Low unstressed | Watu[1] ＼, |
| II | Mid stressed | High fall | Watu -＼ |
| III | High stressed | High | Watu ⁻. |
| IV | Stressed | Stressed | Watu ⁻⌡ |

Of these four patterns, two are required as soon as the study of Swahili begins.

[1] **Watu** people.

# REFERENCE TABLE OF CLASS AND CONCORD PREFIXES

| | Class Prefixes used with:<br>i. Noun roots<br>ii. Deverbatives, i.e. nouns derived from verb stems | | Concordial Prefixes used with:<br>i. Roots functioning as adjectives<br>ii. Certain numeral roots | | Various roots and stems, i.e.<br>i. Possessive<br>ii. Demonstrative<br>iii. Interrogative<br>iv. -O of Reference<br>v. -ote<br>vi. -enye<br>vii. -A of Relationship<br>viii. Verbs, i.e.<br>Subject Prefix<br>Object Prefix. | |
|---|---|---|---|---|---|---|
| Before: | *Sing.* | *Plur.* | *Sing.* | *Plur.* | *Sing.* | *Plur.* |
| Cons't | m- | wa- | m- | wa- | yu- a- m- | wa- |
| Vowel | m(w)- | w(a)- | m(w)- | w(a)- | w- mw- | w- |
| Cons't | m- | mi- | m- | mi- | u- | i- |
| Vowel | m(w)- | mi- | m(w)- | my- | w- | y- |
| Cons't | ki- | vi- | ki- | vi- | ki- | vi- |
| Vowel | ch- | vy- | ch- | vy- | ch- | vy- |
| Cons't | ji- *or* no prefix | ma- | ji- *or* no prefix | ma- | li- | ya- |
| Vowel | j- *or* no prefix | ma- | j- *or* no prefix | m- | l- | y- |
| Cons't | n- m- | n- m- | n- m- | n- m- | i- | zi- |
| Vowel | ny- | ny- | ny- | ny- | y- | z- |
| Cons't | u- | n- m- | u- m- | n- m- | u- | zi- |
| Vowel | u- w- uw- | ny- | w- mw- | ny- | w- | z- |
| Cons't | ku- | | ku- | | ku- | |
| Vowel | kw- | | kw- | | kw- | |
| Cons't | mahali | | pa- | | pa- | |
| Vowel | | | p- | | p- | |

Variations, for which see text, occur chiefly in:
Prefixes of nouns formed on verb roots beginning with a vowel.
N- Class Prefixes. Words of foreign origin.
Pronominal concords functioning as subject or object prefix before verb roots beginning with a vowel.
In addition a few roots beginning with -i, -o, -u, affect certain prefixes.

12

# CHAPTER V

## THE KI- AND VI- CLASSES

### REFERENCE TABLE

| Class Prefixes | | Pronominal Concords | |
|---|---|---|---|
| *Sing.* | *Plur.* | *Sing.* | *Plur.* |
| **ki-** | **vi-** | **ki-** | **vi-** |

Before a vowel these are replaced by **ch-** and **vy-**.[1]

The KI- VI- Classes of nouns are introduced first, because it so happens that the Pronominal Concords have the same form as the Class Prefixes. This is not the case in all classes. The following are typical nouns in the KI- VI- Classes:

| | | | |
|---|---|---|---|
| **ki-su** | a knife | **vi-su** | knives |
| **ch-umba** | a room | **vy-umba** | rooms |
| **ki-kapu** | a basket | **vi-kapu** | baskets |

### Intonation. Tone Pattern I

The characteristics common to this pattern are a stressed penultimate syllable followed by an unstressed syllable on a low note. This final unstressed syllable is constant, being on the bottom note of the speaker's register, but the stressed penultimate varies.

high level    high falling    mid falling    low level

$$\left[\begin{array}{c}\overline{\phantom{-}} \\ {}_{,}\end{array}\right] \quad \left[\begin{array}{c}\backslash \\ {}_{,}\end{array}\right] \quad \left[\begin{array}{c}\backslash \\ {}_{,}\end{array}\right] \quad \left[\begin{array}{c}- \\ {}_{,}\end{array}\right]$$

Words standing in isolation are characterized by a stressed penultimate syllable on a high or high falling note, followed by an unstressed syllable on a low note. Unstressed syllables preceding the penultimate are of mid tone.

ki-su $\left[\begin{array}{c}\backslash \\ {}_{,}\end{array}\right]$ *or* $\left[\begin{array}{c}\overline{\phantom{-}} \\ {}_{,}\end{array}\right]$ chu-mba $\left[\begin{array}{c}\backslash \\ {}_{,}\end{array}\right]$ *or* $\left[\begin{array}{c}\overline{\phantom{-}} \\ {}_{,}\end{array}\right]$

ki-ka-pu $\left[\begin{array}{c}\cdot\ \backslash \\ {}_{,}\end{array}\right]$ *or* $\left[\begin{array}{c}\cdot\ \overline{\phantom{-}} \\ {}_{,}\end{array}\right]$ ki-ka-pu-ni[2] $\left[\begin{array}{c}\cdot\ \cdot\ \backslash \\ {}_{,}\end{array}\right]$ *or* $\left[\begin{array}{c}\cdot\ \cdot\ \overline{\phantom{-}} \\ {}_{,}\end{array}\right]$

---

[1] There are some exceptions.      [2] In the basket.

## EXERCISE 1a

Read with Tone Pattern I the following words and give
their plural forms. Note the words which do not take **ch** and
**vy** before a vowel.

| | | | | |
|---|---|---|---|---|
| 1. | **kikapu** | basket | 14. **cheti** | note, chit |
| 2. | **kitanda** | bedstead | 15. **kiko** | pipe |
| 3. | **kipofu** | blind person | 16. **kiazi** | potato |
| 4. | **kitabu** | book | 17. **chumba** | room |
| 5. | **kiti** | chair, stool | 18. **kiokosi** | reward for picking |
| 6. | **kikombe** | cup | | something up |
| 7. | **kiziwi** | deaf person | 19. **kiatu** | shoe |
| 8. | **chakula**[1] | food | 20. **kijiko** | spoon |
| 9. | **kidole** | finger | 21. **kizibo** | stopper |
| 10. | **kitoto** | infant | 22. **kitu** | thing |
| 11. | **kisu** | knife | 23. **chombo** | utensil, vessel, |
| 12. | **kioo** | looking-glass | | piece of crockery |
| 13. | **kipimo** | measure | 24. **kiini** | yolk, kernel, etc. |

## Underlying Ideas of the KI- VI- Classes

These are often spoken of as the *thing* Classes, for many
of the nouns are the names of inanimate things as opposed
to animate or sentient beings.

Some words have *noun* roots, others are derived from *verbs*,
and a few are borrowings from other languages.

*With noun roots.* These express (*a*) inanimate as opposed
to living beings, or living things, or (*b*) the diminutive forms
of nouns in other classes. (*c*) Some words appear to come
under no particular category.

(*a*) **kitu** (cf. **mtu** person)    **kiti** (cf. **mti** tree)

(*b*) **kitoto** (cf. **mtoto** child)    **kijiko** (cf. **mwiko** spade, trowel)

(*c*) **kiko, chombo**

**ki-, vi-** before **i** are not replaced by **ch-, vy-**, e.g. kiini, viini.
See p. 322.

*With verb roots.* These frequently express either (*a*) the
instrument or something connected with the action of the
verb from which they are derived, or (*b*) people suffering

---

[1] Plur.: **vyakula**, food, provisions.

some disability. These latter do not take the concords of the KI- VI- Classes.

       (*a*) **kizibo** < **ziba** stop up
       (*b*) **kiziwi** < **ziba** stop up

Nouns made on verb roots beginning with a vowel retain **ki-** and **vi-**, e.g. **kiokosi** < **okota**, pick up.

*Borrowed words.* **kiazi, kitabu, cheti.**

Sound change does not necessarily apply to words of foreign origin.

## Typical Sentences

Typical sentences with the Concords of these classes are:

| | |
|---|---|
| **Kisu ki**-me-anguka. | A *or* the knife has fallen down. (Lit. Knife it has fallen down.) |
| **Visu vi**-me-anguka. | Some *or* the knives have fallen down. (Lit. Knives they have fallen down.) |
| **Chumba ki**-me-chafuka. | The room is untidy. (Lit. Room it is untidy.) |
| **Vyumba vi**-me-chafuka. | The rooms are untidy. (Lit. Rooms they are untidy.) |

Four important points are to be learned from the above sentences:

(i) The use of the Pronominal Concord as Subject Prefix of the verb. In Swahili the verb cannot stand alone as in English, but must be prefixed by the Pronominal Concord proper to the noun which forms its subject. This appositional phrasing is a feature of Bantu speech and contributes to its preciseness.

(ii) Place of the noun subject. This precedes the verb and its subject prefix in simple sentences.

(iii) Lack of article. There are no words to represent English "a", "some" or "the" (but see p. 59). Standing in isolation, the above sentences may represent:

A knife or the knife ... Some knives or the knives ... and only the context will give the clue.

(iv) Use of the verb affixes. The verb stem is **-anguka**, -ME- is a tense prefix, indicating:

(a) Completion of an action. The knife has fallen down.
(b) Resultant state. The room is untidy.

These two ideas must not be kept apart, for state is the result of an action completed. In English these two ideas are expressed by the auxiliaries "is", "are", or "has", "have". Hence in translation the student should think of the meaning to be conveyed rather than any fixed formula of English words.

## Sentence Intonation

Statements, commands, certain types of interrogation and exclamation and answers to questions, all follow Tone Pattern I. In order to simplify the study of this pattern it is presented in three sections: Ia, Ib and Ic.

## Tone Pattern I a. Statements

In contrast to words standing in isolation, words at the beginning or middle of a sentence have level tone for both penultimate and final syllables. In statements such as those already given the stresses form a series of descending steps and the penultimate falls in tone from the last step. Thus:

Kisu kimeanguka.

Vyumba vimechafuka.

From these examples it is seen that the trend of the sentence is downwards, preserving in the last two syllables the pattern characteristic of Tone Pattern I.

## Tone Pattern in Parenthesis

An important feature of intonation should be noted at this early stage. Words such as **Bwana** (Sir), **Bibi (Madam)** and other titles of address,[1] when they occur at the end of a sentence, are not included in the general tone pattern of the sentence, but are spoken on a low note as in English parenthesis. To help students, words spoken in parenthesis are printed in italics.

Kisu kimepotea, *Bwana*   $\left[ \begin{array}{c} - \quad - \cdot \cdot \quad \diagdown \cdot \, \underline{\quad} \cdot \end{array} \right]$
The knife is lost, *Sir*.

### VOCABULARY

Read the following verbs with Tone Pattern I. (KU- is the sign of the Infinitive.)

| | | | |
|---|---|---|---|
| **ku-fika** | to arrive | **ku-pasuka** | to be split, torn |
| **ku-vunjika** | to be broken | **ku-haribika** | to be destroyed, |
| **ku-anguka** | to fall down | | spoilt |
| **ku-potea** | to be lost | **ku-chafuka** | to be in confu- |
| **ku-iva** | to get ripe, be | | sion, untidy |
| | fully cooked, etc. | | |

### EXERCISE 1b

Read, with Tone Pattern Ia the following sentences, then put them into the Singular or Plural, as the case may be. Translate into English. Look at key and translate orally back into Swahili.

1. Kisu kimepotea.
2. Kioo kimevunjika, *Bibi*.
3. Kitabu kimepasuka.
4. Kiko kimeanguka.
5. Viatu vimepasuka.
6. Vikombe vimevunjika.
7. Cheti kimepotea.
8. Viti vimeanguka.
9. Vijiko vimepotea.
10. Chombo kimevunjika.
11. Vitabu vimeharibika.
12. Viazi vimeiva.
13. Vitu vimefika.
14. Kikapu kimepasuka.
15. Vyumba vimechafuka.
16. Vitanda vimevunjika.
17. Chakula kimeiva.
18. Kiatu kimepotea.

---

[1] Among the Swahilis themselves **Bwana** and **Bibi** are polite terms of address, corresponding in use to *Monsieur* and *Madame* in French. **Bwana** is also used by a servant to his European master, but many European women object to being addressed by the term **Bibi** and prefer **Memsab** (from Hindustani *Memsahib*).

## PREDICATION WITHOUT A VERB (Section I)
### PLACE

In Swahili predication in relation to place can be expressed without a verb. It is sufficient to use the subject prefix in relation to the noun with one of the three locative enclitics:[1] -KO, -PO, -MO. Frequently an adverbial noun or an adverb follows.

Kikapu kiko jikoni.    The basket is in the kitchen. Lit.
                              Basket it there in or at kitchen.

Before explaining this further it is necessary to know something about the locative suffix -NI and the enclitics of place, -KO, -PO, -MO.

*The locative suffix -NI.* In Swahili nouns of all classes except the names of persons, animals and places, may be given the status of an adverb by the addition of the suffix NI. The stress on the word is shifted by this suffix thus:

| | | | |
|---|---|---|---|
| nyu'mba | house | nyumba'ni | to, at, in, by, from the house |
| me'za | table | meza'ni | to, at, on, by, from the table |
| kika'pu | basket | kikapu'ni | to, in, out of, from the basket |
| ji'ko | kitchen | jiko'ni | to, at, in, out of, from the kitchen |
| kita'nda | bed | kitanda'ni | in, on, out of, from the bed |

Such words are termed adverbial nouns; they are also known as "Nouns in the Locative Case".[2]

The -NI merely expresses some relation of a locative character. The particular aspect of place is expressed by the use of one of the three enclitics -KO, -PO, -MO.

*The enclitics of place.* These are derived from the adverbial affixes KU-, PA-, MU- and the -O of Reference.

KU- + -O > KO.    PA- + -O > PO.    MU- + -O > MO.

KU- PA- MU- express various aspects of place.

KU- indefiniteness direction, non-proximity, i.e. away from the speaker.

PA- definiteness, position (more specific than KU-).

MU- within-ness, area, an enclosing idea.[3]

---

[1] Enclitic. A leaning-on word which has lost its separate power and has attached itself to another word, partaking of the phonetic entity of that word. (Doke, *Bantu Linguistic Terminology*, p. 99.)

[2] See *Swahili Exercises*, p. 51.

[3] Only withinness is dealt with in these early chapters.

The -O of Reference is so called because it directs attention to some word or words in the sentence already mentioned or about to be mentioned, such as a noun or pronoun, or an adverbial concept of place, time, or manner. At this stage however, only its use with the three aspects of place is dealt with.[1]

Kisu kiko wapi?    Where is the knife? (Lit. Knife it there where?)

Kiko nyumbani.    It is at the house. (Lit. It there at house.)

Kipo mezani.    It is on the table. (Lit. It there on table.)

Kimo sandukuni. It is in the box. (Lit. It there in box.)

-KO directs attention to wapi?—the whereabouts of the knife being indefinite.

-KO directs attention to nyumbani—the whereabouts of the knife being indicated in general terms.

-PO directs attention to mezani—the whereabouts of the knife being specifically defined.

-MO directs attention to sandukuni—emphasizing withinness.

These enclitics of place are easy to understand if it is realized that they represent aspects of place from a Bantu standpoint, and therefore the meaning of each cannot be restricted to one particular word or phrase in English.

Thus -KO, because of its less restricted implication, has a wider and more general use than -PO or -MO and accordingly represents a greater variety of English wording.

For instance, where an English speaker might be tempted to use -MO to express English IN, a Swahili would use -KO if he were merely indicating place in general terms.

Kisu kiko wapi?    Where is the knife?

Kiko kikapuni.    It's in the basket (place not specifically defined).

Kimo kikapuni.    It's in the basket, i.e. not on or by the basket (place specifically defined).

[1] See p. 325.

To sum up it should be remembered that the choice of one enclitic for another has no grammatical significance: the speaker chooses the one which best expresses his meaning. Moreover the omission of -KO in asking a question has no grammatical significance. It is omitted if the speaker is concerned with the absence of a thing rather than its whereabouts.[1]

Kisu ki wapi?    Where is the knife?

## VOCABULARY

| | | | |
|---|---|---|---|
| **nje** | outside, out of doors | **hapa** | here (position) |
| **ndani** | inside, indoors | **kule** | there (direction) |
| **juu** | above, up, upstairs | | |
| **chini** | below, underneath, downstairs | | |

## Tone Pattern I b.   Interrogation

### (with interrogative particle)

In sentences which end in an interrogative and contain no verb, the syllables preceding, if few, are on a high level tone, or may fluctuate in longer words. The trend, however, is immaterial provided the syllable preceding the interrogative has high level or high falling tone.

Kisu kiko wapi? $\left[\begin{array}{c} \end{array}\right]$ or $\left[\begin{array}{c} \end{array}\right]$ [2]
Where is the knife?

Kisahani kiko wapi? $\left[\begin{array}{c} \end{array}\right]$ or $\left[\begin{array}{c} \end{array}\right]$ [2]
Where is the saucer?

---

[1] A good illustration occurs in St. Luke xvii. 17 with the M- WA-Classes.

[2] Other variants are met with but these may be considered typical.

## Tone Pattern I c

In replies to such questions, the stresses are in an *ascending* order, the penultimate syllable having the highest tone.

Kisu kiko chini.                    The knife is

_ . _ . \,    *or*    _ . _ . ‾    downstairs.

or better:

Kiko chini.                         It is downstairs.

_ . \,    *or*    _ . _ . ‾

Naturally, where there is only one word in the reply, Tone Pattern I is used.

Hapa. [ \, ]    Here.

Tone Pattern Ic often alternates with Ia in statements or commands when contrast or climax is indicated. This will be discussed later (p. 76).

### EXERCISE 2

Read the following sentences, using Pattern Ib for the questions and Pattern Ic for the answers. Put into singular or plural. Translate, etc.:

1. Viazi viko wapi?  Viko nje.
2. Kikombe kiko wapi?  Kiko juu.
3. Viatu viko wapi?  Viko chini.
4. Kikapu kiko wapi?  Kimo ndani.
5. Vyombo viko wapi?  Vipo hapa.
6. Viti viko wapi, *Bibi* ?  Viko kule.
7. Kisu kiko wapi?  Kipo mezani.
8. Chakula ki wapi?  Kiko jikoni.
9. Vitabu viko wapi, *Bwana*?  Vipo mezani.
10. Kipimo kiko wapi?  Kiko nyumbani.
11. Vyombo viko wapi?  Vipo sandukuni.
12. Vijiko viko wapi?  Vimo kikapuni.

B

### Sound Change in Vowels

Reference has already been made to the fact of sound change in Swahili (p. 8). As it is impossible to go far without coming across examples of sound change, it is advisable for the student to understand at an early stage how it affects vowels (consonants are dealt with later, p. 82), and to see these changes as an intrinsic part of the language and not as tiresome exceptions. In fact two examples have already occurred in this chapter, viz. contraction and elision.

*Contraction.* The process of shortening a word . . . by a reduction in the number of syllables[1]

p. 13. vyu-mba < vi-u-mba. See also

p. 23. mwa-ka < mu-a-ka

p. 23. kwi-sha < ku-i-sha,
etc., etc.

*Elision.* Effacement or dropping of a sound; in Bantu particularly used of the dropping of one vowel in the presence of another.[2]

p. 18. ko < ku-o; po < pa-o; mo < mu-o.

Two other kinds of sound change will be met with: coalescence and vowel harmony or vowel assimilation.

*Coalescence.* A growing together, a fusion resulting in a new form, contrast elision.[3]

p. 29. we-vi < wa-i-vi.

*Harmony.* A just and pleasing adaptation of the parts to each other.[4]

*Assimilation.* The process by which two sounds in juxtaposition or close proximity tend to become identical, or to acquire common characteristics.

Progressive assimilation is that in which one sound affects a *following* sound.[5]

p. 25. lete < leta. Here the influence of mid **e** on final **a** causes the two vowels to become identical.

---

[1] Doke, *Bantu Linguistic Terminology*, p. 81.
[2] Ibid., p. 98.     [3] Ibid., p. 67.     [4] Ibid., p. 114.     [5] Ibid., p. 55.

Regressive assimilation is that in which one sound affects a *preceding* sound.[1]

p. 25. pikeni < pikani. Here the influence of final vowel **i** causes the preceding vowel **a** to become **e**.

It will be seen from the above examples that the effect of sound change in general is to make the word easier to pronounce. (**Mwa** comes more naturally and easily to the tongue than **mu-a**, **ko** than **ku-o**.) In the case of assimilation the resultant word is, if not easier, at least more harmonious from a Bantu point of view.

[1] Ibid., p. 55.

# CHAPTER VI

## THE M- AND MI- CLASSES

### REFERENCE TABLE

| Class Prefixes | | Pronominal Concords | |
|---|---|---|---|
| *Sing.* | *Plur.* | *Sing.* | *Plur.* |
| **m-** | **mi-** | **u-** | **i-** |

Before a vowel the sound change is:

| **mw-**[1] | **mi-** (unchanged) | **w-** | **y-** |
|---|---|---|---|

The student is now introduced to noun classes in which the Pronominal Concord differs from the Class Prefix. As a general rule it may be stated here that where the Class Prefix contains a nasal, the Pronominal Concord has none; otherwise the prefixes are identical. Exceptions to this general rule will be dealt with as they arise.

The following are typical nouns of the M- MI- Classes:
**m-kate** loaf  **mi-kate** loaves  **mw-aka** year  **mi-aka** years

Typical sentences with the Concords of these classes are:

| Mkate **u**-me-anguka. | The loaf has fallen down. |
|---|---|
| Mikate **i**-me-anguka. | The loaves have fallen down. |
| Mwaka **u**-me-kwisha. | The year is finished. |
| Miaka **i**-me-kwisha. | The years are finished. |

### EXERCISE 3a

Read the following nouns with Tone Pattern I and give their plural forms.

| | | | | | |
|---|---|---|---|---|---|
| 1. | **mkono** | arm, hand | 7. | **mguu** | foot, leg |
| 2. | **mwili** | body | 8. | **mwitu** | forest |
| 3. | **mpaka** | boundary | 9. | **mchezo** | game |
| 4. | **mfereji** | ditch, water channel | 10. | **moyo** | heart |
| 5. | **mlango** | door | 11. | **mzigo** | load, burden |
| 6. | **moto** | fire | 12. | **mkeka** | mat |
| | | | 13. | **msikiti** | mosque |

---

[1] There are some exceptions.

22

| | | | |
|---|---|---|---|
| 14. **mwendo** | motion, journey | 24. **mtambo** | trap with |
| 15. **mwezi** | moon, month | | metal spring |
| 16. **mlima** | mountain | 25. **mtego** | trap, snare |
| 17. **msumari** | nail | 26. **mti** | tree, wood |
| 18. **mchungwa** | orange tree | 27. **mji** | town, village |
| 19. **mto** | pillow | 28. **mwavuli** | umbrella |
| 20. **mto** | river | 29. **mshahara** | wages, month- |
| 21. **msumeno** | saw | | ly payment |
| 22. **moshi** | smoke | 30. **mwaka** | year |
| 23. **mkebe** | tin can | | |

Note that **w** is elided before **o** in **moto, moyo, moshi**. The plural forms are regular, **mioto**, etc. See p. 322.

## Underlying Ideas of the M- MI- Classes

*Words with noun roots.* Nouns which are the names of living things but not human, hence the names of all trees, plants, etc., have these prefixes: **mti, mchungwa, mnanasi** (pineapple plant).

An idea of something that spreads or extends may be seen in words like **mji, mto, mlima, moto, moshi, mwitu**.

*Words with verb roots.* These generally take suffix **-o**.

    **mchezo** < **cheza** play    **mwendo** < **enda** go

For some words no explanation can be given: **mwaka, mwezi**.

Some are borrowed words:—**mfereji, msumari, mkebe**.

VOCABULARY

| | | | |
|---|---|---|---|
| **ku-zimika** | to be extinguished | **kw-isha** | to finish (intr.) |
| **ku-anza** | to begin | **ku-toboka** | be pierced |
| **ku-fa** | to die | **ku-kauka** | become dried up |
| **ku-furika** | to become swollen | **ku-onekana** | become visible |
| | | **kw-enda** | to go |

Note the phonetic change of **-u** to **-w** before the vowel in **isha** and **enda**. These verbs as well as all monosyllabic verbs retain the infinitive particle **ku-** in the **-me-** and in most other tenses.

## Exercise 3b

Read the following sentences with Tone Pattern Ia. Translate into English. Then put into the singular or plural as the case may require, and where the sense allows.

1. Mlango umevunjika.
2. Moto umezimika, *Bibi*.
3. Misumeno imeharibika.
4. Mikeka imepasuka.
5. Mchezo umeanza.
6. Michungwa imekufa.
7. Mto umefurika.
8. Mito imepasuka.
9. Misumari imekwisha.
10. Mtambo umevunjika.
11. Mwavuli umepasuka.
12. Mkebe umetoboka.
13. Miti imekauka.
14. Mizigo imepotea, *Bwana*.
15. Mwezi umeonekana.
16. Mipaka imeharibika.

## Tone Pattern II. Interrogation

### (without interrogative particle)

Statements may be expressed as questions without change in word order. The difference in meaning is indicated by intonation.

Questions such as these take Tone Pattern II in contrast to Ib, which is used only with questions containing an interrogative particle or word (like **wapi?**).

The characteristic of Tone Pattern II is a stressed mid (or slightly rising) penultimate syllable, followed by a long stressed final syllable which generally has high falling tone. Preceding syllables may be mid level or may fluctuate.

In the replies to such questions Tone Pattern Ic with ascending scale is again used—Tone Pattern I if the reply is a single word.

## QUESTION AND ANSWER

| Statement.<br>*Tone Pattern Ia* | Question.<br>*Tone Pattern II* | Answer.<br>*Tone Pattern I<br>or Ic* |
|---|---|---|
| Imekwisha.<br><br>They are finished (i.e. the loaves). | Imekwisha?<br><br>Are they finished? | Imekwisha.<br><br>They are finished. |
| Vikombe vimo sandukuni.<br><br>The cups are in the box. | Vikombe vimo sandukuni?<br><br>Are the cups in the box? | Vimo.<br><br>They are. |
| | Vimo?<br><br>Are they in it? (i.e. the box). | Havimo.<br><br>They are not. |

*Observation.*

When titles of address are added to questions having Tone Pattern II—more particularly in short sentences—they may be incorporated into the pattern and thus end on a high falling note.

Vimo, Bwana?  $\left[ - \cdot \; - \; \diagdown \; \right]$  *or*  $\left[ - \; \cdot \; - \; \diagdown \; \right]$

This should be compared with Tone Pattern I, p. 16, where the title always stands in parenthesis and is outside the sentence.

EXERCISE 3c
Read the sentences in Exercise 3b as questions, using Tone
Pattern II.

## PLACE PREDICATION (cont.)

*Subject Prefixes* = Sing. **u-**, Plur. **i-**.

| | |
|---|---|
| Mwavuli **u-ko** wapi? | Where is the umbrella? |
| **U-ko** juu. | It is upstairs. |
| Misumari **i-mo** kabatini. | The nails are in the cupboard. |

On p. 18 the enclitics have been discussed in relation to
some other adverbial expression in the sentence. However,
when place has been already referred to, they, combined with
a subject prefix alone, suffice to form a sentence, either as a
question with Tone Pattern II or as an answer with Tone
Pattern I.

| | |
|---|---|
| (II) Vikombe **vimo**? (i.e. sandu-kuni) | Are the cups inside? (the box) |
| (I) **Vimo.** | They are. (inside) |

The noun need not be repeated if already mentioned.

| | |
|---|---|
| (II) **Vimo?** | Are they inside? |
| (II) Kisu **kipo**? (i.e. mezani) | Is the knife there? (on table) |
| (I) **Kipo.** | It is. (there) |
| (II) Misumari **iko**? | Are the nails there? |
| (I) **Iko.** | They are there. |

**ko** has a wide usage and may be used to inquire whether a
certain commodity is available. Word order may then be
reversed.

| | |
|---|---|
| (II) **Iko** misumari? **Iko.** | Are there any nails? There are. |

NEGATIVE PREDICATION is expressed by prefixing HA-
to the positive form.

| | |
|---|---|
| Vikombe **ha**-vimo sandukuni. | The cups are not in the box. |
| Kisu **ha**-kipo mezani. | The knife is not on the table. |
| Mtego **ha**-upo hapa. | The trap is not here. |
| Mizigo **ha**-iko nje. | The loads are not outside. |

### EXERCISE 4

Read the following sentences using Tone Pattern II for
questions and I or Ic for replies. Put into singular or plural
as case may be. Translate into English. Translate orally
into Swahili from key.

| | | |
|---|---|---|
| 1. | Mchezo umekwisha? | Umekwisha. |
| 2. | Miti imekufa? | Imekufa. |
| 3. | Kiti kiko juu? | Hakiko. |
| 4. | Viatu viko chini? | Haviko. |
| 5. | Mlango umevunjika? | Umevunjika. |
| 6. | Mkeka umeharibika? | Umeharibika. |
| 7. | Moto umezimika? | Umezimika. |
| 8. | Mikebe iko *Bibi*? | Iko *Bibi*. |
| 9. | Vijiko vimo sandukuni? | Vimo. |
| 10. | Mwavuli uko? | Hauko. |

## COMMANDS

| *Infinitive* | | *Imperative* | | *Neg. Subjunctive* | |
|---|---|---|---|---|---|
| Kupika | to cook | Pika | Cook! | **Usi**pike | Don't cook! |
| | | Pik**eni** | Cook! pl. | **Msi**pike | Don't cook! pl. |
| Kununua | to buy | Nunua | Buy! | **Usi**nunue | Don't buy! |
| | | Nunu**eni** | Buy! pl. | **Msi**nunue | Don't buy! pl. |
| Kuondoa | to take away, | Ondoa | Take away! | **Usi**ondoe | Don't take away! |
| | remove | Ondo**eni** | Take away! pl. | **Msi**ondoe | Don't take away! pl. |
| Kuleta | to bring | Lete | Bring! | **Usi**lete | Don't bring! |
| | | Let**eni** | Bring! pl. | **Msi**lete | Don't bring! pl. |
| Kwenda | to go | Enda | Go! | **Usi**ende | Don't go! |
| | | End**eni** | Go! pl. | **Msi**ende | Don't go! pl. |

The Imperative is generally used to express a command in
the affirmative. In the singular the verb stem is used by

B*

itself, in the plural it is given a suffix **-ni**, which causes Vowel Harmony **-a > -e** in the final stem vowel.

For prohibition the negative subjunctive form is used. This ends in **-e**. Note that **-si-** is the negative particle and that **u-** and **m-** are the 2nd person subject prefixes, sing. and pl. respectively.

**ku** is *not* required with **enda**, **isha**, and monosyllabic verbs in the Imperative and Subjunctive forms.

## Imperative Intonation

When standing alone, both Imperative and Negative Subjunctive forms have Tone Pattern I.

Pika! $\left[ \begin{array}{c} \diagdown \\ {}_{\scriptstyle\mathsf{I}} \end{array} \right]$ Cook (it)!   Usipike! $\left[ \begin{array}{c} \cdots \diagdown \\ {}_{\scriptstyle\mathsf{I}} \end{array} \right]$ Don't cook (it)!

Pikeni! $\left[ \begin{array}{c} \cdot \diagdown \\ {}_{\scriptstyle\mathsf{I}} \end{array} \right]$ Cook ye (it)!   Msipike! $\left[ \begin{array}{c} \cdots \diagdown \\ {}_{\scriptstyle\mathsf{I}} \end{array} \right]$ Don't (pl.) cook (it)!

When standing at the head of a longer sentence, Tone Pattern Ia (with descending stresses) is used.

Pika viazi! $\left[ \begin{array}{c} {}^{-} \cdots \diagdown \\ {}_{\scriptstyle\mathsf{I}} \end{array} \right]$ Cook potatoes!

Pikeni viazi! $\left[ \begin{array}{c} \cdot {}^{-} \cdots \diagdown \\ {}_{\scriptstyle\mathsf{I}} \end{array} \right]$ Cook ye potatoes!

### EXERCISE 5

Read with appropriate tone patterns (indicated in brackets), translate into English, then look at the key and retranslate orally into Swahili.

1. (Ia)      Pikeni viazi.
2. (Ia)      Msipike chakula hapa.
3. (Ia)      Ondoa vyombo.

#### COMMANDS

4. (Ia)      Usilete kiti.
5. (Ia)      Lete vijiko na visu.
6. (Ia)      Usiondoe msumeno.
7. (Ia, Ia) Leteni kitanda, msilete viti.
8. (Ia, Ia) Ondoeni visu, msiondoe vijiko.
9. (Ia, Ia) Ondoa mkate, usiondoe vikombe.

### Further Notes on Tone Pattern II

Tone Pattern II has two forms of which only one has been treated up till now in this book. For a complete picture, and in order to straighten out the confusion that has already arisen, it is highly necessary to describe the other (and more common) form.

The tone pattern already shown in this book is characteristic of deliberate speech, and is much used when pressing for an answer. It is also very common when "talking down" to people, especially children or strangers learning the language, and was unconsciously used by the author's first informants in order to make the questions obvious.

The second form, to be described here, seems to be the normal form used between Swahili speakers when asking questions which do not contain an interrogative particle or word. It is very like Tone Pattern I, except that the penultimate syllable does not fall but has a high and slightly rising note, e.g.

Vimo?  $\left[\begin{array}{c} \acute{} \\ | \end{array}\right]$          Are they inside?

Vikombe vimo sandukuni?  $\left[._-._-..._{\diagup}|\right]$  Are the cups in the box?

Mikate imekwisha?  $\left[._{-}..._{\diagup}|\right]$  Are the loaves finished?

The impression is of Tone Pattern I pronounced with a faint air of surprise, a mental "raising of the eyebrows", on the penultimate syllable. (This should not be overdone by the learner, as any exaggeration would give the impression of actual surprise—"Are they really inside?")

If the question is not at first understood, or if for any other reason the speaker wishes to repeat his question, the form of Tone Pattern II as described in the book is almost invariably used. A similar form, in such or similar circumstances, may even be used with questions ending in an interrogative particle and normally employing Tone Pattern Ib.

Kiko wapi?  $\left[- - ._\diagdown\right]$          Where is it then?

# CHAPTER VII

## THE M- AND WA- CLASSES

| Class Prefixes | | Pronominal Concords | |
|---|---|---|---|
| *Sing.* | *Plur.* | *Sing.* | *Plur.* |
| m- | wa- | yu- a- | wa- |

Before a vowel:
mw-[1]    w(a)

a is used as Subject Prefix before a verb, while yu- occurs before ko, po, mo and other stems.

The following are typical nouns of the M- WA- classes:

| | | | |
|---|---|---|---|
| **m-tu** | a person | **wa-tu** | people |
| **mw-ana** | a son, daughter, child | **w-ana** | children |

Typical sentences:

**M**-geni **a**-me-fika    A *or* the stranger has arrived.
**Wa**-geni **wa**-me-fika.   Some *or* the strangers have arrived.

## EXERCISE 6

Study notes below then read the following words with Tone Pattern I and give their plurals.

| | | | |
|---|---|---|---|
| Mwarabu | Arab | mchunga | herdsman |
| mwana | child, son, daughter | mume | husband |
| | | mwanamume | man |
| mtoto | child | mwenyewe | owner |
| mpishi | cook | mwanafunzi | pupil, apprentice |
| mwoga | coward | | |
| mwenzi | companion | mpagazi | porter |
| Muumba | Creator | Mwokozi | Saviour |
| mlevi | drunkard | mtumishi | servant |
| Mzungu | European | mwimbaji | singer |
| mzee | elder | mgonjwa | sick person |
| mnyapara | headman | mgeni | stranger, guest |

[1] There are some exceptions.

28

| Mswahili | Swahili person | mwanamke | woman |
| mwashi | stonemason | mke | wife |
| mwalimu | teacher | mwandikaji | writer |
| mwivi | thief | | |

## Underlying Ideas

These classes are generally spoken of as the Living Classes, because they contain the names of human beings. Some of these words are made on noun roots, but the majority are derived from verb stems. Such nouns generally have as suffix -i, -ji or -a, and indicate the doer of the action.

| mpishi | < pika | cook | mwimbaji | < imba | sing |
| mlevi | < lewa | be drunk | mchunga | < chunga | take care of |
| mwivi | < iba | steal | | | animals, etc. |

Some nouns in these classes are of foreign origin:

mwalimu (teacher), pl. waalimu or- walimu.

mw does not always replace m before u:—mu-umba or mw-umba.

wa + a > wa in nouns made on noun roots but the full form is generally retained in nouns made on verb stems. Thus:

| w-ana | wa-ashi | < (w)aka | build in stone |
| w-anafunzi | wa-andikaji | < andika | write |
| w-anawake | wa-imbaji | < imba | sing |
| w-ana(wa)ume[1] | wa-okozi | < okoa | save |

wa + e > we w-enzi w-enyewe

Note coalescence in wevi < wa-ivi < iba, steal. Names of persons also occur in other classes, but generally take the concords of the Living Classes, e.g. kijana (child), kipofu, kiziwi, etc. See also Chapter XV.

## PLACE PREDICATION (cont.)

*Subject Prefixes* = Sing. yu-, Plur. wa-.

| Hamisi yu-ko wapi? | Where is Hamisi? |
| Yu-ko juu? Ha-yu-ko. | Is he upstairs? He is not (there). |

[1] Each part of the compound noun takes the plural form in wana-(wa)ume and wanawake. It is, however, frequently omitted in wa-naume.

Wageni **wa**-ko wapi?     Where are the strangers?
**Wa**-ko nje? Ha-**wa**-ko.  Are they outside? They are not
                             (there).

### VOCABULARY

**ku-lala**  to lie down, to sleep  **ku-simama**  to stand
**ku-amka**  to awake               **ku-kaa kitako** to sit down
                                    **ku-lewa**     to be drunk

Verbs indicating *posture* are much used in the -ME- tense
where in English the present tense would be used. This from
a Bantu viewpoint is logical, for posture implies the completion of an action resulting in a state.

### EXERCISE 7a

Read, using appropriate tone patterns indicated. Put into
singular or plural. Translate into English and retranslate
orally from key.

1. (II) Wagonjwa wamelala?   (I) Wamelala.
2. (II) Mwalimu ameamka?     (I) Ameamka.
3. (II) Mzungu yuko chini?   (I) Hayuko.
4. (II) Wapagazi wamefika?   (I) Wamefika.
5. (Ib) Wako wapi?           (Ic) Wako nje.
6. (II) Mgeni amefika?       (I) Amefika.
7. (II) Mzee amesimama?      (I) Amesimama.
8. (Ib) Amesimama wapi?      (Ic) Amesimama kule.
9. (Ib) Watoto wako wapi?    (Ic) Wako juu, (I) wamelala.
10. (II) Mgeni amekaa kitako?  (Ic) Amekaa kitako.
11. (II) Mzee amelewa?       (I) Amelewa.
12. (Ib) Yuko wapi?          (Ic) Yuko nje.
13. (II) Mgonjwa amekufa?    (I) Amekufa.

The replies to these questions have Tone Pattern I where
there is only one stress, and Tone Pattern Ic[1] in sentences
containing more than one stress.

### EXERCISE 7b

Translate, bearing in mind the significance of **ko, po** and
**mo**:

---

[1] Or Ia; a fair amount of variety may be expected here.

1. Where are the porters? They are not here, they are sitting down over there, i.e. they are over there, they are sitting down.
2. Where is the chair? It's upstairs, it's not here.
3. Where is the child? He is upstairs, asleep.
4. Where are the sick people? They are indoors, they are not here.
5. The umbrella is not here, it is upstairs.
6. The teachers are not here, they are outside.
7. The women are not inside, they are here.

## THE SUBJUNCTIVE

The Subjunctive verb stem is obtained by substituting **-e** for final **-a** of the Infinitive stem. The Subjunctive is much used in asking questions of a permissive nature; it is also used in permission and prohibition. It has other functions, which are indicated by the context or by the tone pattern of the sentence. The following are typical examples. (Tone Pattern is shown in the margin.)

Note that the personal subject prefixes are distinguished in number but not in gender.

| | | |
|---|---|---|
| (II) | Ni-pike? | Am I to cook? Shall I cook? |
| (I) | Ni-pike. | Let me cook. |
| (I) | U-pike. | Do thou cook. |
| (II) | A-pike? | Is he/she to cook? Shall he/she cook? |
| (I) | A-pike. | Let him/her cook. |
| (II) | Tu-pike? | Are we to cook? Shall we cook? |
| (I) | Tu-pike. | Let us cook. Let's cook. |
| (I) | M-pike. | Do ye cook. |
| (II) | Wa-pike? | Are they to cook? Shall they cook? |
| (I) | Wa-pike. | Let them cook. |

Further examples:

| | | |
|---|---|---|
| (II) | Ninunue kikapu? | Shall I buy a basket? |
| (I) | Nunua. | Buy (one). |
| (II) | Watoto waondoe viti? | Are the children to take away the chairs? |
| (I) | Waondoe. | They are to take (them). |

Monosyllabic verbs, together with **kwisha** and **kwenda**, do not retain the infinitive particle in the Subjunctive. Verb stems beginning with a vowel cause the following phonetic changes in the personal prefixes:—**Ni**-ende, **w**-ende *or* **u**-ende, **a**-ende; **tw**-ende, **mw**-ende *or* **mu**-ende, **wa**-ende.

The *negative* form inserts **-si-** after the subject prefix. Remember that in the second person this form may correspond to the negative imperative in English.

| | | |
|---|---|---|
| (II) | Ni-si-pike? | Am I not to cook? |
| (I) | Ni-si-pike. | Let me not cook. |
| (I) | U-si-pike. | Do thou not cook. Don't cook. |
| (II) | A-si-pike? | Is he not to cook? |
| (I) | A-si-pike. | Let him not cook. He is not to cook. |
| (II) | Tu-si-pike? | Are we not to cook? |
| (I) | Tu-si-pike. | Let us not cook. Let's not cook. |
| (I) | M-si-pike. | Ye are not to cook. Don't cook (pl.). |
| (II) | Wa-si-pike? | Are they not to cook? |
| (I) | Wa-si-pike. | They are not to cook. Don't let them cook. |

Further examples:

| | | |
|---|---|---|
| (II) | Nisinunue kikapu? | Am I not to buy a basket? |
| (I) | Usinunue. | Don't buy (one). |
| (Ic) | Usinunue kitu. | Don't buy anything (lit. a thing). |
| (II) | Watoto wasiondoe viti? | Aren't the children to take away the chairs? |
| (I) | Wasiondoe. | They are not to take (them) away. |

Other and further uses of the Subjunctive are discussed later (Chapter XX).

## Tone Pattern I b *(cont.)*

On page 20 Tone Pattern Ib is illustrated with **wapi** in predication without a verb. When this and other interrogatives, such as **nini** (what?), **lini** (when?), follow a verb, the general pattern is much the same, but it is the stressed penultimate of the verb rather than the unstressed syllable immediately preceding the interrogative which has high tone, and this high tone is level rather than falling.

Tusome lini? [· ‾ · ___.]    When shall we read?

Mpishi anunue nini?                    What shall the cook buy?

Amekwenda wapi?[1]                    Where has he gone?

Variants within this Tone Pattern frequently occur but at this stage should not be taken too seriously.

For instance, sometimes the interrogative itself starts on a high note. This is particularly noticeable when followed by a parenthesis.

Tusome lini Bwana?                    Amekwenda wapi Bwana?

Or again, Swahili speakers under some circumstances may superimpose Tone Pattern II on Ib.

Ulifika lini? $[\cdot\cdot\ \bar{}\ \bar{}\ \_\ \backslash\ ]$      When did you arrive?

Nilete nini Bwana? $[\cdot\ \bar{}\ \cdot\cdot\ \_\ \backslash\ ]$ What am I to bring, sir?

As these differences depend upon the immediate context, the mood of the speaker or other factors, hard and fast rules cannot be given for them all. They can best be learnt—especially the finer nuances—by careful listening.

## VOCABULARY

| | | | |
|---|---|---|---|
| ku-lima | to cultivate | kesho | to-morrow |
| wapi? | where? | nini? | what? |
| ku-nunua | to buy | kesho kutwa | day after to-morrow |
| ku-leta | to bring | ku-pika | to cook |
| ku-soma | to read | ku-la | to eat |
| sasa | now | ku-ondoa | to take away |
| ku-ja | to come | asubuhi | morning |
| lini? | when? | jioni | evening |

### EXERCISE 8a

Do as with previous exercises:

1. (Ib) Watoto walime wapi?        (Ic) Walime hapa.
2. (Ib) Wagonjwa walale wapi?      (Ic) Walale nyumbani.

[1] With verb kwenda the enclitic form -pi is met with. See p. 153.

3. (II) Mzee anunue viazi?      (I)    Anunue.
4. (II) Tulete visu?      (I)    Leteni.
5. (II) Nisome sasa?      (I)    Soma.
6. (Ib) Mwalimu aje lini?      (Ic) Aje kesho.
7. (Ib) Watoto waje lini?      (Ic) Waje kesho kutwa.
8. (II) Waswahili walete chakula?   (I)    Walete.
9. (II) Mgonjwa asome?      (I)    Asome.
10. (Ib) Mgonjwa ale lini?      (Ic) Ale sasa.
11. (II) Leo nisipike viazi?      (I)    Usipike.
12. (Ia) Watoto wasiondoe viti.
13. (Ia) Mgonjwa asinunue kiko.
14. (Ia & Ic) Tusisome asubuhi, tusome jioni.

### EXERCISE 8b

When the Interrogative **nini?** (what?) is used as the object of a verb, it stands after the verb.

Do as with previous exercises:

1. (Ib) Mpishi amepika nini?      (Ic) Amepika mikate.
2.      Watoto wapike nini?      Wapike viazi.
3.      Wazungu wamenunua nini?      Wamenunua vitabu.
4.      Mpishi anunue nini?      Anunue mkate.
5.      Mwalimu ameondoa nini?      Ameondoa kiti.
6.      Niondoe nini?      Usiondoe kitu.
7.      Wanawake wameleta nini?      Wameleta viazi.
8.      Mtoto amekula nini?      Amekula viazi.
9.      Mzee ameleta nini?      Ameleta kiko.

### EXERCISE 8c

Translate, and supply answers to the following questions, selecting nouns from the **ki- vi-** and **m- mi-** classes:

1. What have the men brought?
2. What has the cook eaten?
3. What have the children cooked?
4. What have the elders brought?
5. What have the sick people eaten?
6. What have the women cooked?
7. What are the sick people to eat?
8. What are we to bring?

# CHAPTER VIII

## VERBS AND THEIR TENSES (Section I)

### Preliminary Remarks

TENSES of the verb in Swahili are expressed by formative prefixes attached to the verb stem. Like other affixes each expresses a certain idea.

Except for a few *time* tenses it is a mistake to equate any one Swahili tense with any one particular tense in English for several reasons:

(i) *Some tenses do not refer specifically to time, but merely to some aspect of the action or state*—e.g. whether the action is completed or going on, or whether it takes place before another action or after another action. For tenses such as these there is no counterpart in English tense forms.

(ii) Frequently two or more tenses in Swahili are covered by one tense in English, or conversely one Swahili tense may be represented by several tenses in English. The -ME- tense (p. 15) admirably illustrates this point.

### Observation

After the prefixes **-li-**, **-ta-** and **-na-** the Infinitive prefix **ku-** is retained with monosyllabic verbs (and **kwisha** and **kwenda**), but not after the prefix **-a-**, thus:

| | | | |
|---|---|---|---|
| Nilikuja. | I came. | Naja. | I come. |
| Nitakuja. | I shall come. | Waja. | You come. |
| Ninakuja. | I am coming. | Yuaja.[1] | He comes. |

[1] Preferred to **aja**. Note alternative forms **yuenda** and **aenda** (he goes).

Six primary tenses of the Swahili verb **kutaka** (to want or need).[1]

| | Singular | | | Plural | | |
|---|---|---|---|---|---|---|
| The -LI- of Past Time | Ni-li-taka U-,, ,, A-,, ,, Ki-,, ,, U-,, ,, etc. | I you he, she it (chair) it (tree) | } wanted | Tu- li-taka M-,, ,, Wa-,, ,, Vi-,, ,, I-,, ,, etc. | We you they they (chairs) they (trees) | } wanted |
| The -TA- of Future Time | Ni-ta-taka U-,, ,, A-,, ,, Ki-,, ,, U-,, ,, etc. | I shall you will he, she will it will it will | } want | Tu-ta-taka M-,, ,, Wa-,, ,, Vi-,, ,, I-,, ,, etc. | We shall you will they will they will they will | } want |
| The -NA- of Definite Time, mostly Present | Ni-na-taka[2] U-,, ,, Ki ,, ,, U-,, ,, etc. | I am you are he, she is it is it is | } want-ing | Tu-na-taka M-,, ,, Wa-,, ,, Vi-,, ,, I-,, ,, etc. | We you they they they | } are want-ing |

*NOTE* how vowel **a** causes phonetic change in the Subject Prefixes:

| | Singular | | | Plural | | |
|---|---|---|---|---|---|---|
| The -A- of Indefi- nite Time | Ni + a > Na-taka[3] U + a > Wa ,, A + a > A ,, Ki + a > Cha ,, U + a > Wa ,, | I want You want he, she wants } it wants | | Tu + a > Twa-taka M + a > Mwa ,, Wa+ a > Wa ,, Vi + a > Vya ,, I + a > Ya ,, | We you they they they | } wan |
| -ME- of com- pleted action or state | Ni-me-taka, etc. Ni-me-choka, etc. | I, etc., have wanted I, etc., am tired | | Tu-me-taka, etc. Tu-me-choka, etc. | We, etc., have wanted We, etc., are tired | |
| HU- of habitual or repe- titive action | Hu-taka. I want, you want, etc. Used for all persons sing. and plur. and for all classes. | | | | | |

[1] Kutaka also means "to be about to . . ."
    Unataka kuanguka.        You are about to fall.
    Ngoma inataka kupasuka.   The drum is about to split.
[2] Frequently heard as: (N)-na-taka. Similarly: (N)-na-kuja and (N)-na-kwenda
[3] Similarly: Na-ja and N(a)-enda.

## The Uses of the Six Primary Tenses

The -ME- tense has already been shown on p. 15 to express the completion of an action and/or the resultant state. Though it corresponds to many tense forms in English, the underlying concept is constant:

| | | |
|---|---|---|
| Amefika. | He has arrived. | |
| Amechoka. | He is tired. | Completion of action |
| Amesimama. | He is standing. | and/or resultant |
| Amesikia. | He understands, i.e. | state. |
| | he has heard. | |

The -LI- tense refers to verbal activity in the past. Sometimes -ali- is heard instead of -li-, but not so frequently now as in former years, except in the 1st person singular:

> Nilisoma jana. ⎫
> Nalisoma jana. ⎬ I read yesterday.

The -TA- tense refers to verbal activity in the future.
> Nitasoma kesho.   I shall read to-morrow.

The -NA- tense refers to an action taking place within a period or at a point in time. If nothing in the context indicates past or future time, it refers to the present. This is its most frequent usage, and because of this it is often spoken of as the "Present Definite". At a later stage it will be seen to have a wider significance than that of the Present Definite.
> Ninasoma.   I am reading (now).

The -A- tense is used to state facts and ask questions without relation to any particular time, and is therefore the opposite of the -NA- tense, which refers to a point or period in time. The -A- tense is often spoken of as the "Present Indefinite". A more comprehensive term is "Indefinite Time Tense". Its use as a simple present is well described in *Steere's Exercises*, pp. 37–8. It should always be used in present time unless the speaker wishes to indicate clearly that the action is in process of going on at the moment of speaking.

The right use of -A- may be be learnt by comparing it with -NA-.
> Mpishi asema ataka sukari.   The cook says he wants some sugar.

Here **asema** and **ataka** both state facts, without relation to time.

Mpishi asema anataka sukari. The cook says he wants some sugar.

The use of **anataka** indicates that the cook is in immediate need of sugar for his work.

Ataka kiasi gani? How much does he want?

Here **ataka** merely asks the question.

The HU- tense takes no Subject Prefix, and is used for all Classes, singular and plural. It occurs in contexts which imply habitual or recurrent action, apart from time. It can often be rendered in English by adverbs such as "generally", "usually", "always", and is much met with in proverbs and everyday maxims.

In the following sentences it is compared to the -A- tense:

Ng'ombe **wala** chakula gani? What sort of food do cows eat?
    Wala nyasi. They eat grass.

The use of the -A- tense shows a general question and its answer.

Ng'ombe **hula** chakula gani? What sort of food do cows eat
    Hula nyasi. as their staple food? They eat grass.

Mayai **yapatikana** wapi? Ya-patikana sokoni. Where are eggs procurable? They are procurable in the market.

Compare:

Mayai **hupatikana** sokoni? Are eggs usually to be got in the market?

For use in compound tenses see p. 256.

**hu** is a contraction of **ni+ku**. Nikula > hula.

## Aphorisms Illustrating the HU- Tense[1]

At this early stage the aphorisms should not be studied too intently, for they cover a vocabulary beyond the scope of the present chapter. It suffices for the student to compare the words illustrating the point under discussion with the thought conveyed by the English translation, e.g. in this par-

[1] The numbers refer to paragraphs in Taylor's *African Aphorisms*.

ticular instance the use of HU- to express what is general, normal or habitual.

| | | |
|---|---|---|
| 515. | Ubishi mwingi **huleta** mateto. | Much joking generally brings on quarrelling. |
| 44. | Bandu bandu, **humala** gogo. | Chip, chip, the block finishes. |
| 70. | Haba na haba **hujaza** kibaba. | A little and a little fills up the kibaba measure. (Many a mickle . . .) |
| 260. | Mgema akisifiwa tembo, **hulitia** maji. | The palm-wine tapper, if he has his wine praised, puts water into it. |
| 394. | Mwivi **hushikwa** na mwivi mwenziwe. | A thief is caught by a thief his companion. (Set a thief to catch a thief.) |
| 279. | Mla-mbuzi **hulipa** ng'o-mbe. | The eater of a goat pays a cow. |
| 475. | Shauku nyingi **huondoa** maarifa. | Too great eagerness bereaves one of understanding. |

### VOCABULARY

| | | | |
|---|---|---|---|
| **ku-soma** | to read | **juzi** | day before yesterday |
| **ku-fika** | to arrive | **kesho** | to-morrow |
| **jana** | yesterday | **sasa hivi** | just now |

EXERCISE 9a (Verb Drill on the six primary tenses)

Translate the following sentences as a written exercise. Then do it again and again orally until the change of tense and person becomes automatic. Two verbs only are used: kufika, to arrive, and kusoma, to read.

*Note*—**Lini?** = When? comes immediately after the verb.

1. What are you reading?
2. I am reading a book.
3. The porters have arrived.
4. Has Ali arrived?
5. Did Ali read yesterday?
6. Did the strangers arrive yesterday?
7. They will arrive to-morrow.
8. They have just now arrived.
9. Ali will read to-morrow.
10. When will you arrive?
11. I shall arrive to-morrow.

12. When did the strangers arrive?

13. Did Hamisi arrive yesterday?

14. He arrived yesterday.

15. Hamisi reads well.

16. Will Hamisi arrive to morrow?

*Word order.* Remember to put the noun which forms the topic first and the point about the topic last.

### VOCABULARY

| ku-rudi | to return | ku-lima | to cultivate |
|---------|-----------|---------|--------------|
| ku-fanya | to do | kw-enda | to go |
| ku-andika | to write | vizuri | well |
| ku-imba | to sing | ku-la | to eat |

### EXERCISE 9b

Do as with previous exercises:

1. (II) Bwana amerudi?     (Ic) Amerudi.
2. (Ib) Alirudi lini?     (Ic) Alirudi jana.
3. (Ib) Unafanya nini?     (Ic) Ninaandika.
4. (Ib) Unaandika nini?     (Ic) Ninaandika kitabu.
5. (Ib) Wataka nini?     (Ic) Nataka viazi.
6. (Ib) Mizigo iko wapi?     (Ic) Imepotea.
7. (Ia) Watoto wanaimba vizuri.
8. (II) Watoto waimba vizuri?     (Ic) Waimba vizuri.
9. (Ia) Wanawake wanalima shambani.
10. (Ia) Mpishi amekwenda sokoni.

### EXERCISE 9c

Translate:

1. Have the porters arrived? They have arrived.
2. What are the sick folks doing? They are lying down.
3. What have you taken away? I have taken some chairs away.
4. What are you taking away? I am taking the utensils away.
5. The sick man died the day before yesterday.
6. What do you (pl.) want? We want some food.
7. What has he eaten? He has eaten some potatoes.

8. What did he eat yesterday?   He ate some potatoes.
9. Have you (pl.) read to-day?   We have read.
10. When did you cultivate?   I cultivated the day before yesterday.
11. Did you go to the market yesterday?   I went.

# CHAPTER IX

## PRONOUNS (Section I)

### PERSONAL AND NON-PERSONAL PRONOUNS

In Swahili there are three forms of personal pronouns:

| (i) | | (ii) | | (iii) | |
|---|---|---|---|---|---|
| *Subject Prefix* | | *Object Prefix* | | *Self-standing Pronoun* | |
| ni- | I | -ni- | me | **mimi** | I, me |
| u- | you (thou) | -ku- | you (thee) | **wewe** | you |
| a- | he, she | -m- | him, her | **yeye** | he, she, him, her |
| tu- | we | -tu- | us | **sisi** | we, us |
| m- | you | -wa-[1] | you | **ninyi** | you, ye |
| wa- | they | -wa- | them | **wao** | they, them |

(i) *The Subject Prefix* has been discussed on p. 31.

(ii) *The Object Prefix.*

The Object Prefix stands immediately in front of the verb stem, and consequently follows all tense prefixes.

Note that the Object Prefixes for 2nd person sing. and plur., and for the 3rd person sing. are different from the Subject Prefixes.

> **Ulimwona?** Did you (sing.) see him?
> **Alikuona?** Did he see you (sing.)?
> **Mlituona.** You (pl.) saw us.
> **Tuliwaona** We saw you (pl.).

No distinction is made for gender.

> **Nilimwona.** I saw him (or her).
> **Aliniona.** He (or she) saw me.

Sound change in the object prefix before a verb stem beginning with a vowel is not entirely subject to the rules

---

[1] The 2nd pers. plur. form has several variations.
I shall hit you (pl.) = Nitawapiga, nitawapigeni, nitakupigeni.
Compare -eni of the Imperative plural form.

governing classificatory and concordial prefixes. Thus:—**ni** and **wa** generally remain unchanged; **mw** replaces **m**; **kw** and **tw** may replace **ku** and **tu** before **a, e, i.**

Where neuter non-personal pronouns are concerned, the Subject and Object Prefixes are alike in form, being the Pronominal Concord of the noun concerned. There is no sound change before a verb stem beginning with a vowel.

| | |
|---|---|
| Kiti **ki**mevunjika. | The chair is broken. |
| Uli**ki**vunja? | Did you break it? |
| Vikombe **vi**mepotea. | The cups are lost. |
| Ume**vi**ona? | Have you seen them? |
| Mti **u**lianguka. | The tree fell down. |
| Nili**u**ona. | I saw it. |
| Mizigo **i**ko wapi? | Where are the loads? |
| Wame**i**ondoa. | They have taken them away. |

The Object Prefix -**ji**- is reflexive,[1] and can be used for any person sing. or plur. It corresponds to nouns of all classes where the sense allows.

| | |
|---|---|
| Nili**ji**ficha. | I hid myself. |
| Wali**ji**ficha. | They hid themselves. |
| Kijidudu kili**ji**ficha. | The insect hid itself. |

### EXERCISE 10

Translate as a written exercise, then do again orally, using the correct tone patterns. Ku-ona = to see.

1. They have seen it. (tree)
2. They have seen them. (people)
3. They have seen us.
4. They have seen you. (pl.)
5. They have seen you. (sing.)
6. They have seen them. (chairs)
7. Did you (sing.) see them? (people)
8. Did you (sing.) see it? (fire)
9. Did you (sing.) see her?
10. Did you (sing.) see us?
11. Did you (sing.) see it? (chair)
12. Did you (sing.) see me?
13. He will see you. (pl.)
14. He will see us.
15. He will see him.
16. He will see me.
17. He will see it. (cup)
18. He will see himself.

[1] For wider uses of Reflexive -**ji**- see p. 220 and the *Standard Swahili-English Dictionary*, p. 154, section 3.

19. Do you (pl.) see them? (trees)
20. Do you (pl.) see me?
21. Do you (pl.) see them? (spoons)

22. Shall we see you? (pl.)
23. Shall we see you? (sing.)
24. Shall we see him?

(iii) *The Self-standing Pronouns.*

The Self-standing Personal Pronouns may stand alone or in apposition to a noun.

| Nani yuko? **Mimi**. | Who is there? I. |
| **Mimi**, Hamisi. | I, Hamisi. |

They may also be used with either the Subject or Object Prefix to give emphasis. In this connection they should be used sparingly by beginners, as emphatic speech should be avoided at this stage.

| Subj. | **Mimi** nimekwisha. | As for me, I have finished. |
| | **Yeye** asema . . . | He himself says . . . |
| Obj. | Nilimwona **yeye** na Hamisi pia. | I saw both him and Hamisi. |

The corresponding Neuter forms are not required at this stage; they are set out on p. 304.

## The Noun Object and its Object Prefix

*Position in the Sentence.*

The noun object normally follows the verb, but it may precede the verb in certain circumstances. As already stated the object prefix always stands immediately in front of the verb stem and after the tense prefix.

*Occurrence.*

Direction of emphasis dictates the position of the noun object, and the use or omission of the object prefix. Two general principles are concerned:

(a) In questions of a general nature, the noun object follows the verb.

Umeleta chakula?        Have you brought (the) food?

The important element here is the action, not the object. In replies to such question, no object is usually expressed.

| Nimeleta Bwana. | I have brought (it), sir. |
|---|---|

(*b*) In statements or questions in which attention is directed to the object rather than to the action, the object prefix is used as well as the noun. The noun in these cases may follow or precede the verb.

| Hamisi amekileta chakula. | Hamisi has brought the food. (which you asked for) |
|---|---|
| Umekileta chakula? | Have you brought the food? |
| Chakula umekileta? | (which I asked you to bring) |

In replies to such questions the noun is omitted but the object prefix is usually retained.

| Nimekileta Bwana. | I have brought it, sir. |
|---|---|

As the degree of definiteness to be conveyed is entirely dependent on the context, and is further expressed by tone and gesture, the above principles must be regarded as very general in scope; isolated examples in print may often bear more than one interpretation. Beginners should err rather on the side of omission in regard to the object prefix, and not imagine that it should be used every time the English translation contains an "it" or a "them".

Note the direction of emphasis in the following Aphorisms, indicated by the place of the noun and the use of the object prefix.

| Chombo amekipanza (*or* amekipandisha) mwamba. | He has run (it) the vessel on the rock (i.e. ruined the scheme). |
|---|---|
| 66. Farasi hamwawezi, ndovu mtawalishani? | (As for) horses, you can't manage for them, with what will you feed elephants? |

# CHAPTER X

## ADJECTIVAL CONCEPTS (Section I)

In Swahili there are few words which may be termed "Adjectives". There are, however, many ways of expressing an adjectival concept. The following will be discussed in this section:

    (A) Roots and stems taking the Adjectival Concord (A.C.).

    (B) Uninflected loan words.

These two categories of qualifiers approach nearest to the conception of "Adjective" in English grammar.

### (A) The Adjectival Concord

Certain roots and stems are given adjectival function by the addition of a concordial prefix termed the Adjectival Concord (A.C.). This concord, except with certain nouns in the U- Class, is the same as the Class Prefix, and virtually converts the "Adjective" stem into a noun in apposition.

Examples: Note that the adjective follows its noun.

| | | | |
|---|---|---|---|
| **-refu** long | **Kisu kirefu.** | A long knife. | (Lit. Knife, a long one.) |
| | **Visu virefu.** | Long knives. | (Lit. Knives, long ones.) |
| **-vivu** lazy | **Mtu mvivu.** | A lazy man. | (Lit. Man, a lazy one.) |
| **-wili** two | **Watu wawili.** | Two people. | (Lit. People two.) |
| **-zuri** fine | **Mti mzuri.** | A fine tree. | (Lit. Tree, a fine one.) |
| **-tatu** three | **Miti mitatu.** | Three trees. | (Lit. Trees three.) |

Some adjective stems are derived from verbs.

| | | | |
|---|---|---|---|
| **-bivu** | ripe | **kuiva** | to ripen |
| **-bovu** | rotten | **kuoza** | to rot |
| **-kuu** | great | **kukua** | to grow |

46

Others give rise to verb forms by the addition of suffixes:

| **-nene** | fat | **kunenepa** | to get fat |
| **-refu** | long | **kurefusha** | to lengthen |
| **-fupi** | short | **kufupiza** | to shorten |

Nearly all these adjective stems have cognate abstract nouns with the **u-** (< **bu**) Prefix.

| Mtu **m**-zuri. | A fine man. | **u**-zuri | beauty, nice- |
| Watoto **wa**-zuri. | Beautiful | | ness, fineness |
| | children. | | |
| Chakula **ki**-zuri. | Nice food. | | |
| Watu **wa**-chache. | A few people. | **u**-chache | scarcity, few- |
| Miti **mi**-chache. | A few trees. | | ness |

*Sound change.*

Adjectives and their prefixes are subject to more or less the same rules of sound change as Nouns. The following are the sound changes before Adjective stems beginning with the vowels **-i** and **-e**.

| ki | | ki | Chakula **ki**ngine. | Other food. |
| vi | | vi | Vitu **vi**ngine.[1] | Other things. |
| mi | + i > | mi | Miti **mi**ngi. | Many trees. |
| m | | mwi | Mtu **mwi**ngine. | Another person. |
| | | | Mwitu **mwi**ngi. | Dense forest. |
| wa | | we | Watu **we**ngi. | Many people. |

| ki | | che | Kikombe **che**upe. | A white cup. |
| vi | | vye | Viti **vye**ma. | Good chairs. |
| mi | + e > | mye | Miti **mye**kundu.[2] | Red trees. |
| m | | mwe | Mtu **mwe**ma. | A good person. |
| | | | Mti **mwe**ma. | A good tree. |
| wa | | we | Watu **we**usi. | Black people. |

It will be noticed that most adjective stems beginning with a vowel begin with **i-** or **e-**. There are only two or three

[1] Contrast noun kiini. Note that in Mombasa, chengine and vyengine are used.
[2] Contrast noun miezi.

beginning with **a-**, **o-** or **u-** in common use, and their meaning is so restricted that they cannot be used with nouns of every class. The following are typical examples:

| | | |
|---|---|---|
| Mtu mwanana. | A gentle person. | pl. Watu waanana. |
| Mtu mwororo. | A mild person. | pl. Watu waororo. |
| Mtu mume. | A man. | pl. Watu waume. |
| Mti mwororo. | Soft yielding wood. | pl. Miti myororo. |
| Kitu chororo. | A soft substance. | pl. Vitu vyororo. |
| Kijana kiume. | A young man. | pl. Vijana viume. |

The following list of roots and stems taking the Adjectival Concord is more or less exhaustive. They are arranged so as to help the student in making the various sound changes necessary in the N- Classes (p. 85).

| | | | |
|---|---|---|---|
| -dogo | little, small | -zee | old |
| -gumu | hard | -zuri | nice, fine, beautiful |
| -geni | foreign | -zima | sound, whole |
| | | -zito | heavy |
| | | -baya | bad |
| -vivu | idle | -bichi | raw, unripe |
| | | -bivu | ripe |
| | | -bovu[1] | rotten |
| -eupe | white, light | -ingi | many |
| -eusi | black, dark | -ingine | other |
| -ema | good | -ume | male |
| -erevu | cunning | -anana | gentle |
| -epesi | easy, light | -ororo | soft |
| -embamba | narrow, slender | -ovu[1] | evil |
| -ekundu | red | -angavu | bright |
| -pana | broad | -fupi | short |
| -tatu | three | -nene | fat (of people) |
| -tano | five | -nono | fat (of animals) |
| -tamu | sweet | -moja | one |
| -tupu | bare, empty, mere | -ngapi | how many? |

---

[1] Mtu mw-ovu = An evil man.
Mti m-bovu  = A rotten tree.

| -chungu | bitter | | |
|---------|--------|---|---|
| -chache | few | | |
| -kuu | great, chief | | |
| -kubwa | big | | |
| -kali | fierce, savage, sharp, acid | | |
| -kuukuu | old, worn out | | |
| -kavu | dry | | |
| | | | |
| -wivu | jealous | **-refu** | long |
| -wili | two | | |
| | | | |
| -pya | new | **-ne** | four |
| -ke | female | | |

The meaning of these qualifying words should not be confined to the English translations given above, for many express an elemental idea. For instance, the elemental idea of **-bichi** is "a natural state", but in its wider uses it may denote unripe fruit, new-laid eggs, damp clothes, milk which has not been boiled or otherwise heated, a raw recruit, etc., etc. The Dictionary should be consulted at this stage for further examples of a similar nature.

## EXERCISE 11

Combine the adjective stems: -pya, -ema, -ingine, -baya -fupi, -dogo, with the nouns mtu, milango, vitanda.

### (B) Uninflected Loan Words

These are mostly loan words from Arabic. The following few examples should be sufficient:[1]

| **hodari** | clever, strong, able | **Mtu hodari.** | A clever man. |
|------------|---------------------|-----------------|---------------|
| | | **Mti hodari.** | Strong, hard wood. |
| **tele** | plenty | **Watu tele.** | Many people. |
| | | **Maji tele.** | Plenty of water. |

[1] Nouns from other Classes are included in these examples to show the absence of concord.

C

| **safi** | clean, honest | **Chumba safi.** | A clean room. |
| | | **Maneno safi.** | A straightforward statement. |
| **kamili** | complete | **Mwezi kamili.** | A full month. |
| **haba** | few | **Maneno haba.** | A few words. |

Many of these words have abstract nouns corresponding to them:

| **u**-hodari (U- Class) | courage, capability |
| tele (N- Class) | abundance, plenty |
| **u**-safi | cleanliness, purity, honesty |
| **u**-kamili | completeness |
| (**u**-)haba | scarcity, rarity |

## THE NUMERALS

In counting, the numbers are:

| 1. moja *or* mosi[1] | 12. kumi na mbili |
| 2. mbili *or* pili[1] | 20. ishirini |
| 3. tatu | 30. thelathini |
| 4. nne | 40. arobaini |
| 5. tano | 50. hamsini |
| 6. sita | 60. sitini |
| 7. saba | 70. sabini |
| 8. nane | 80. themanini |
| 9. kenda *or* tisa | 90. tisini |
| 10. kumi | 100. mia |
| 11. kumi na moja | 1,000. elfu |

When used as noun qualifiers, only the following numeral stems take the Adjectival Concord:

| 1. -moja | Mwaka mmoja. | One year. |
| 2. -wili | Viti viwili. | Two chairs. |
| 3. -tatu | Watu watatu. | Three people. |
| 4. -ne | Vijiko vine. | Four spoons. |
| 5. -tano | Watoto watano. | Five children. |
| 8. -nane | Miaka minane. | Eight years. |
| and -ngapi (how many?) | Milango mingapi? | How many doors? |

---

[1] In Mombasa only, but note in Zanzibar Swahili:
 Juma-mosi (Saturday), Juma-pili (Sunday).

The following numerals take no prefix:

| | | |
|---|---|---|
| 6. **sita** | Miaka sita. | Six years. |
| 7. **saba** | Viti saba. | Seven chairs. |
| 9. **tisa** *or* **kenda** | Watu tisa. | Nine people. |
| 10. **kumi** | Vijiko kumi. | Ten spoons. |

Also all multiples of ten:

**Watu** ishirini.  Twenty people.    **Miti** mia.  A hundred trees.

In compound numerals, 11–19, 21–9, etc., the "tens" are not declined, but the declinable "units" receive the appropriate Adjectival Concord.

| | |
|---|---|
| Viti kumi na **ki**-moja. | Eleven chairs. |
| Miaka ishirini na **mi**-wili. | Twenty-two years. |
| Watu thelathini na **wa**-tatu. | Thirty-three people. |
| Viti sitini na **vi**-nane. | Sixty-eight chairs. |

But:

| | |
|---|---|
| Viti sitini na sita. | Sixty-six chairs. |

Sometimes the Arabic numerals are used instead of the Bantu compound forms for 11–19.

| | | |
|---|---|---|
| 11. edashara | *instead of* | kumi na -moja |
| 12. thenashara | | kumi na -wili |
| 13. thelatashara | | kumi na -tatu |
| 14. arobatashara | | kumi na -ne |
| 15. hamstashara | | kumi na -tano |
| 16. sitashara | | kumi na sita |
| 17. sabatashara | | kumi na saba |
| 18. themantashara | | kumi na -nane |
| 19. tisatashara | | kumi na kenda |

In such cases there is no concord.  Compare:

**Watu** kumi na **m**-moja *or* **Watu** edashara.    Eleven people.
**Miti** kumi na **mi**-ne    *or* **Miti** arobatashara.  Fourteen trees.
For the ordinals see p. 146.

### EXERCISE 12

Combine the following numeral qualifiers: -moja, kumi na -wili, thelathini na -nane, sita, mia na -tatu with: mtu, mlango, kitanda respectively (using plural forms where necessary).

## Uses of Adjectives

Adjectives have a twofold use:

1. They may follow and qualify a noun:
   Lete visu vikubwa.    Bring some big knives.
2. They may stand alone, when the noun to which they refer is known:
   Lete vikubwa.        Bring big ones.

## Word Order in Adjectives

*In ordinary i.e. unemphatic speech.*

When two qualifiers are used with one noun, the word which is most closely connected with the noun follows it immediately, and the word which defines or embraces the other two follows.

In "two white cups", the word "two" embraces or defines "white cups", and therefore stands last.

Vikombe vyeupe viwili.        Lit. Cups white ones two of them.

In "large white cups", the word "large" embraces or defines "white cups", and therefore stands last.

Vikombe vyeupe vikubwa.  Lit. Cups white ones large.

*In emphatic speech.*

Here the same principle holds good, in that the definining or important word comes last.

In "two *white* cups", the word "white" embraces or defines "two cups", and therefore stands last.

Vikombe viwili vyeupe.    Lit. Cups two white ones.

In "large *white* cups", the word "white" embraces or defines "large cups", and therefore stands last.

Vikombe vikubwa vyeupe.  Lit. Cups large ones, white.

Beginners are advised to confine themselves to *unemphatic* speech in doing the exercises in this book.

**ku-ingia ufa** to be(come) cracked   **La!** No!

### EXERCISE 13

Translate:

1. Some cunning thieves have stolen a trap.
2. Ten tall trees have died.
3. Yesterday we bought two umbrellas and some new shoes.
4. Three white cups are cracked, five small saucers are broken.
5. The cook wants a new knife.
6. Bring eight little loaves.
7. How many cups am I to bring? Bring five.
8. Am I to bring white ones? No, bring red ones.

# CHAPTER XI

## PRONOUNS (Section II)

## PRONOMINAL ROOTS

THE following roots and stems are brought into concordial relationship with the Noun to which they refer by the Pronominal Concord (P.C.):

| | | | |
|---|---|---|---|
| (i) | Possessive (including the -A of Relationship) | **-angu**, etc. | my, mine, etc. |
| (ii) | Demonstrative | **-le** | that yonder |
| (iii) | Interrogative | **-pi?** | which? |
| (iv) | -O of Reference | **-o** | who, whom, etc. |
| (v) | | **-ote** | whole, all |
| | | **-o -ote** | any whatsoever |
| (vi) | -enye | **-enye** | having, possessing |
| | | **-enyewe** | itself |

These roots and stems have a twofold usage:

1. They may be used with nouns to qualify or define them, and are thus termed "adjectives" by some grammarians.

2. They may stand alone as pronouns.

These two uses will be illustrated as each root or stem comes under discussion.

The -A of Relationship also takes the P.C. in certain contexts. Only one of its many uses is discussed here, viz. to express possessive relationship.

The -O of Reference also occurs in many contexts, but only two of its uses are discussed at this stage.

Study the table on the next page, which refers to three Classes only, in connection with the Reference Table on p. 12, noting that in all cases where the Class Prefix is non-nasal, the form of the Pronominal Concord is identical (except in the JI- Class, which see later).

### SOUND CHANGE IN PRONOMINAL CONCORDS

| Class Prefix | Pronominal Concord | | | |
|---|---|---|---|---|
| | Before Consonant | With following vowel | | |
| | | -a- | -o- | -e- |
| ki- | ki- | cha | cho | che |
| vi- | vi- | vya | vyo | vye |
| m- | u- | wa | (w)o | we |
| mi- | i- | ya | yo | ye |
| m- | yu- | wa | yo | we |
| wa- | wa- | wa | (w)o | we |

### (I) Possessives

The -A of Relationship expresses possessive relationship between its noun antecedent and:

(a) *Another noun.* **-a Hamisi** Hamisi's; **-a wapagazi** porters'.
Kiti **cha** Hamisi.   Hamisi's chair. (Chair it-of Hamisi.)
Mizigo **ya** wapagazi. The porters' loads. (Loads they-of porters.)

(b) *A pronominal root or stem.*
**-a-ngu** of me, my, mine     **-etu**[1] of us, our, ours
**-a-ko** of you, your, yours   **-enu**[1] of you, your, yours (pl.)
**-a-ke** of him, his       **-a-o** of them, their, theirs
      Viti **vyangu.** My chairs. (Chairs they-of me.)
      Mguu **wake.** His leg.   (Leg it-of him.)

(c) *An interrogative.* **-a nani?** of whom, whose?

   Kiti **cha** nani?  Whose chair?  (Chair it-of whom?)
   Viti **vya** nani?  Whose chairs?  (Chairs they-of whom?)

These roots and stems may also be used without a preceding noun.
Lete kitabu changu.    Bring my book.
Kimepotea. Nilete **changu?** It's lost. Shall I bring mine?

[1] < -a-itu, -a-inu

Note that in ordinary speech, the possessive stems, being the most closely connected with their antecedent, take precedence over other qualifying stems, and come next to the noun.

Vikombe **vyangu** vikubwa.   My big cups. (Cups mine, big ones.)

Watoto **wao** watatu.   Their three children. (Children their, three.)

Emphatic speech, however, may involve a different word order.

### EXERCISE 14a

Translate as a written exercise, then practise this drill orally, substituting singular or plural nouns as the case may be.

1. Their room.
2. His children.
3. My porter.
4. (Other) people's things.
5. Ali's basket.
6. Whose cup?
7. Our guest.
8. My hands.
9. My large cup.
10. His tall trees.
11. The stranger's knife.
12. The strangers' loaves.
13. Whose cook?
14. Your (sing.) fire.
15. Your (pl.) fires.
16. Their town.
17. Whose pipe?
18. The old man's chair.
19. Their long knives.
20. Our few guests.

### Notes on Possessive Constructions

Names of near relatives and certain other words take a shortened form of the possessive.

Mwenz**angu** < mwenzi wangu.   My companion.
Mwenz**io** < mwenzi wako.   Your companion.
Mwenz**iwe** < mwenzi wake.   His companion.
Mwenz**etu** < mwenzi wetu.   Our companion.

For fuller list see p. 308.

Sometimes the full pronominal possessive form is used as an alternative to P.C. + -A, when referring to persons.

Mtoto **wake** Hamisi. ⎫
Mtoto **wa** Hamisi. ⎭ Hamisi's child.

*Concerning the use of -ao.*

This possessive form can only be used in relation to living beings.

> Visahani vy**ao**.   Their, i.e. people's saucers.

For inanimate things **-ake** is used, both for singular and plural.

> Kikombe na kisahani ch**ake**.   A cup and its saucer.
> Vikombe na visahani vy**ake**.   Cups and their saucers.

*Peke.*

This word, when followed by the appropriate possessive stem, expresses "by oneself, I alone", etc. Note that the concord prefix is invariably **y-**.

> Mimi peke **yangu**.   I alone, I only.
> Wewe peke **yako**.   You alone, you only.
> Mtu peke **yake**.   The man by himself.
> Watu peke **yao**.   The people alone.

Note here again the use of **-ake**, for both singular and plural, when referring to inanimate things.

> Kisu peke **yake**.   The knife only.
> Visu peke **yake**.   The knives by themselves.

Note also the following expressions:

> Mtu **wa pekee**.   A solitary man.
> Mwenda **pekee**.   One who goes alone, used of either man or beast.

*Possessive Stem after Kwenda.*

The use of the possessive stem with **z-** as prefix is frequently heard with **kwenda** to give force to the meaning. It somewhat resembles the English expression "to go off".

> Nenda (*or* naenda) **zangu**.   I'm off.
> Enda **zako**.   Be off with you.
> Amekwenda **zake**.   He's gone off.
> Twende **zetu**.   Let's get off.
> Endeni **zenu**.   Be off with you.
> Wamekwenda **zao**.   They've gone away.

c*

The same idiom is found in Shona but with a wider implication (see J. O'Neill, *A Shona Grammar*, p. 162).

*The Object Prefix.*

The Object Prefix is generally used with noun objects of the Personal Classes when followed by a Possessive.

Umem**wo**na mpishi wangu? Have you seen my cook?
Uli**wa**ona wagonjwa wetu? Did you see our sick folk?

With nouns indicating inanimate objects it may be used or omitted according to the degree of emphasis to be conveyed.

Umeona kisu changu? Have you seen my knife?
Kisu changu ume**ki**ona? My knife, have you seen it?

### EXERCISE 14b

Translate:

1. His two guests arrived yesterday.
2. Our new basket is split.
3. The stranger's pipe has fallen down. Is it broken?
4. Your (pl.) three trees are dead.
5. Two cups and their saucers are broken.
6. Has your companion taken away my basket?
7. Did Hamisi's child arrive yesterday?
8. When did Ali's child come?
9. Have you seen our porters? I have seen them.
10. Have they read your book? They have read it.
11. Put the knives by themselves.
12. Did he come alone?
13. Take yourselves off.

### (II) Demonstratives

The Demonstrative root **-le** denotes some person or thing at a distance or in "Non-proximity", or in a direction **away** from the speaker. Thus:

Kisu **ki**le. That knife. Vyumba **vi**le. Those rooms.
Mti **u**le. That tree. Milango **i**le. Those doors.
Mtoto **yu**le. That child. Watu **wa**le. Those men.

The corresponding "Proximity" forms of the Demonstrative are composed of the P.C. as a suffix, preceded by **h-** which is invariable, plus the same vowel as that which occurs in the P.C.

| | | | |
|---|---|---|---|
| Kisu hiki. | This knife. | Vyumba hivi. | These rooms. |
| Mti huu. | This tree. | Milango hii. | These doors. |
| Mtoto huyu. | This child. | Watu hawa. | These men. |

These Demonstratives may stand with a noun as in the above examples, or they may stand alone as demonstrative pronouns.

> Nataka **kile**.    I want that one (i.e. knife).
> Namtaka **huyu**.    I want this one (i.e. child).

### Exercise 15a

Translate:

| | | | |
|---|---|---|---|
| This pipe, | that pipe. | This month, | that month. |
| This teacher, | that teacher. | This mountain, | that mountain. |
| This load, | that load. | This shoe, | that shoe. |

Practise this drill in the plural forms also.

## Notes on Demonstratives

The **-le** and **h-** forms cannot be used in conjunction to sharpen a contrast as in English.

92. **Hii** yafutika, **hii** haifutiki.    *That* (sin) can be blotted out, *this* one cannot be.

The Demonstrative form **-le** may either precede or follow the noun it qualifies. When it precedes the noun, its function corresponds to that of the definite article in English.

> **Yule** mtu.    The man (away from speaker).

When it follows the noun, its function is generally demonstrative.

> Mtu **yule**.    That man (over there).
> Mtu **yuleee**.    That man (right over there).

At this stage it must suffice to draw attention to the two positions. A wider context than is here possible is required to illustrate fully the difference indicated in the two positions. (See p. 181.)

The "Proximity" demonstrative is found mostly after the noun.

Mtu huyu.   This man.

The Object Prefix is generally used with noun objects in the Personal Classes when followed by a Demonstrative.

Ulimpiga mtoto huyu?   Did you strike this child?

With nouns indicating inanimate objects it may be used or omitted according to the degree of emphasis to be conveyed.

| | |
|---|---|
| Wataka kitabu hiki? | Do you want this book? |
| Nakitaka. | I want it. |
| Kitabu hiki wakitaka? | Do you want *this* book? |

EXERCISE 15b

Translate:

1. Lete kile kisu kidogo.
2. Viatu hivi vipya vyaniumiza.
3. Ondoa vyombo vile.
4. Kisu hiki chanipendeza.
5. Watoto hawa wasoma vizuri?
6. Mzee yule amelala?
7. Mlango huu umevunjika.
8. Mpishi huyu apika vizuri.
9. Miti hii miwili imekufa.
10. Viazi hivi vimeiva?
11. Alimpiga mtoto yule.
12. Nataka hiki na hiki.

## (III) Interrogative -pi

This root expresses a selective idea.

| | |
|---|---|
| Kitabu **ki**pi? | Which book? |
| Mti **u**pi? | Which tree? |
| Mtu **yu**pi? | Which man? |
| Viazi **vi**pi? | Which potatoes? |
| Mikate **i**pi? | Which loaves? |
| Watoto **we**pi?[1] | Which children. |

[1] **Wepi** is more common than **wapi**.

It may be used with a noun, or it may stand alone as an interrogative pronoun.

> **Wataka kipi?** Which one (i.e. book) do you want?

<h3 style="text-align:center">EXERCISE 16a</h3>

Translate:

| | |
|---|---|
| Which sick man? | Which towns? |
| Which month? | Which strangers? |
| Which cup? | Which pipes? |

The Object Prefix is generally used with the noun object in the Living Classes when followed by the Interrogative.
**Waliwapiga** watoto wepi?   Which children did they beat?
**Wamtaka yupi?**   Which one (i.e. boy) do you want?

<h3 style="text-align:center">EXERCISE 16b</h3>

Translate:

1. Which child did you see? I saw yours.
2. Which book did you buy?
3. Which mountain did they see?
4. Which potatoes did the women bring?
5. Which one (i.e. basket) am I to bring?
6. Which cup does the cook want?
7. Which porter do you want?

### (IV) -O of Reference

This will be discussed in Chapters XVII, XIX and XXIX.

### (V) -ote and -o -ote

The conception underlying **-ote** is one of "wholeness", completeness. It may be used with a noun, or it may stand alone as a pronoun.

Its use in the singular is restricted.
Mwili **wote** waniuma.   My whole body pains me.
Chakula **cho**te kimeharibika? Is all the food spoilt?
**Cho**te Bwana.   All of it, sir.

It is more often found in plural forms.

Lete visu **vyote**.   Bring all the knives.

Lete vyote.          Bring all of them.

Watu wote wamefika.      All the people have come.

Compare:

Mwili wote.    The whole body.    Mi(w)ili yote.    All the bodies.

Chumba chote.   The whole room.    Vyumba vyote.   All the rooms.

Note the alliterative forms of **-ote** in the 1st and 2nd person plural.

Sisi sote.      All of us.      Ninyi nyote.    All of you.

These forms are frequently used with numerals.

Sote **wawili**.   Both of us.      Nyote **wawili**.   Both of you.

Vyote **viwili**.   Both of them (books).    Yote **mitatu**.   All three of them (trees).

The phrase **-o -ote** has the meaning "anyone whosoever" or "anything whatsoever". Note that the singular Personal Class is irregular.

Kitu **cho chote**.      Anything whatever.

Viti **vyo vyote**.     Any chairs whatever.

Mti **wo wote**.      Any tree whatever.

Miti **yo yote**.      Any trees whatever.

Watu **wo wote**.     Any people whatever.

Mtu **ye yote**.[1]      Any person whatever.

The phrase may be used to qualify a noun, or it may stand alone as a pronoun.

Lete kisu **cho chote**.   Bring any knife.

Nilete **cho chote**?    Am I to bring any one of them?

## EXERCISE 17

Translate:

1. All the shoes.
2. Any cups.
3. All the towns.
4. Any spoon whatever.
5. Any child whatever.
6. All sick folks.
7. Any shoes whatever.
8. All the cups.
9. Any town whatever.
10. All the spoons.
11. All children.
12. Any sick person whatever.

[1] yo yote in Mombasa.

## (VI) -enye[1] and -enyewe

**-enye** expresses "having" or "becoming". It requires an object, which may be a noun or its equivalent. The resultant phrase usually expresses state or condition. Note that the Singular Personal Class is irregular.

**-enye** is not usually used without a preceding noun, except when referring to persons (or places).

| | |
|---|---|
| Chumba **chenye** giza. | A dark room, i.e. a room having darkness. |
| Vyumba **vyenye** giza. | Dark rooms. |
| Mlima **wenye** mawe. | A stony hill, i.e. a hill with stones. |
| Mti **wenye** miiba. | A thorny tree, i.e. a tree with thorns. |
| (Mtu) **mwenye** mali. | A rich man, i.e. a man having money. |
| (Watu) **wenye** maarifa. | Well-informed people, i.e. people with knowledge. |

**-enyewe** expresses "himself" or "itself" in an emphasizing (non-reflexive) sense. In the Personal Class it may also mean "the owner".

| | |
|---|---|
| Chumba **chenyewe**. | The room itself. |
| Viti **vyenyewe**. | The chairs themselves. |
| Mti **wenyewe**. | The tree itself. |
| Milango **yenyewe**. | The doors themselves. |
| (Mtu) **mwenyewe**. | The man himself. |
| (Watu) **wenyewe**. | The people themselves. |

Note also **mwenyeji** pl. **wenyeji**—the inhabitants of a town, or the natives of a country, the owner or occupier of a house, a host in relation to guests.

## EXERCISE 18

Translate:

1. The thorn itself.
2. Knives with long handles.
3. A room with two doors.
4. The pipe itself.
5. The moon itself.
6. A three-legged chair.
7. Porters with loads.
8. The shoes themselves.

[1] See p. 147. Excellent notes are also given in the *Standard Swahili-English Dictionary*, p. 85.

# CHAPTER XII

## THE JI- AND MA- CLASSES

### REFERENCE TABLE

|  | Class Prefixes | | Concordial Prefixes | | | |
|  |  |  | Adjectival | | Pronominal | |
|  | Sing. | Plur. | Sing. | Plur. | Sing. | Plur. |
| Before consonant: | ji- or no pref. | ma- | ji- or no pref. | ma- | li- | ya- |
| Before vowel: | j- or no pref. | ma- | j- | m- | l- | y- |

The prefix of the JI- Class needs care.

1. **ji-** occurs before monosyllabic stems.

2. The prefix is absent before disyllabic, or polysyllabic stems beginning with a consonant (but see "Augmentatives", pp. 297).

3. **j-** occurs before most disyllabic or polysyllabic stems beginning with a vowel, except that

4. There is generally no prefix before stems derived from verbs.[1]

The plural prefix **ma-** occurs before all stems, and occasionally, as will be seen from later examples, is added to the singular **j(i)-** prefix.

### Examples

|  (1) | (2) | (3) | (4) |
|  |  |  |  |

Sing.:

**ji-we** (stone)   **tawi** (branch)   **j-ino** (tooth)     **onyo** (warning)

Plur.:

**ma-we**     **ma-tawi**     **meno** (< **ma-ino**)   **ma-onyo**

---

[1] Jambo (< amba) appears to be an exception.

Typical sentences with concords of these classes are:

Tawi **li**-mevunjika.    The branch is broken.

**Matawi ya**-mevunjika.    The branches are broken.

## Underlying Ideas

In these classes are found:

1. The names of things which occur in quantities, but which may be thought of singly as well, i.e.:

(a) Parts of the body which go in pairs or in sets:

**jino**, pl. **meno** tooth; **sikio**, pl. **masikio** ear.

(b) Constituent parts of trees, bushes, etc.:

**jani**, pl. **majani** leaf; **tunda**, pl. **matunda** fruit.

(c) Phenomena which occur in quantities:

**jiwe**, pl. **mawe** stone; **yai**, pl. **mayai** egg.

(d) Nouns describing actions, etc., derived from verbs:

**neno**, pl. **maneno** word < **kunena** to speak.

**pigo**, pl. **mapigo** blow, stroke < **kupiga** to hit.

2. Miscellaneous words, some of foreign origin.

**shoka**, pl. **mashoka** axe; **shamba**, pl. **mashamba** plantation; **soko**, pl. **masoko** market.

Other words which will be dealt with at a later stage are:

3. Names of foreign titles and ranks. See p. 89.

**Bwana**, pl. **Mabwana** master, sir.

4. Some relationship terms. See p. 89.

**shangazi**, pl. **mashangazi** aunt.

5. Words expressing an amplicative idea. See p. 297.

**j-oka**, pl. **majoka** huge snake; cf. **ny-oka** snake.

**ji-guu**, pl. **majiguu** big leg; cf. **m-guu** leg.

In the plural class, note that sometimes **ma-** takes the place of the **ji-** prefix, but that sometimes it is itself prefixed to this prefix.

Study these further examples with their plurals:

| | | | |
|---|---|---|---|
| 1. (a) | **bawa** | wing | **mabawa** |
| | **bavu** | side | **mabavu** |
| | **bega** | shoulder | **mabega** |
| | **jicho** | eye | **macho** |
| (b) | **ua** | flower | **maua** |

|   | boga | pumpkin | maboga |
|---|------|---------|--------|
|   | kuti | frond of coconut palm | makuti |
|   | pera | guava | mapera |
|   | embe | mango[1] | maembe |
|   | limau | lemon | malimau |
|   | nanasi | pineapple | mananasi |
|   | zao | crop | mazao |
| (c) | wingu | cloud | mawingu |
|   | jipu | boil | majipu |
|   | kaa | charcoal | makaa |
|   | tofali | brick | matofali |
| (d) | wazo | thought | mawazo |
|   | vazi | garment | mavazi |
|   | shauri | advice, plan | mashauri |
|   | elezo | explanation | maelezo |
|   | agano | covenant, testament | maagano |
|   | kosa | mistake | makosa |
| 2. | juma | week | majuma |
|   | duka | shop | maduka |
|   | jembe | hoe | majembe |
|   | gunia | sack | magunia |
| 3. | waziri | vizier | mawaziri |
|   | kadhi | Mohammedan judge | makadhi |
|   | boi | houseboy | maboi |
|   | fundi | skilled workman | mafundi |
|   | bibi | lady, mistress | mabibi |

Since Section 3 nouns refer to living beings, they are followed by the *personal* subject prefixes.

Bwana amefika.      The master has arrived.
Mabwana wamefika.    The gentlemen have arrived.

Such words will be discussed later, but are introduced at this stage because of their frequent occurrence in speech.

[1] Also sometimes heard as an N- Class word.

*Further Notes on the MA- Class.*

In this class are also found words which often express a collective idea, but which have no corresponding singular form in the JI- class. Such words are:

(*a*) Names of liquids, etc.:

| | | | |
|---|---|---|---|
| **maji** | water | **manukato** | scent |
| **mate** | saliva | **mavumbi** | dust |
| **maziwa** | milk | **mafuta** | fat, oil |

(*b*) Specialized forms of words normally occurring in the U- or N- Classes. These forms impart a collective idea.

pesa   pl. pesa   pice   **ma**-pesa   small change
**u**-nyasi pl. nyasi   grass   **ma**-nyasi   grass and weeds in
general

(*c*) Words derived from verbs with cognate forms in the U- class. The MA- form expresses the process, method, etc., of action in contrast to the purely abstract idea expressed by U-.

ku-gomba   to scold   **u**-gomvi   quarrelling
**ma**-gomvi   quarrels

(*d*) Certain abstract nouns of Arabic origin:

| | | | |
|---|---|---|---|
| **maisha**[1] | life | **maana** | meaning |
| **mauti** | death | **majonzi** | grief |
| **mali**[1] | wealth | **maridhawa** | abundance |

## EXERCISE 19a

Do as with other exercises (viz. Exercise 7a, etc., in so far as the sense allows):

1. (II) Mananasi yameiva?    (I)  Yameiva.
2. (II) Shoka liko kibandani?    (I)  Haliko, limepotea.
3. (Ia) Lete mafuta.    (Ic) Mafuta yamekwisha.

4. (Ia) Tia mayai bakulini.
5. (Ia) Wapagazi wasilete maji.

---

[1] Also as N- Class words when given a plural meaning.
Maisha **mengi,** long life; but maisha **nyingi,** many lives.
Mali **mengi,** great wealth; but mali **nyingi,** much property, etc.

6. (Ib) Hamisi ameleta nini?    (Ic) Ameleta majembe.
7. (Ia) Mabwana hawako shambani.
8. (Ia) Maboi wako jikoni.
9. (Ib) Mpishi anunue nini?    (Ic) Anunue malimau.
10. (Ia) Maziwa yamo ghalani?
11. (Ib) Mabibi wako wapi?    (Ic) Wako nyumbani.

## The Adjectival Concords

The same rules of sound change, but with fewer irregularities, may be found here as with the Class Prefixes.

| Before monosyllabic stem | Before Consonant | Before Vowel |
|---|---|---|
| Jembe **ji-pya** <br> Majembe **ma-pya** | Jembe **refu** <br> Majembe **ma-refu** | Jembe **j-ema** <br> Majembe **m-ema** |

Irregular Adjectival forms:

Bata **d-ume** drake  pl. Mabata **maume** *or* **madume** drakes.
Mabata **ma-ji-ke** ducks  sing. Bata **ji-ke** is regular.
**-ingine** has two forms in the singular: jingine and lingine,
                    pl. mengine.

### EXERCISE 19b

Give the Swahili of the following, together with the plural forms. (List of Adjective Stems on pp. 48-9.)

1. A new leaf.
2. One red pineapple.
3. Much water.
4. A large white tooth.
5. A long axe.
6. A fresh egg.
7. A fine eye.
8. A new name.

## The Pronominal Concords

These are **li-** and **ya-** before consonants and **l-** and **y-** before vowels (except before verb stems beginning with a vowel).

| Possessives | Demonstratives | -o root | -enye |
|---|---|---|---|
| Jembe langu | Jembe lile | Jembe lote | Jembe lenye kipini |
| Majembe yangu | Majembe yale | Majembe yote | Majembe yenye vipini |
| Jembe la Hamisi | Jembe hili | Jembe lo lote | Jembe le-nyewe |
| Majembe ya Hamisi | Majembe haya | Majembe yo yote | Majembe yenyewe |

| Interrogative | Subject Pref. | Object Pref. |
|---|---|---|
| Jembe lipi? Majembe yapi?[1] Jembe la nani? Majembe ya nani? | Jembe limeanguka Majembe yameanguka | Nimeliona Nimeyaona |

## VOCABULARY

| | | | |
|---|---|---|---|
| **toka** | come out, come from | **zidi** | increase |
| **kauka** | dry up, cf. **kavu** | **furika** | boil over, |
| **angalia** | take care | | overflow |

## EXERCISE 19c

Do as with previous exercises:

1. Jino lake limetoka?  Limetoka.
2. Tawi hili limevunjika.
3. Maji yote yamekauka.
4. Lete mayai mabichi matano.
5. Magomvi yao yamezidi.
6. Wataka jembe lipi?  Lo lote.
7. Wataka hili kubwa?  Nalitaka.
8. Maboi wote wamelala?
9. Bwana wako ameamka?
10. Wataka machungwa haya?  Nayataka.
11. Maziwa haya yamefurika: angalia yasifurike tena.

[1] Also heard as **yepi**.

# CHAPTER XIII

## VERBS AND THEIR TENSES (Section II)

## THE NEGATIVE FORMS OF THE PRIMARY TENSES

### General Remarks

NEGATION is expressed by means of two particles, either **ha-** or **-si-**, but never by both in the same verb form.

**ha-** is prefixed to the Subject Prefix and is used in the tenses of the Indicative Mood.

| | |
|---|---|
| Ha-wa-imbi. | They do not sing. |
| Ha-wa-ta-imba. | They will not sing. |
| Ha-wa-ku-imba. | They did not sing. |
| Ha-wa-ja-imba. | They have not yet sung. |

**si-** is prefixed to the verb stem, and occurs in the Subjunctive and Imperative forms.

| | |
|---|---|
| Wa-**si**-ende. | Let them not go. |
| **Si**-endeni. | Don't go (pl.). |

Both **ha** and **si** are subject to phonetic change before a vowel. This is clearly indicated in the reference table on the next page.

An important point to remember is that one negative tense in Swahili often corresponds to several affirmative tenses. Negation, being negation, cannot always express the finer shades of meaning conveyed in the different affirmative tenses.

### Notes on certain Negative Tenses

1. In the *General Negative*, which has no tense prefix, the final vowel **-a** of the verb is replaced by **-i**.[2]

Ha-wa-taki.  They do not want.

---

[1] It will also be seen that si replaces ha-ni for the 1st person singular in these tenses. This si is to be kept distinct from the si of the Subjunctive and Imperative forms.

[2] Borrowed verbs from Arabic do not undergo this sound change. Hawatubu, they do not repent.

The function of this form is to express the *fact* of negation without reference to time. It is not merely the negative of the present tense.

## REFERENCE TABLE—NEGATIVE

| | Singular | | Plural | |
|---|---|---|---|---|
| egative the I- of st me eynote A-KU- | Si-   ku-taka Hu-[1]   ,, Ha-   ,, | I did not you did not he, she did not } want | Hatu-ku-taka Ham-   ,, Hawa-   ,, | We did not you did not they did not } want |
| | Haki-   ,, Hau-[2]   ,, Hali-   ,, | } It did not want | Havi   ,, Hai-   ,, Haya-   ,, | } They did not want |
| egative the A- of uture me eynote A-TA- | Si-   ta-taka Hu-[1]   ,, Ha-   ,, | I shall not you will not he, she will not } want | Hatu-ta-taka Ham-   ,, Hawa   ,, | We shall not you will not they will not } want |
| | Haki-   ,, Hau-[2]   ,, Hali-   ,, | } It will not want | Havi-   ,, Hai-   ,, Haya-   ,, | } They will not want |
| eneral egative d egative the A- and NA- enses eynote A- - -I | Si-   taki Hu-[1]   ,, Ha-   ,, | I do not you do not he, she, does not } want (am not wanting, etc.) | Hatu-taki Ham-  ,, Hawa-  ,, | We do not you do not they do not } want (are not wanting, etc.) |
| | Haki-   ,, Hau-[2]   ,, Hali-   ,, | } It does not want (is not wanting) | Havi-   ,, Hai-   ,, Haya-  ,, | } They do not want (are not wanting) |
| he A- or OT ET ense eynote A- | Si-   ja-taka Hu-[1]   ,, Ha-   ,, Haki-   ,, Hau-[2]   ,, Hali-   ,, | I, you, etc., do not yet want, or have not yet wanted. | Hatu-ja-taka Ham-   ,, Hawa-   ,, Havi-   ,, Hai-   ,, Haya-   ,, | We, you, they do not yet want, or have not yet wanted. |

[1] Note elision HA + U > HU.
[2] No elision HA + U > HAU.

2. Two tenses are employed to express the negative equivalent of the **-me-** tense, according to what the speaker wishes to imply.

(i) The **ha- -ja-** or "not yet" tense is used if the speaker implies that the action may yet take place.

| | |
|---|---|
| Amerudi? | Has he returned? |
| Hajarudi. | He has not yet returned. |

Often **bado** (= not yet) is added.

(ii) Or the Negative Past Tense **ha-ku-** may be used. This is quite logical, for negation of a completed action is necessarily in past time.

| | |
|---|---|
| Amerudi? | Has he returned? |
| Hakurudi. | He has not returned. |

This same tense is also the negative counterpart of the **-li-** tense:

| | |
|---|---|
| Alirudi? | Did he return? |
| Hakurudi. | He did not return. |

3. **ku-** in monosyllabic verbs and in **kw-isha** and **kw-enda** is not retained in all tenses. Thus:

| | | | |
|---|---|---|---|
| General Negative. | Siji, | haji, | hawaji, etc. |
| Past. | Sikuja, | hakuja, | hawakuja, etc. |
| | (-ku- here is the tense prefix) | | |
| Compare: | | | |
| Future | Sitakuja, | hatakuja, | hawatakuja, etc. |
| "Not yet" tense. | Sijaja, | hajaja, | hawajaja, etc. or |
| | Sijakuja, | hajakuja, | hawajakuja, etc. |

## Aphorisms illustrating Negation without reference to Time

116. Jitahidi **haiondoi** amri ya Mungu.

Diligence annuls not the decree of God.

139. Kidole kimoja **hakivunji** chawa.

One finger will not kill a louse.

173. Kuku **hawekwi** shahidi wala **hajui** sheria.

A fowl is not set (as) witness nor does it know the law.

| | |
|---|---|
| 267. Mjumbe **hauawi**. | A messenger is not (i.e. must not be) slain. |
| 311. Msema kweli **hakosi**. | A truth-teller makes no mistakes. (Honesty is the best policy.) |
| 330. Mchimba kisima **hakatazwi** maji. | The digger of the well is not forbidden the water (cf. 1 Cor. ix, 7). |
| 359. Mwungwana **hanuni** kwa mashavu, hununa moyoni. | The man of birth pouts not with his lips, he pouts in his heart. |
| 370. Mwana wa kuku **hafunzwi** kuchakura. | A chick (child of a fowl) is not taught how to scratch up the ground. |
| 444. Nyungu kuu **haikosi** ukoko. | A big pot is sure to have (lacks not) some burnt rice (inside it). |

## VOCABULARY

| | | | |
|---|---|---|---|
| **kumbuka** | remember | **waka** | burn (intrans.) |
| **lia** | emit a sound, cry, etc. | **toka** | come out |

## EXERCISE 20a

Verb Drill, Negative Tenses.

Translate as a written exercise, then use as a drill verbally until some degree of fluency is attained.

1. We shall not want anything (kitu).
2. Will you not want something (kitu)?
3. Do you not want something?
4. I do not want anything.
5. I want nothing.
6. Did he not want anything?
7. They will not want anything.
8. Did they not want something?
9. They do not want anything.
10. He does not want anything.
11. I do not remember.
12. They did not remember.
13. He will not remember.
14. Do you not remember?

15. Does he not remember?
16. They will not remember.
17. Did you (pl.) not remember?

18. We did not remember.
19. We remember.
20. We do not remember.

## EXERCISE 20b

Put into the negative:

1. Tulikwenda mjini jana.
2. Nitapika kesho.
3. Mtoto alilia?
4. Moto unawaka vizuri?
5. Ninaandika.
6. Mananasi yameoza.
7. Mlikuja jana?
8. Kesho ataleta viazi.
9. Watakuja kesho.
10. Mpishi apika vizuri.
11. Tunasoma.
12. Ataandika kesho.
13. Mtoto analia.
14. Twataka kitu.
15. Tutakuja kesho.

## EXERCISE 20c

Give corresponding affirmative forms for:

1. Hatutaki kusoma.
2. Hamkununua viazi?
3. Viazi havikuoza.
4. Jino halikutoka.
5. Mpishi hataki maji.
6. Sitanunua jembe.
7. Hamisi hakuondoa vyombo?
8. Watoto hawasomi.
9. Jana sikula nanasi.
10. Hasomi vizuri.
11. Hatulii. Hatuli kitu.
12. Siendi mjini leo.

### Intonation. Tone Pattern in Parenthesis

As stated before, on p. 16, when a word like **Bwana** or **Bibi** is added to the end of a sentence or phrase, especially in a question or a reply, it is not included in the general tone pattern of the sentence, but is pronounced without much stress on a low tone level. In the following examples parenthetical words are written in italics:

(I) Hapa, *Bwana*.                     Here, sir.

\ . _ .

(Ia) Kisu kimepotea *Bwana*.          The knife is lost, sir.

_ . _ . . \ . _ .

(Ib) Kisu kiko wapi *Bwana*?[1]       Where is the knife, sir?

(Ic) Kisu kiko hapa *Bwana*.       It is here, sir.

The same tone pattern is found when interrogative sentences are reversed in word order, so that the interrogative word is not at the end. All words following the interrogative word are pronounced on a low tone level, being in apposition to the subject of the sentence.

(Ib) Kiko wapi *kisu*?       Where is the knife?

*or*

Amekwenda wapi *Hamisi*?[1]       Where has Hamisi gone?

Note also:
    Kwa nini *amekwenda jikoni*?       Why has he gone to the kitchen?

Certain adverbs, coming at the end of a sentence, and when not emphasized, have the same intonation pattern.

(Ia) Watu wamelala *tu*.       The people are just sleeping.

(Ib) Ulikwenda wapi *jana*?       Where did you go yesterday?

---

[1] See note on the interrogative starting on a high note, p. 33.
[2] Compare with **Kisu kiko wapi?** p. 20.

This tone pattern is often bound up with *direction of emphasis,* in that everything that follows the emphasized element in the sentence is pronounced with low tone. The following occasions are typical:

Hawataki *kitu.*　　　They don't want anything.

Compare:
Hawataki kitu.　　　They don't want *anything*.

Siji tena.　　　I certainly won't come again.

Siji *tena.*　　　I won't come again.

In this connection it should be noticed that any following sentence which implies a contradiction or contrast takes Tone Pattern Ic.

(Ia) Sikununua *mananasi.*　　　I didn't buy pineapples,

　　(Ic) nilinunua machungwa.　　　I bought oranges.

(Ia) Usipike viazi *leo.*　　　Don't cook potatoes to-day,

　　(Ic) pika mikate.　　　cook loaves.

In the foregoing examples, Tone Pattern in parenthesis is shown as occurring at the end of sentences. It may also occur, however, in the middle of a sentence or phrase, with usually a slightly higher tone level.

Vyombo *Bwana* vimeondolewa kitambo.   The tea things, sir, have been removed some time ago.

It may even be found initially in short introductory sentences, especially in a -ka- tense.

*Akasema* Vyema.     And he said, Very well.

VOCABULARY

| | | | |
|---|---|---|---|
| letwa | be brought | tena | again, also |
| patikana | be procurable | gunia (ma-) | sack |
| choka | be tired | faa | be of use, be |
| tu | merely, only, just | | suitable |

EXERCISE 21

Read and translate:

1. (Ib) Yametoka wapi *maji haya*?
2. (Ib) Yuko wapi *bwana wako*?
3. (Ib) Yaliletwa lini *machungwa haya*?
4. (Ib) Alifika lini *mgeni huyu*?
5. (Ib) Mawe makubwa yapatikana wapi?   (Ic) Hayapatikani *Bwana*.
6. (Ia) Jembe langu limepotea *tena*.
7. (Ib) Wataka mayai mangapi?   (Ic) Nataka mawili *tu*.
8. (Ib) Umeleta matunda mengine?   (I) La (I) sikuleta *mengine*, (Ic) nimeleta haya *tu*.
9. (II) Umeleta maji?   (Ic) Sikuleta, *Bwana*, (Ic) maji yamekwisha.
10. (II) Umenunua magunia?   (Ic) Sikununua, (Ic) dukani hayapatikani (Ic) ila moja *tu*.
11. (Ia) Jembe hili halinifai, (Ia) lete jingine (Ia) *lenye* kipini kirefu.
12. (Ia) Siendi *leo* (Ic) nilikwenda jana.

## Tone Pattern III

The sentences dealt with up till now have all been short and mostly on an ascending or a descending scale.  In longer sentences, whether simple, complex or compound, it would be impossible to follow such a scale without going outside the range of the speaker's voice. To obviate this, suitable "breaks" or pauses are introduced, which enable the speaker to readjust his scale. The last two syllables of each "break" have a characteristic "carry on" Tone Pattern, which indicates that the sentence is not finished.

This pattern is characterized by a stressed penultimate syllable on a high note, followed by a less stressed final syllable on the same note or on a higher note. Preceding syllables are usually pronounced on a mid level or a rising scale.

(III) Mpishi asema (III) hawezi kupakua   The cook says he cannot dish up the food because chakula (Ic) sababu mayai hayatoshi.   there are not enough eggs.

It is often used in giving lists of objects or actions:

(III) Nunua vikombe, (III) visahani,   Buy cups, saucers, knives and spoons.

(III) visu (Ia) na vijiko.

For list of actions, see p. 135.

Initial adverbs and pronouns very often have this pattern.
(III) Leo (Ia) nitasoma, (III) kesho   To-day I shall read, to-morrow I shall play.

(Ia) nitacheza.

(III) Mimi (Ia) nimekwisha.   As for me I have finished.

It is also much used in subordinate conditional clauses. See p. 138.

## EXERCISE 22

Read and translate:

1. (III) Leo (Ia) nimechoka *sana*.
2. (III) Mpishi asema (Ia) ataka viazi vikubwa.
3. (Ib) Umenunua mayai mangapi? (I) Matano *Bwana*.
    (III) Nimemwambia mpishi (I) asipike *yote ma-*
    *tano*, (Ic) apike matatu *tu*.
4. (III) Jana (Ia) tulilima, (III) kesho (Ia) tutacheza mpira.
5. (II) Mashoka yote yako? (I) Yote *Bwana* (I) yako.
6. (III) Mti huu (Ia) umezaa matunda mengi *sana*.
7. (Ib) Umeleta nini? (III) Nimeleta machungwa matatu
    (Ia) na mayai manane.

## NDIYO AND SIYO

These two words are much used in answer to questions;
**ndiyo** expresses assent to, and **siyo** dissent from, what is
asked in the question.

If the question is asked affirmatively, these two words
correspond to English "yes" and "no" respectively.

Ninunue mkate?    Am I to buy a loaf?

**Ndiyo**, nunua.    It is as you say, buy.

$\qquad$ = Yes, buy one.

**Siyo**, usinunue.    It is not as you say, don't buy.

$\qquad$ = No, don't buy one.

If, however, the question is asked negatively, these words
correspond to English "no" and "yes" respectively.

Nisinunue mkate?    Am I not to buy a loaf?

**Ndiyo**, usinunue.    It is as you say, don't buy.

$\qquad$ = No, don't buy one.

**Siyo**, nunua.    It is not as you say, buy.

$\qquad$ = Yes, buy one.

Note that the Arabic **la** corresponds to "no" as used in
English.

## EXERCISE 23

Read and translate:

1. (II) Hutaki malimau haya?    (I) Siyo, (Ic) nayataka.
2. (II) Wataka malimau haya?    (I) Ndiyo, (Ic) nataka.

3. (II) Umelitumia hili jembe ji-    (I) Ndiyo, (Ic) nimelitu-
       pya?                                 mia.

4. (II) Umeleta maji?                (I) Siyo *Bwana* (Ic) siku-
                                          leta.

5. (II) Hataki kuuza viazi vyake?    (I) Ndiyo *Bwana* (Ia) ha-
                                          taki.

### VOCABULARY

| | | | |
|---|---|---|---|
| **panda** | plant | **anza** | begin |
| **msumeno (mi-)** | saw | **chemka** | boil (intrans.) |
| **mchele** | rice | **washa** | light a fire, lamp, etc. |
| **pita** | pass | **boga** | pumpkin |
| **sahau** | forget | **lab(u)da** | perhaps |

### EXERCISE 24

(Revision of Tenses.) Translate:

1. What are you planting?  What are you selling?  I am
   selling pineapples.
2. They are not selling potatoes, they are selling pineapples.
3. We shall not want any milk to-morrow.
4. Lemons are not procurable in the market to-day.
5. Were any to be had yesterday (were they procurable
   yesterday)?
6. There were none to be had yesterday.
7. He says he does not want a saw, he wants an axe.
8. What is Hamisi doing?  He is cultivating.
9. Yesterday Ali went to the market, to-morrow he will go
   again.
10. The women are cooking some rice.
11. What is the sick man doing?  He is reading a book.
12. Does he read well?  He does not read well.
13. Did you see him yesterday?  No, I saw him to-day early
    in the morning.
14. Where are the hoes?  Did you put them in the shed?
15. The mountain is not visible to-day.
16. Did you (sing.) get them (oranges)?
17. Have you (pl.) seen them (stones)?
18. Some people are passing.

19. I will buy them (cups) to-morrow.
20. Has he forgotten us?
21. Where did you see him?
22. Will you go to town to-morrow or the day after to-morrow?
23. I'm not going to-morrow, I went yesterday.
24. We have not begun to read yet.
25. Ali says he cannot carry a load.
26. Has the water boiled?
27. The milk is boiling (now).
28. The cook is cooking some small pumpkins.
29. Has Hamisi lit the fire? No, he has not yet returned.
30. The fire will not burn (does not burn, is not burning), it needs a little oil.
31. Where is the oil? I don't know, perhaps it is finished.
32. My father is in the house, he has not left yet.

# CHAPTER XIV

## THE N- CLASSES (Singular and Plural)

| | | Concordial Prefixes | | | |
|---|---|---|---|---|---|
| *Class Prefixes* | | *Adjectival* | | *Pronominal* | |
| *Sing.*    *Plur.* | | *Sing.*    *Plur.* | | *Sing.* | *Plur.* |
| (n-) (m-)   (n-) (m-) | | (n-) (m-)    (n-) (m-) | | i- | zi- |
| Subject to many phonetic changes | | Subject to many phonetic changes | | Before vowels:[1] | |
| | | | | y- | z- |

### Underlying Ideas

To the N- Class Singular belong words which are the names of common objects and of animals. The plural forms of these nouns are the same as the singular forms, but the Pronominal Concords are different.

Typical sentences illustrating the concords are:

> Ngoma **i**mepasuka.     The drum is split.
> Ngoma **zi**mepasuka.    The drums are split.

Note that most animals take the Concordial Prefixes of the M- WA- Classes. For exceptions see Chapter XV.

> Ng'ombe **a**mekufa.     The cow is dead.
> Ng'ombe **wa**mekufa.   The cows are dead.

*Phonetic change.*

Although it is usual to talk about the "N- Class", actually there are relatively few nouns which have **n-** as a Classificatory Prefix. The reason for this is twofold:

1. Many nouns of these classes are of foreign origin, mainly Arabic, and, being loan words, do not come under the rules governing phonetic change in Swahili. Many such words have no prefix at all.

2. In words of Bantu origin the initial sound of the word

---

[1] No sound change before verb stems beginning with a vowel.

stem causes sound change in the prefix, often causing it to disappear altogether. When used, the prefix has three forms: **n-**, **m-** and **ny-**. Note the following phonetic laws:

(a) N- occurs before **-d-**, **-g-**, **-j-**, **-z-** in disyllabic and polysyllabic stems.

| | | | |
|---|---|---|---|
| **n-jaa** | hunger | **n-gurumo** | roaring, as of an animal |

(b) M- occurs before the labial consonants **-v-** and **-b-** under the same conditions.

| | | | |
|---|---|---|---|
| **m-vua** | rain | **m-begu** | seed |

(c) NY- occurs before vowels.

| | | | |
|---|---|---|---|
| **ny-undo** | hammer | **ny-umba** | house |

(d) The prefix is absent before other consonants (**ch, f, k, m, n, p, s, t**), but the consonants **p, t, ch** and **k** are pronounced with considerable aspiration (not recorded in the Standard spelling, but written **p′ t′ ch′ k′** by Taylor and Burt).

| | | | |
|---|---|---|---|
| **kuku (k′uku)** | chicken | **pembe (p′embe)** | horn |
| **siku** | day | **fisi** | hyena |

(e) The prefix occurs before *all* consonants in monosyllabic stems, being **m-** before labial consonants and **n-** before other consonants. Here again **p, t, ch** and **k** are aspirated.

| | | | |
|---|---|---|---|
| **n-ta (nt′a)** | wax | **m-vi** | grey hair |

Study the following nouns with the foregoing rules in mind:

*Words of foreign origin.*

| | | | |
|---|---|---|---|
| **barua** | letter | **senti** | cent |
| **dawa** | medicine | **safari** | journey |
| **jinsi** | kind, sort | **saa** | hour, watch |
| **daraja** | bridge | **sahani** | plate |
| **kazi** | work | **sabuni** | soap |
| **kofia** | fez, hat | **motakaa** | motor-car |

*Disyllabic or polysyllabic stems.*

| | | | |
|---|---|---|---|
| (a) **n-dizi** | banana | **n-goma** | drum |
| **n-jia** | road, path, way | **ng'ombe** | cow, cattle |
| **n-zige** | locust | | |

| (b) **m-vua** | rain | **m-boga**[1] | vegetable |
| (c) **ny-ama** | meat | **ny-uki** | bee |
| (d) **chumvi** | salt | **fimbo** | stick |
| **kengele** | bell | **simba** | lion |
| **nazi** | coconut | **mende** | cockroach |
| **tembo, n-dovu** | elephant | **pesa** | pice |

*Monosyllabic stems.*

| (e) **n-cha** | point | **m-bu** | mosquito |
| **n-chi** | country | | |

The N- Class Plural, as said before, does not differ in form from the N- Class Singular, and only the concord will show, in any given sentence, which Class is intended.

The N- Class Plural, besides functioning as the plural of the N- Class Singular, may also function as the plural of certain words in one of the U- Classes. Here sound change plays an important part, which will be described on p. 106.

### VOCABULARY

| **nywa** | drink | **zima** | extinguish |
| **kitambo** | a short period | **sababu** | because |
| **zimika** | be extinguished | **kwa nini?** | why? |
| **tengeneza** | put in order | **mwambie** | tell him |

### EXERCISE 25

Read and translate:

1. (II) Mwataka chumvi?     (I) Ndiyo (Ic) twataka.
2. (II) Motakaa iko nje?     (Ia) Haiko *Bwana*.
3. (II) Kazi imekwisha?     (Ia) Haijakwisha *bado*.
4. (Ia) Lete nyundo.     (Ia) Haipo (Ic) labuda imepotea.
5. (Ib) Wagonjwa wanakunywa nini?     (Ic) Wanakunywa chai.
6. (Ia) Wasinywe chai, (Ia) wanywe maziwa *tu*.
7. (Ib) Mafundi wanafanya nini?     (Ic) Wanatengeneza daraja.
8. (II) Mafundi wasije tena?     (I) Siyo (I) waje.

---

[1] Contrast boga pl. maboga (pumpkin).

9. (II) Kengele imeli∂ ?           (Ic) Imelia kitambo.
10. (III) Mwambie boi (Ia) awashe taa.
11. (I)  Hamisi, (Ia) zima taa. (III) Taa *Bibi* (Ic) ime-
                                            zimika.
12. (Ib) Kwa nini *taa hii imezimika*? (Ic) Kwa sababu yataka
                                            mafuta.

## The Adjectival Concord

Here there is great sound change, and the student is referred to p. 83 for the rules with the following additions:
n + r > **nd**; n + w > **mb**. Examples:

(*a*) Ngoma **n-dogo.** Kazi **n-gumu.** Sahani **n-zuri.**
    Fimbo **n-defu.**   (< **-refu**)
(*b*) Ngoma **m-baya.**
    Senti **m-bili.**   (< **-wili**)
(*c*) Taa **ny-eupe.** Mvua **ny-ingi.**
(*d*) Ndizi **chache.** Nyundo **fupi.** Njia **pana.** Kengele **tatu.**
(*e*) Senti **n-ne.** Saa **m-pya.**

Exceptions: Ng'ombe **dume.** (< **-ume**)
            Hali **njema.**   (< **-ema**)

## EXERCISE 26

Combine the following roots with the noun "njia":
    -pana, -pya, -refu, -wili, -tatu, -zuri, -eupe, -baya, -fupi,
    -gumu, -nane, -embamba.

## The Pronominal Concords

These are **i-** and **zi-** before consonants and **y-** and **z-** before
vowels (except before verb stems beginning with a vowel).

| Possessives | Demonstratives | o- root | -enye |
|---|---|---|---|
| Sahani yangu | Sahani ile | Sahani yote | Sahani yenye taka |
| Sahani zangu | Sahani zile | Sahani zote | Sahani zenye taka |
| Sahani ya mtoto | Sahani hii | Sahani yo yote | Sahani yenyewe |
| Sahani za mtoto | Sahani hizi | Sahani zo zote | Sahani zenyewe |

| Interrogative | Subject Prefix | Object Prefix |
|---|---|---|
| Sahani ipi? | Sahani imevunjika | Nimeiona |
| Sahani zipi? | Sahani zimevunjika | Nimeziona |
| Sahani ya nani? | | |
| Sahani za nani? | | |

## VOCABULARY

| | | | |
|---|---|---|---|
| **kandarinya** | kettle | **tuma** | send (a person) |
| **maana** | because | **kila** | every (comes be- |
| **toboka** | be pierced | | fore noun) Aı |
| **vuja** | leak | **supu** | soup |
| **peleka** | convey, take | **kutu** | rust |
| **kwa** | to (in this con- | **ingia kutu**[1] | get rusty |
| | text) | **bunduki** | gun |
| **ngoja** | wait, wait for | **ingia moshi**[1] | be smoked |
| **majibu** | answer | **twaa** | take (to oneself) |
| **funga safari** | set out on a jour- | **katika** | in, in the midst |
| | ney | **sikia kiu** | feel thirsty |
| **alfajiri** | dawn, daybreak | **poa moto** | get cool |
| **chukua** | take, carry away | **sikia njaa** | feel hungry |
| **hitaji** | need | **shona** | sew |
| **hema** | tent | | |
| **chandalua** | mosquito net | | |
| (vy-) | | | |

## EXERCISE 27a

Read and translate:

1. (Ia) Twende sokoni. (Ib) Wataka kununua nini *sokoni*? (Ia) Nataka kununua kandarinya, (Ia) *maana* yetu imetoboka, (Ia) tena yavuja.
2. (Ia) Peleka barua hii kwa Bwana Ali. (II) Ningoje majibu *Bwana*? (I) La, (Ia) usingoje *majibu*.
3. (Ia) Tufunge safari kesho alfajiri. (Ib) Nichukue nini na nini? (III) Utahitaji hema, (III) meza, (III) mablanketi, (III) chandalua, (III) ndoo (Ia) na bakuli.
4. (Ia) Tuma mtu anunue kuku, (III) mwambie alete viazi, (III) maziwa (Ia) na mboga.

[1] Cf. ingia ufa. See also p. 281.

5. (II) Nyama hupatikana sokoni? (III) Leo (Ia) yapatikana, (III) jana (Ia) hai*kupatikana*. (Ic) Haipatikani
   *kila siku*.
6. (III) Sahani hizi mbili (Ia) zimevunjika, (III) na hii
   moja (Ia) imeingia ufa.
7. (Ia) Supu imeingia moshi.
8. (III) Msumeno huu (Ia) umeingia kutu.
9. (Ib) Ninunue wapi *bunduki nzuri*?
10. (Ib) Unakwenda wapi? (Ic) Ninakwenda kutwaa saa
    yangu, (III) iko juu (Ia) katika chumba changu. (Ia)
    Haiko *juu* (Ic) ipo hapa mezani.
11. (Ia) Nasikia kiu, (Ia) nataka chai. (Ia) Chai hii imepoa
    moto. (Ia) Nasikia njaa, (Ia) lete chakula.
12. (III) Watoto wasema (Ib) washone nguo zipi? (Ic) Wa-
    shone hizi mbili.
13. (Ib) Wataka kofia ipi? (Ia) Yo yote *yanifaa*. (II) Wai-
    penda hii? (Ic) Naipenda.
14. (Ib) Yu wapi *mwenye motakaa ile*?

### VOCABULARY

| | | | |
|---|---|---|---|
| **shona** | sew | **uma** | hurt, bite |
| **fua nguo** | wash clothes | **tele** | plenty |
| **piga pasi** | iron (verb) | **debe** | tin container for oil, etc. |
| **makaa** | charcoal | **fagia** | sweep |

### EXERCISE 27b

(Revision of Tenses.) Translate:

1. Are the children playing? They are not playing, they are
   sitting down.
2. What are the women sewing? They are sewing clothes.
3. Did they sew yesterday? No, they didn't sew yesterday,
   they washed clothes.
4. Has Ali ironed the clothes? Not yet, he says the charcoal
   is finished.
5. Why is the child crying? He says he does not want to
   read.
6. Why does he not want to read? He says his head aches.
   (Head it hurts him.)

7. The sick man wants some food, he is hungry.

8. I am not cooking to-day, I will cook to-morrow.

9. The lamp is not burning well, it has gone out, it needs oil. The oil is finished, Bibi.

10. Is the cook in the kitchen? He is not there, Bibi. He has gone to the market to buy some eggs. Has he returned? Not yet, Bibi.

11. Bibi, the cook has returned, he has not got any eggs, he says they are not procurable to-day.

12. Where is Hamisi? He is downstairs sweeping the room.

# CHAPTER XV

## NOUNS OF NON-PERSONAL CLASSES DENOTING LIVING BEINGS

NOUNS denoting animates are also found in classes other than the Personal Classes. These fall into two divisions:

1. Nouns denoting relationships, titles, and people suffering some disability, which take the concords of the Personal Classes, except sometimes in the possessives. This, as already pointed out, also applies to names of animals.

| (JI-) MA- | | N- | KI- VI- | M- MI- |
|---|---|---|---|---|
| *Titles* | | *Relation-ships* | *People with a disability* | *Title* |
| **Bwana** | Mr., sir Master gentleman | **mama** mother  **baba** father | **kipofu** blind person  **kiziwi** deaf person | **mtume** apostle |
| **Bibi** | Mrs., ma'am mistress lady | **ndugu** brother (in wide sense) | **kiwete** lame person | |
| **boi** | houseboy | | | |
| **baharia** | sailor | | | |
| **seremala** | carpenter | | | |

| *Relationships* | | *Animals, etc.* | |
|---|---|---|---|
| **umbu** | sister | **ng'ombe** | ox |
| **shangazi** | aunt | **kuku** | fowl |
| | | **samaki** | fish |
| | | **simba** | lion |

The possessive concords appear to be a law unto themselves and may be thus summarized:

| | *Singular* | *Plural* |
|---|---|---|
| Titles | bwana wangu | mabwana zetu |
| | bibi yangu | mabibi wetu |
| Relationships | baba yangu | baba zetu |
| | rafiki yangu | rafiki zetu |
| Animals | ng'ombe wangu | ng'ombe zangu |
| Persons | kipofu wetu | vipofu wetu |
| | kijana wangu | vijana wangu |

Some words in the N- Class denoting relationship take a plural form in **ma-** to denote collectiveness. Such words retain the P.C. of the plural N- Class.

> **ma**baba zetu. Our ancestors or forefathers.
> **ma**rafiki zake. His circle of acquaintances.

Note also in M- WA- Classes: **wake zetu.** Our wives.

2. Nouns used distinctively as diminutives and augmentatives, which take the concords of the KI- VI- and JI- MA- Classes respectively (especially if used with a derogatory implication). See Chapter XLIII.

> Joka hili baya limekufa. This monstrous snake is dead.
> Kitoto hiki kizuri kimekufa. This fine infant is dead.
> Kitwana kile kibaya. That slave is a bad one.

But note: **kijana** takes the concords of the Personal Classes:
Vijana hawa wema. These children are good.

It should be noted, however, that up-country natives when speaking Swahili do not always adhere to the rules governing concords of nouns belonging to other classes, for in some Bantu languages concordial agreement is more regular. At the coast also, latitude in concordial agreement is noticeable.

### VOCABULARY

| | | | |
|---|---|---|---|
| kongoni | hartebeest | **pigana** | fight |
| kondoo | sheep | **kaa** | live, dwell |
| mbwa | dog | **lisha** | browse |
| mbuzi | goat | **winda** | hunt |
| farasi | horse | **mwindaji** | hunter |
| nyumbu | mule | **wawindaji** | hunters |
| simba . | lion | **mnyama** | |
| chui | leopard | **(wa-)** | animal |

## EXERCISE 28a

Translate:

1. These three hartebeest.
2. Your fierce oxen.
3. This fine sheep.
4. Five huge snakes.
5. Their fathers.
6. Our red ox.
7. Your tall brother.

## EXERCISE 28b

Translate:

1. Your two dogs are fighting.
2. All the sailors returned yesterday.
3. Your friends do not live here.
4. Their wives arrived yesterday.
5. When will your master arrive?
6. Where are your goats? They are browsing on the hillside.
7. My little brother is not here. He has gone to market.
8. Sesota the great snake is dead.
9. This infant is sleeping.

# CHAPTER XVI

## PREDICATION WITHOUT A VERB (Section II)

### IDENTIFICATION

PREDICATION in relation to Place without the help of a verb has been discussed in Chapters V and VI.

When the complement identifies the subject, it is introduced in two ways:

(a) By the Subject Prefix, for 1st and 2nd persons.

| | | | |
|---|---|---|---|
| **Ni** mpishi. | I am a cook. | **Tu** wapishi. | We are cooks. |
| **U** nani? | Who are you? | **M** nani? | Who are you? |
| **U** mpishi? | Are you a cook? | **M** wapishi? | Are you cooks? |

(b) By the invariable copula NI[1] for the 3rd person only, but for all Classes. Before words beginning with **n-** it is often heard as a syllabic nasal.

| | | | |
|---|---|---|---|
| **Ni** mtu. | It is a man. | **Ni** watu. | They are people. |
| **Ni** mti. | It is a tree. | **Ni** viti. | They are chairs. |
| Hamisi **ni** mpishi. | Hamisi is a cook. | Hamisi na Ali **ni** wapishi. | Hamisi and Ali are cooks. |
| **N(i)** nani? | Who is it? | **N(i)** nini? | What is it? |

### DESCRIPTION

When the complement *describes* the subject, i.e. is an adjective, the construction is similar, except that the Subject Prefix may alternate with the copula NI in the 3rd person.

| | |
|---|---|
| Hamisi **ni** mrefu. | Hamisi is (a) tall (one). |
| Hamisi **yu** mrefu. | Hamisi is tall. |
| **Ni** mbovu. | It is (a) rotten (one) (i.e. tree). |
| **U** mbovu. | It is rotten. |

*Important Note.*

Both Subject Prefix and copula NI are frequently omitted when the subject itself is a pronoun or is followed by a demonstrative or possessive.

[1] Not to be confused with the 1st pers. prefix NI above.

| Mimi Hamisi. | I am Hamisi. |
| Sisi wapagazi. | We are porters. |
| Hiki kizuri. | This is (a) nice (one). |
| Mizigo hii mizito. | These loads are heavy. |
| Mti huu mbovu. | This tree is rotten. |
| Kisu changu hiki. | This is my knife. |
| Mzigo huu wangu. | This load is mine. |

## Negation

NEGATION is expressed by SI.

| Mimi si mwivi. | I am not a thief. |
| Hamisi si mpishi wetu. | Hamisi is not our cook. |
| Si kitabu. | It is not a book. |
| Si chako, ni changu. | It is not yours, it is mine. |

| Ali si mrefu. | Ali is not tall. |
| Mti huu si mdogo. | This tree is not small. |
| Chakula hiki si kizuri. | This food is not nice. |
| Si kizuri. | It is not nice. |

## STATE

When the complement expresses State or Condition, it is linked to its Subject by the Subject Prefix only, and NI cannot be used as an alternative. Thus:

| **Yu** dhaifu. | He is weak. |
| Nyoka **yu** hai? | Is the snake alive? |
| Mtoto **yu** macho. | The child is awake. (Lit. eyes.) |
| Hamisi **yu** maji. | Hamisi is in trouble. (Lit. water.) |
| Chai hii **i** maji maji. | This tea is weak. (Lit. water water.) |
| Sukari **i** tamu. | Sugar is sweet. |
| Nyumba **i** tupu. | The house is empty. |
| Sahani **zi** safi. | The plates are clean. |
| Mlango **u** wazi? | Is the door open? |
| **Tu** tayari. | We are ready. |
| Kwinini **i** chungu. | Quinine is bitter. |

In certain of the above sentences the Subject Prefix may again be omitted.

| Sahani hizi safi. | These plates are clean. |
| Sisi tayari. | We are ready. |

It will be noticed that uninflected adjectives (see p. 49) usually come under the heading of State. Certain adjectives, however, like **-tamu**, **-tupu** and **-chungu**, have alternative constructions.

| | |
|---|---|
| Mkate huu **u** tamu. | This loaf is sweet. |
| Mkate huu **ni** mtamu. | This loaf is (a) sweet (one). |

There is no one way of expressing State negatively.

| | |
|---|---|
| Sisi si tayari. | |
| Hatu tayari. | We are not ready. |

## Word Order and Intonation

Word order in copulative phrasing varies according to the direction of emphasis. No fixed rules can be laid down, but certain guiding principles should be noted, viz. that the topic comes first and the detail concerning it comes last. Thus, the sentence "whose is this knife?" may be rendered in two ways according to direction of emphasis (with corresponding variations in Tone Pattern):

Kisu hiki (ni) cha nani?  — ·  ̄ ·  (·) · \\,

(Ni) Kisu cha nani *hiki*?  (·) —  ·· \\. _.

Similarly the sentence "you (pl.) are lazy" may be rendered:

Ninyi (m) wavivu.   ̄ · (·) · \\,

(M) wavivu *ninyi*.   (·) · \\. _.

## Aphorisms illustrating Phases of Predication

| | | |
|---|---|---|
| 4. | Ahadi **ni** deni. | A promise is a debt. |
| 7. | Akili mali. | Wits are wealth. |
| 57. | Dalili ya mvua **ni** ma-wingu. | A sign of rain is clouds—Clouds are a sign of rain. |
| 410. | Njia ya mwongo fupi. | The way of a liar is short. |

503. Chembe na chembe **ni** mkate.

A grain and a grain are (i.e. make) a cake.

131. Kawaida **ni** kama sheria.

Etiquette (or custom) is like the law.

195. Kusikia **si** kuona.

Hearing is not seeing.

48. Cha kichwa **ki** tamu, na cha mkia **ki** tamu.

The head piece is sweet also the tail piece is sweet—If the head is good eating, there can be no doubt about the tail.

155. Kipya **ki** nyemi kingawa kidonda.

A new thing is a joy, though it may be a sore.

514. U mwana **u** kamange we?

Are you a child or a grit now (i.e. altogether shameless)?

The retention of the verb LI, generally omitted in modern Swahili (see p. 282), is seen in:

516. Udongo upatize **uli** maji.

Take advantage of the clay while it is wet.

180. Kila muacha samboye hwenda **ali** mwanamaji.

Every one leaving his own vessel goes as a common sailor.

562. Utakufa na Laiti! na chanda **kili** kinywani.[1]

Thou wilt die with an Alas! and your finger yet at your mouth.

## Exercise 29a

Read the following sentences, using Tone Pattern indicated. Then put into the plural. Then substitute (1) "shoka", (2) "mwavuli" for "kitabu", and rewrite as an exercise.

1. (Ib) Kiko wapi *kitabu changu*? (Ib) Kitabu kipi? (Ic) Kile kipya.
2. (Ib) Kitabu cha nani *hiki*? (Ic) Ni chake Hamisi.
3. (Ia) Kitabu chetu kimepotea. (II) Umekiona?
4. (Ia) Lete kitabu. (Ib) Nilete kipi *Bwana*? (Ic) Lete cho chote. (III) Hiki, *Bwana*, (I) kizuri.

Do the same with the following sentences. For the written

[1] A native gesture of vexation.

exercise substitute (1) "kikapu", (2) "ngoma" for "mwavuli".

1. (Ia) Mwavuli huu umepasuka: (Ia) lete mwingine.
2. (III) Ule mwingine (Ib) uko wapi *Bwana*? (Ic) Uko juu.
3. (Ib) Huu hapa *Bwana*, (Ic) nimeuleta.
4. (III) Huu (I) si wangu. (III) Ule wangu (Ic) mzuri, (III) huu (Ic) mbaya.

Read and translate:

1. (Ib) Watoto wako wako wapi? (Ic) Wako juu, (III) wawili (Ic) wanaandika, (III) mmoja (Ic) anasoma.
2. (Ib) Umemwona mpishi wetu? (Ic) Nimemwona, (Ic) yuko jikoni (Ic) anapika. (III) Yule (Ic) si mpishi *wetu*. (Ia) Mpishi wangu ametoka kazini. (Ia) Nataka mpishi mwingine. (III) Yuko mtu nje (Ic) asema ni mpishi. (Ib) Mtu yupi? (Ic) Yule mfupi.

## EXERCISE 29b

Translate. (Note that some sentences admit of more than one translation.)

1. The chairs are upstairs.
2. Whose hat is this?
3. Which hat is yours?
4. These are my trees.
5. The children are awake.
6. They are not upstairs.
7. Are you (sing.) ready?
8. It is an animal.
9. Are you lazy?
10. This knife is a good one.
11. Are these people Swahilis?
12. We are lazy folk.
13. My knives are few, yours are many.
14. Are you ready?
15. The room is empty.
16. This work is easy.
17. The cups are clean.
18. Are they (snakes) alive?
19. The porters are outside.
20. These shoes are not mine.
21. The spoons are in the cupboard.
22. Is the Bwana about?
23. He is not in the house.
24. The lion is a fierce animal.

## SWAHILI GREETINGS

Swahili greetings are easy to understand when it is borne in mind that they express State or Condition (p. 93).

| (Ib) U hali gani? | You are what state? How are you? | (Ib) M hali gani? | How are you? |
| (Ic) Ni hali njema. | I am a good state. Very well (thank you). | (Ic) Tu hali njema. | We are well. |
| (Ib) Yu hali gani? | How is he? | (Ib) Wa hali gani? | How are they? |
| (Ic) Yu hali njema, *or* nzuri. | He is well (thank you). | (Ic) Wa hali nzuri. | They are well. |

The Subject Prefixes are often omitted in the 1st and 2nd person sing. Likewise the subject prefixes and **hali** are frequently omitted in the reply.

(Ib) Hali gani?    (I) Njema *or* nzuri.

Another set of greetings is phrased negatively:

| (II) Hujambo? | You have not anything the matter?—Are you well? |
| (I)  Sijambo. | I have not anything the matter.—I am well. |
| (II) Hajambo? | He has not anything the matter?—Is he well? |
| (I)  Hajambo. | He has not anything the matter.—He is well. |
| (II) Hamjambo? | You have not anything the matter?—Are ye well? |
| (Ic) Hatujambo. | We have not anything the matter.—We are well. |
| (II) Hawajambo? | They have not anything the matter?—Are they well? |
| (Ic) Hawajambo. | They have not anything the matter.—They are well. |

The adverbial prefix **ku** is sometimes used in place of the personal prefix **wa**:

(II) Hakujambo?   Are all well at home?

An abbreviated form is in common use:

> **Jambo.**

This may be used both in greeting and replying.

The answer to a greeting in plural form should be given in the plural and in chorus.

| (II) Hamjambo *Mabwana*? | How do you do, gentlemen? |
| (Ic) Hatujambo. | We are well (thank you). |

Titles are much used:

(II) Bwana jambo?  *or*  (II) **Jambo** *Bwana*?

Arabic greetings are in common use at the coast.

| (I) Sabalkheri *or* Subulkheri. | Good morning. |
| Masalkheri. | Good evening. |

# CHAPTER XVII

## PREDICATION WITHOUT A VERB (Section III)

### ASSOCIATION

The Subject Prefix, followed by the NA of Association, is used to express the association of a subject with its object. This construction has two functions:

1. It describes Possession.

| | |
|---|---|
| **Nina** kisu. | I have a knife. (I-with knife.) |
| **Una** nguo? | Have you any clothes? (You-with clothes?) |
| **Ana** chakula. | He has food. (He-with food.) |
| **Tuna** watoto wawili. | We have two children. (We-with children two.) |
| **Mna** kazi? | Have you work? (You-with work?) |
| **Wana** senti ngapi? | How many cents have they? (They-with cents how-many?) |

2. It describes state or condition, especially if acquired rather than inherent.[1]

| | |
|---|---|
| **Nina** kiu. | I am thirsty. (I-with thirst.) |
| **Una** njaa? | Are you hungry? (You-with hunger?) |
| **Ana** wazimu. | He is mad. (He-with madness.) |
| **Tuna** homa. | We have fever. (We-with fever.) |
| **Wana** nini? | What is the matter with them? (They-with what?) |
| Mtoto **ana** baridi. | The child is cold. (Child he-with cold.) |
| Chai hii **ina** moto. | This tea is hot. (Tea this it-with heat.) |
| Sahani hizi **zina** taka. | These plates are dirty. (Plates these they-with dirt.) |

Negation is expressed by the prefix HA- with phonetic change in the three persons singular.

[1] Compare Predication of State (p. 93): Sukari i tamu (Sugar is sweet), where the condition is inherent rather than acquired.

98

| | |
|---|---|
| **Sina** kitu. | I have nothing.  (Not-I-with thing.) |
| **Huna** dawa? | Have you no medicine? |
| **Hana** wazimu. | He is not mad. |
| **Hatuna** neno. | We have no complaint to make.  (Not-we-with word.) |
| **Hamna** fedha? | Have you no money? |
| **Hawana** senti. | They have no cents. |

Further examples, positive and negative:

| | |
|---|---|
| Sina nafasi. | I have no time. |
| Mti huu hauna miiba. | This tree has no thorns. |
| Miti hii ina mizizi mingi. | These trees have numerous roots. |
| Kisu hiki kina kipini kifupi. | This knife has a short handle. |
| Taa hii ina utambi? | Has this lamp a wick? |
| Taa hizi hazina mafuta. | These lamps have no oil. |
| Chai hii haina moto. | This tea is not hot. |

That **na** stresses association rather than possession is seen in sentences in which subject and object may be reversed without materially altering the sense.

| | |
|---|---|
| Kitabu changu kipo mezani? | Is my book on the table? |
| Hakipo, **kina** Ali. | It isn't, Ali has it. (i.e. it -with Ali.) |

Note also the following:

| | |
|---|---|
| Ugonjwa **una** mtu mmoja? | Does illness concern one person only?  (Lit. Illness it-with one man?) |
| Utukufu **una** Mungu. | Glory belongeth unto God. (Lit. Glory it-with God.) |
| 191. Kupata **kuna** Mungu. | Getting depends on God. |
| Amri **ina** Mungu. | Commanding is of God. |

### The -O of Reference as Pronominal Object of NA

Whereas the pronominal object of a transitive verb is the Object Prefix, that of NA is a suffix consisting in the P.C. and the -O of Reference (except in the Singular Personal Class, where the suffix is -YE) as in the following table.[1]

[1] This table is set out for all Classes and will be needed again when further uses of -O come under discussion.

TABLE OF THE -O OF REFERENCE WITH P.C.

| Class | Singular | Plural |
|---|---|---|
| M- pl. WA- | -ye | wa + o > wo > o[1] |
| M- pl. MI- | u + o > wo > o[1] | i + o > yo |
| KI- pl. VI- | ki + o > **cho** | vi + o > **vyo** |
| JI- pl. MA- | li + o > **lo** | ya + o > **yo** |
| N- pl. N- | i + o > **yo** | zi + o > **zo** |
| U- (pl. N-) | u + o > wo > o[1] | (zi + o > **zo**) |
| KU- | ku + o > **ko** | |

| | Adverbial |
|---|---|
| KU- | ku + o > **ko** |
| PA- | pa + o > **po** |
| MU- | mu + o > **mo** |
| VI- | vi + o > **vyo** |

The use or omission of this pronominal object closely follows that of the Object Prefix, set out on pp. 44-5. Thus:

(a) In a general statement or question the nominal object stands alone.

> Hamisi ana kitabu.  Hamisi has a book.
> Una kitabu?  Have you a book?

In an affirmative answer to a general question a pronominal object is required.

> Ninacho.  I have one.

In a negative answer no pronominal object is needed.

> Sina.  I haven't (one).

(b) When attention is directed to the noun object whether in a statement or in a question, the pronominal object is also required. (The nominal object itself may either precede or follow NA.)

> Hamisi anavyo vitabu vyangu.  Hamisi has my books. (Hamisi he-with-them books my.)
> Vitabu vyangu anavyo Hamisi.

---

[1] Note that w- is an elusive sound in Swahili, and often disappears Hence: wa + o > wo > o; compare u + o > wo > o. Compare also: ya + o > yo and i + o > yo.

Kitabu changu unacho?        Have you my book? (Book my
                               you-with-it?)

Punda anaye[1] Ali?          Has Ali the donkey? or Is the
                               donkey with Ali? (Donkey
                               he-with-him Ali?)

In an affirmative answer the pronominal object is naturally
required.

Ninacho.        I have it (book).
Anaye.          He has it (donkey) or it is with him.

In a negative answer there is usually no pronominal object,
though it may be introduced if attention is directed to the
lack of it.[2]

Sina.           I haven't it.
Hana.           He hasn't it.

## Exercise 30a

Translate. Show emphasis by putting the noun first in (a).

(a) I have the hammer.        We have the screws.
    Have you the nails?       Have you (pl.) the axe?
    He has the saw.           Have they the string?

(b) 1. I haven't the hammer, Ali has it.
    2. We haven't any fruit, but (lakini) Ali has some.
    3. Ali hasn't a book, nor (wala) have I.

## Exercise 30b

Translate:

1. Our cat has large feet.
2. Every porter has his load.
3. The cook has two children.
4. How many fingers have
   you?
5. All birds have wings.
6. An elephant has no tongue.
7. We have no money.
8. How many cents have you?
9. She has two fine rings.
10. What is the matter with
    these children?
11. Is the cat hungry?

[1] Names of animals generally take the concords of the Personal
Classes.
[2] ... ikawa hanacho tena. .... and then he no longer has it.

12. The lamp is not on the table, perhaps the Bwana has it.

13. Have you my books? Yes, here they are, sir.

### Exercise 30c

Read and translate:

1. Aliwauliza Mna kitu cha kula? Wakasema Hatuna.
2. Alimwambia Sultani, Wezi wamenishinda, wameninyang'anya mbuzi na asali pia. Sultani akasema (and the Sultan said) Mimi ninayo asali.
3. Namtaka Bwana, maana ninayo barua yake hapa.
4. Alimkuta mkewe, ana majonzi. Akamwuliza (and he asked her) Je Bibi, una nini?
5. Mbuzi anaye nani?

### Other Aspects of Association based on NA

**na** occurs after finite verbs, and in other contexts also. Its translation is dependent on its context.

| | |
|---|---|
| Enda **na** Hamisi. | Go with Hamisi. |
| Walikaa karibu **na** ziwa. | They lived near a lake. |
| Alipigwa **na** askari. | He was struck by a soldier. |
| Lete chai **na** sukari. | Bring tea and sugar. |
| Lete **na** maziwa pia. | Bring some milk also. |
| Mimi **na** Hamisi. | Hamisi and I. |

The concept underlying **na** in these foregoing sentences is constant, i.e. that of Association; also in sentences like:

| | |
|---|---|
| Walikaa mbali **na** Nairobi. | They lived far away from Nairobi. |
| Jilindeni **na** Mafarisayo. | Beware of (i.e. guard yourselves from) the Pharisees. |

Where *personal pronouns* are concerned, the suffix to **na** is a shortened form of the Self-standing Pronoun.

| | | |
|---|---|---|
| **Mimi.** | Enda **nami.** | Go with me. |
| **Wewe.** | Nitakwenda **nawe.** | I shall go with you. |
| **Yeye.** | Mimi **naye.**[1] | He and I. |

[1] It is customary to name oneself first in Swahili.

| | | |
|---|---|---|
| **Sisi.** | Walikaa mbali **nasi**. | They lived far away from us. |
| **Ninyi.** | Atakwenda **nanyi**. | He will go with you. |
| **Wao.** | Mashahidi **nao** pia walikwenda **nao**. | The witnesses also went along with them. |

Examples with other Classes:

| | |
|---|---|
| Alipewa sufuria akakaa **nayo** siku tatu. | He was given a metal saucepan and kept it (stayed with it) three days. |
| Alitwaa moto akashuka **nao** mbugani. | He took some fire and took **it** down to the plains. |
| Nakupa joho hili la dhahabu ujivike **nalo**. | I give you this robe of gold for you to wear (that you **may** clothe yourself with it). |

## Exercise 31

Translate:

1. Bring a lamp and my stick.
2. They want some rice, some tea and some sugar.
3. Do they also want some bananas?
4. Take a basket with you to the market. (Go with basket to market.)
5. Juma and Muhamadi are cultivating.
6. I do not want to go alone. Very well then, go with **Ali**.
7. Come with me.
8. Go with them.
9. They are standing near the door.
10. I have bought some oranges and lemons.

# CHAPTER XVIII

## THE U- CLASSES

THERE are two U- Classes in Swahili, corresponding to the BU- and LU- Classes respectively in other Bantu languages. The concords of these two classes are identical except in the case of adjectives.

REFERENCE TABLE

U- (< BU-)

| | Class Prefix | Concordial Prefixes | |
| | | Adjectival | Pronominal |
|---|---|---|---|
| Before consonant: | u- | u-   m- | u- |
| Before vowel: | u-  w-  uw- | w-   mw- | w- |

## Underlying Ideas

To the U- (< BU-) Class belong:

1. Words which admit of no singular or plural concept, such as abstract nouns denoting qualities or states. These often have a common root with nouns of the M- WA- and MA- Classes, or with adjectives or with verbs.

| u-toto | childhood | cf. | m-toto | child |
|---|---|---|---|---|
| u-falme | kingdom | | m-falme | king |
| u-zee | old age | | m-zee | old man |
| | | | | |
| u-zuri | beauty | | -zuri | beautiful |
| u-chache | scarcity | | -chache | few |
| u-baya | badness, evil | | -baya | bad |
| w-ema | goodness | | -ema | good |
| w-ingi | plentitude | | -ingi | much, many |
| | | | | |
| u-wezo | power, ability | | ku-weza | to be able |
| u-ombi | intercession | | ku-omba | to pray |
| | | | ma-ombi | prayers |
| uw-ongo | falsehood | | ku-ongopa | to lie |

104

2. The names of some countries.

**U-ganda** Uganda        **U-laya** Europe

REFERENCE TABLE

U- (< LU-) CLASS. Pl. = N- CLASS

|  |  |  | Concordial Prefixes | | | | |
|---|---|---|---|---|---|---|---|
|  | Class Prefixes | | Adjectival | | | Pronominal | |
|  | Sing. | Plur. | Sing. | Plur. | | Sing. | Plur. |
| Before consonant: | u- | (n-)[1] (m-) | m- | (n-) (m-) | | u- | zi- |
| Before vowel: | u- w- uw | ny- | mw- | ny- | | w- | z- |

## Underlying Ideas

The ideas underlying words of the U- (< LU-) Class are somewhat confused. All words, however, refer to concrete objects, with a further implication of length or mass.

Words denoting long objects have their plural forms in the Plural N- Class.

| | | | |
|---|---|---|---|
| **u-tambi** | wick | **tambi (t'ambi)** | wicks |
| **u-kuta** | wall | **kuta (k'uta)** | walls |

Words expressing something in the mass may be studied under two heads:

(a) Those which express something as a composite whole, the component parts of which are not usually thought of as existing singly. Such words have no plural.

| | | | |
|---|---|---|---|
| **u-ji** | porridge | **u-dongo** | clay |
| **w-ali** | cooked rice | **u-mande** | dew |

(b) Those which express a single item or particle of the whole mass. Here the Plural N- noun indicates the mass itself.

| | | | |
|---|---|---|---|
| **u-nywele** | a hair | **nywele** | hair |
| **u-shanga** | a bead | **shanga** | beads |

[1] This, being the Plural N- Class, is subject to many phonetic changes.

Occasionally a single form will express both meanings, i.e. the mass and one particle of the mass.

**u-vumbi**  dust, a grain of dust     **vumbi**  dust

(c) There are also one or two words indicating the instrument of verbal action.

**u-funguo** key            **funguo** keys    cf. **ku-fungua** (to open)

**u-fagio** sweeping-       **fagio** brushes cf. **ku-fagia** (to
          brush                                   sweep)

*Phonetic change in Plural of U- Class nouns.*

When the Plural N- Class is used to express the plural of U- Class nouns, the same rules of sound change apply as already discussed on p. 83, allowing, however, for certain modifications of the prefix U-.

This prefix U- is elided before all stems other than monosyllabic, and rules (*a*), (*b*), (*c*) and (*d*) are applicable to the word stem. Thus:

(*a*) **u-devu** a single hair of      **n-devu**   beard
              beard
(*b*) **u-bao** plank, form            **m-bao**    planks
(*c*) **w-embe** razor                 **ny-embe**  razors
(*d*) **u-fagio** sweeping-brush       **fagio**    brushes
      **u-kuni** stick of firewood     **kuni (k'uni)** firewood

In addition two other sound changes are to be noticed, this time in the stem consonant:

n + -w- > mb-   **u-wati** hut-pole    **mbati** hut poles
n + -l- > nd-   **u-limi** tongue      **ndimi** tongues

With monosyllabic stems the **u-** is retained, and is itself preceded by **ny-**. This is a different process from that described on p. 83.

**u-so** face          **ny-uso** faces

## Exercise 32a

Using the above rules as a guide, give the plural of:

| | | | |
|---|---|---|---|
| uapo | oath | ukucha | finger-nail |
| ukuta | wall | ufito | stick for building |
| uma | fork | unyoya | a single hair of wool, etc. |
| ubavu | rib | uta | bow |
| upanga | sword | wavu | net |
| uwanda | open space | upande | side |
| ua | courtyard | utepe | stripe, chevron |
| utambi | wick | ufa | crack |
| upepo | wind | wayo | sole, footprint |
| wimbo | song | uteo | tray for sifting grain |

## Exercise 32b

Read and translate:

1. (II) Wembe upo mezani? (I) Haupo, (Ic) umo sandu-kuni.
2. (II) Wanawake wameleta fito? (Ic) Wameleta.
   (Ib) Ziko wapi? (Ic) Ziko nje. (I) Je,[1] Bwana, (II) wa-lete tena kesho? (I) La, (Ic) wasilete tena.
3. (II) Uma umo sandukuni? (Ic) Haumo (Ic) upo mezani.
4. (Ib) Funguo ziko wapi? (Ic) Ziko chini.
   (I) La, (I) haziko chini, (Ic) ziko juu.
5. (Ia) Sipendi uji, (I) usipike tena.
6. (Ib) Mswahili ameleta nini? (Ic) Ameleta panga.
7. (Ia) Mabibi hawataki wali.
8. (Ia) Ukuta umeingia ufa.
9. (III) Pikeni wali, (III) uji (I) na viazi.
10. (II) Panga ziko kibandani? (I) Haziko Bwana.
11. (Ia) Ondoeni mbao, (Ic) hazifai tena.
12. (Ia) Wanawake wataka uteo.
13. (Ia) Upepo unavuma (Ia) unarusha uvumbi.
14. (II) Uma wapatikana sokoni? (I) Ndiyo Bibi, (Ic) wapa-tikana.
15. (II) Watoto wanaimba nyimbo? (I) La, (Ic) wanapiga kelele tu.
16. (II) Utambi umekwisha? (I) Haukwisha.

[1] See p. 151.

17. (Ia) Hamisi yupo mlangoni (Ia) auza *fagio*.
18. (Ia) Funguo zimepotea, (Ia) hazimo sandukuni.
19. (III) Jana, (Ia) nilileta kuni, (III) kesho (II) nilete tena?
    (Ic) Usilete *tena*.
20. (II) Hamisi alete kuni kesho? (Ic) Asilete *kesho*, (Ic)
    labuda kesho kutwa.

## The Adjectival Concord

The A.C. of the two U- Classes is generally **m-** before
consonants and **mw-** before vowels, though **u-** is sometimes
used in reference to abstract nouns.

| | |
|---|---|
| Uzuri mwingi. | Much beauty. |
| Ushirika utakatifu. | Holy Communion. |
| Utu uzima. | Full-grown manhood. |

Many abstract nouns do not lend themselves to qualifying
by adjectives.

**m-** (**mw-**) is always used in reference to U- (< LU-)
nouns.

| | |
|---|---|
| Ufunguo mfupi. | A short key. |
| Ufagio mbaya. | A bad brush. |

Sound change in adjectives referring to the plural N- Class
is as already described under that class (p. 85).

Compare:

| U- (< BU-) | utu **u**ke | ubishi **mw**ingi | |
|---|---|---|---|
| | | | *Plur.* |
| U- (< LU-) | uta**m**bi **m**zuri | | ta**m**bi **n**zuri |
| | ufa **m**baya | | nyufa **m**baya |
| | ulimi **m**kali | | ndimi **k**ali |
| | wembe **m**moja | | nyembe **m**bili |
| | ubao **m**refu | | mbao **n**defu |
| | ukuta **mw**eupe | | kuta **ny**eupe |

## EXERCISE 33

Combine the following adjectives with the noun "wembe"
and its plural form:

-gumu, -eusi, -fupi, -dogo, -bovu, -ne (pl. only)

## The Pronominal Concord

There is nothing new to learn in this section. The Concord **u-** in the singular is the same in form as that of the "mti" Class, and the plural **zi-** is that of the Plural N- Class, already discussed.

| Possessives | Demonstratives | -o root | -enye |
|---|---|---|---|
| Wembe wangu | Wembe ule | Wembe wote | Wembe wenye kipini |
| Nyembe zangu | Nyembe zile | Nyembe zote | Nyembe zenye vipini |
| Wembe wa Ali | Wembe huu | Wembe wo wote | Wembe wenyewe |
| Nyembe za Ali | Nyembe hizi | Nyembe zo zote | Nyembe zenyewe |

| Interrogative -pi | Subject Prefix | Object Prefix |
|---|---|---|
| Wembe upi? | Wembe umepotea | Nimeuona[1] |
| Nyembe zipi? | Nyembe zimepotea | Nimeziona[1] |

### EXERCISE 34a

Using "wembe", rewrite the sentences on p. 95. Use verb "haribika".

### EXERCISE 34b

Read and translate:

1. Taa hizi mbili zataka tambi mpya.
2. Taa yako utambi wake mfupi sana, ninunue utambi mpya?
3. Mbao hizi ndefu mno, hazifai kitu.
4. Wapagazi wasema wataka panga tatu na fagio mbili. Wapeni basi.
5. Ufunguo huu si wangu. Wangu (ni) mdogo, huu (ni) mrefu tena mwembamba sana.
6. Uji huu mzuri, wanifaa sana.

[1] No sound change before verb stem.

# CHAPTER XIX

## PRONOUNS (Section III)

## THE -O OF REFERENCE AS RELATIVE PARTICLE

THE -O of Reference is found in many contexts. Its use has already been discussed as an adverbial enclitic in Chapter V and as object suffix to the NA of Association in Chapter XVII. The table setting out the phonetic changes caused by -O in the P.C. is on p. 100.

The -O of Reference functions as a relative particle when used with a verb, or with **amba**, i.e.:

It is a *pronominal* relative when prefixed by the P.C. and may refer to either the subject or object of the verb. (This use of -O is discussed here.)

It is an *adverbial* relative when prefixed by the adverbial prefixes **pa-**, **ku-**, **mu-** of place and time, or by the **vi-** of manner. (This use of -O will be discussed in a later section.)

The relative particle combines with the verb or verb particle in five tenses only:

The "no time" tense (with no tense prefix).

The negative **-si-** tense.

The **-na-**, **-li-**, and **-ta-** tenses.

If required in tenses other than the above, **amba-** is used.

## (A) -O AS PRONOMINAL RELATIVE REFERRING TO THE SUBJECT

The following sentences illustrate the relative particle in concord with nouns of the Personal and N- Classes respectively. Note the form **-ye** for the Singular Personal Class.[1]

### Combined with the -NA-, -LI- and -TA- Tenses

Mtu a- $\begin{Bmatrix} \text{na} \\ \text{li} \\ \text{taka} \end{Bmatrix}$ -YE-soma.     A person who $\begin{cases} \text{is reading.} \\ \text{read.} \\ \text{will read.} \end{cases}$

[1] In old Swahili and in poetry the form is -O, e.g.:

> 38. Asoweza kutuumba, kutuumbua hawezi.
> He that cannot create us, cannot deface us.

110

| | | | | | |
|---|---|---|---|---|---|
| Watu wa- | $\begin{cases} \text{na} \\ \text{li} \\ \text{taka} \end{cases}$ | -O-soma. | People who | $\begin{cases} \text{are reading.} \\ \text{read.} \\ \text{will read.} \end{cases}$ | |
| Kengele i- | $\begin{cases} \text{na} \\ \text{li} \\ \text{taka} \end{cases}$ | -YO-lia. | A bell which | $\begin{cases} \text{is ringing.} \\ \text{rang.} \\ \text{will ring.} \end{cases}$ | |
| Kengele zi- | $\begin{cases} \text{na} \\ \text{li} \\ \text{taka} \end{cases}$ | -ZO-lia. | Bells which | $\begin{cases} \text{are ringing.} \\ \text{rang.} \\ \text{will ring.} \end{cases}$ | |
| Mtu a- | $\begin{cases} \text{na} \\ \text{li} \\ \text{taka} \end{cases}$ | -YE-ki-soma kitabu hiki. | A man who | $\begin{cases} \text{is reading} \\ \text{read} \\ \text{will read} \end{cases}$ | this book. |
| Kazi i- | $\begin{cases} \text{na} \\ \text{li} \\ \text{taka} \end{cases}$ | -YO-m-faa. | Work which | $\begin{cases} \text{suits}[1] \\ \text{suited} \\ \text{will suit} \end{cases}$ | him. |

[1] At the moment of speaking.

*Notes.*

(i) The relative particle always follows the tense prefix.

(ii) The Object Prefix, when used, stands next to the verb and follows the relative particle.

(iii) -TAKA-, in the future tense, is the verb = to be on the point of . . . In the simple future it is shortened to -TA-, but in the relative future the full form is retained and carries a secondary stress, e.g. **ataka′yeso′ma**, he who will read.

## Without a tense prefix

| | |
|---|---|
| Mtu a-soma-YE. | A man who reads. |
| Watu wa-soma-O. | People who read. |
| Kengele i-lia-YO. | A bell which rings. |
| Kengele zi-lia-ZO. | Bells which ring. |
| Mtu a-ki-soma-YE kitabu hiki. | A person who reads this book. |
| Kazi i-tu-faa-YO. | Work which suits us. |

*Notes.*

(i) When joined to a verb stem without a tense prefix, the relative particle is suffixed to the verb. This form carries no time implication.[1]

(ii) The Object Prefix retains its place before the verb.

Relative Prefixes of the Personal Classes are the same for all persons, viz.: -YE and -O.

[1] In the new edition of *Swahili Exercises* it is termed "The General Relative": in the old edition, "The Relative without note of Time".

| Ni-<br>U-<br>A- } li-YE-andika. | I<br>You<br>He } who<br>wrote. | Tu-<br>M-<br>Wa- } li-O-andika. | We<br>You<br>They } who<br>wrote. |
|---|---|---|---|
| Ni-<br>U-<br>A- } andika-YE. | I<br>You<br>He } who<br>write(s). | Tu-<br>Mu-<br>Wa- } andika-O. | We<br>You<br>They } who<br>write. |

## Combined with the negative SI

Mtu a-si-YE-soma.          A man who doesn't read.

Kengele i-si-YO-lia.       A bell which doesn't ring.

Kazi i-si-YO-tu-faa.       Work which doesn't suit us.

*Notes.*

(i) With negative SI this form expresses no time, but rather description of a negative character. Hence it may also be used to translate an English past or future tense: A man who did not or who will not read—provided that time is not the point to be stressed. If past or future time is to be stressed, AMBA- is used.

(ii) The Object Prefix stands between the relative particle and the verb stem.

## (B)  -O AS PRONOMINAL RELATIVE REFERRING TO THE OBJECT

When the relative particle refers to the object, the corresponding Object Prefix is generally required.

The following sentences illustrate the relative particle in concord with nouns of the Personal and KI- VI- Classes respectively.

### Combined with the -NA-, -LI- and -TA- tenses

| Kitabu a- { na<br>li<br>taka } -CHO-ki-<br>soma<br>Hamisi. | The book which<br>Hamisi { is reading.<br>read.<br>will read. |
|---|---|
| Watoto a- { na<br>li<br>taka } -O-wa-ita<br>Hamisi. | The boys whom<br>Hamisi { is calling.<br>called.<br>will call. |

Wewe ni-li-YE-**ku**-amini.       You whom I trusted.

### Without a tense prefix.

Kitabu a-**ki**-taka-CHO Ha-       The book which Hamisi wants.
misi.

| | |
|---|---|
| Watoto a-**wa**-taka-Q Hamisi. | The boys whom Hamisi wants. |
| Sisi u-**tu**-funza-O. | We whom you teach. |

### Combined with the negative SI:

| | |
|---|---|
| Vitabu a-si-**VYO**-**vi**-taka Hamisi. | The books which Hamisi doesn't want. |
| Watoto a-si-O-**wa**-taka Hamisi. | The boys whom Hamisi doesn't want. |

The word order is important:

The verb containing the relative follows close after its antecedent. It may not be separated from it by a nominal subject. Such a subject, if used (i.e. Hamisi in the above sentences), follows the verb and does not precede it.

Note that when both subject and object are of the same number, and both refer to a Personal Class, there is no difference in the two forms of relative. No confusion arises in conversation, however, as context always gives the clue and intonation differs.

| | |
|---|---|
| Mtoto ali**YE**mw**o**na Hamisi. | The child who saw Hamisi, *or* The child whom Hamisi saw. |
| Watoto wa**wa**penda**O** wazee wao. | Children who love their parents, *or* Children whom their parents love.[1] |

### Amba-

When relative phrasing is required with verb forms other than the foregoing, the relative particle is suffixed to the stem AMBA-. Its use also directs attention to the antecedent.

Subject relative:

| | |
|---|---|
| Watu amba-O wamechoka wapumzike. | Let the people who are tired rest. |

Object relative:

| | |
|---|---|
| Kazi amba-YO huku-i-fanya jana ameifanya Hamisi. | The work which you did not do yesterday Hamisi has done. |

---

[1] Passive construction preferred here:
**Watoto wapendwao na wazazi wao.**

E

| Vitu amba-VYO huta-vitaka kesho viweke sandukuni. | Put the things which you will not want to-morrow in the box. |

For other contexts in which AMBA- is used see p. 309. These require a wider knowledge of Swahili than this stage affords.

## Aphorisms illustrating the Relative Particle

| 531. Ulichokiacha pwani kakingoje ufuoni. | (As to) what you left at the shore, just go and wait for it on the beach. |
| 13. Alimaye njiani sharti alinde, ndege asipate chembe. | He who cultivates by the wayside must needs watch that a bird gets no grain. |
| 219. Liandikwalo halifutiki. | That which is written cannot be blotted out. |
| 36. Asiyeona kwa yeye (mwenyewe) na akionywa haoni. | He who sees not of himself sees not (even) if he be shown. |
| 33. Ivushayo ni mbovu. | That which ferries one across is rotten. (The paddle or punting-pole may be rotten, but it does get you across.) |
| 123. Kafiri akufaaye si Isilamu asiyekufaa. | An infidel who is of use to you is better than a Moslem who isn't. (SI is often used in Aphorisms to express "is better than") |
| 146. Kikulacho ki nguoni mwako. | That which bites (eats) you is in your clothes. |
| 231. Maji yaliyomwagika hayazoeleki. | Water that is spilt cannot be scooped up (like grain). |
| 34. Asiyekuridhi mridhi. | He who does not please you, do you please him. |
| 412. Ndovu wawili wakisongana ziumiazo ni nyika. | When two elephants jostle that which is hurt is the grass. |

### Intonation. Tone Pattern in Relative Clauses

The Tone Pattern of a relative clause depends on its position in the sentence.

If the clause occurs at the beginning or in the middle of the sentence, it requires the "carry on" Tone Pattern III.

Mtoto aliyerudi jana amekwenda zake.    The boy who returned yesterday has gone off.

If it occurs finally, the Tone Pattern is **Ia**.

Mwite mtoto aliyerudi jana.    Call the boy who returned yesterday.

### VOCABULARY

| | | | |
|---|---|---|---|
| kando | aside | rejesha | return (trans.) |
| kwa nini? | why? in respect to what? | tumiwa | be used |
| | | mwagika | be spilt |
| weka | place, put in position | futika | be wiped up |
| | | upesi | quickly |
| tupa | throw away | somesha | teach (lit. help to read) |
| mche (mi-) | cutting, shoot, etc. | fungua | open, unfasten |
| tiwa | be put | funga | shut, close, fasten |
| shika | take hold | liwa | be eaten |
| sitawi | flourish | mpaka | until |
| angaliwa | be taken care of | azima | borrow |
| tengenezwa | be mended | kimbia | run away |
| takikana | be required | pandwa | be planted |
| chakula cha jioni | evening meal | itwa | be called |
| faida | profit | pata[1] | get (used here to express "cut") |
| gani? | what, or what kind? | funguka | become un-fastened |
| kata | cut | | |

[1] Kisu hiki chapata, hiki hakipati. This knife cuts, this one doesn't.

## EXERCISE 35a

Read and translate:

1. Wageni waliokuja jana wamerudi? Wamerudi.
2. Mtakao kazi simameni kando, msiotaka kazi rudini.
3. Usiweke mkebe usiofaa kitu. Kama haufai, utupe.
4. Miche iliyotiwa maji vizuri imeshika, tena imesitawi, lakini ile isiyoangaliwa imekufa yote.
5. Kitanda kilichorudi kutengenezwa kimevunjika.
6. Viazi hivi vidogo viweke mbali na hivi vikubwa vitaka-vyotakikana kwa chakula cha jioni.
7. Yafaa nini kengele isiyolia?
8. Yako wapi magunia? Yapi Bwana? Yale niliyoyanunua jana.
9. Irejeshe sabuni isiyotumiwa.
10. Wino uliomwagika jana haufutiki upesi.
11. Yule kijana unayemsomesha Kiswahili akili zake nzuri?
12. Wageni wale niliowaona jana wanakaa wapi?
13. Hamisi amefungua mlango nilioufunga.
14. Mikate aliyoipika mpishi isiliwe mpaka kesho.
15. Je, kile kisu ulichoazima kwa Sefu kizuri? Kizuri.
16. Visu hivi nilivyovinunua jana vibaya, havipati.
17. Sabuni ile nzuri uliyonipa imekwisha.
18. Je, barua nilizoziweka mezani zimetiwa posta?

## EXERCISE 35b

Translate:

1. The children who ran away have all returned.
2. The knife which was lost has been found.
3. The sick man who arrived yesterday returned to-day.
4. Where are the boys who wanted work?
5. The trees which were planted last year are growing well.
6. We have eaten all the potatoes which were cooked yesterday.
7. Bring the hoes which were used yesterday.
8. Is the sugar you bought yesterday finished?
9. Men who carry loads are called Wapagazi.
10. We want people who cultivate well.
11. What good is a knife which won't cut?

12. I do not want a good-for-nothing hoe (hoe which is useless).
13. Is the soap which I gave you finished?
14. The strangers whom you saw yesterday live at Mombasa.
15. The door which you shut has come open.
16. The loaves I cooked have all been eaten.
17. Where are the sacks which Hamisi has brought?
18. I have removed the plates which are not required for the evening meal.

# CHAPTER XX

## MORE ABOUT THE IMPERATIVE AND SUBJUNCTIVE

THESE two forms of the verb are so closely connected, and their uses so interwoven, that a comparison is necessary.

*Imperative.*

Sing. verb stem in **-a**.[1]  Piga.  Beat.
Pl. verb stem in **-eni**.  Pig**eni**.  Beat.

*Subjunctive.*

Subj. Pref. + verb stem in **-e**.

|  |  |
|---|---|
| U̇pig**e**. | That you may beat. |
| Mpig**e**. | That you may beat (pl.). |

### The Uses Compared (positive)

*Imperative.*

To give a command in general terms.

Ondoa vyombo.     Clear away the crockery, etc.

If an object prefix is used, final **-a** is replaced by **-e** in the singular.[2]

**Vi**ondo**e**. (vyombo)  Clear them away. (the crockery, etc.)
**Mwit**e Hamisi.     Call Hamisi.

*Subjunctive.*

1. To correspond to such English forms as "Shall I . . .?" "Am I to . . .?" "May I . . .?" "I may . . .". "Thou shalt . . .". "Let him . . .".

Nisome?          Shall I read? May I read?
Waende?          Are they to go?

---

[1] Note the following three irregular imperative forms in constant use:
Lete pl. leteni   = bring.  cf. kuleta  = to bring.
Njoo pl. njoni   = come.  cf. kuja   = to come.
Nenda pl. nendeni = go.  cf. kwenda  = to go.
                    cf. kwenenda = to go (more forceful form).

[2] Not always in Mombasa. -a is generally retained if the object prefix is the 1st pers. sing.
          Nipa.  Give me.          Niambia.  Tell me.

118

| | |
|---|---|
| Waende. | Let them go. |
| Twende. | Let's go. |

2. To express the second of two commands.

| | |
|---|---|
| Kaa kitako usome. | Sit down and read. |
| Lete chai, kisha uondoe vyombo. | Bring the tea, then take away the things. |
| Mwambie apike nyama. | Tell him to cook meat. |

3. To express purpose.

| | |
|---|---|
| Mwite niseme naye. | Call him that I may speak to him. |

4. After words expressing obligation.

| | |
|---|---|
| Sharti aende. | He must go. |

## NEGATIVE FORMS

*Imperative.*

Sing. **Si** + verb in **-e**.    **Si**pige.    Don't beat.
Pl.  **Si** + verb in **-eni**.    **Si**pig**eni**.

*Subjunctive.*

Subj. Pref. + **si** + verb in **-e**.

                       **Tusi**pige.    That we may not beat.

## The Uses Compared (negative)

*Imperative.*

Used in general prohibition. This form is often met with in proverbs.

| | |
|---|---|
| 497a. Sicheze na paka-vue. | Do not play with a wild cat. |
| (pl.) Siendeni sokoni bila ruhusa. | Never go to the market without permission. |

*Subjunctive.*

To express particular prohibition. Therefore, in ordinary speech, this form is much more common than the negative imperative.

| | |
|---|---|
| Usiondoe vyombo. | Don't take the things away. |
| Leo msiende sokoni. | Don't (pl.) go to market today. |
| Msimpige. | Don't (pl.) beat him. |

Compare also with positive forms above :

1. Nisisome?      Shan't I read? Mayn't I read?
   Wasiende?      Are they not to go?
   Wasiende.      Don't let them go. They are not to go.
   Tusiende.      Let us not go.

2. Mwambie asipike nyama.      Tell him not to cook meat.

3. Simama hapa asikuone.      Stand here so that he won't see you.

## Aphorisms illustrating the uses of the Imperative and Subjunctive

3. Adui **mpende**.      Love an enemy.

523. Ukimpa mtu kazi **pata-neni** na ujira.      If you give a man work (first) agree about the wages.

483. **Sifanye** mashindano na mtu.      Never match thyself emulously with (any) man. (Lit. Do not make strivings with . . .)

486. Silaha **chukua** siku zote, sikuye (ye < yake) ita-kufaa.      Carry a weapon always, in its day it will be useful to you.

490. **Sione** tanga la nguo, ka-sahau la miaa.      Do not find a cloth sail and then forget the matting one.

548. **Usende** (usiende) pahali bila huja, ghalibu hu-kasirika.      Never go to a place needlessly, you will almost always be vexed.

588a. **Usiweke** msingi mwovu.      Do not lay a bad foundation (make a bad precedent).

491. Siri yako **usimwambie** mwanamke.      Don't tell your secret to a woman.

### VOCABULARY

| | | | |
|---|---|---|---|
| **sasa hivi** | at once | **usikose** | do not miss, i.e. be sure to |
| **pakua** | dish up | | |
| **chelewa** | be late | **andika meza** | lay the table |
| **karani** | clerk | **kunja** | fold |
| **kalamu** | pen | **kunja kunja** | crumple |
| **pia** | also | **dirisha** | window |

| | | | |
|---|---|---|---|
| **posta** | post | **tumbako** | tobacco |
| **bahasha** | envelope | **desturi** | custom |
| **ovyo** | carelessly, anyhow | **chupa** | bottle |
| **vuta** | pull, draw | | |

## EXERCISE 36a

Read and translate:

1. Mwite Hamisi, mwambie aende sokoni sasa hivi.
2. Mimi hapa Bibi, ninunue nini?
3. Nunua mkate, sukari na samaki.
4. Ninunue mikate mingapi Bibi?  Nunua mmoja tu.
5. Ijaze kandarinya maji.
6. Mwambie mpishi apakue chakula.
7. Mpishi apakue chakula lini Bibi?
8. Mwambie apakue saa sita, asichelewe.
9. Boi asilete maji sasa.
10. Kwa nini asilete?
11. Haya, rudini.
12. Msipige kelele.
13. Piga kengele, ipige sana.
14. Waiteni rafiki zenu.
15. Tuwaambie nini?
16. Waambieni waje kesho asubuhi na mapema.
17. Nifunge mlango?  La, usifunge.
18. Jipeni moyo.
19. Watoto waende zao?  Wasiende bado.
20. Njoni hapa.
21. Bwana asema usipike viazi leo.
22. Haya, nenda zako.
23. Amkeni, saa imekwisha.
24. Sisemeni ovyo, semeni vizuri.
25. Avutaye tumbako sharti atumie kiko.
26. Ni desturi hapa kila mtu atakaye dawa sharti aje na chupa.

E*

## EXERCISE 36b

Translate:

1. These clothes are very dirty, be sure to wash them (do not miss to wash them).
2. Fold them carefully.
3. Lay the table, do not crumple the cloth.
4. Fill the lamp with oil. (It fill lamp oil.)
5. Tell him to come early.
6. Fill this kettle with water.
7. Take this letter to the Bwana.
8. Don't loiter on the way (in the road).
9. Buy fish, meat and eggs.
10. Tell him not to cook anything to-day.
11. Boil two fresh-laid eggs.
12. Don't throw away food.
13. Tell Ali to make the tea.
14. Give Hamisi a lamp.
15. Shut the window.
16. Count the loads.
17. Tell the porters not to be late.
18. Call the clerk, tell him to take away this pen.
19. Take these letters (to the) post.
20. Give me some long envelopes.

# CHAPTER XXI

## THE INFINITIVE FORM OF THE VERB

THE Infinitive form of the verb in Swahili has two usages which must be clearly distinguished.

(a) That of a verbal infinitive in such sentences as:

Ataka kusoma. He wants to read.

This usage is so closely paralleled in English that it needs no further explanation.

(b) That of a verbal noun, as such it forms a class of nouns known as the KU- Class.

## THE KU- CLASS

### REFERENCE TABLE

|  | Class Prefix | Adjectival Concord | Pronominal Concord |
|---|---|---|---|
| Before consonant:<br>Before vowel | ku-<br>ku-[1] | ku-<br>kw- | ku-<br>k(w-) |

These verbal nouns cannot be thought of in terms of singular and plural. They express the act of doing, of becoming or the state of being, and correspond to both Infinitive and Gerund in English. Thus:

Infinitive form:      *To sing* is pleasant.
Gerund form:      *Singing* is pleasant.
                He has finished *singing*.

These forms, being nominal in function where Swahili is concerned, require concordial prefixes. Thus:

Kuimba kumekwisha. The singing is finished.
Kuimba ku wapi? Where is the singing?

[1] kw- in a few verbs like kw-enda and kw-isha.

## The Adjectival Concord

Not all verbs used as nouns lend themselves to qualification, but note:

> Kuimba kuzuri.   Fine singing.
> Kuimba kwema.   Good singing.

## The Pronominal Concord

| Possessives | Demonstratives | -o root | -enye |
|---|---|---|---|
| Kuimba kwetu Kuimba kwa watoto | Kuimba kule Kuimba huku | Kuimba kwote Kuimba ko kote | Kuimba kwenye Kuimba kwenyewe |

| Interrogative | Subject pref. | Object pref. |
|---|---|---|
| Kuimba kupi? | Kuimba kumekwisha | Unakusikia kule kuimba kwao? |

## Aphorisms illustrating the use of the KU- Class

171. **Kufaa hakudhuru.**   Being of use (to be of use) does no harm.

176. **Kulekeza si kufuma.**   Aiming is not hitting. To aim is not to hit.

195. **Kusikia si kuona.**   Hearing is not seeing. To hear is not to see.

# CHAPTER XXII

# THE MAHALI CLASS AND THE ADVERBIAL CLASSES

## THE MAHALI CLASS

THERE is only one word belonging to this class, viz.: **mahali** = place(s).[1] It takes **pa-** as its Subject Prefix.

### REFERENCE TABLE

|  | Noun | Adjectival Concord | Pronominal Concord |
|---|---|---|---|
| Before consonant:<br>Before vowel: | **Mahali** | pa-<br>p- | pa-<br>p- |

Typical sentence:

**Mahali pote pameharibika.** The whole place has been spoilt.

### Underlying Idea

Reference to a definite place.

### The Pronominal Concord

| Possessives | Demonstratives | -o root | -enye |
|---|---|---|---|
| Mahali pangu<br>My place[2] | Mahali hapa<br>This place<br>Mahali pale<br>That place | Mahali pote<br>The whole place<br>Mahali po pote<br>Any place what-<br>soever | Mahali penye watu<br>A place with people<br>Mahali penyewe<br>The place itself |

| Interrogative | Subject Prefix | Object Prefix |
|---|---|---|
| Mahali papi? (or wapi?)<br>Which place? | Mahali pote pataka maji.<br>The whole place needs water. | Sipaoni.<br>I do not see it. |

[1] Mombasa Swahili: pahali pl. mwahali.
[2] Also: In my stead, instead of me.

125

## The Adjectival Concord

| | |
|---|---|
| Mahali **pa**zuri. | A beautiful place. |
| Mahali **pe**ma. | A good place. |
| Mahali **pa**ngapi? | How many places? |

### EXAMPLES

| | |
|---|---|
| Akajificha[1] mahali mwituni. | He hid himself at a place in the forest. |
| Hata siku moja simba akatoka kwenda tembea mahali pa mbali. | Now one day the lion went for a walk to a place some distance away. |
| Yule Mwarabu mahali pa kukasirika akacheka sana. | The Arab instead of being angry laughed heartily. |
| Alimtoa matopeni akamweka mahali pakavu. | He took him out of the mud and put him in a dry spot. |
| Mahali pote pamejaa watu. | The whole place is full of people. |

## THE ADVERBIAL PLACE CLASSES KU-, PA-, MU-

Place may also be expressed adverbially, as:

| | | |
|---|---|---|
| An adverbial noun. | mezani | on, by, at, etc., a table |
| A simple adverb. | chini | below, underneath |
| An adverbial phrase. | chini ya meza | under the table |
| An adverbial pronoun. | pale | there |

Such words belong to the Adverbial Classes, and take either **ku-**, **pa-** or **mu-** as Concordial Prefixes.

### Underlying Ideas

| | |
|---|---|
| **ku-** | Indefinite place, direction |
| **pa-** | Definite place, position |
| **mu-** | Area, "alongness", "withinness" |

*Adverbial nouns* have been discussed on p. 18. Their form is constant, no matter what the implication.

*Simple adverbs* require no comment.

---

[1] For the significance of the **-ka-** prefix see p. 133.

*Adverbial phrases.*

Simple adverbs, such as **juu** (above), **chini** (below), may be extended into phrases by the -A of Relationship, which generally takes **y-** as its prefix, followed by a noun or pronoun. Note that **mbali** (far) and **karibu** (near) generally take **na**. Thus:

| | | | |
|---|---|---|---|
| **chini** | below | chini **ya** meza | under the table |
| **juu** | above | juu **ya** picha | above the picture |
| **nyuma** | behind | nyuma **ya** kabati | behind the cupboard |
| **mbele** | before | mbele **ya** mlima | beyond the mountain |
| **mbali** | far | mbali **na** mji | far from the town |
| **karibu** | near | karibu **na** shamba | near the plantation |

*Adverbial pronouns.*

These are formed from certain pronominal roots by means of the prefixes **ku-**, **pa-** and **mu-**. They may stand alone, or may be used as adjuncts of an Adverbial Noun or another Adverbial Pronoun.

| | Demonstratives | | | | Possessives | |
|---|---|---|---|---|---|---|
| Direction, etc. | **Ku**le | that place (there) | **Hu**ku | this place (here) | **Kw**etu, etc. | to or at our . . . |
| Position, etc. | **Pa**le | that spot (there) | **Ha**pa | this spot (here) | **Pe**tu, etc. | at our . . . |
| Withinness, etc. | **M**le | inside, etc. (there within) | **Hu**mu | inside, etc. (here within) | **Mw**etu, etc. | in our . . . |

For other roots taking these prefixes see p. 159.

## Adverbial Subject

All adverbial forms may stand as *subject* of a sentence in exactly the same way as nouns in the Noun Classes, except that they require **ku-**, **pa-** or **mu-** as Concordial Prefixes. The construction too is somewhat different. Study the following sentences:

| | |
|---|---|
| Mwituni **m**-me-lala wa-nyama. | Animals are asleep in the wood. (In wood there-are-asleep animals.) |

| | |
|---|---|
| Kule mjini **ku**-me-kufa watu wengi. | Many people have died in the town over there. (There in-town there-have-died . . .) |
| Hapa **pa**-me-kufa simba. | A lion has died here. (On-this-spot there-has-died lion.) |

This construction has no counterpart in English. In Swahili the adverbial form is the subject of the sentence, with **ku-**, **pa-** or **mu-** as Subject Prefix to the verb. The noun which in English would be the subject of the sentence stands here as adding some necessary detail to the meaning expressed by the verb. (See the "Nominal Construction", p. 299.)

An adverbial subject may also be used in Predication of Association. Here the construction follows that of noun or pronoun subjects, except that the concord prefixes are again **ku-**, **pa-** or **mu-**.

| | |
|---|---|
| Kisimani **m**-na maji. | There is water in the well. (In-well therein-with water.) |
| Nje **ku**-na watu. | There are some people outside. (Outside there-with people.) |
| Juu ya kioo **pa**-na picha. | There is a picture above the mirror. (Above of mirror there-with picture.) |
| Hapa **pa**-na miti. | There are trees here. (Here here-with trees.) |

This construction is much used in Swahili. Often the word order is reversed.

| | |
|---|---|
| Ku-na watu nje. | There are some people outside. (There-with people outside.) |

## Negation

Negation is expressed by **ha-**.

| | |
|---|---|
| Kwetu ha-**ku**-na mahindi mengi. | There is not much maize at our (home). |
| Ha-**pa**-na watu nje. | There are no people outside. (Not-there-with . . .) |
| Ha-**m**-na maji kisimani. | There is no water in the well. (Not-therein-with water . . .) |

Ha-pa-na miti hapa.    There are no trees here.

Ha-m-na kitu sanduku-ni?    Is there nothing in the box?

Frequently a Demonstrative is used to particularize still further. It generally precedes the word to which it refers.

Hapa petu hapana mahindi.    Here at our house there is no maize.

### Intonation

Adverbial subjects are often pronounced with Tone Pattern III.

Humu nyumbani, mmekufa watu.    People have died in this house.

— ·  ·  ‾ ‾ · · — · ＼,

(In this house there have died people.)

In the reversed sentence order, the adverbial subject has the Tone Pattern of parenthesis.

Kuna watu *nje*. [ — · ＼ . _ ]

*Further Notes.*

(i) The Possessive forms standing alone indicate "home". They may take **pa-** or **ku-** as concord prefix.

Hapa (ni) **petu**.    This is our home.

Twende **kwetu**.    Let us go home.

Amerudi **kwao**.    He has returned home (lit. to theirs).

**Kwenu** ku wapi?    Where is your home?

**Kwao** may sometimes be given the status of a noun with plural form in the MA- Class.

Watu wamerudi **ma-kwao**?    Have the people returned to their homes?

Note also the expression:

Hana **kwao**.    He has no home.

(ii) **Kwangu, kwako**, etc., may also mean "to my way of thinking", "as far as I am concerned", etc.

**Kwangu**, jambo hili (ni) baya sana.　　To my way of thinking this is a bad affair.

**Kwake**, kazi hii si nzito.　　This work to him is not difficult.

### The Adjectival Concord

Adjectives can only be used predicatively in these Classes.

Hapa (ni) **pazuri**.　　Here it is beautiful.

Kwetu (ni) **kuzuri**.　　At our place it is nice.

VOCABULARY

| | |
|---|---|
| **wekwa** | be placed, stationed, appointed |
| **pakwa chokaa** | be whitewashed |
| **jaa** | be full |
| **sanduku** | box |
| **kauka** | be dry, dry up |
| **hospitali** | hospital |
| **duka (ma-)** | shop |

EXERCISE 37a

Read and translate:

1. Mjini kumewekwa askari.
2. Nyumbani mmepakwa chokaa.
3. Hapa pamelimwa.
4. Kule mjini kumekufa wagonjwa.
5. Pale mlimani pamesimama watu.
6. Nyumbani mmejaa watu.
7. Hamna kitu kisimani.
8. Leo hakuna kitu sokoni.
9. Kuna watu shambani.
10. Mwituni mna nyoka? Mna.
11. Mjini kuna maduka? Hakuna.
12. Mjini mna maduka? Hamna.
13. Pale chini pana nyoka.
14. Mezani hapana kitu? Hapana.
15. Hapa mbele ya sanduku hapana kitu.
16. Sandukuni hamna kitu.

17. Hapa pana wageni?
18. Kule kuna miti.
19. Hapa pana mto.
20. Sandukuni mna vitabu.

### EXERCISE 37b

Translate, using an Adverbial Subject.

1. Is there anything in the box?
2. There is nothing here.
3. There is a lamp behind the box.
4. Are there any houses over there?
5. There are no towns hereabouts.
6. There is no well here.
7. There is nothing upstairs.
8. Are there any people here?
9. There are flowers in the forest.
10. In this forest there are no people.
11. There are no animals in this forest.
12. Is there any firewood in the house?
13. Outside there is much firewood.
14. Are there any oranges at the market?
15. There is no water here.
16. In this kitchen there are no utensils.
17. Is there any sugar in the basin?
18. There are snakes under the tree.

## Nominal and Adverbial Subject compared

Study the following sentences, noting how the choice of the subject varies according to whether attention is directed to the thing itself or to place and its association (or disassociation) with the thing.

| | |
|---|---|
| Sukari iko? | Is there any sugar? (Lit. Sugar it there.) |
| Iko. | There is some. (Lit. It there.) |
| Haiko. | It is not there. |
| Hakuna *or* hapana. | There isn't any. (i.e. No.) |
| Sukari imo kabatini? | Is the sugar in the cupboard? |
| Imo. | It is in. |
| Haimo. | It is not in. |

| Hamna. | There is none in (the cupboard). |
| Bakulini mna sukari? | Is there any sugar in the basin? |
| Mna. | There is some in. |
| Hamna. | There is none in. (i.e. No.) |

The frequent use of **hakuna**, **hapana** and to a lesser degree of **hamna** to express an English *no* should be noted. They should not be used in reply to a question containing a finite verb, i.e. like Amekuja?

## EXERCISE 37c

Read and translate:

1. Mpishi yuko? Hayuko Bibi, amekwenda sokoni.
2. Sokoni kuna samaki? Leo hakuna.
3. Sabuni iko juu? Haiko juu; juu hakuna kitu.
4. Mchele upo mezani? Haupo, mezani hapana kitu.
5. Mafuta yako? Ndiyo, yako ghalani.
6. Mafuta hayako ghalani; ghalani hamna kitu.
7. Lete maji. Maji hapana Bibi, kisimani hamna maji, yame-kauka.
8. Bakulini mna sukari? Hamna, imekwisha.

## EXERCISE 37d

Translate, using the subject indicated. (*N.* = Nominal Subj. *A.* = Adverbial Subj.)

| | |
|---|---|
| 1. *N.* Is there any firewood? | *N.* There is some. |
| | *A.* There is none. |
| 2. *N.* Is the firewood outside? | *N.* It is not outside, it is in the shed. |
| 3. *A.* Is there any firewood at the market? | *A.* There is none there. |
| 4. *N.* Is anyone there? | *N.* Someone is there. |
| 5. *N.* Is Hamisi outside? | *N.* He is not outside, he is upstairs. |
| 6. *A.* Are there any sick people here? | *A.* There are no sick people here. |
| | *N.* They are at the hospital. |
| 7. *N.* Are the sick people here? | *N.* They are not here. |

# CHAPTER XXIII

## VERBS AND THEIR TENSES (Section III)

### (-KA-, -KI-, -SIPO-)

### THE -KA- TENSES

THE prefix -KA- may occur in the Indicative Mood, also in the Subjunctive. Wherever it occurs, it expresses an action or state which follows another action. Therefore its time implication is consecutive to the time expressed in the preceding verb.

(a) *Simple Indicative form*

Ni-
U-
A-        } -ka-nunua {  And I,
Tu-                       you,
M-                        he, she,
Wa-                       etc.
                          bought

(b) *Subjunctive form*

Ni-
U-
A-        } -ka-nunue {  That I,
Tu-                       you,
M-                        he, she,
Wa-                       etc.
                          may or
                          might
                          buy.

(a) *Simple Indicative form*.

This form follows the -LI- tense or another -KA- tense, to indicate that one action is subsequent to the other in time and/or place.

Nilikwenda sokoni, nikanunua ndizi sita, nikala tatu, nikampa mwenzangu tatu.

I went to market, and bought six bananas; I ate three and three I gave to my companion.

It also expresses action or state *resultant* from or *consequent* upon that mentioned in the preceding sentence.

Huwezi kutupa jiwe kwa teo likafika mpakani kwa shamba.

You cannot sling a stone far enough for it to reach the boundary of a shamba.

Ni nani aliyekosa, mtu huyu au wazazi wake, hata akazaliwa kipofu?

Who sinned, this man or his parents, that he was born blind?

133

It may occasionally follow a HU- tense as well and carries on the force of that tense.

| | |
|---|---|
| Paka huyu mzuri sana, kila siku hukamata panya aka- wala. | He's a fine cat, he is always catching rats and eating them. |

Note that a -KA- tense is not used at the beginning of a sentence unless it is closely allied to the verb in the previous sentence.

*(b) Subjunctive form.*

This form may be used after the Future Tense -TA- to express purpose, to be carried out subsequent in time and away from the speaker in place.

| | |
|---|---|
| Nitakwenda sokoni, nikanu- nue ndizi. | I shall go to market and buy some bananas. |

It may also follow an Imperative or a Subjunctive, to indicate that the second order is to be carried out subsequent to the first in time and/or away from the speaker in place.

| | |
|---|---|
| Nenda sokoni ukanunue ndi- zi. | Go to the market and buy some bananas. |
| Mwambie mpishi aende soko- ni akanunue ndizi. | Tell the cook to go to the market and buy some bananas. |

In certain types of sentences the verb of motion may be omitted.

| | |
|---|---|
| Nimeambiwa (niende) nika- tafute kuni. | I have been told to go and search for firewood. |
| Cf.  Nimeambiwa  nitafute kuni. | I have been told to search for firewood. |

## Omission of Subject Prefix

The Subject Prefix is sometimes omitted:

*(a)* In the Indicative apparently to express some emotional quality like mild surprise:

| | |
|---|---|
| **Kasema nani?** | Who spoke? (Implication is that nobody should have been speaking at the time.) |

Nani katenda haya?                  Who did this?

Aliiba watoto kakimbia nao.         He stole the children and actually ran off with them.

(b) In the Subjunctive when motion is implied:

Nenda kalete maji.                  Go and bring some water.

Here also the verb of motion may be omitted:

Hamisi, kalete maji.                Hamisi, (go and) fetch some water. (The water is not at hand.)

Cf. Hamisi, lete maji.              Hamisi, bring some water. (Water not far away.)

## Negation

The negative counterpart of -KA- is identical in form with the Negative Subjunctive.

Alimtafuta asimwone.                He looked for him but did not find him.

107. Hutumiaje mchuzi nya-          How can one get gravy with-
ma usile?                           out eating meat?

## Verb ku-wa to be)

In the -KA- form of ku-wa the meaning is "become".

Akarudi akasoma akawa               So he went home and studied
sheikh mkuu.                        and became a great chief.

Hapa tulikaa wiki mbili na          We stayed here two weeks and
pakawa kama stesheni ya             it became like a centre for
kuondokea.                          excursions.

*Note.* The ku- of the infinitive is not retained in mono-syllabic, etc., verbs here.

## Intonation. Tone Patterns with -KA- tenses

As has already been stated, Tone Pattern III is a "carry on" pattern, much used in giving lists of objects. It occurs also in describing a series of actions, and is thus often found in narration in connection with the -KA- tense.[1]

[1] It is also used with other tenses in narration, when they occur in the first of two co-ordinate sentences.

(III) Nilikwenda sokoni, (Ia) nikanunua ndizi sita.

I went to the market, and I bought six bananas.

Wakaenda, wakamkamata, wakamleta   So they went, and arrested him, and brought him before the judge.

mbele ya kadhi.

Note that this Tone Pattern cannot occur finally in a sentence.

Alisema Nitarudi nikasome.   He said I shall go home and read.

The pattern of the syllables preceding a Tone Pattern III depends greatly on individual speakers. Usually these syllables are pronounced with low tone, even when stressed, though there is occasionally a slightly rising sequence leading towards the high Tone Pattern III on the last two syllables of the phrase.

In short introductory sentences a -KA- tense may be pronounced with the tone pattern of parenthesis.

Akanena Vyema.   And he said, Very well.

## VOCABULARY

| | | | |
|---|---|---|---|
| enda tembea | go for a walk | gereza | prison |
| kuta | come across, meet with | halafu | later on, presently |
| sungura | hare | uliza | ask |
| kanga | guinea-fowl | amkia | greet |
| cheche | animal like a mongoose | msiba (mi-) | misfortune |
| | | pata | get |
| tega | set a trap | ambiwa | be told |
| naswa | be snared | tafuta | search for |
| somo | friend | shika njia | take the road |
| choma | roast | fuatia | follow after |
| sinzia | take a nap | kahawa | coffee |
| kiumbizi | name of a game | paka | cat |
| tazama | look at, see | tembo | elephant |
| jamaa | relative | urafiki | friendship |

| usiku | night | kataa | refuse |
|---|---|---|---|
| askari | soldier | vyema | very well |
| jogoo | cock | jibu | answer |
| sema | say | waziri (ma-) | vizier |
| majonzi | grief | fahamu | understand |

### EXERCISE 38a

Read and translate the following extracts from vernacular texts:

(a) *Simple Indicative.*

1. (III) Siku moja (III) walikwenda tembea mahali (Ia) wakakuta mayai ya kanga. (Ia) Sungura akasema (Ia) Na tumtege *huyu kanga.* (Ia) Cheche akasema Vyema. (III) Sungura akaenda (III) akafanya mtego (Ia) akatega. (Ia) Akaja kanga (Ia) akanaswa, (Ia) wakamchukua nyumbani. (Ia) Sungura akamwambia Cheche (I) Somo, (Ia) huyu kanga mchome (Ia) mimi nimechoka *kidogo* (Ic) nataka kusinzia. (Ia) Cheche akasema Vyema.

2. (Ia) Cheche akasema (Ia) Kaja mtu hapa (Ia) kanifunga (III) tena (Ic) kanipiga sana, (III) kisha (Ia) kaenda zake.

(b) *Subjunctive.*

3. (III) Hata siku moja (Ic) Cheche akamwambia Sungura (Ia) Twende tukacheze kiumbizi leo. (Ia) Sungura akasema Vyema (III) lakini (Ic) nataka nifike kwetu *kwanza* (Ia) nikatazame jamaa.

4. (III) Usiku ule akatoka, (Ia) askari wakamkamata. (III) Akasema (Ic) Msinipeleke *gerezani*, (Ic) nipelekeni kwetu *kwanza* (Ic) nikale chakula (III) halafu (Ia) mnipeleke gerezani.

5. (Ia) Twende kwa mama yetu *tena*, (Ic) tukamwulize *kazi ya baba.*

6. (III) Sultani akamwambia Fikirini, (Ia) Nenda ndani (Ia) kamwamkie mama yako.

7. (Ia) Mume wangu (II) twende ndani (III) nikakupe habari za msiba (Ia) ulionipata.

*Without verb of motion.*

8. (III) Nikamwambia mke wangu (Ia) Kafunge mlango.
   (III) Mke wangu akaniambia (Ia) Kafunge wewe.

9. (III) Nimeambiwa (Ia) nikatafute ndege, (Ia) *mwenye*
   mbawa za dhahabu.

*Negative.*

10. (III) Mara yule Sultani (III) akashika njia (Ia) kumfua-
    tia yule mwivi, (III) akamtafuta (Ia) asimwone.

11. (Ia) Wakakaa hata jioni (Ia) wasipate hata kahawa.

12. (III) Paka akatoka (Ia) akaenda kumtafuta Tembo, (III)
    akamwona (III) akamwambia (Ia) Nataka urafiki.
    (III) Tembo asikatae (Ia) akamwambia Vyema.

13. (III) Jogoo akasikia maneno yake (Ia) asiseme neno, (Ic)
    akakaa kimya *tu.*

14. (Ia) Akamkuta mkewe ana majonzi. (Ia) Akamwuliza
    (I) Je *Bibi*, una nini? (Ia) Yule Bibi asijibu neno.

15. (III) Njiani (Ia) Sultan akamwambia waziri (II) Ume-
    fahamu maneno yale? (Ic) Akasema La (I) Si*kufahamu.*
    *Akasema* (III) Wewe waziri mzima (II) usifahamu ma-
    neno yale?

## THE -KI- TENSE

-KI- expresses imperfect, continuous or incomplete action.
The -KI- tense, as a simple tense, corresponds to two totally
different forms in English:

(i) A Present Participle, when that participle refers to an
incomplete action.

Tuliwaona watoto **waki-**        We saw the children playing. (Lit.
cheza.                           they-playing.)

(ii) A conditional clause, when used without reference to
any definite time. Here Tone Pattern III is used.

Ukimwona Hamisi, mwambie namtaka.   If or should you see
                                     (lit. you-him-see-
                                     ing) Hamisi, tell
                                     him I want him.

Both these sentences are consistent with the basic meaning
of -KI-. For -KI- expressing a continuous or repetitive action
in past or future time, see pp. 250-1.

## THE -SIPO- TENSE

The negative form of -KI- tense, expressing an "if" idea, is indicated in two ways:

1. By inserting -SIPO- between Subject Prefix and the root. This in English is generally translated by "unless":

**Asipo**soma.    Unless he reads.

This **-sipo-** consists of the negative **si** plus the **po** relative of time and place, and means literally "when not". (See also the **-japo-** tense, p. 186 and for **po**, p. 168.)

2. By using the general negative form with KAMA (if):

**Kama** hasomi.   If he does not read.

For compound forms see later, pp. 257–8.

*Note.* The **ku-** of the Infinitive is retained in the -SIPO- tense of monosyllabic verbs (and **kwisha** and **kwenda**), but not in the -KI- tense, e.g. Wasipo**ku**wa but Wakiwa.

## Aphorisms illustrating the -KI- and -SIPO- tenses

143. Kijana **aki**lilia kisu mpe.

If a child cries for a knife give it to him.

144. Kijana **uki**mnyang'anya kisu mpe kijiti.

If you take away a knife from a child, give him a stick (instead).

145. Kikiharibika ni cha Fundi, kikifaa ni cha Bwana Suudi.

If it is spoilt, it is the artisan's; if it will do, it is Mr. Suudi's.

221. Likitoka lote. ( <liote)

When (the sun) comes out, bask in it. (Make hay while the sun shines.)

260. Mgema **aki**sifiwa tembo hulitia maji.

When the palm wine tapper has his toddy praised (in his hearing) he puts water to it.

448. Paka **aki**ondoka panya hutawala

When the cat's away the rat holds sway.

473. Samaki akioza ni mtungo pia.

If a fish rots, the whole string (rots) also. (Lit. it is the string also.) (Fish are often strung together on a spit of wood, or on fibre.)

525. Ukiona neno, usiposema neno, hupatikani na neno.

When you see something, if you do not say something, you will not suffer something.

527. Ukitaja nyoka, shika kigongo.

When you mention a snake, get hold of a cudgel.

528. Ukiwa mkazi jenga.

If you are going to stay in a place (Lit. are a stayer), build.

557. Usipoziba ufa utajenga ukuta.

Unless you stop up the crack you will build a wall. (A stitch in time saves nine.)

## VOCABULARY

| | | | |
|---|---|---|---|
| kaa kimya | sit still and silent | tayari | ready |
| | | fungu (ma-) | portion |
| sikiliza | listen attentively | pona | get well |
| | | mapema | early |
| mwisho (mi-) | end | maliza | finish (tr.) |
| masikini | poor person | cheza mpira | play football |
| jini | genie | mara moja | at once |
| bin Adamu | man | msimamizi (wa-) | overseer |
| zungumza | converse | saidia | help |
| nyamaza | keep quiet | lipa | pay |
| mwinda (wa-) | hunter | nya | fall like rain |
| katika | during | lipwa | be paid |
| mazungumzo | conversation | kutoka mji | from the town |
| ila | except | kimbia | run away |
| ku-cha | to dawn | ona | see, find |

EXERCISE 38b

Read and translate the following extracts:

1. (Ia) Jogoo akakaa kimya (Ia) akisikiliza mwisho wa ma·neno yao.

2. (Ia) Yule masikini akaenda zake (Ia) akilia.

3. (Ia) Akatokea Jini mrefu (Ia) akasimama karibu yake
   *akamwambia* (Ia) Bin Adamu (III) ukitaka (Ia) umekufa, (III) usitake (Ia) umekufa.

4. (III) Ukisikia watu wənazungumza (Ic) basi wamelala
   (III) na ukisikia wamenyamaza (Ic) basi wa macho.

5. (III) Mwinda akiona ni Paka tu, (I) *akamjibu* Vyema, (Ia)
   twende zetu kwangu.

6. (III) Jogoo (III) katika yale mazungumzo yao (Ia) akamwambia Sungura (I) Je *rafiki yangu* (II) usiku huni-
   sikia nikisema? (Ia) Sungura akamjibu (III) Hata siku
   moja (Ia) sijakusikia ukisema (III) ila karibu na asubuhi tu, (III) nakusikia ukisema (Ia) Kucha kucheree.

7. (III) Msiba huu, (III) usipoondoa (III) utakufa wewe (Ia)
   au mume wako.

8. (I) Vyema (Ia) mimi ni tayari kukupa fungu lako, (I) *lakini* je? (II) mtoto wangu asipopona?

## EXERCISE 38c
Translate:

1. If you look for (it), you will find it (book.)
2. Unless he comes early, he will not finish his work.
3. If you are not careful, you will spoil your book.
4. If you don't know, you will be told.
5. We saw the porters playing football.
6. Should the tree fall, return at once.
7. If you see the overseer, tell him to come to my house
   to-morrow.
8. If bananas are procurable, buy some.
9. Unless you tell me, I cannot help you.
10. If they do not return, I shall not pay them.
11. If rain does not fall to-morrow, all the flowers will die.
12. If they do not carry (any) loads, they will not be paid.
13. I saw them cultivating.
14. We saw them returning from town.
15. If you look, you will see the animals running away.
16. If the police find the thief, they will arrest him.

# CHAPTER XXIV

## VERBS AND THEIR TENSES (Section IV)

### MONOSYLLABIC VERBS

THESE are ten in number.

| | | | |
|---|---|---|---|
| **ku-cha** | to fear | **ku-la** | to eat |
| **ku-cha** | to rise, i.e. of sun | **ku-nya** | to drop like rain |
| **ku-chwa** | to set | **ku-nywa** | to drink |
| **ku-fa** | to die | **ku-pa** | to give to |
| **ku-ja** | to come | **ku-wa** | to be or become |

Two disyllabic verbs with vowel stems—**isha** and **enda**—follow the rules for monosyllabic verbs, and in some localities other verbs also, such as **iba** (steal), **oga** (bathe).

The retention of **ku-** in certain tenses has been mentioned as the various forms have come under discussion. The reasons for this are now summarized.

In Swahili the penultimate syllable usually carries the stress. But certain tense prefixes and the relative particles **-o** and **-ye** cannot carry the stress; therefore **ku-** is inserted to prevent the stress falling on these particles. Note, how-

---

| *Particles which cannot be stressed* | | *Particles which can be stressed* | |
|---|---|---|---|
| NA | Anakula | KI | Akila |
| ME | Amekula | KA | Akala |
| LI | Alikula | KU | Hakula |
| TA | Atakula | SI | Asile |
| NGE[1] | Angekula | HU | Hula |
| NGALI[1] | Angalikula | A | Yuala |
| Relative | Aliyekula | Subj. Pref. | Ale |
| | Asipokula | | Hali |
| | Alipokula | Obj. Pref. | Ameyala |
| | Ajapokula[1] | | |

One tense takes both forms:—**Hajakula** *or* **Hajala**

[1] See p. 186 for this tense.

ever, that the tense prefixes **-ki-**, **-ka-** and **-ku-** can carry stress, and do not need the insertion of **ku-**. Subject and object prefixes and **hu-** and **si-** can also take the stress; therefore no **ku-** is required if the stress falls on these.

## VOCABULARY

| | | | |
|---|---|---|---|
| **mtoto wa mbwa** | puppy | **panda** | plant (verb) |
| **mshahara (mi-)** | wages | | |

## EXERCISE 39a

Translate:

1. Have you given Hamisi the cents for these eggs?
2. When will you eat these bananas?
3. When are we to eat these bananas?
4. The sick man did not drink his medicine yesterday.
5. Tell him to drink it to-morrow.
6. Where is the cat who ate the rat?
7. When did this tree die?
8. It is not dead, it is alive.
9. I will give you your wages to-morrow.
10. Do not let the puppy drink up all the milk.
11. The money I gave him is not enough.
12. The sun is setting, let us get off.
13. I do not fear him.
14. If this tree dies, I will plant another.

## REFERENCE TABLE

Primary tenses of the monosyllabic verb KUWA (to be *or* become).

| Wawa[1] | They are | Hawawi | They are not |
|---|---|---|---|
| Wanakuwa | They are being | | |
| Wamekuwa | They have been or have become | Hawakuwa | They have not been |
| Walikuwa | They were | | They were not |
| Watakuwa | They will be | Hawatakuwa | They will not be |
| Huwa | They usually are | | |
| Wakawa | And they became | (Wasiwe | And they were not) |
| Wakiwa | If they are | Wasipokuwa | Unless they are |
| Wajapokuwa | Although they are | | |

[1] In relative constructions only.

| Wangekuwa | (If) they would be | Hawangekuwa | (If) they would not be |
| | | Wasingekuwa | |
| Wangalikuwa | (If) they would have been | Hawangalikuwa | (If) they had not been |
| | | Wasingalikuwa | |
| Wangawa | Even if they be | | |
| Wawe | That they may be | Wasiwe | That they may not be |
| Iwe[1] | Be thou | Usiwe | Be thou not |
| Iweni | Be ye | Msiwe | Be ye not |

When NA is added to any of these tenses, it expresses association, i.e. "to be with", or possession, i.e. "to have".

Alikuwa **na** watoto wengi.   He had many children.

Hakuwa **na** kitu.   He hadn't anything.

## EXERCISE 39b

Translate:

1. The loads have been ready some time.
2. The loads were ready yesterday.
3. The loads will be ready at noon.
4. If the loads are ready, I will leave this afternoon.
5. They will not be ready until to-morrow.
6. Let the loads be ready early to-morrow morning (to-morrow morning and early).
7. Where were the loads?
8. They were there by the door yesterday.
9. When will your loads be ready?
10. Where is the cook's load?
11. It is outside, near the coconut tree.
12. One load is missing (i.e. is not here).

[1] This is the only verb which takes the prefix **i-** in the imperative.

# CHAPTER XXV

## ADJECTIVAL CONCEPTS (Section II)

In Section I two ways of qualifying nouns have been discussed, viz.:

(A) By roots and stems taking the Adjectival Concord.
(B) By uninflected loan words.

The present section will discuss the remaining ways of expressing adjectival concepts.

### (C) By Phrases based on the -A of Relationship

*-A + noun.*

This construction is identical with the possessive construction in form (p. 55).

| | |
|---|---|
| Kiti cha mti. | A wooden chair. (Lit. a chair of wood.) |
| Mtu wa haki. | A just man. |
| Pete ya dhahabu. | A golden ring. |
| Maji ya moto. | Hot water. |
| Mtoto wa watu. | A child or person of good lineage. |
| Neno la mwisho. | The last word. |
| Ratli mbili za sukari. | Two pounds of sugar. |
| Kisa cha kuku na kanga. | The story of a fowl and a guinea-fowl. |
| Alimpiga kofi la shavu. | He hit him a blow on the cheek. |

*-A + verb in the Infinitive.*

| | |
|---|---|
| Chakula cha kutosha. | Sufficient food. |
| Maneno ya kupendeza. | Pleasing words. |
| Bakuli ya kutilia mayai. | A basin for putting eggs in. |
| Wa kupigwa wakapigwa, wa kukimbia wakakimbia. | Those destined to be beaten (lit. of being beaten) were beaten, and those who were to get away got away. |

F

*-A + cardinal number*.

In this way ordinal numbers are formed.

| | |
|---|---|
| Mtoto wa tatu. | The third child. |
| Yai la tano. | The fifth egg. |

Note that **-a pili** and **-a kwanza** (**kwanza** = to begin) **are** used instead of **-a mbili** and **-a moja**.

| | |
|---|---|
| Nyumba ya pili. | The second house. |
| Mlango wa kwanza. | The first door. |

From eleven to nineteen the Arabic forms are often used in the ordinals:

| | |
|---|---|
| Mtu wa edashara. | The eleventh man. |
| Mtu wa thelatashara. | The thirteenth man. |

*-A + adverb*.

This includes simple adverbs, adverbs formed by prefixes **ku-, pa-, ki-**[1] and adverbial nouns.

| | |
|---|---|
| Mashamba ya mbali. | Distant plantations. |
| Chakula cha jana. | Yesterday's food. |
| Vitu vya juu. | The top things. |
| Desturi za kwetu. | Our native customs. |
| Watu wa hapa. | People of these parts. |
| Nyimbo za kizungu. | European songs. |
| Pambo ya kike. | Female adornment, cosmetics. |
| Vyombo vya jikoni. | Kitchen utensils (. . . of in the kitchen). |
| Chumba cha mezani. | The dining-room (room of at-table). |
| Njia za mjini. | Town thoroughfares. |

Note the different implication given by the addition of **ki-**.

| | |
|---|---|
| Nguo za shamba. | Clothes for working in the plantation. |
| Nguo za kishamba. | Countrified or "shamba-like" clothes. |
| Desturi za kale. | Old customs. |
| Desturi za kikale. | Old-fashioned customs. |

---

[1] See further, p. 165.

## (D) By Phrases based on the -O of Reference as a relative particle

| | |
|---|---|
| Sauti iliyosikilika. | An audible voice. |
| Mtungi uliojaa. | A full water-jar. |
| Mwezi ujao. | Next month. |

## (E) By other Nouns

| | |
|---|---|
| Kijana mwanamke. | A young girl. |
| Mtu tajiri. | A rich man, merchant. |
| Mbwa mwitu. | A wild dog. |
| Paka mwitu. | A wild cat. |
| Bata maji. | A water-fowl. |
| Askari kanzu. | A plain-clothes policeman. |
| Askari koti. | A uniformed policeman. |
| Mwaka jana.[1] | Last year. |

## (F) By means of -ENYE + Object[2]

| | |
|---|---|
| Mti wenye mi(i)ba. | A thorny tree. (Lit. tree having thorns.) |
| Samaki mwenye mafuta. | A fish rich in oil. |
| Mwenye mali. | A wealthy (person). |
| Penye uvuli. | A shady (place). |

There is actually a slight difference between such phrases as:

Mtu mwenye maarifa—expressing state—a learned man.
Chumba chenye giza                    a dark room (always dark).

*and*

Mtu wa maarifa—describing his qualifications                    —a well informed man.
Chumba cha giza                    a dark room (as opposed to a light one).

---

[1] Jana = yesterday, may be used as both noun and adverb.
[2] Cf. p. 63.

Some typical adjectives of type C:

| | | | |
|---|---|---|---|
| -a baridi | cold | -a kizungu | European |
| -a hila | crafty | -a kiswahili | Swahili |
| -a dhahabu | golden | -a kiungwana | well bred |
| -a giza | dark | -a kienyeji | native |
| -a moto | hot | | |
| -a mwisho | last | -a kweli | true |
| -a kawaida | customary, regular | -a juu | top, upstairs |
| | | -a chini | under, downstairs |
| -a chumvi | salt | | |
| -a thamani | valuable | | |
| -a haki | just | -a mwituni | forest, wild |
| -a maji maji | watery | -a nyumbani | house, household |
| -a kwanza | first | -a jikoni | kitchen |
| -a kulia¹ | right (hand), viz. hand to eat with | -a shambani | plantation |
| | | -a kondeni | field |
| | | -a baharini | ocean, sea |
| | | -a mtoni | river |
| -a kitoto | childish | | |
| -a kiume | male | -a kuume | right |
| -a kike | female | -a kushoto | left |
| -a kishenzi | uncivilized, uncouth | | |

## EXERCISE 40

Translate:

1. Royal robes
2. Hot water
3. Hard work (lit. hot work)
4. Regular (or customary) wages
5. Valuable rings
6. European customs
7. Swahili words
8. Well-bred people
9. Uncouth children
10. Male children
11. Female teachers
12. Upstairs rooms
13. Downstairs work
14. Wild animals
15. Household jobs
16. Kitchen utensils
17. Kitchen work

¹ Used only with **mkono**.

18. Wild flowers
19. Plantation crops
20. The right hand
21. Left hands
22. Watery soup
23. Salt-water fish (sea)
24. Sea water
25. Salt water
26. Enough chairs
27. A room with many windows
28. The fifth mistake
29. The twelfth bird
30. The fourth child
31. The third lamp
32. The eleventh porter
33. The second door
34. The first page
35. Cold meat
36. Crafty children
37. A gold ring
38. The last page
39. A just man
40. Childish games
41. True news
42. The top place
43. The under blanket
44. River fish
45. Sufficient food
46. Pleasing work
47. Full cups
48. Audible words
49. Next year
50. Last year

## More Notes on Word Order

Principles already laid down on p. 52 indicate that variation in word order is connected with degree of emphasis. The following sentences illustrate the possibilities of such variation. In some examples the context is not full enough to indicate the reason for that order.

| | |
|---|---|
| Nimeona mambo haya kwa macho **yangu mawili** aliyonipa Mungu. | I have seen these things with my two eyes which God has given me. |
| Tulipokewa kwa wema mwingi sana na nduguze **wa kike wawili**. | We were received with much kindness by his two sisters. |
| Muda **wote huu** tulikuwa tukienda[1] kichwa wazi. | During the whole of this period we were going bareheaded. |
| Wakati **wote huu** simba walikuwa wanatoka[1] tu mapangoni, wakitazama safari. | All this time lions kept on coming out from caves, watching the caravan. |
| Maneno **yangu haya machache** yamekwisha. | My few words are finished. |

[1] These are compound verb forms. See p. 250.

| | |
|---|---|
| Wakati **huu wote** London huingia[1] giza saa tatu za usiku au saa nne. | The whole of this time it gets dark at about 9 or 10 o'clock in London. |
| Wanyama **waovu hawa**. | These bad beasts. |
| Muda **wa miaka mine ya** vita. | A period of four years of war. |
| Watu **wa bara wengi**. | Many people from up country. |
| Nisameheni kwa **huu** ujinga **wangu**. | Forgive my lack of knowledge. |
| **Wale** vijana **watano**. | The five youths. |
| Akapewa ng'ombe **mzuri mweupe mwenye pembe** ndefu. | He was given a fine white cow with long horns. |
| Nduguze **wake wote**. | All her (his) sisters. |
| Mambo **hayo mengi ya kwao**. | These many matters concerning their home. |
| Yatwae **haya** manyoya **yangu mawili mazuri marefu ya mkiani**. | Take these two fine long tail feathers of mine. |

TENA is frequently used to join two adjectives. When NA is used, the second adjective is replaced by an abstract noun.

| | |
|---|---|
| Maembe haya mazuri **tena** mabivu, *or* Maembe haya mazuri **na** ubivu. | These mangoes are fine and ripe. |

The tendency in modern Swahili, however, is to use NA in both cases.

[1] See p. 281.

# CHAPTER XXVI

## INTERROGATIVES

QUESTIONS in Swahili are asked in one of three ways:

(i) By means of a statement without any change in the word order but with a different Tone Pattern (Pattern II as already described, p. 23).

Kazi imekwisha?                Is the work finished?

Questions such as these are sometimes introduced by the particle JE.

Je, kazi imekwisha?

(ii) By the use of the Interrogative roots -NI and -PI, which take various prefixes, and function as Adverbs, Pronouns and as Adjectives. Here Tone Pattern Ib is used.

(iii) By the use of -JE, -NI and -PI as enclitics suffixed to the verb again with Tone Pattern Ib.

### REFERENCE TABLE OF INTERROGATIVE ROOTS

| Adverbs | Pronouns | | Adjectives | | Enclitics |
|---|---|---|---|---|---|
| *Time* <br> **Lini?** When? | *Personal* <br> **Nani?** Who? | | *Defining* <br> **Gani?** What? <br> What sort? | | |
| | *Neuter* <br> **Nini?** What? | | | | *Neuter* <br> **-ni?** |
| *Place* <br> **Wapi?** Where? | *Selective* <br> **-pi?**[1] Which one? | | *Selective* <br> **-pi?**[1] Which? | | *Place* <br> **-pi?** |
| | *Enumerative* <br> **-ngapi?**[2] How many? | | *Enumerative* <br> **-ngapi?**[2] How many? | | |
| *Manner, etc.* <br> **Vipi?** How? | | | | | *Manner* <br> **-je?** |

### Interrogative Adverbs, lini? wapi? vipi?

These follow the verb to which they refer.

Alifika lini?                When did he arrive?

[1] Takes the P.C.                [2] Takes the A.C.

| Amekwenda wapi? | Where has he gone? |
| Alikutukana vipi? | In what way did he abuse you? |

*Note.* Adverbial vi- in vipi must be distinguished from the plural vi- prefix in phrases like Vitu vipi? Which things?

### Interrogative Pronouns, nani? nini? -pi? -ngapi?

(a) As object of the verb they follow the verb.

| Umemwona nani? | Whom did you see? |
| Ataka nini? | What does he want? |
| Ameleta ipi? (taa) | Which one has he brought? (lamp) |
| Ameleta ngapi? (taa) | How many has he brought? (lamps) |

(b) When required as subject of a sentence, copulative phrasing is employed, and the interrogative forms the complement of NI. This NI is, however, generally omitted.

In copulative phrasing, as already pointed out on p. 94, word order varies.

| (Ni) Nini *bei ya kawaida*? <br> Bei ya kawaida (ni) nini? | } What is the ordinary price? |
| (Ni) Nani *watoto hawa*? <br> Watoto hawa (ni) nani? | } Who are these children? |

As can be seen, the tone patterns of such sentences also vary; if the interrogative comes first, the remainder of the sentence takes the tone pattern of parenthesis.

A few sentences generally follow a stereotyped pattern:[1]

| Nani *huyu*? | Who is this? |
| Nini *hii*? | What is this? |
| Jina lako nani? | What (lit. who) is your name? |

With finite verbs also, the interrogative may stand either at the beginning or end of the sentence.

| (Ni) nani *amesema*? <br> Kasema nani? | } Who spoke? |

[1] A change of word order in sentences such as these would imply a reversal of the normal direction of emphasis from nani, nini and jina to huyu, hii and nani respectively.

Relative phrasing is often employed with interrogatives. The position of the interrogative again varies with the sense.

Aliyekupiga (ni) nani? ⎫
(Ni) Nani *aliyekupiga*? ⎬ Who struck you?

## Interrogative Adjectives, gani? -pi? -ngapi?

Interrogatives used as qualificatives follow the noun to which they relate.

| | |
|---|---|
| Nilete mti gani? | What tree am I to bring? |
| Wataka taa zipi? | Which lamps do you want? |

When occurring in copulative phrasing, they and their noun generally form the topic of the sentence.

| | |
|---|---|
| (Ni) Mti gani *huu*? | What tree is this? |
| (Ni) Mtu gani *huyu*?[1] | Of what tribe is this man? |
| (Ni) Taa zipi *hizi*? | Which lamps are these? |
| (Ni) Mashoka mangapi *haya*? | How many are these axes? |

## Interrogative Enclitics, -pi? -ni? -je?

Here the main sentence stress falls on the syllable immediately preceding the enclitic, though it itself may also be preceded by a secondary stress.

| | |
|---|---|
| Amekwendapi? | Where has he gone? |
| Waniitiani? | What are you calling me for? i.e. Why are you calling me? |
| Alifanyaje? | What (lit. how) did he do? |

## Interrogative Phrases

Interrogative phrases based on the simple forms are numerous. They too function as Adverbs, Pronouns or Adjectives according to their context.

| | |
|---|---|
| -a nini? | For what? For what purpose? |
| -a nani? | Of whom? Whose? |

[1] Cf. Mtu namna gani *huyu*? What sort of person is this man?
[2] Je is also found in auje and kwaje.

F*

| **-a wapi?** | From where? Whence? |
|---|---|
| **kama nini?** | Like what? As for instance? |
| **muda gani?** | What space of time? For how long? |
| **namna gani?** | What kind? |
| **kiasi gani?** | What amount? How much? |
| **kadiri gani?** | What degree? How much? |
| **mahali gani?** | What place? Where? |
| **kwa nini?** | In respect to what? Why? |
| **kwani?** | Why? |
| **mbona?**[1] | Why? |

*Examples.*

| Taa hii ya nini?<br>Ya nini *taa hii*? } | What is this lamp for? |
|---|---|
| Taa ya nani *hii*? | Whose lamp is this? |
| Mahindi ya wapi *haya*? | Where does this maize come from? |
| | |
| Nauli kiasi gani? | How much is the fare? |
| Moja kiasi gani? (maembe) | How much each? (mangoes) |
| Jumla kiasi gani? | How much for the lot? |
| Kwa muda gani *umekaa hapa*? | How long have you lived here? |
| Kwa sababu gani *hukurudi jana*? | Why did you not return yesterday? |
| Kwa nini *alifanya hasira*? | Why did he become angry? |
| Kwa nini *umechelewa*?<br>Mbona *umechelewa*? } | Why are you late? |

**Kwa nini** merely asks why. **Mbona** conveys an element of surprise and implies that matters are different from what the speaker expects.

| Umechelewa, mbona? | How is it that you are late? |
|---|---|

## VOCABULARY

| | | | |
|---|---|---|---|
| **nauli** | fare | **pata** | attain |
| **bei** | price | **ng'ambo** | other side |
| **mwendo (mi-)** | journey | **takiwa** | be required |
| **kufuli** | padlock | **kamba** | rope |
| **hali** | state | **ziwa (ma-)** | lake |

[1] Origin **uncertain**, but probably related to **ona** = see.

| upana | width | mkeka (mi-) | mat |
| kadiri | extent | rat(i)li | pound, lb. |
| gari | train | mahudhurio | attendance (at |
| tikti | ticket | | school, etc.) |

## EXERCISE 41a

Read and translate, noticing how the position of the interrogative affects the tone pattern.

1. (Ib) Ninunue wapi *kofia*?
2. (Ib) Unasemaje? (Ib) Anasema nini?
3. (Ib) Nauli kiasi gani?
4. (Ib) Mwenyewe yuko wapi?
5. (Ib) Unauza nini *hapa*?
6. (Ib) Bei ya kawaida nini?
7. (Ib) Wauzaje *machungwa haya*?
8. (Ib) Nyumba gani *ile*?
9. (Ib) Ni mwendo wa saa ngapi *mpaka Maweni*?
10. (III) Miti hii mizuri (Ib) ni miti gani?
11. (I) Nani *hawa wafanyao kazi hapa*?
12. (Ib) Njia iendayo mjini ipi?
13. (Ib) Itachukua muda gani *kufika*?
14. (Ib) Utanunua nini *sokoni*?
15. (Ib) Umetumia shilingi ngapi?
16. (Ib) Kufuli i wapi?
17. (Ib) Una nini? (Ib) Huwezi[1] nini?
18. (Ib) Waonaje *hali yako leo*?
19. (Ib) Tangu lini *umekuwa mgonjwa*?
20. (Ib) Saa ngapi *kufika ng'ambo*?
21. (Ib) Wapagazi wangapi *wanatakiwa*?
22. (Ia) Nichukue nini na nini?
23. (Ib) Kipimo gani *kila mzigo*?
24. (Ib) Mzigo huu wa nani?
25. (Ib) Kamba hii ya nini?
26. (Ib) Wako watu wangapi *Tanga*?
27. (III) Nyumba ile yenye saa (Ib) ni nyumba gani?
28. (Ib) Ziwa hili lapata urefu gani? (Ib) Upana wake kadiri gani?

[1] Used idiomatically. Siwezi, huwezi, hawezi, etc. I am not well, you are not well, etc.

29. (Ib) Mvua itakwisha lini?
30. (Ib) Mvua itakunya lini?
31. (Ib) Saa ngapi *hata chakula tayari*?
32. (Ib) Kwa nini *unataka kazi*?
33. (I) Mbona *unataka sabuni tena*?
34. (Ib) Yametoka wapi *maji haya*?
35. (Ib) Kuna chakula gani *jikoni*?
36. (Ib) Kwa nini *hukupika viazi*?
37. (Ib) Gari itaondoka lini?
38. (Ib) Tukate tikti wapi?
39. (Ib) Tutengeze vipi *mahudhurio*?
0. (Ib) Jina lako waitwaje?

## Exercise 41b

Translate:

1. Who is this man?
2. Whose clothes are these?
3. Who broke this cup?
4. Who has broken this cup?
5. What do you sell here?
6. How do you sell these mats?
7. How much each?
8. How much for the lot?
9. What is the ordinary price?
10. What is that noise?
11. What animal is this?
12. What fruit is this?
13. What wages do you want?
14. How many porters do you want?
15. How many loads are there at the house?
16. What is the name of this child?
17. What sort of meat is procurable in the market to-day?
18. How much per pound?
19. How much fruit have you bought?
20. How many eggs am I to buy to-day?
21. What are these women carrying?
22. Where do these things come from?
23. What are they for?

24. Which is your lamp?
25. Which way shall we go?
26. Why did you not go yesterday?
27. How comes it about that you did not work yesterday?
28. What are you up to? (fanya)

# CHAPTER XXVII

## ADVERBS (Section I)

### ADVERBIAL CONCEPTS

BANTU roots basically adverbial are comparatively few in Swahili, e.g.:

| | |
|---|---|
| Mzigo huu mzito **mno**. | This load is very heavy. |
| Wataka viti vingapi? Nataka viwili **tu**. | How many chairs do you want? I want only two. |

Adverbial function, however, is shown in a variety of ways:

1. By nouns:

Alifika **usiku**.        He arrived at night.

2. By adverbial nouns with suffix -**ni**:

Amerudi **nyumbani**.[1]        He has returned to the house.

3. By loan words, mostly Arabic in origin. Many of these are nouns also.

Atarudi **halafu**.        He will come back later.

4. By ideophones (see Chapter XLV).

Ilibwatika **bwata**.        It dropped down with a bang.

5. By phrases introduced by **kwa**, also to a lesser extent by **katika**, **tangu**, **tokea**, **mpaka**.

**Kwa siri**.        Secretly.

6. By an enclitic -**to** found in proverbs, etc.

157. (U)kitema kuni tema**to**.    If you cut firewood (in the bush), cut it well.

7. By nominal and pronominal roots taking adverbial prefixes. Only these need detailed discussion at this stage. The prefixes concerned are:

| *Place and Time* | *Manner* | *Likeness* | *State* |
|---|---|---|---|
| ku- pa- mu- | vi- | ki- | u- |

[1] Locative -**ni** is sometimes omitted, thereby giving the noun the status of a Proper Noun.

| | |
|---|---|
| Amekwenda shamba. | He has gone to the plantation. |
| Amekwenda posta. | He has gone to the post. |
| Amekwenda Bara. | He has gone up country. |

## THE ADVERBIAL PREFIXES KU-, PA-, MU-, VI-

As adverbial formatives, these prefixes may be used with the pronominal roots and stems given below.

KU- PA- and MU- denote both Place and Time, but KU- and MU- have greatly restricted usages in reference to Time.

MU- expresses area, "alongness" in addition to "withinness".

VI- expresses Manner, Likeness, etc. It must be distinguished from the plural VI- Class.

REFERENCE TABLE

| Possessives | Demonstratives | | -enye + noun | -ingine | -A of Relationship |
|---|---|---|---|---|---|
| kwangu, etc. | kule | huku | kwenye | kwingine | kwa |
| pangu, etc. | pale | hapa | penye | pengine | pa |
| mwangu, etc. | mle | humu | mwenye | mwingine | mwa |
| | vile | hivi | | vingine | |

With -O of Reference:

| Reference Demonstratives[1] | Enclitic after Subject Pref. | Enclitic after NA- | -ote | -o -ote |
|---|---|---|---|---|
| huko | yuko, etc. | nako | kote | ko kote |
| hapo | yupo, etc. | napo | pote | po pote |
| humo | yumo, etc. | namo | m(w)ote | mo mote |
| hivyo | | navyo | | vyo vyote |

In addition a few of the more common reduplicated forms will be found among the examples which follow. For full list see p. 304.

### Ku-, Pa- and Mu- of Place and Time

As *formative* prefixes KU- and PA- give certain of these roots the status of an Adverbial Pronoun (see p. 127).

| | |
|---|---|
| Simameni **hapa**. | Stand here. |
| Wamerudi **kwao**. | They have returned home. |

[1] See p. 181.

As *concordial* prefixes they bring words into concordial relationship with all adverbial forms.

| | |
|---|---|
| Wamerudi nyumbani **kwa** mpishi. | They have returned to the cook's house. |
| Hapa **pa**itwa Maweni. | This (place) is called Maweni. |
| Ha**m**na kitu ndani. | There is nothing inside. |

Study the following sentences, noting the dual function of the prefixes, also the reference to Time.

### KU- in reference to Place and Time

| | |
|---|---|
| Twende **kw**ingine. | Let us go in another direction. |
| **Kw**enye miti ha**ku**na wajenzi. | Where there are trees (i.e. a place having trees) there are no builders. |
| Wamerudi **kwa**o? | Have they returned home? |
| **Kwa**o **ku** wapi? | Where is their home? |
| **Ko**te kote aliona nzige tu, makundi makundi. | In every direction he saw nothing but swarms of locusts. |
| Vitabu hivi vipeleke nyumbani **kwa**ngu. | Take these books to my house. |
| **Ku**le **ku**melimwa vizuri. | Over there has been well cultivated. |
| Alitoka nyumbani **mw**ake akawafuata hu**ku** anaimba. | He went out of his house and followed them meanwhile singing. |
| Huta**ku**ona **kw**enu tena. | You will not see your home again. |
| **Ku** hali gani nje? | What is it (i.e. the weather) like outside. |

### PA- in reference to Place and Time

| | |
|---|---|
| Weka ha**pa**. Weka **pa**le. | Put it down here. Put it down over there. |
| **Pe**ngine hatusomi. | Sometimes we do not read. |
| Alimuangukia miguuni **pa**ke. | He fell down at his feet. |
| Kikombe ki**po** mezani. | The cup is on the table. |
| Amesimama mlangoni **pa** nyumba yake. | He is standing at the door of his house. |

Wapaona? Sipaoni. | Do you see it? I don't see it.

Penye uvuli panipendeza. | A shady spot pleases me.

Pote pote pana taka. | The whole place is dirty.

Mahali pengine hapafai. | Another place won't do.

Mimi ni radhi kukaa papa hapa. | I am content to stay right here.

Siendi po pote mpaka nione ng'ombe wangu kwanza; nieleze papa hapa. | I will go nowhere until I have seen my cow. Tell me right now on the spot (what has happened).

Mara pale pale Dunduvule akafufuka. | Just then Dunduvule came to life again.

Siku moja niliona mlangoni pao ghasia na kelele nyingi. | One day I noticed a disturbance at their door and a great noise.

Hapo zamani paliondoka mtu. | Once upon a time there arose a man.

### MU- in reference to Place and Time

Bwana hayumo chumbani mwake. | The Bwana is not in his room.

Hawakuvaa kofia vichwani mwao. | They wore no hats on their heads.

Tuliingia mipakani mwa Uganda. | We entered the borders of Uganda.

Lile joka . . . liliingia mle mtungini. | The snake entered the water-jar.

Humu nyumbani hamkai mtu. | There is no one living in this house.

Mnara mkubwa wa Westminster wenye saa kubwa yenye sifa ulimwenguni mwote. | The Tower of Westminster with the great clock well known throughout the world.

Katika mto wa Thames tukaona vyombo vingi na ghala kubwa sana ukingoni mwake. | On the Thames we saw many vessels and huge warehouses along its banks.

Tulifika mnamo saa tano. | We arrived about 11 o'clock.

KU- and PA- may also be used without an adverbial subject. Here ideas of Time and Place often overlap.

| | |
|---|---|
| Kumefunga mawingu. | It is cloudy. |
| Kumekuwa kweupe. | It has cleared up. |
| Kumekucha. | It has dawned. |
| Tuliwatazama hata kukawa giza. | We watched them until it became dark. |
| Upepo ukavunja kukawa shwari kuu. | The wind ceased and there was a great calm. |
| Siku ya Jumapili mwezi tatu huu kulivuma upepo mkali hata mashua moja ilizama. | On Sunday the third of this month there was such a great gale blowing that one boat sank. |

## VOCABULARY

| | | | |
|---|---|---|---|
| kisiwa (vi-) | island | shimo (ma-) | pit |
| mbogo | buffalo | piga mbiu | make a proclamation |
| skuli | school | | |
| uvuli | shade | ruksa | |
| mshale (mi-) | arrow | ruhusa | permission |
| vaa[1] | wear, i.e. put on clothes | tembea | go for a walk |
| | | ndani | inside, interior |
| wayo (nyayo) | footprint | bega (ma-) | shoulder |
| telemka | descend | useja | string of beads |
| mfuko (mi-) | bag, pocket | shingo | neck |
| baraza | veranda, council | kabati | cupboard |

### EXERCISE 42a

Translate, noting the force of the adverbial formatives and concords:

1. Alirudi kisiwani kwake katika ziwa.
2. Wamo chumbani mwao.
3. Walifika kwenye nyumba ya Mbogo.
4. Mtoto hayuko skuli amekwenda kwao.
5. Penye moto hapakosi moshi.
6. Penye miti hapakosi uvuli.
7. Mshale wake hauanguki chini patupu.
8. Hawakuvaa kitu kichwani mwao.

[1] Contrast vua, (take off clothes).

9. Mahali pengine, zile nyayo hazikuonekana.
10. Amani (child's name) aliteremka kuangalia kote kote.
11. Kwenu ku wapi?
12. Iweke mizigo pale uvulini.
13. Waliondoka wakaenda kwingine.
14. Akatwaa mfuko wa fedha, akaenda akauweka barazani pa Abunawas.
15. Akauliza habari ya Wazungu, akaambiwa La, hapa hawapo.
16. Akamwambia, Kwenu unakujua? Akasema Nitakujuaje nami nimo ndani ya shimo.
17. Alimwambia, Bwana mjini mna wevi humu?
18. Sultani akapiga mbiu kama baada ya saa nne hapana ruksa kutembea.
19. Huku nyuma Kedhab akachukua nguo zote akaenda zake.
20. Tukakaa hata akaja punda mle nyumbani. Akaja mbwa akaingia nyumbani akaja pale mezani.

## Exercise 42b

Translate:

1. There is nothing inside.
2. A place where children are never lacks noise.
3. He carried the load on his shoulders.
4. This is my home.
5. She wore a string of beads round her neck.
6. They have gone in another direction.
7. Did they go into their house?
8. Has he returned to his village?
9. They are standing at the door of my house.
10. Are you (sing.) going to their house?
11. Put the letters down there.
12. Sometimes I forget, at other times I remember.
13. The cups are here in this cupboard.

## The VI- of Manner

A study of the table on p. 159 shows that **vi-** as a formative affix has a more limited usage than **ku-**, **pa-**, **mu-**, but it can often tersely and graphically represent a whole English phrase.

Kuona **vile**, . . .     On seeing how matters were, . . .

In addition **vi-** may be prefixed to certain of the "Adjectival" stems (see pp. 48–9) with adverbial function.

| | |
|---|---|
| **vizuri** | nicely |
| **vibaya** | badly |
| **vyema** | well |

**Vi-** is occasionally met with as Subject Prefix; here it refers to no actual subject word, but to some implied adverbial concept.

**Vi**likuwaje ukafika mapema?     How came it about (*or* how was it) that you came early?

## Other Examples

| | |
|---|---|
| Akawasalisha hi**vi** mpaka mwisho wakatoka. | He led them in worship in this manner until the end and then they went out. |
| Mke aliposikia **vile** akafanyiza hofu. | When she heard how matters were she became alarmed. |
| Aliandika barua kwa mjomba wake akaandika hi**vi**, Salaam mjomba wangu . . . | She wrote a letter to her uncle and wrote after this fashion: Salaams my Uncle . . . |
| Kusikia **vile** . . . | On hearing how matters stood . . . |
| Kwa nini kusema hi**vi**? | Why speak in this way? |
| Tumjaribu **vingine**. | Let us test him in some other way. |
| Ah, watu watanifikiri **vipi** mimi? | Ah, what will people think of me? |
| **Vipi** ni bora, hivi au hivi? | Which is the best, this way or that? |
| Kama nimesema **viovu**, nisamehe. | If I have spoken evil, forgive me. |

Ukijipitia ovyo,[1] waweza ku-pondwa mara moja.

If you cross (the street) care-lessly, you are liable to be run over straight away.

Lakini katika ila hii vile vile hatuna haki kuwalaumu sana watoto. Wazee vile vile wana makosa katika haya.

But concerning this defect likewise we are not justified in blaming the children. The parents in like manner are to blame in this.

Wachezaji wa nyuma vile vile hawakuonyesha mapa-tano na watu wa mbele, wakapiga mpira ovyo tu badala ya kuwatupia we-nzi wao.

In the same way the backs showed no combination with the forwards, they kicked the ball aimlessly instead of passing it to their fellow-players.

Chewa akajibu, Hiyo ni kazi ya Mungu . . . Chewa aka-sema vile vile.

The rock-cod replied, This is God's doing. . . . The rock-cod said exactly as before.

Kila siku hufanya vivi hivi.

Every day they do exactly like this.

## OTHER ADVERBIAL PREFIXES

### The U- of State

This has a limited usage.

Nenda upesi.

Go quickly.

Usile wima.

Don't eat standing up (ima, an old root, meaning to stand upright).

Mstari huu umekwenda upa-nde.

This line is crooked (has gone askew).

### The KI- of Likeness

This is prefixed to a number of roots, mostly nominal.

-toto   Alicheza na kucheka kitoto.

He played and laughed in a childish way.

-zungu  Aliniamkia kizungu.

He greeted me in European fashion.

---

[1] The word ovyo is obviously derived from vi-. It means "just anyhow".

169. Kufa **ki**kondoo ndiko    To die like a sheep (i.e.
     kufa **ki**ungwana.         silently), that is to die in
                        the noble manner.

This same adverbial **ki-** when used with the **-a** of relationship helps to express an adjectival concept as given on p. 146.

## Adverbial Prefix KA-

This prefix is common to many Bantu languages but is lacking in Swahili except in the one word **kamwe. ka** = times; **mwe** is an old Swahili root for "one". It can only be used in negative sentences.

Sipendi kamwe.           I do not like it at all (not once).

### VOCABULARY

**mdudu (wa-)** insect
**kamatwa** be caught hold of
**tenda** do, act, perform
**siri** a secret
**funzana** instruct one another
**angika** suspend, hang up
**picha** picture
**lishwa** be fed
**kuchwa** whole day
**zaliwa** be born
**kipofu (vi-)** a blind person; adv. in a blind condition

**kiwete (vi-)** a lame person, cripple; adv. in a lamed or crippled condition
**kidogo** adv. a little
**kidogo kidogo** by degrees
**kaa kitako** sit down
**tako (ma-)** buttock
**kisirisiri** stealthily
**lala kifulifuli** or **kifudifudi** lie on face
**sadiki** believe
**onyesha** show
**jaribu** try

### EXERCISE 43a

Translate:

1. Sasa amenipa fedha vile vile.
2. Kwa nini ukafanya hivi?
3. Wadudu hawa si wazuri wakikamatwa ovyo.
4. Usifanye kazi yako ovyo.

5. Mfalme wetu hanywi maji ovyo.
6. Alipotenda haya aliyatenda kisirisiri.
7. Nenda upesi.
8. Walifunzana kiume.
9. Usiangike picha upande.
10. Kuku hulishwa hivi mara mbili kuchwa.
11. Waliniamkia kiswahili.
12. Mtu huyu alizaliwa kipofu.
13. Mtoto huyu aenda kiwete.
14. Atajua kidogo kidogo.
15. Wamekaa kitako.
16. Usilale kifulifuli (*or* kifudifudi).
17. Jini akasema, Kama hamsadiki ngojeni niwaonyeshe. Akaingia ndani ya chupa akasema, Nalikaa hivi.

## EXERCISE 43b

Translate:

1. Hamisi does his work nicely.
2. He spoke thus.
3. Do (it) like this.
4. They sang after this manner.
5. Try some other way.
6. They greeted us in European fashion.
7. He speaks in a kingly way.
8. These people cultivate just anyhow.
9. How do I know?
10. Go and do likewise.
11. Do it just like this.
12. He spoke in a childish way.
13. Play the man.

# CHAPTER XXVIII

## ADVERBS (Section II)

ADVERBIAL relatives are formed on the -O of Reference with prefixes KU-, PA-, MU- and VI-, in the same way as pronominal relatives (already described in Chapter XIX).

In addition the adverbial prefix KU- may combine with the -A of Relationship to form adverbial phrases.

## ADVERBIAL RELATIVES

### REFERENCE TABLE

| -KO | -PO | | -MO | | -VYO |
|---|---|---|---|---|---|
| *Place* | *Place* | *Time* | *Place* | *Time* | *Manner, etc.* |
| Indefiniteness Direction Motion to or from | Definiteness Rest at Position | A point A going on | Withinness Aroundness Alongness | | Manner Likeness Reason Cause Degree |
| English equivalents: Where | where at which on which etc. | when | wherein | round about | as just as even as how according as in proportion as, etc. |

*Place.*

**-ko**, **-po** and **-mo** are used to indicate that aspect of Place which the speaker wishes to particularize:

| | |
|---|---|
| Kote kote tuli**ko**tazama tu-kaona watu. | In every direction where we looked we saw people. |
| Po pote nisimama**po** huni-fuata. | Wherever I stand he follows me. |
| Tumepaona pale ali**po**pigana na simba. | We have seen the spot where he fought with a lion. |

168

| | |
|---|---|
| Sipajui anapokaa. | I don't know where he lives. |
| Hamna kitanda chumbani anamolala. | There is no bed in the room in which he is sleeping. |

## Time.

-ko is not met with as a relative particle of time, but -po is used both for a "point" and a "going on" in time. The difference is indicated by the verb form. -mo has a restricted usage.

| | |
|---|---|
| Aliposema. | When he spoke (point). |
| Alipokuwa akisema.[1] | While he was speaking (duration). |
| Mnamo saa sita. | Round about 12 o'clock.[2] |

## Manner, etc.

-vyo as a relative is easy to understand if it is realized that it has a very wide application. It may refer to any adverbial concept expressing Manner, Likeness, Reason, Cause, Degree, whether stated or understood. Its translation therefore depends upon what is expressed in the antecedent.

| | |
|---|---|
| *Manner*. Fanya vyo vyote upendavyo. | Do (it) just however you like. |
| Vyo vyote walivyotaka wao wenyewe. | In whatever way they themselves desired. |
| *Likeness*. Sema kama asemavyo yeye. | Say it as he does. |
| *Reason*. Alifurahi mno kwa jinsi alivyompendeza rafiki yake. | She was overjoyed at having pleased her friend. |
| *Cause*. Hakuwa na furaha kwa vile alivyongurumiwa na Bwana wake. | He was unhappy because of the way in which he had been stormed at by his master. |
| *Degree*. Nichukue yote? La, chukua kadiri uwezavyo. | Am I to carry all? No, carry as many as you are able. |

---

[1] See Compound Tenses, Chapter XXXVI.
[2] For hours of the day see p. 319.

Ni heri nifanye wema ijapo-    It behoves me to do good,
kuwa kidogo kwa kadiri         even though it be little, in
niwezavyo.                     so far as I am able.

On no account must these subdivisions of Manner, Likeness, etc., be pressed too far, for a glance at the examples
suffices to show that they often overlap.

### Intonation of Adverbial Relative Sentences

Tone Pattern varies as with the pronominal relative, viz.
according to whether the relative clause occupies a final or
non-final position in the sentence.

If non-final, the tone pattern is III.

Alipofika, watu wote wakakimbia.     When he arrived, the
                                     people all fled.

If final, the tone pattern is Ia.

Tumepaona pale alipofika.            We have seen the spot
                                     where he arrived.

### Aphorisms

465. Riziki kama ajali, huita-    One's providences are like
     mbui ijapo.                   one's fate—(for) you know
                                   not when that comes.

549. Ushikwapo, shikamana,        When thou art caught hold
     uchwewapo na jua,             of, hold on; when thou
     lala.                         hast the sun set on thee
                                   (stay and) sleep there.

211. Kwendako mema, hu-           Whither good (things) go,
     rudi mema.                    (thence) good things are
                                   wont to return.

#### VOCABULARY

| | | | |
|---|---|---|---|
| wonyesho | exhibition | kuta | come upon, meet |
| shinda | surpass, etc. | | |
| weza | be able | mkulima (wa-) | peasant, cultivator |
| asali | honey | | |

| tangu | since, from (mostly in relation to time) | **mwanzo (mi-)** | beginning |
| | | **nusa harufu** | follow the scent |
| | | **majonzi** | grief |

## EXERCISE 44

Read and translate:

1. Wembley ni mahali palipofanywa wonyesho.
2. Hapa tukaapo pazuri; sijapaona pengine pa kushinda hapa.
3. Watakaporudi wapagazi, wape chakula.
4. Huku wakaako, hatukujui.
5. Pale tulipokaa zamani pabaya, kwani ni mahali pasipo maji mengi.
6. Sungura akaenda zake, mpaka akafika katika soko, ambako akamkuta mchinja nyama.
7. Mtu huyu jinsi aimbavyo vizuri!
8. Nitafanya kama niwezavyo kukusaidia.
9. Kama nionavyo mimi kazi hii imekwisha.
10. Ko kote alikotazama hakuona kitu.
11. Na Ali kule alikokwenda hakumpata mbuzi, akarudi kwenye asali, asikute asali wala masikini.
12. Mkulima akampa habari zote tangu mwanzo, alivyokuja na alivyosema.
13. Basi mbwa akaanza kunusa harufu ya paka na kutafuta alimopita.
14. Hapo zamani Kalungu ni mahali palipojaa majonzi.
15. Hemedi akajibu, Ah, Bwana wangu, sijui ninakokwenda. Kisha Hemedi akamwuliza Fikirini, Je, wewe, unakwendapi? Akamwambia, Na mimi, Bwana wangu, sijui niendako.
16. Niliposema naye, hakunijibu.

## ADVERBIAL PHRASES BASED ON KWA
### The KWA of State, Reason, etc.

Adverbial phrases introduced by KWA are commonly used in Swahili to express Cause, Reason or Purpose, and to a lesser extent Manner or State. Such phrases indicate (i) By means of, (ii) By reason of, (iii) In respect to. KWA is formed from the -A of Relationship with prefix KU-, which must be distinguished from the KU- of Place.

These functions must not be looked upon as mutually exclusive, for one often overlaps another, as a study of the following sentences will show:

| | |
|---|---|
| Alikwenda **kwa** miguu. | He went *on* foot. |
| Alikwenda **kwa** gari. | He went *by* train. |
| Alikufa **kwa** njaa. | He died *of* hunger. |
| Alikichonga **kwa** teso. | He shaped it *with* an adze. |
| Alimtambua **kwa** sauti yake. | He recognized him *by* his voice. |
| Alikosa **kwa** ujinga. | He failed *through* ignorance. |
| Alistaajabu **kwa** uzuri wake. | He was astonished *at* its beauty. |
| **Kwa** ajili hii siendi tena. | *For* this reason I am not going again. |
| Nguo hizi hazimfai **kwa** kazi. | These clothes are no use to him *for* work. |
| Alikwenda zake **kwa** furaha. | He went off *with* joy. (in a state of joy, joyfully) |
| Fanya kazi yako **kwa** bidii. | Do your work *with* zest. (thoroughly) |
| Aliondoka **kwa** haraka. | He left *with* haste. (in a hurry) |
| **Kwa** nini hukwenda? | Why did you not go? (*in respect to* what?) |
| **Kwa** sababu gani hukuniita? | *For* what reason did you not call me? |
| Sikukwita (**kwa**[1]) sababu nilisahau. | I did not call you because I forgot. |
| Sikukwita **kwa** kuwa umechoka. | I did not call you because you were tired. |

## The KWA of Place or Direction

When built upon the KU- of Place, KWA has a directional significance. Note, however, that it is used only in reference to people.[2]

---

[1] **Kwa** is often omitted before **sababu**.
[2] This use of **kwa** corresponds almost exactly with the French "chez" —"Allez chez Monsieur; Il vient de chez Madame; Il est chez Muhamadi."

| | |
|---|---|
| Enda **kwa** Bwana. | Go *to* the Bwana. |
| Ametoka **kwa** Bibi. | He has come *from* the Bibi. |
| Yuko **kwa** Muhamadi. | He is *at* Muhamadi's. |

It is not used before place-names nor with adverbial nouns.[1]

| | |
|---|---|
| Ametoka Tanga. | He has come from Tanga. |
| Ametoka nyumbani. | He has come from the house. |

## Aphorisms illustrating KWA

18. Amani haiji ila **kwa** ncha ya upanga. — Peace comes not save by the point of the sword.

22. Fulani amejifunga **kwa** ulimi wake. — So-and-So has bound himself with his tongue.

192. Kupata si **kwa** werevu, na kukosa si ujinga. — Getting is not of cunning and lacking is not (necessarily) unskilfulness.

KWA before a possessive stem has already been mentioned on p. 129.

| | |
|---|---|
| Enda **kwake** saa tano. | Go to him at 11 o'clock. |
| Njoo **kwangu** kesho. | Come to me to-morrow. |

Also the extended meaning of home:

| | |
|---|---|
| **Kwao** hakuna ng'ombe wengi. | At their (home) there are not many cattle. |

## Other Uses of KWA

The following uses of KWA should be noted, although it does not here introduce an adverbial phrase.

| | |
|---|---|
| Wengi walifika wakubwa **kwa** wadogo. | Many arrived, both old and young. |
| Wakapewa chakula kingi, wali **kwa** mchuzi. | They were given much food, rice with curry. |
| Maneno haya **kwa** haya. | These same words over and over again. |
| Mia **kwa** tano. | 5 per cent. |
| Shika njia moja **kwa** moja. | Keep straight on. |
| **Kwa** siku nyingi mvua ilikunya moja **kwa** moja. | For many days the rain poured down without a break. |

[1] In the latter case **katika** is sometimes used: Ametoka **katika** nyumba.

## VOCABULARY

| | | | |
|---|---|---|---|
| **huruma** | pity (sb.) | **shina (ma-)** | root and stem of a tree |
| **uawa** | be killed | | |
| **pigwa mawe** | be stoned | **ishi** | live |
| **mzinga (mi-)** | native beehive | **furaha** | joy |
| **Mfereji (mi-)** | ditch (here refers to Suez Canal) | **uangalifu** | care |
| | | **utaratibu** | slowness, gentleness |
| **pasulika** | capable of being split, cf. **pasua** split | **maarifa** (pl.) | knowledge |
| | | **maana** | because, meaning |
| **isipokuwa** | except | **sharti** | it is necessary |
| **fasiri** | translate | **fundisha** | teach |
| **Kiingereza** | English | **omba ruksa** | ask permission |
| **amuru** | order (vb.) | **fundi (ma-)** | a person skilled in art or trade |
| **gugu (ma-)** | weed | | |
| **tema** | cut | **kasi** | violence |

## EXERCISE 45a

Translate:

1. Alimchukua kwa huruma zake.
2. Mchawi aliuawa kwa kupigwa mawe.
3. Maji yalipita kwa kasi.
4. Mzinga wa nyuki umevunja tawi kwa wingi wa asali.
5. Katika mfereji huu utakuta meli kubwa kwa ndogo.
6. Kuta hizi kwa Kiingereza huitwa Breakwater.
7. Kuni hizi hazipasuliki isipokuwa kwa shoka.
8. Fasiri kwa Kiingereza.
9. Mkubwa wetu aliamuru ngoma ipigwe kwa siku nyingi.
10. Mimea yote imekauka kwa jua kali, hata magugu na majani na miiba pia.
11. Tema lile shina kwa jembe.
12. Watu wa nchi hii hupigana kwa nyuta na mishale.
13. Barua hii ipeleke kwa Bwana.
14. Njoo kwangu kesho saa sita.
15. Wanawake wote wamerudi makwao.
16. Kintu na Nambi wakaishi pamoja kwa furaha wakazaa watoto wengi wake kwa waume.

17. Fanya kazi yako kwa uangalifu.
18. Chukua vitu hivi kwa utaratibu.
19. Ndizi hizi zimetoka kwa nani?
20. Anakaa kwa ndugu yake.

## EXERCISE 45b

Read and translate:

Hapo kale maarifa ya kufuata kitu kwa kunusa harufu ilikuwa kazi ya Paka. . . . Mbwa akaona Paka ana njia nzuri ya kupata chakula, maana wengine sharti wakione chakula chao kwa macho lakini Paka kwa harufu. Basi Mbwa akatoka akaenda kwa Paka akamwambia, Nifundishe na mimi kazi hii. . . . Paka akamwambia, Vyema. Mbwa akakaa kwa Paka. . . . Mbwa alipoona siku nyingi zimepita, naye kazi anajua, akaomba ruksa kwa fundi wake Paka kwenda zake.

## Some Useful Adverbs and Adverbial Phrases

### TIME

| | | | |
|---|---|---|---|
| alfajiri | at dawn, at day-break | juzi juzi | the other day |
| alasiri | in the afternoon | kabula ⎫<br>kabla ⎭ | (foll. by ja tense) ere, before |
| adhuhuri | at noon | kati kati | in the middle |
| baadaye | afterwards, later | kesho | to-morrow |
| bado | not yet, still, as yet | kesho kutwa | day after to-morrow |
| bado kidogo | soon, presently | kila siku | daily, every day |
| daima | continually, perpetually | kwanza | first, firstly, to begin with |
| hapo kale | long ago | leo | to-day |
| halafu | afterwards, presently | lini? | when? |
| | | mapema | early |
| hatima ⎫<br>hatimaye ⎭ | finally, in the end | mara | (precedes verbs) immediately |
| jana | yesterday | mara moja | once, at once |
| jioni | in the evening, at dusk | mbele | before, first, earlier |
| juzi | day before yesterday | mchana | in the daytime |
| | | milele | for ever and ever |

| mtondo | three days hence | -po- | (adverbial affix) when |
| mwisho | lastly, finally | | |
| nyuma | hereafter, later | sasa | now |
| pale pale | at that very moment | sasa hivi | } now, at once |
| | | hivi sasa | |
| papo hapo | immediately, just then | siku hizi | nowadays |
| | | siku zote | always |
| pengine | sometimes, other times | zamani | formerly |

## PLACE

| chini | down below, downstairs | kule kule | in the same direction |
| hapa | here | ko kote | in any direction |
| huku | here, in this direction | kote kote | everywhere, on all sides |
| huko | there (place in mind) | kwingine | elsewhere, in another direction |
| huko juu | up there | | |
| humu | in here | mbali | far away |
| humo | in there (place in mind) | mbele | in front |
| | | mle | in there, inside there |
| juu | up above, upstairs | mumu humu | just in here |
| kando | aside | pale | there, over there |
| kando kando | alongside, all round | pale pale | in the same spot |
| | | papa hapa | just here |
| karibu | near | pengine | elsewhere |
| kuku huku | just there | -po- | (adverbial affix) where |
| kule | there, in that direction | po pote | anywhere |
| | | wapi? | where? |

## MANNER, STATE, DEGREE

| bure | to no purpose, freely | halisi | exactly |
| | | haraka | hurriedly |
| ghafula | suddenly, abruptly | hata kidogo | not any, not even a little |
| haba | very little | hivi, hivyo | thus |

| | | | |
|---|---|---|---|
| jinsi...-vyo | as, how | sawasawa | properly |
| kadiri (ya)... -vyo | according as | taratibu | carefully |
| | | tu | only, simply |
| kama...-vyo | as | upande | on one side, crookedly |
| kama vile ...-vyo | even as | upesi | quickly, rapidly |
| kamwe | never, not at all | vibaya | badly, ill |
| kabisa | entirely, not at all | vile, vivyo | thus, so |
| | | vile vile | just so, just the same |
| kadhalika | in like manner | | |
| kidogo | a little, somewhat | vile...-vyo | just so |
| | | vivyo | likewise |
| kidogo kidogo | by degrees | vivyo hivyo | precisely the same |
| kwa kweli | thoroughly | vizuri | well, nicely |
| kweli | truly | vyema | well, nicely |
| mbali mbali | separately | vingine | in a different way |
| mno | exceedingly | | |
| polepole | slowly, gently | vyepesi | easily |
| sana | very, very much, thoroughly | wima | upright |
| | | zaidi | more |

## Affirmation and Negation

| | | | |
|---|---|---|---|
| la | no | ndivyo | it is so, it is thus |
| naam | yes | siyo | no, not so |
| ndiyo | yes, it is so | sivyo | not so, not thus |

G

# CHAPTER XXIX

## PRONOUNS (Section IV)

## FURTHER USES OF THE -O OF REFERENCE

### REFERENCE TABLE

| Noun Classes | 1 It is he, she, it, they, etc. | 2 This, these already mentioned | 3 Other such-like | 4 By means of him, it, them, etc. |
|---|---|---|---|---|
| M- WA- | Ndiye Ndio | Huyo Hao | Wengineo | Kwake Kwao |
| M- MI- | Ndio Ndiyo | Huo Hiyo | Mwingineo Mingineyo | Kwao Kwayo |
| KI- VI- | Ndicho Ndivyo | Hicho Hivyo | Kinginecho Vinginevyo | Kwacho Kwavyo |
| JI- MA- | Ndilo Ndiyo | Hilo Hayo | Jinginelo Mengineyo | Kwalo Kwayo |
| N- N- | Ndiyo Ndizo | Hiyo Hizo | Nyingineyo Nyinginezo | Kwayo Kwazo |
| U- (N- | Ndio Ndizo | Huo Hizo | Mwingineo Nyinginezo | Kwao Kwazo) |
| KU- | Ndiko | Huko | Kwingineko | Kwako |
| Mahali | Ndipo | Hapo | Penginepo | Kwapo |

| Adverbial Classes | It is here, there, then, thus | Here, there, then, thus, already referred to | Other such-like (place, time, manner) |
|---|---|---|---|
| KU- PA- | Ndiko Ndipo | Huko Hapo | Kwingineko Penginepo |
| MU- | Ndimo | Humo | Mwinginemo |
| VI- | Ndivyo | Hivyo | Vinginevyo |

THIS particle may function as:

1. An enclitic complement of copula NDI-.
2. A suffix to demonstrative forms.
3. A suffix to -INGINE.
4. A suffix to KWA and NA.[1]

In each case the -O is preceded by the appropriate concord, except in the Singular Personal Class.

## 1. Complement of NDI- (<NI)

The -O of Reference, preceded by the appropriate concord, forms a pronominal or adverbial complement of the copula except in the Singular Personal Class.

Note the replacement of **ni** by **ndi-**, which takes the word stress. (**ni** as copula is never stressed.)

These forms are often spoken of as the "Emphatic" forms of the copula **ni-**. They are used to define more sharply the nominal, pronominal or adverbial antecedent to which they refer.

| | |
|---|---|
| Kitabu hiki ndi**cho** nikitakacho. | This is the book I want. (Lit. Book this it is the one I want.) |
| Huyu ndi**ye** asiyefanya kazi yake leo. | This is the one who didn't do his work to-day. (Lit. This one it is he who, etc.) |
| Hivi ndi**vyo** alivyosema. | It was after this manner he spoke. (Lit. This manner it is thus how he spoke.) |
| Hapa ndi**po** aliposimama. | It was (or is) here where he stood. |
| 193. Kupotea njia ndi**ko** kujua njia. | To lose the road, that is to know the road. |
| 369. Mwana umleavyo, ndi**vyo** akuavyo. | As you nurse your child so he grows up. |
| 152. Kinga na kinga ndi**po** moto uwakapo. | Firebrand and firebrand, then it is the fire burns. |

---

[1] As suffix to NA it has already been discussed in Chapter XVII.

358a. Muumba ndiye Muu-    The Creator is the (only) De-
    mbua.                    facer.
95. Hindi ndiko kwenye      India is the country of clothes
    nguo, na waendao         and yet there are those who
    tupu wako.               go naked there.

The Personal forms are built up on the Personal Pronouns.

| | | | |
|---|---|---|---|
| **Ndimi** | It is I | **Ndisi** | It is we |
| **Ndiwe** | It is you | **Ndinyi** | It is you |
| **Ndiye** | It is he, she | **Ndio** | It is they |

The negative construction is expressed by SI:

Huyu siye asiyefanya kazi    This is not the one who didn't
leo.                          do any work to-day.
Kitabu hiki sicho nitakacho.  This is not the book I want.

Note that the **-yo** in the forms **ndiyo** and **siyo**, expressing assent or dissent (see p. 79), probably refers to **maneno** (words).

Shortened forms of the Personal Pronoun are only used in the 3rd person.

| | |
|---|---|
| Si mimi | Si sisi |
| Si wewe | Si ninyi |
| Si yeye *or* **Siye** | Si wao *or* **Sio** |

## VOCABULARY

| | | | |
|---|---|---|---|
| **kizalia** | one born at a | **mashaka** | hardships |
| **(vi-)** | place or to a | **shauri** | affair, plan |
| **mzalia** | person, hence | | |
| **(wa-)** | offspring or | **radi** | thunderbolt |
| | descendants | **mtihani** | a school examina- |
| **teka (ma-)** | captive | **(mi-)** | tion |
| **eleza** | give a full ac- | **tambua** | discern, recognize |
| | count of | **kosa** | offend against |
| **shaka** | doubt | **shtaki** | accuse |

## EXERCISE 46

Read and translate:

1. Mimi ndiye mwanao baba, huyu, siye.

2. Vizalia vya mateka tu ndio wawezao kueleza mashaka yale wazee wao waliyopata.
3. Mume wangu hayupo; naye ndiye mwenye shauri ya pesa.
4. Chukua huu, ukampe Sultan, mwambie ndio upanga wa radi.
5. Njia ya kuondoa shaka hii ni moja tu, nayo ndiyo mtihani.
6. Wakatambua kuwa baba yao ndiye aliyemchukua kondoo.
7. Wao ndio walionikosa, asiyenikosa siwezi kumshtaki.

## 2. Demonstrative of Reference

The right use of the Demonstrative of Reference lies in a fuller understanding of the function of the Simple Demonstratives, which are here recapitulated.

*Simple forms.*

These are used in contexts where Proximity or Non-proximity of Place or Time is implied.

They precede or follow the noun, or may stand alone.

When these forms precede the noun, this noun has already been introduced or implied, and their function approximates to that of English *the* in similar circumstances.

When they follow the noun or stand alone, their function is similar to that of English *this*, *these*, and *that*, *those*.

*Proximity.*

| | |
|---|---|
| Akasema, **Hii** kamba imekata jiwe kwa sababu kila siku hupita juu yake. | And he said, *The* rope has cut the stone because it passes over it daily. |
| Kadhi akampa haki mwivi, akanena **Hizi** lulu ni zake. | The judge gave judgment in favour of the thief and said, *The* pearls are his. |
| Akamwambia Chukua nyoya **hili**. | And he said, Take *this* feather. |
| Mke wa Sultani akasema, A, a, a, **huyu** si mtoto wangu. | The Sultan's wife said, No, no, no, *this* is not my son. |

*Non-proximity.*

| | |
|---|---|
| Akamwambia Niazime sufuria. Akampa sufuria. Siku ya nne akatwaa **ile** sufuria akampelekea mwenyewe. | And he said, Lend me a saucepan. And he gave him a saucepan. On the fourth day he took *the* saucepan back to its owner. |
| Alipomwona Sultan akamwambia **Ile** nyumba nimekwisha jenga. | When he saw the Sultan he said, I have finished building *the* house. |
| Siku zikipita Sungura akaja kwa Jogoo, wakaamkiana, wakakaa wakazungumza sana. Hata katika mazungumzo yao **yule** Jogoo akamwambia Sungura . . . | Days passed and the Hare came to the Cock, and they exchanged greetings, and sat down and talked. Now in the course of conversation *the* Cock said to the Hare . . . |
| Alipoona mambo **yale**, . . . | When he saw what had happened, . . . |
| Nenda upesi ukamtazame mtu **yule** ana nini? | Go quickly and find out what is the matter with *that* man. |

*Reference form.*

The question of proximity or non-proximity is immaterial here, for the implication of **-O** is the keynote, viz. that it always refers to something previously mentioned. The form may be rendered by *this, these, that, those* and occasionally *the.*

| | |
|---|---|
| Akamwambia, **Fulani** yupo pamoja nao? Akasema **Huyo** sikumwona, wala simjui. | And he asked him, Is So-and-So with them? He replied, I haven't seen *the said person*, nor do I know him. |
| Natafuta ndege mwenye mbawa za dhahabu. Nikipata **huyo** ndege, vyema. | I am looking for a bird with wings of gold. If I get *such a* bird, well and good. |
| **Huyo** unayemtaka yupo ndani ya tundu. | *This* (bird) which you desire is here inside a cage. |
| Tangu siku **hizo** za **huyo** mhunzi, maneno **hayo** yamekuwa kama fumbo. | Since *the* days of *the* blacksmith *these* words have become a saying. |

Tangu siku **hiyo** urafiki wa Jogoo na Sungura ukakatika.

From *that* day onwards the friendship of the Cock and the Hare was severed.

Mwewe akaona furaha kusikia maneno **hayo**.

The hawk was pleased at hearing *these* words.

Basi walimpa mikuki na miunde, lakini **hivyo** vyote alivikataa.

They gave him spears and hatchets, but all *these* he refused.

Yeye alisafiri mpaka kontinenti hili ili afungue Parliament ya kwanza ya Australia. Wakati **huo** alionana na watu wengi wa kontinenti **hilo**.

He travelled to this continent for the special purpose of opening the first parliament of Australia. During *this* time he met many people of *this* continent.

It will be seen from the examples that the functions of the **-le** and **-o** forms appear sometimes to overlap. One important point should be remembered, viz. that whereas Simple forms are often used for reference, Reference forms may *only* be used for reference.

VOCABULARY

| | | | |
|---|---|---|---|
| **kutosikilizana** | lack of agreement (Lit. not to listen to one another) | **mganga (wa-)** | native doctor |
| | | **mwanafunzi (wa-)** | pupil, apprentice |
| **fumua** | undo (Fig. let loose) | **zawadi** | present |
| | | **ruhusu** | give permission |
| | | **naam** | yes |
| **dhahiri** | evident, clear | **sakafu** | floor |
| **mtama** | millet | **okota** | pick up |
| **zamani** | long ago | **ulizwa** | be asked |
| **bubu (ma-)** | dumb person | **rupia** | rupee |
| **kubali** | accept | **fedha** | money, silver |
| | | **mlio** | sound, clink |

## EXERCISE 47a

Read and translate, noting the force of the demonstratives used:

1. Huko **kutosikilizana** kwao ndiko kulikofumua vita.

2. Ni dhahiri, Kintu hatakuwa na mtama, na hivyo kuku zangu watakufa kwa njaa.

3. Alikuwa na watoto na desturi ya watoto hao ilikuwa ...

4. Hapo zamani Kuku na Jogoo hawakuwa nyama wa mjini, walikuwa nyama wa mwituni.

5. Tangu wakati huo Nyoka na Jongoo hawakupatana tena.

6. Mwanangu nataka ujifanye bubu. Mtoto akakubali. Mama yake akamchukua akampeleka mpaka kwa mganga, akamwambia, Nimekuletea mwanafunzi. Akamwuliza, Huyu mtoto bubu? Akanena, Bubu tangu kuzaliwa. Akamwambia, Unaona, hivyo ndivyo nilivyotaka.

7. Mahali pa kuwafunga akawapa zawadi akawaruhusu kwenda zao, lakini pamoja na hayo hakutaka kuwaacha wale watoto warudi kwao.

8. Unasikia vitu vinalia? Sultani akanena, Naam, nasikia. Abunawas akasema: Hao ndio mafundi, wanatengeneza sakafu na hivyo vinavyolia ni nyundo na misumari.

## Exercise 47b

Translate, noting the force of the demonstratives used:

1. Akaondoka akaenda kwa ndugu zake. Akawaeleza mambo yote. Na wale ndugu zake wakamwuliza, Ndugu yetu, huyu mwanamke ni mwanamke gani? Yule kijana asiseme jina lake yule mwanamke, akasema Nimemwokota njiani tu, na upanga huu nimeukuta na huyu ndege ndiye anayemtaka baba ...

Na wale ndugu zake wakaulizwa na baba yao, Mwanamke huyu jina lake nani? Wakasema Hatumjui, tumemwokota njiani na upanga wake.

2. Akatwaa Abunawas rupia zake thenashara akampa yule masikini. Akamwambia, Nakupa hizi, nenda kalipe. Asubuhi wakakutana wote kwa Sultan. Masikini akasema amekuja kulipa zile fedha. Abunawas akamwuliza masikini, Unazo rupia thenashara? Akajibu Ninazo. Abunawas akatwaa zile fedha akazishika akamwita tajiri atwae fedha zake. Alipotaka kupokea akamwambia Ngoja. Akazitupa chini,

akamwambia, Haya chukua mlio wa hizo rupia, maana masikini naye hakula nyama, amekula harufu tu.

## 3. -ingine-o

Here two sets of prefixes are used, **-ingine** taking the A.C.
and **-o** the P.C.

This is a useful form, which may best be translated by
"such like people or things", etc., or occasionally by "and so
on and so forth".

| | |
|---|---|
| Ah, walimu wa Nairobi wa macho kwa jambo hili na jinginelo. | Ah, the teachers at Nairobi are awake as regards this matter and any other like it. |
| Katika shamba letu mna mindimu, michungwa na mingineyo. | In our plantation are lime and orange trees and various other (fruit trees). |
| Walikuja askari na mabaharia na watu wengineo. | Soldiers and sailors and other such people came. |
| Hao wazungu mashujaa Dr. Livingstone na wengineo waliona mambo maovu sana. | These adventurous Englishmen such as Dr. Livingstone and others like him saw many evil things. |

## 4. kwa-o

This form is not often found outside the Living Classes.

| | |
|---|---|
| Na hata akipata mtu wa ku- mtunza, ataweza kusali- mika na ile aibu waliyo- mtia chapa kwayo wazee wake? | And even should he get some- one to look after him, will he be able to escape the stigma with which his parents have branded him? |

G*

# CHAPTER XXX

## VERBS AND THEIR TENSES (Section V)

### (-NGA-, -JAPO-, -NGE-, -NGALI-)

### THE -NGA- AND -JAPO- TENSES

Both these tenses represent English "though, although, even
though, even if". In the case of -NGA- the concession is
actual, whereas in the case of -JAPO- it is suppositional;
hence the use of the verb (KU)JA (come) and relative -PO-
of time.[1]

*Examples of -NGA-.*

| | |
|---|---|
| 29. **Ang**(a)enda juu kipu-ngu, hafikilii mbingu-ni. | Though the osprey goes high, she does not reach to heaven. |
| 155. Kipya ki nyemi, ki**nga**wa kidonda. | A new (thing) is a joy (source of pleasure) even though it be a sore. |
| 210. Kweli **inga**wa uchungu niambie, usinifiche. | The truth, even though it is bitter, tell it me, and do not hide it from me. |
| Uchumi wa karafuu u**nga**wa ni mkubwa haulipi faida. | The turnover from cloves, although high, does not yield any profit. |

*Examples of -JAPO-.*

| | |
|---|---|
| 310. Msafiri maskini a**japo**-kuwa mfalme. | A traveller is a poor man, even though he be a king. |
| 11. (Fulani) a**japo**shikwa mafungo, hwenda te-na. | So-and-so, although he has a narrow escape, he goes again. |
| U**japo**mwambia hasikii. | Even though you tell him, he pays no attention. |

[1] Modern writers often appear to use -JAPO- for both forms of concession.

186

| Nijapomkataza, hufa-<br>nya vile vile. | Even though I forbid him, he<br>goes on doing it just the<br>same |
|---|---|

**-japo-** expresses no time; if time or negation is to be expressed, a compound form is used. See p. 260.

The **ku-** of the infinitive is retained with monosyllabic verbs.

## THE -NGE- AND -NGALI- TENSES

These tenses are used in a suppositional condition.

When the supposition is possible of realization the -NGE-tense is used both in the protasis (condition) of a sentence and in the apodosis (consequence). The protasis is sometimes introduced by **kama**.

| Mti huu (kama) ungeanguka<br>ungeniua. | If this tree should fall (*or*<br>were to fall), it would kill<br>me. |
|---|---|
| (Kama) ungekitafuta, unge-<br>kiona. | If you would look for it, you<br>would find it. (book) |

If the supposition is regarded as not having been realized, the -NGALI- tense is used—both in the protasis and apodosis.[1]

| Mti huu (kama) ungaliangu-<br>ka ungaliniua. | If this tree had fallen, it would<br>have killed me. |
|---|---|
| (Kama) ungalikitafuta unga-<br>likiona. | If you had looked for it, you<br>would have found it. |

Note, however, in simple condition the -KI- tense is used, followed usually by a Future tense, or the Imperative.

| Ukikitafuta utakiona. | If you look for it, you will see<br>it. |
|---|---|
| Mti huu ukianguka utaniua. | If this tree falls, it will kill me. |
| Mti huu ukianguka, nipe ha-<br>bari. | If this tree falls, let me know. |

These forms may also be used in compound tenses. See p. 259.

---

[1] In actual practice there is considerable laxity in the use of **-nge-** and **-ngali-**.

## Negative

Two alternative forms are in use in the spoken and written word.

(i) With -SI- following the subject prefix.

(ii) With HA- prefixed to the subject prefix.

| If I, you, he, they, etc., were not to know, did not know. | | If I, you, he, they, etc., had not known, would not have known. | |
| --- | --- | --- | --- |
| Nisingejua | Singejua | Nisingalijua | Singalijua |
| Usingejua | Hungejua | Usingalijua | Hungalijua |
| Asingejua | Hangejua | Asingalijua | Hangalijua |
| Tusingejua | Hatungejua | Tusingalijua | Hatungalijua |
| etc. | etc. | etc. | etc. |

The use of the -SI- form is advocated in present-day Swahili.[1]

| | |
| --- | --- |
| Asingejua angeniuliza. | If he did not know (or does not know), he would ask me. |
| Asingejua asingeniuliza. | If he did not know, he would not ask me. |
| Asingalijua angaliniuliza. | If he had not known, he would have asked me. |
| Kama angalijua asingaliondoka mapema? | If he had known, would he not have left early? |
| Kama ningalijua nisingalikwambia? | If I had known, would I not have told you? |

*Note.* The **ku-** of the Infinitive is retained with monosyllabic verbs (and **kwisha** and **kwenda**) in these tenses.

### VOCABULARY

| | | | |
| --- | --- | --- | --- |
| **pumbaa kazi** | take no pains with work | **bila** | without |
| **futwa** | be dismissed | **kiri** | acknowledge |
| **kutana** | meet together | **samehe** | forgive |

[1] *Steere's Exercises* (revised), p. 75.

Translate:

1. Kama mngalifika jana mngalisikia habari zote.
2. Ungaliniambia wakati huo ya kuwa hupendi kusafiri, nisingalikuamuru uende.
3. Kile kisu kama ungalikitafuta sana, kingalipatikana.
4. Kama ningalisikia neno lo lote ningalikuambia.
5. Ningalipumbaa kazi yangu ningalifutwa.
6. Kama ungalikwenda mara moja kukutana naye angali-kulipa wala usingalirudi bila kitu.
7. Kama ningalijua singalimpa senti zangu.
8. Ungalikiri kosa lako labda Bwana angalikusamehe.
9. Kama angalikuja jana ningalimwona.
10. Kama ungekula kidogo usingesikia njaa.
11. Kama ungefanya kazi hii ungepata faida.
12. Asingalikuwa mwivi asingalichukua zote.

## FURTHER USES OF THE -TA-, -NA- AND -ME-TENSES

-TA- may be used when referring to time, future to that already mentioned or implied in the context. Such a construction does not necessarily correspond to the Future Tense in English.

| | |
|---|---|
| Atakaporudi Bwana, mpikie chai. | When the Bwana *comes* (Lit. shall come) make him some tea. |
| Aliniuliza kama nitapenda kumchukua rafiki yangu pamoja nami. | He asked me if I *would like* to take my friend with me. |
| Mwanzo tulidhani kama "—" Team itashinda. | At first we thought that the "—" Team *would win*. |
| Alimwahidi kuwa meli yetu itakapoondoka ataishusha bendera yake nyumbani kwake. | He promised him that when our boat *left* he *would lower* the flag on his house. |

Kiwanjani walikuwako Mabwana waganga tayari kuwatazama watu ambao wataumia katika mchezo wa mpira.

Doctors were there on the field, ready to tend people who *might be* hurt in the football match.

-NA- may similarly refer to a definite or particular time *in the past* when the rest of the context indicates past time.

Manyani walitambua ya kuwa safari inaondoka.

The apes realized that the caravan *was leaving*.

Simba alinyamaza kimya kwa kuwa mkono unamwuma.

The lion kept quiet, for his paw *was paining* him.

Tense sequence in English requires a past tense to follow a past tense. This is not so in Swahili, and if both tenses in the above examples were past, it would mean that the action or state was already completed, i.e. that the caravan *had left*, and that the paw *had been giving* pain.

-ME-, similarly, when used with a past tense, may express action completed at the time indicated in the context. It should then be translated by an English Pluperfect.

Yule mchawi aliposikia kuwa Kintu amewasili, alimpelekea mjumbe.

When the witch doctor heard that Kintu *had arrived*, he sent a messenger to him.

-NA- and -ME-, like -KI-, may also represent an English Present Participle, the context indicating the particular form to be used. Thus:

-NA- is required if the action referred to is taking place at a definite time.

Hata siku moja amekaa anatazama mto wa maji, akamwona mtu anakuja.

Now one day he sat *looking* at the river, and he saw a man *coming*.

-KI- is used when the action referred to is not limited to a particular time.[1]

Tuliwaona watoto wakicheza.

We saw the children *playing*.

[1] It should be noted, however, that -KI- is frequently used instead of -NA-.

-ME- is required when state or completed action is implied rather than the action itself.

| | |
|---|---|
| Alimwona mtu amechukua kuni. | He saw a man *carrying* some firewood. (State, i.e. laden with, not the act of carrying.) |

In addition -ME- may represent an English Past Participle.

| | |
|---|---|
| Walimkuta amekufa. | They found him *dead*. |

*Further Examples.*

| | |
|---|---|
| Na kule chumbani, akisimama dirishani, huwaona wale wenzake wanacheza chini ya mti. Na mara hukumbuka akicheza pamoja nao. | There in her room, *standing* by the window, she saw her companions *playing* under the tree. And at once she would remember *playing* with them. |
| Wakamkuta mvuvi anatengeneza mishipi yake tayari kwenda baharini. | They came across a fisherman *mending* his lines ready to go to sea. |
| Wakati huu wote mume yuko shamba analima. | All this time the husband was at his plantation *cultivating*. |
| Mfalme akamwambia, Nimekupa ruksa, kila utakapomwona inzi ametua, mpige. | The king said, I give you permission, every time you see a fly *settle*, to strike it. |
| Basi akachukua sinia na sahani zimefunikwa vile vile mpaka kwa Haruni Rashidi. | So he took a tray and a plate likewise *covered* to Harun Rashid. |

## Intonation. Tone Pattern IV

This pattern is characterized by a stressed penultimate syllable on a high or falling tone followed by a final stressed syllable on a low rising or low level tone.

Its use is to direct attention to some particular word in a phrase or sentence.

It most frequently occurs as an alternative to Tone Pattern III when extra antithesis or emphasis is required.

Huu mzuri, **huu** mbaya.

This is good, this is bad.

Hapo **kwanza**, nyoka alikuwa ana

**mi**g**uu**, ila macho hana.

In early days the snake had legs but no eyes.

Ngoma ilipo**kwisha**, nyoka akarudi.

When the dance was over, the snake returned.

Tangu wakati **huo**, nyoka na jongoo

hawakupatana tena.

From that time onward the snake and the millipede have not got on well together.

**Leo** sipiki, nitapika kesho.

I'm not cooking today. I shall cook tomorrow.

The following sentences have already been given with Tone Pattern III. They could, however, just as readily be said with Tone Pattern IV. Thus:

(IV) Leo (Ic) yapatikana, (IV) jana (I) hai*kupatikana*.

(IV) Huu (I) si *wangu*; (IV) ule wangu (Ic) mzuri; (IV) huu (Ic) mbaya.

(III) Akasema (Ic) msinipeleke gerezani, (Ic) nipelekeni kwetu *kwanza*, (Ic) nikale chakula (IV) halafu (Ia) mnipeleke gerezani.

(Ia) Sungura akasema Vyema (IV) lakini (Ic) nataka nifike kwetu *kwanza*, (Ia) nikatazama jamaa.

(IV) Jana (Ic) tulilima, (IV) kesho (Ic) tutacheza mpira.

(IV) Mti huu (Ic) umezaa matunda mengi *sana*.

Note how in these examples Tone Pattern Ic often replaces Ia.

## Other Emphatic Tone Patterns

Other tone patterns in emphatic speech are met with, such as:

*Alternative to Tone Pattern II*—very high-stressed penultimate syllable followed by low final syllable. It sounds like an exaggerated Tone Pattern IV.

| | |
|---|---|
| Shilingi **tano**? | What, five shillings? |
| Amekula **yote**? | Do you mean to say he has eaten them all? |
| Haikubakia hata **kidogo**? | Not even a scrap remained? |

*Alternative to Tone Pattern Ic*—last two syllables both stressed, the penultimate being mid-high and the final syllable mid.

| | |
|---|---|
| Nani *wewe*? Mimi ni **Muhumadi**. | And who are you? Oh, I'm Muhamadi, of course. |
| La, nilikuwa siwezi **tumbo**. | No, I was ill in my stomach (not my head). |

*Another alternative to Ic*—this sounds like Tone Pattern II, but is pronounced faster and with more vigour.

| | |
|---|---|
| Siipendi **kamwe**! | I don't like it at all. |

In addition all four standard tone patterns may naturally be emphasized by increasing the range of the voice, without however, altering the essential patterns themselves.

## Vocative Intonation

In calling people by name, either Tone Pattern I or III may be used, with variations according to the degree or urgency.

The reply takes the form of a stressed mid tone penultimate syllable followed by a less stressed final syllable on a high note. Monosyllabic replies take a rising tone.

Ali! $\left[\begin{array}{c}\searrow\end{array}\right]$ *or* $\left[\begin{array}{c}\frown\end{array}\right]$ Bibi? $\left[\begin{array}{c}-\ ^-\end{array}\right]$

Hamisi! $\left[\begin{array}{c}\cdot\ ^-\ ^-\end{array}\right]$ Labbek? $\left[\begin{array}{c}-\ ^-\end{array}\right]$

In calling out people's names in places like courts of law, all syllables may be sung on a fairly high note.

Huseini bin Juma! $\left[\begin{array}{c}\cdot\ ^-\ \cdot\ \cdot\ ^-\ \cdot\end{array}\right]$ Naam? $\left[\begin{array}{c}\diagup\end{array}\right]$

# CHAPTER XXXI

## PREPOSITIONS AND CONJUNCTIONS

### PREPOSITIONS

In Swahili there are no Bantu words which are basically prepositions, but there are a few words based on the -A of Relationship which may be termed so. These are:

**kwa**      by means of, by, with, through, for, to, at, from
**na**         with, by
**P.C. + -a**  of, for

There are also numerous phrases, i.e. compound prepositions, based on **kwa, na** and **-a**.

| | | | |
|---|---|---|---|
| **kwa habari ya** | about, concerning | **chini ya** | below |
| **kwa sababu ya** | because of | **juu ya** | on, over |
| **kwa ajili ya** | for the sake of | **kabla ya** | before (time) |
| | | **mbele ya** | before (place) |
| | | **baada ya** | after (time) |
| **karibu na** | near | **nyuma ya** | after (place) |
| **mbali na** | far from | **ndani ya** | inside |
| **pamoja na** | together with | **nje ya** | outside |
| | | **katikati ya** | among |
| **mahali pa** | instead of | **kati ya** | between |
| | | **zaidi ya** | more than |

199. Kuchinja mbuzi kwa ajili ya kinofu.    To slaughter a goat for the sake of a chop.

Note that **na** is followed by personal pronouns, while **kwa** and **-a** are followed by possessive forms, in the Personal Classes.

| | | | |
|---|---|---|---|
| Pamoja na**mi**. | Together with me. | Chini y**angu**. | Under me. |
| | | Mahali p**etu**. | Instead of us. |
| Mbali na**si**. | Far from us. | **Kwake**. | Through him. |

In addition a few Bantu noun and verb forms are used as prepositions and some words are borrowed from Arabic.

| mpaka | till, as far as | hata | till |
| kutoka | } from | bila | without |
| toka, tokea | | kama | like |

Some forms such as **na, hata, kama**, are also used as conjunctions.

The following preposition needs particular attention:

### Katika

This word has a very wide usage. Although written as one word, it is a compound preposition. Its root meaning is "in", and it refers to both *time* and *place*.

In reference to *place* it indicates locality in much the same way as **-ni**, and the two may often alternate.

### Nyumbani *or* Katika nyumba.

When the noun is qualified by an adjective, however, only one construction is possible.

Katika nyumba hii ndogo.      In this little house.

**Katika** is translated by many different prepositions in English.

| Kuingia katika nyumba. | To go into a house. |
| Kutoka katika nyumba. | To come out from (within) a house. |
| Kupanda katika mti. | To climb up (into) a tree. |
| Kuondoka katika kitanda. | To get up from a bed. |
| Kuandika katika karatasi. | To write on paper. |

In the same way **katika** represents any English preposition denoting duration of *time*, such as "whilst, during, in the act of", etc.

| Katika safari yetu. | During our journey. |
| Katika kusema alisahau . . . | In speaking he forgot . . . |
| Katika mwaka ule . . . | During that year . . . In the year . . . |
| Hapana ghasia wala magomvi katika kuingia na kutoka. | There is no confusion or quarrelling while entering or leaving. |

It also occurs in contexts such as:

| | |
|---|---|
| Alikuwa katika usingizi mzito. | He was in a deep sleep. |
| Alikuwa katika kazi. | He was engaged in work. |
| Katika visu hivi viwili wataka kipi? | Of these two knives which one do you want? |
| Katika watu weusi walichaguliwa watu watatu. | From among the black people three were chosen. |

## CONJUNCTIONS

In Swahili there are no Bantu words which are basically conjunctions except NA which is composed of the -A of relationship and N- of association.

There are, however, various ways of joining words and sentences:

By phrases, many of which are based on **kwa.**

By borrowings from Arabic.

By the use of certain tense forms, e.g. **-ka-**, **-ki-**, **-japo-**, etc.

In Swahili the choice of the right conjunction is closely bound up with the kind of words or sentences to be joined.

Conjunctions fall into two main classes:

A. **Co-ordinating Conjunctions** which join sentences of co-ordinate rank. They may be subdivided according as they express the following:

(i) *Addition.*

| | |
|---|---|
| **na** | and, also |
| **pia** | also, too |
| **tena** | again, furthermore, besides |
| **juu ya hayo** ⎫ | in addition, |
| **pamoja na** ⎬ | furthermore |
| **hayo** ⎭ | |

(ii) *Choice*

| | |
|---|---|
| **ama** . . . **ama** | either . . . or |
| **au** | or |
| **wala** . . . **wala** | neither . . . nor |

**Wala** is often followed by a negative where in English the affirmative is used.

| | |
|---|---|
| Hakuna maji **wala** hakuna maziwa. | There is no water neither is there any milk. |

(iii) *Contrast*　　　　　　(iv) *Inference or Reason*

| | | | |
|---|---|---|---|
| **lakini** | but, nevertheless | **kwa hivyo** ⎫ | because of this, |
| **ila** | but, except, unless | **kwa vile** ⎭ | in that |
| **bali** | but rather, on the | **kwa kuwa** ⎫ | for, because, foras- |
| | contrary | **kwa sababu** ⎪ | much as, the |
| | | **kwani** ⎬ | reason being, |
| | | **kwa maana** ⎭ | etc. |
| | | **basi** | well, then, so, etc. |
| | | **kwa ajili ya** | wherefore |
| | | **hayo** | |

**B. Subordinating Conjunctions.** These introduce clauses which are subordinate to the main sentence.

(i) *Purpose*　　　　　　　　(ii) *Condition*

| | | | |
|---|---|---|---|
| **ili** ⎫ | so that, in | **kama** ⎫ | if, whether |
| **ili kwamba** ⎭ | order that | **kwamba** ⎭ | |
| | | **kama kwamba** ⎫ | as if |
| | | **kana kwamba** ⎭ | |

(iii) *Mere Introduction*

| | |
|---|---|
| **kwamba** ⎫ | |
| **ya kuwa** ⎬ | that |
| **kama** ⎭ | |

Note also that **kana**, **hata** and **na** also function as prepositions.

**Kisha** (< **kwisha** to finish) is used as a conjunction to express "in addition, moreover," etc.

Kumekuwa giza, **kisha** giza kuu.
It was dark, indeed very dark.

Pwanali akamwambia Mrere, M wevi, **kisha** m waongo.
Pwanali said to Mrere, Ye are thieves and in addition liars.

Basi aliazimia vita na huyo Chaliwali, **kisha** vita vya kumwangamiza.
He planned to make war on Chaliwali, and what is more to destroy him utterly.

**Kisha** also expresses "then, afterwards."

| | |
|---|---|
| Fanya kazi nyumbani (u)ki-sha nenda sokoni. | Do the housework first and then go to the market. |

## VOCABULARY

| | | | |
|---|---|---|---|
| **bandari** | harbour | **kadhi (ma-)** | judge |
| **shukia** { | descend (at) | **bendera** | flag |
| | disembark (at) | **shushwa** | be lowered |
| **jabali (ma-)** | rock | **ahidi** | promise (vb.) |
| **funua** | open (eyes) | **sheria** | law |
| **bara bara** | exactly, abso-lutely | **taraji** | expect, hope |
| | | **tende** | date (fruit) |
| **mamba** | crocodile | **lazimu** | be necessary |
| **kiboko (vi-)** | hippopotamus | **tembezwa** | be conducted |
| **ruka** | fly | **kiwanda (vi-)** | workshop, or (work) yard |
| **tangulia** | go in front, pre-cede | **ghali** | expensive |

Note idiomatic construction: **Kama + si.**
    Kama si wewe.    If it were not for you.

## EXERCISE 49

Translate and note the force of the conjunctions:
1. Lete kisu na kikombe.  Lete na vijiko pia.
2. Ngoma hailii kwa kuwa imepasuka.
3. Bandari yenyewe si nzuri kwa kushukia kwa kuwa ni jabali.
4. Lazima tumfukuze kwa sababu atatuharibia furaha yetu.
5. Hii kamba imekata jiwe sababu kila siku kamba hupita juu yake.
6. Tuliambiwa tufunue macho bara bara kwani tutapita walipo mamba na viboko.
7. Aliruka kumtangulia mbele kwa kusudi ya kumwonyesha njia.
8. Tuliambiwa mamba halii ila anapotoka yaini tu.
9. Siku moja Panya alikwenda kushtaki kwa Paka, maana yeye amekuwa kadhi.
10. Alikwenda kutazama kama pana maji.
11. Bendera yake ilishushwa kama alivyoahidi.

12. Alisema kama kwa sheria ya Isilamu . . .
13. Sina shaka kwamba wasomaji wengi watataraji kusikia habari za safari yetu.
14. Kama si tende hizi, wangalikufa kwa njaa.
15. Ilitulazimu kutembezwa katika viwanda kwa motakaa, kwa jinsi vilivyo vingi.
16. . . . juu ya hayo chakula kilikuwa ghali.

# CHAPTER XXXII

## COMPARISON

IN Swahili there are no special forms to express degrees of comparison as there are in English.

**The Positive Degree** (viz. equality) is expressed by the help of the Arabic word **sawa**, or by the Swahili verb **pungua** (get less) expressed negatively.

| | |
|---|---|
| Mtoto wangu ni hodari **sawa** na wako. *Or* | My child is as clever as yours. |
| Mtoto wangu **sawa** na wako kwa uhodari. | |
| Tulikuta kanga wengi hawa-**pungui** ishirini. | We came across many guinea-fowl, no less than twenty. |

**The Comparative Degree** (viz. inequality) in adverbs and adjectives is expressed in two ways:

A. By inference: (*a*) by placing two statements side by side,

(*b*) by using an adjective or adverb in an absolute sense.

| | |
|---|---|
| Nyumba yake **nzuri**, yangu **nzuri sana**. | His house is a fine one, but mine is better. (His house is fine, mine is very fine.) |
| Upi mwezi **mkubwa**, Mei au Juni? | Which is the long(er) month, May or June? |
| Masawa una gati kama Kilindini, ila gati yake ni **ndogo**. | Masawa has a landing-stage the same as Kilindini, but it is small(er). |
| Sahani hii **ndogo**, hii **kubwa**. | This plate is small, this is large(r). |
| Ipi njia **nzuri** ya kwenda mjini? | Which is the better road for getting to the town? |

B. By the use of certain words and phrases, such as **kuliko** (where there is), **kushinda**, **kupita** (to surpass), **kuzidi** (to ex-

201

ceed), **zaidi** (more), **bora** (better, best), **heri** (better) and the negative particle **si**.

| | |
|---|---|
| Nyumba yake nzuri sana **ku-liko** nyumba yangu. | His house is finer than mine. |
| Nani katika ninyi wawili **amempita** mwenziwe kwa miaka? | Which of you two is the elder? |
| Kazi yako **imezidi** yangu kwa ugumu. | Your work is harder than mine. (Your work exceeds mine in hardness). |
| Wapi mbali **zaidi**, kutoka A mpaka B au kutoka C mpaka D? | Which is the greater distance, from A to B or from C to D? |
| Yupi **bora**, Hamisi au Ali? | Which is the better (man), Hamisi or Ali? |
| Hiari **hushinda** utumwa. | Choice is better than compulsion (slavery). |

**Si** qualifies the word which follows it. When used in comparison it indicates the less preferable person, thing or state named.

| | |
|---|---|
| 123. Kafiri akufaaye **si** Isilamu asiyekufaa. | An unbeliever who is of use to you is better than a Moslem who is of no use to you. |
| 134. Kazi mbi[1] **si** mchezo mwema. | Bad work is better than good play. |

**Superlative Degree.** This is expressed in the same way as the Comparative, but if the context is insufficient, a word such as **-ote** or **sana** is added. Relative phrasing is also employed to give definiteness.

| | |
|---|---|
| 46. **Bora** afya. | Health is the chief thing. |
| Hapa katika vijiko hivi vitatu nilete kipi? Lete kile **kilicho** kikubwa sana. Hiki, Bwana, ni kikubwa sana. | Of these three spoons which spoon am I to bring? Bring the largest. This one, Bwana, is the largest. |

---

[1] **-bi,** old root for "bad".

| Ana sauti nzuri **kushinda** waimbaji **wote** hapa. | He has the best voice of all the singers about here, *or*, He has a better voice than all the singers about here. |
| Soko la London ni kubwa **kuliko** masoko **yote** ya ulimwenguni. | The London Market is the greatest market in the world. |
| Neno **lililo** kubwa kuliko **yote**. | The greatest thing of all. |
| Haya matatu—ila katika hayo matatu **lililo** kubwa ni mapenzi. | These three—but the greatest of these is love. |

The word **mno** (very, exceedingly) is often used with the meaning of "too".

| Kisu hiki kikubwa **mno**. | This knife is too big. |

| **simulia** talk about | **barabara** highway |
| **kitendo** action | **sifa** renown |

### EXERCISE 50a

Translate:

1. Hamisi ni mdogo wake Ali.
2. Nduguye Juma (Juma's brother) amshinda kwa akili, lakini kijana huyu awashinda wote wawili.
3. Kusimulia si kitendo, bora kuona mwenyewe.
4. Huyu ndiye mtoto aliyependwa zaidi kuliko wenziwe.
5. Hali yake ni bora kuliko ya rafiki yake.
6. Mji wao ni mdogo sana, tena una vijumba vidogo vidogo sana kuliko vya kwetu.
7. Barabara za Paris zina sifa kwa kuwa ni pana sana kuliko barabara za nchi nyingine.
8. Katika wanyama wote wa mwituni hakuna amshindaye sungura kwa ujanja.
9. Heri kufa macho kuliko kufa moyo.
10. Bora kwenda kwa motakaa kuliko reli.
11. Jana tulifanya kazi nyingi, leo tumezidi.
12. Hamisi amshinda Ali kwa nguvu

## EXERCISE 50b

Translate:

1. Ali is taller than Juma.
2. Who is the taller, Juma or Ali?  Ali is the taller.
3. A dog is bigger than a cat.
4. This is the highest tree.
5. The elephant is the strongest of all animals.
6. This is the best work.
7. My child is as tall as yours but older.

# CHAPTER XXXIII

# VERBS AND THEIR TENSES (Section VI)

## VERBS LI AND KUWA

THERE are two verbs "to be" in Swahili, LI and KUWA, each used in a particular context. Both these verbs are common to other Bantu languages.

Predication without reference to Time and without a verb has already been discussed. When, however, a relative particle is used, LI is required in affirmative sentences. This LI should be carefully distinguished from the -li- prefix of Past Time.[1]

Compare the following:

|  | *Non-relative* | *Relative* |
|---|---|---|
|  | He is { here / a cook / ready <br> He has many people <br> He is thirsty | He who is { here / a cook / ready <br> He who has many people <br> He who is thirsty |
| Place <br> Identification <br> State <br> Association | **Yupo** <br> **Ni mpishi** <br> **Yu tayari** <br> **Ana watu wengi** <br> **Ana kiu** | **A-LI-yepo** <br> **A-LI-ye (ni) mpishi** <br> **A-LI-ye tayari** <br> **A-LI-ye na watu wengi** <br> **A-LI-ye na kiu** |

*Negation.*

Here relative constructions are not all of one pattern, but KUWA predominates.

|  | *Non-relative* | *Relative* |
|---|---|---|
|  | He is not { there / a cook / ready <br> He hasn't anything <br> He is not thirsty | He who is not { there / a cook / ready <br> He who hasn't anything <br> He who is not thirsty |
| Place <br> Identification <br> State <br> Association | **Hayuko** <br> **Si mpishi** <br> **Hayu tayari** <br> **Hana kitu** <br> **Hana kiu** | **AsiyeKUWAko** <br> **A-LI-ye si mpishi** <br> **AsiyeKUWA tayari** <br> **Asiye(KUWA) (na) kitu** <br> **Asiye(KUWA) (na) kiu** |

[1] These two particles probably have the same origin however.

205

A study of the foregoing sentences indicates that in the negative relative construction:

(*a*) LI with the negative copula **si** is required to express non-identification.

| | |
|---|---|
| WaLIo **si** watoto. | They who are not children. |

(*b*) **-si-kuwa** is used to express Place.

| | |
|---|---|
| Wasiokuwamo. | They who are not within. (Also: They who are not concerned in the matter.) |

(*c*) **-si-kuwa na** is generally used to express negation of Association, although **kuwa** is sometimes omitted.

| | |
|---|---|
| Wasio(**kuwa**) **na** watoto. | They who have no children. |

But note that neither **kuwa** nor **na** is required if attention is directed to a state of lacking rather than to the object itself.

| | |
|---|---|
| Wasio watoto. | They who are childless. |

(*d*) There is no one set way of expressing negation of State.

| | |
|---|---|
| WaLIo **si** safi. | They who are not clean. |
| Wasiokuwa tayari. | They who are not ready. |

Alternative forms with **amba** are also heard.

| | |
|---|---|
| Wale **ambao** si tayari. | Those who are not ready. |

In the following proverbs note how the emphasis is on the state of lacking.

| | |
|---|---|
| 133. Kazi **isiyo** kipimo mwishowe watu huteta. | Work that has no measure, at the end of it people quarrel. |
| 32. Kazi **isiyo** faida kutenda si ada. | Profitless work (work without profit) it is not customary to do (such as that). |
| 77. Hakuna msiba **usio** mwenziwe. | There is no misfortune but has its fellow. (Troubles never come singly). |

| | |
|---|---|
| 118. Msikiti **usio** maji hausa- liwi. | A waterless mosque is not prayed in. |
| 75. Hakuna kubwa **lisilo** mwisho. | There is no matter so great as to have no end. (It's a long lane that has no turning). |
| 489. Simpandi punda **asiye** matandiko. | I do not mount a donkey which has no saddle (a saddleless donkey). |
| 32. **Asiye** nadhari sianda- mani naye. | He that hath not common sense I do not go in his company. |
| Hakuna masika **yasiyo** mbu. | No rainy season is without mosquitoes. |

KUWA must be used in Past and Future tenses, both with and without the relative particle. The examples given here are in the Past Tense only.

| | *Non-relative* | *Relative* |
|---|---|---|
| | We were $\left\{\begin{array}{l}\text{there}\\ \text{children}\\ \text{ready}\end{array}\right.$ <br> We had some food <br> We were hungry | We who were $\left\{\begin{array}{l}\text{there}\\ \text{children}\\ \text{ready}\end{array}\right.$ <br> We who had some food <br> We who were hungry |
| Place <br> Identification <br> State <br> Association | **Tulikuwako** <br> **Tulikuwa (tu) watoto**[1] <br> **Tulikuwa tayari** <br> **Tulikuwa na chakula** <br> **Tulikuwa na njaa** | **Tuliokuwako** <br> **Tuliokuwa (tu) watoto**[1] <br> **Tuliokuwa tayari** <br> **Tuliokuwa na chakula** <br> **Tuliokuwa na njaa** |

*Negation.*

The following corresponding negative forms express a *general* statement in past time. When a *particular* time in past is to be indicated, compound tenses are more frequently used. These will be discussed on p. 265.

---

[1] Third pers.: Walikuwa (**ni**) watoto, Waliokuwa (**ni**) watoto, etc.

Note here again that the phrases are not all of one pattern, **amba** being often preferred.

|  | *Non-relative* | *Relative* |
|---|---|---|
|  | We were not { there / children / ready }<br>We had no food<br>We were not hungry | We who were not { there / children / ready }<br>We who had no food<br>We who were not hungry |
| Place<br>Identification<br>State<br>Association | **Hatukuwako**<br>**Tulikuwa si watoto**<br>**Hatukuwa tayari**<br>**Hatukuwa na chakula**<br><br>**Hatukuwa na njaa** | **Sisi ambao hatukuwako**[1]<br>**Tuliokuwa si watoto**<br>**Sisi ambao hatukuwa tayari**[1]<br>**Sisi ambao hatukuwa na cha-**<br>**kula**[1]<br>**Sisi ambao hatukuwa na njaa**[1] |

# LI AND KUWA WITH ADVERBIAL PARTICLES

## 1. -ko, -po, -mo, -vyo as Relative Particles

| *Relative referring to Subject*[2] | *Relative referring to Time and Place* | *Relative referring to Manner* |
|---|---|---|
| TuLIo<br>We who are | TuLIpo<br>Where or when we are | TuLIvyo<br>As we are |
| Tuliokuwa<br>We who were | Tulipokuwa<br>Where or when we were | Tulivyokuwa<br>As we were |
| Tutakaokuwa<br>We who will be | Tutakapokuwa<br>Where or when we shall be | Tutakavyokuwa<br>As we shall be |
| Tusio *or* Tusiokuwa<br>We who are not<br>were not<br>will not be | Tusipokuwa<br>When we are not,<br>i.e. Unless we are | Tusivyokuwa<br>As we are not<br>were not<br>will not be |

## 2. -ko, -po, -mo as Adverbial Enclitics

| *Without relative* | *With Pronominal relative* |
|---|---|
| Tupo<br>We are here | TuLIopo<br>We who are here |
| Tulikuwako<br>We were there | Tuliokuwako<br>We who were there |
| Tutakuwamo<br>We shall be within | Tutakaokuwamo<br>We who will be within |

---

[1] Also Tusiokuwako, tusiokuwa tayari, tusiokuwa na chakula.
[2] This column is given for comparison.

| *Without relative* | *With Pronominal relative* |
|---|---|
| **Hatumo** | **Tusiokuwako** |
| We are not within | We who are not, were not, will not be there |
| **Hatukuwapo** | **Ambao hatukuwapo** |
| We were not here | We who were not here |
| **Hatutakuwako** | **Ambao hatutakuwapo** |
| We shall not be there | We who will not be here |

The double function of **-po**, **-ko** and **-mo** should be noted:

| **TuLIpo** | *Where* we are | Relative |
|---|---|---|
| **Tupo** | We are *here* | } Complement of verb |
| **TuLIopo** | We who are *here* | |

Sometimes the relative affix **-ye-** in the singular of the Living Class is replaced by **-o-**, as in the expressions **niliopo**, **uliopo, aliopo**. These examples afford good illustrations of Vowel Harmony.

### VOCABULARY

| | | | |
|---|---|---|---|
| **milki** | dominion, | **namna** | kind |
| **idadi** | number | **uzwa** | be sold |
| **salaam** | greetings | **kundi (ma-)** | batch, crowd |
| **mjomba (wa-)** | uncle | **chagua** | choose |
| **ahera** | the next world | **mjinga (wa-)** | ignoramus |
| **kumbe** | lo and behold | **sukuma** | push away |
| **juha (ma-)** | simpleton | **panya** | rat |
| **alama** | mark, sign | **mtego (mi-)** | trap |
| **mahudhurio** | attendance | **endelea** | progress (vb.) |
| | | **enea** | spread |

### Exercise 51a

Translate:

1. Akarudi pale alipo rafiki yake.
2. Visiwa vyote vile vilivyomo katika ziwa kubwa havimo katika milki yangu.
3. Mfalme akampa zawadi nyingi na ng'ombe wasio idadi.
4. Halafu mtaona kipi kilicho kizuri zaidi.
5. Salaam mjomba, mimi huku ahera si jambo na jamaa wote waliopo wazima.
6. Mkubwa wa manowari alijua kwamba hao waliomo ni watumwa.

H

7. Akasema Kumbe majuha wapo wengi nikadhani ni mke wangu tu. Kumbe hata katika watu wakubwa wamo majuha. Wakaenda zao mbali mahali pasipo watu.

8. Wote walikuwa na alama ya namna moja, ndiyo alama sita, alama tatu kila tako. Hiyo ndiyo iliyokuwa alama ya watumwa wa Mwinyi Rashidi.

9. Mrere, ambaye alikuwa ni mmoja wa watumwa wale waliouzwa na M——, alikuwamo katika kundi hili.

10. Kwa kusikia hivi sote tuliokuwapo tukatoka.

11. Alichagua kwenda shamba kwa Wahadimu kwa kuwa huko ndiko walikokuwa wajinga wasiojua kusoma.

12. Mara Hemedi akatoka mahali alipokuwa, akawasukuma watu akaingia mpaka alikokuwa mama yake.

13. Lakini alipofika bandani alikokuwako punda, ng'ombe hakusema habari za kazi.

14. Alipokufa, wazee wake na watu waliokuwapo wakauliza, Nini maana yake maneno waliyosema?

15. Simba naye wakati huo alikuwamo njiani.

16. Panya akanena, Kweli huu ni mtego wa panya, lakini tena ni mtego wa kuingia waliomo na wasiokuwamo.

17. Manung'uniko yameenea kwa kuwa mahudhurio katika skuli hayaendelei kama vilivyo.

18. Angekuwapo Abunawas angetuambia maana yake mkono huu.

19. Kwa vile nisivyo mweupe, waniona si mtu auje?

## LI AND KUWA IN RELATIVE PHRASING WITH NA

Here the relative particle **-o** may refer either to the Subject or the Object. Thus:

Watu wa**LI**o na vitabu.          People *who* have books.
**-o** refers here to the subject **watu**.

Vitabu wa**LI**vyo navyo.          The books *which* they have.

The first **-vyo** functions as relative particle to **vitabu**, the second as pronominal object of **na**, also referring to **vitabu**.

The same construction holds good for Past and Future Tenses:

Vitabu walivyokuwa navyo.          The books which they had.

| Vitabu watakavyokuwa na-vyo. | The books which they will have. |

**-enye.**

The use of **-enye** as an alternative to relative phrasing is often met with. See p. 63.

| Wenye vitabu, simameni ka-ndo. | Those of you who have books (Lit. owners of books) stand on one side. |

### VOCABULARY

| | | | |
|---|---|---|---|
| **parafujo** | screw | **zaa** | bear, bring forth |
| **mwafikano** | contract, pact | **ondolewa** | be taken from |
| **sadiki** | believe | **mazungumzo** | conversations |
| **afadhali** | preferably | **udhika** | be annoyed |
| **maskani** | home, dwelling-place | **ras il mali** | one's possess-ions, **capital** |
| **rejea** | return | **jazi** | reward, fulfil |
| **fungwa** | be fastened | **imani** | faith |
| **mwishowe** | finally | **gamba (ma-)** | shell |
| **poteza** | lose (trans.) | **funika** | cover (vb.) |
| **tabia** | nature, character | **kasa** | turtle |
| | | **wasiwasi** | perplexity |

### EXERCISE 51b

Translate as a written exercise, then do orally:
1. The hammer which I have, which I had, which I shall have.
2. The nails which you have, which you had, which you will have.
3. The saw which he has, which he had, which he will have.
4. The screws which we have, which we had, which we shall have.
5. The axe which ye have, which ye had, which ye will have.
6. The string which they have, which they had, which they will have.

## EXERCISE 51c

Translate:

1. Huu ndio mwafikano wao waliokuwa nao.
2. Mtu akikwambia hali hii niliyo nayo sasa naipenda, usi-msadiki.
3. Afadhali sisi tufanye maskani hapa, tujenge mji wetu, watu tulio nao wanatutosha.
4. Jogoo kuona vile hakuwa na neno ila kurejea nyumbani kwake.
5. Ng'ombe akasema, Mimi leo sikupewa kazi, nalifungwa panapo majani nikila tu.
6. Basi mwishowe akapoteza vyote alivyo navyo.
7. Kila mti ulio na tabia njema huzaa matunda mema na mti mwovu huzaa matunda maovu.
8. Aliye nacho atapewa, na asiyekuwa nacho, hata hicho alicho nacho ataondolewa.
9. Kwa ule wasiwasi aliokuwa nao, hakusema neno.
10. Njiani hawakuwa na mazungumzo mema, maana Sultani ameudhika.
11. Alikuwako mtu mmoja na mkewe, hawakuwa na kitu, ras il mali yao ni kondoo na jogoo.
12. Mwenyiezi Mungu akamjazi imani yake, akatwaa lile gamba alilo nalo akamfunika (kasa), miguu na kichwa akatia ndani.

## KUWA NA WITH ADVERBIAL SUBJECT

Adverbial Subjects are much used. Here **pa-** and **ku-** may refer to both Time and Place.

| | |
|---|---|
| Hapo kale **palikuwa na** mtu. | Once upon a time there was a man. |
| Hapa Kisauni pana mahali paitwapo Miembeni, ndipo **palipokuwa na** uwanja mkubwa. | At Kisauni there is a place called "At the mango trees" and it was here where there was a big open space. |

Mahali pengine zile nyayo hazikuonekana kwa ajili ya mawe mengi. Humo **mlimokuwa na** mchanga ndimo mlimoonyesha kule watumwa waliko.

Elsewhere the footprints were not visible because of the many stones. It was the sandy places (Lit. where there was sand) which indicated where the slaves were (gone).

| Non-relative | | Relative | |
|---|---|---|---|
| There is<br>Kuna<br>Pana<br>Ina | There is not<br>Hakuna<br>Hapana<br>Hamna | Where there is<br>Kunako<br>Panapo<br>Mnamo | Where there is not<br>Kusiko (na)<br>Pasipo (na)<br>Msimo (na) |
| There was<br>Kulikuwa na<br>Palikuwa na<br>Mlikuwa na | There was not<br>Hakukuwa na[1]<br>Hapakuwa na[1]<br>Hamkuwa na[1] | Where there was<br>Kulikokuwa na<br>Palipokuwa na<br>Mlimokuwa na | Where there was not<br>(Constructions with **amba** used) |
| There will be<br>Kutakuwana<br>Patakuwa na<br>Mtakuwa na | There will not be<br>Hakutakuwa na<br>Hapatakuwa na<br>Hamtakuwa na | Where there will be<br>Kutakakokuwa na<br>Patakapokuwa na<br>Mtakamokuwa na | Where there will not be<br>(Constructions with **amba** used) |

The simple forms **kunako** and **panapo** express State without reference to Time.

Alirudi **kunako** kondoo wake.

He returned to *where* his sheep *was*.

Walikaa pale **panapo** miti mingi.

They stayed there *where* there *were* many trees.

The use of the Past Tense here would imply that there *had been* a sheep, trees, etc., there in the past.

[1] Negative forms are frequently expressed as Compound Tenses, e.g palikuwa hapana, etc. See p. 265.

# PART TWO

## CHAPTER XXXIV

### DERIVATIVE VERBS

### FORMATIVE SUFFIXES

#### Reference Table

| Root fung-kam- | Simple | Prepositional (Applied) | Passive | Stative (Neuter) | Causative |
|---|---|---|---|---|---|
| Suffix: | -A | -IA  -EA | -WA | -IKA -EKA | -YA -FYA -VYA -SA -SHA -‖ |
| | | -ILIA -ELEA | -IWA -EWA | -IKANA -EKANA | -ISHA -ESH -IZA  -EZA |
| Examples: | funga kama | fungia kamia | fungwa kamwa | fungika kamika | fungisha kamisha |

| | Static | Contactive (Tenacious) | Conversive | Inceptive | Associati (Reciproca |
|---|---|---|---|---|---|
| Suffix: | -MA | -TA | -UA  -OA -UKA -OKA | -PA | -NA |
| Examples: | fungama | kamata | fungua funguka | nenepa < -nene | fungana |

| | Augmentative (Intensive, Durative) | | Diminutive |
|---|---|---|---|
| Suffix: | Same in form as certain Causative, Prepositional and Conversive suffixes | | Reduplication verb stem |
| Examples: | chomoza shikilia kamua | | pigapiga |

*General Introductory Remarks.*

In the foregoing sections, prefixes, with one or two exceptions, have played the dominant part in modifying the meanings of words. It is, however, by means of formative suffixes mostly that the root form of a verb takes on different shades of meaning. These suffixes are set out in tabular form above, with the verbs **funga** (bind), **kama** (squeeze) for the most part.

Before passing on to a consideration of each form individually, the following points should be noted:

(i) Modifications in the form of individual suffixes may all be accounted for on phonetic grounds. These modifications are treated under their several headings.

(ii) Verbs which express an elemental idea such as hitting, fastening, going, are those which have the greatest variety of forms.

(iii) Each suffix expresses a particular meaning. This must be read into the concept expressed in the root. Thus:

| | |
|---|---|
| kufung**a** | to fasten, bind, etc. |
| kufung**ua** | to unfasten |
| kufung**wa** | to be fastened |
| kufung**ia** | to tie for (someone), etc., etc. |

(iv) Two or more suffixes may be added to one root. When such is the case *the meaning of each suffix must be read into the root*. The concept thus expressed often requires to be translated in English by a word entirely different from that which represents the simple form. Thus:

**kupata**             to get

**kupata** + Associative **-na** = **kupatana**
            to get together, to agree

**kupatana** + Causative **-isha** = **kupatanisha**
            to cause agreement, to reconcile.

(v) Suffixes which form derivative stems are also found in the simple form as an inherent part of that form; these do not necessarily convey the idea expressed by a derivative suffix, e.g. -ma in **soma, choma, pima**, etc., does not convey a static idea.[1]

(vi) In these illustrations verbs have been chosen which allow of a fairly precise translation, but it is often impossible to express the meaning conveyed by the root and suffix in a single word which suits all contexts. This is admirably expressed by Madan in the Introduction to his Swahili Dictionary. He says:

"The Swahili verb root is capable of . . . a rich and varied development in the form of additional verb stems—each with its complement of conjugations, moods, tenses, etc. Shades of meaning are so numerous and their differences so delicate that appropriate renderings in English suited to each particular case have to be left very largely to the student's appreciation of each form separately. . . . The following considerations may enable him to infer for himself the meaning of verb forms not stated under the verb itself. And if he is still inclined to complain of vagueness and inadequacy in their interpretations, it may be remembered that language unwritten (like Swahili) is the speech of a living people, and so carries its own simultaneous commentary of look, gesture and tone as well as sound, thus appealing to four senses in sympathetic and intelligent relation to the speaker, and not only to the eye in interpreting a written character. The full meaning of any written statement has at best often to be guessed, and a Swahili if he writes, writes as he speaks, assuming a hearer and not a reader."

Moreover, as Swahili words frequently require a much wider vocabulary in English, the reader must on no account restrict the meaning of words to those given in the vocabulary or in a particular context. Many words have a figurative meaning also. The use of the *Standard Swahili-English Dictionary* is as enlightening and entertaining as it is essential in the study of this language.

---

[1] On the other hand the final syllable of a simple verb often gives a clue to its meaning, thus -ga expresses a repetitive idea as in

| **kanyaga** | tread | **koroga** | stir |
| **mwaga** | pour out | **taga** | lay eggs |

See p. 285. An interesting field of investigation awaits the research worker here.

## THE PREPOSITIONAL (OR APPLIED) FORM

The characteristic of this form is the suffix -(L)IA or -(L)EA.

The principles of Vowel Harmony are well illustrated here, for the vowel in the suffix has to be in harmony with that in the root, the final vowel of the latter being replaced as follows:

| Verbs with -A-, -I-, -U- in root | | -IA |
| --- | --- | --- |
| fanya | do | fanyia |
| pika | cook | pikia |
| ruka | jump | rukia |
| Verbs with -E- or -O- in root | | -EA |
| enda | go | endea |
| soma | read | somea |
| Verbs ending in -AA, -IA, -UA | | -LIA |
| twaa | take | twalia |
| kimbia | run | kimbilia |
| chukua | carry | chukulia |
| Verbs ending in -EA or -OA | | -LEA |
| pokea | receive | pokelea |
| ondoa | take away | ondolea |
| Verbs of non-Bantu origin ending in -I or -U | | -IA |
| rudi | return | rudia |
| tubu | repent | tubia |
| Verbs of non-Bantu origin ending in -E | | -EA |
| samehe | forgive | samehea |
| Verbs of non-Bantu origin ending in -AU add | | -LIA |
| sahau | forget | sahaulia |

In the above examples no English translation of the Prepositional form is given, as it is unwise to try to associate these verbs with any one English preposition.

Occasionally Prepositional verbs are made on nouns borrowed from Arabic:

      **huruma** pity     **hurumia** have pity on

The same principles of Vowel Harmony will be found to govern the Passive, Stative, and to a lesser degree the Causative forms.

H*

### EXERCISE 52a

Give the prepositional forms of:

(a)
| jibu | leta | ponya | ingia | eleza | funga |
|------|------|-------|-------|-------|-------|
| fungua | jongea | pasua | dhani | zuia | tubu |

and the simple forms of:

(b)
| nyolea | kalia | nunulia | pigia | endea | vukia |
|--------|-------|---------|-------|-------|-------|
| chagulia | sokotea | inulia | fasiria | fumbulia | shuhudia |

## Uses of the Prepositional Form

This form, as the name implies, gives a prepositional concept to the simple form of the verb. Its functions are as follows:

1. *To express "to do to, for, or on behalf of someone, or to the detriment of such a one".*

| imba · sing | Watoto walitu**imba** nyimbo. | The children sang songs to us. |
|------|------|------|
| pika cook | Niku**pikie** chakula? | Shall I cook some food for you? |
| lima cultivate | Amem**limia** shamba lake. | He has cultivated his plantation for him. |
| kasirika be angry | Chura alim**kasirikia** mjusi. | The frog was angry with the lizard. |
| haribu destroy | Atatu**haribia** furaha yetu. | He will spoil (for us) our pleasure. |
| dhani think | Ulini**dhania** kuwa ni mwivi mimi! | So you thought me to be a thief! |

Note that the Pronominal Object of the Prepositional verb is that of the corresponding English preposition. The object, if any, of the English verb stands in the Nominal Construction.[1]

| *Prepositional verb* | *Object* | *Noun in Nominal Construction* |
|------|------|------|
| The children sang to | us | songs. |
| Shall I cook for | you | food? |
| He was angry with | him, | lizard. |
| He will spoil for | us | our pleasure. |

[1] See p. 299.

A few verbs have a hostile implication in the *simple* form if taking an object prefix, though implying "to do for", or "on behalf of someone", if used similarly in the *prepositional* form.

| | |
|---|---|
| **Kumwamba** mtu. | **Kumwambia** mtu. |
| To speak against someone. | To tell someone. |
| **Kumsema** mtu. | **Kumsemea** mtu. |
| To speak against someone. | To speak on behalf of some-one. |

10. Akutendaye, mtende, si-mche akutendaye.

He that does ill to thee, do thou to him, fear not him who does it thee.

Usijiweke pekeyo hata wa-kaku**sema**, Mtazame, hata hataki kujuana na watu, anajidhani yeye ni mzu-ngu tu, sisi ni wajinga.

Do not keep yourself aloof so that people say of you, "Look at him, he doesn't even want to know people, he considers himself a Euro-pean and us fools."

2. *To express motion towards*. In certain contexts verbs expressing *motion towards* take the Prepositional form but re-quire the simple form if *motion from* is indicated. This Prepo-sitional form represents the particular preposition which is called for in the English context.

| | | |
|---|---|---|
| **tupa**<br>throw | Yule mchawi aliwa**tu-pia** mapande mapa-nde yá majabali. | The wizard hurled great blocks of rock at them. |
| **panda**<br>climb | Walipo**pandia** ile mi-buyu . . . | When they climbed up the baobab trees . . . |
| **kimbia**<br>run away | Mtoto alim**kimbilia** mama wake. | The child ran off to his mother. |
| **geuka**<br>turn | Yule mfalme akali-**geukia** Jua akase-ma . . . | The king turned to the Sun and said . . . |
| **fuata**<br>follow | Aliambiwa awa**fuatie** wale wapagazi. | He was told to follow (after) the porters (with the idea of catching them up). |

| angusha let fall, drop | Nyani mmoja alimwa-**ngushia** Pwanali buyu bichi la¹ kichwa. | One baboon dropped a green baobab fruit on Pwanali's head. |
|---|---|---|

3. *To express purpose.* In this connection the verb in the infinitive is used, preceded by the -A of Relationship.

| jenga build | Kamba hizi kama ni za ku**jengea**, hazitafaa. | If these ropes are for building with, they will be useless. |
|---|---|---|
| kata cut | Nataka kisu cha ku**katia** nyama. | I want a knife for cutting meat. |

4. *To express finality or completeness.* When thus used the verb is generally followed by an adverb such as **sana, mbali.**

| tupa throw away | Mikebe hii nii**tupe**? | Am I to throw away these tin cans? |
|---|---|---|
| | **Itupie** mbali. | Throw them right away. |

Note that the Prepositional suffix is sometimes reduplicated to strengthen further the sense of completeness. See Augmentative forms, p. 243. They should not, however, be confused with such forms as **kimbilia, ondolea, chukulia** and **pokelea** already mentioned.

5. The Prepositional form of the verb with the interrogative **nini** or enclitic **-ni** (what?) expresses "Why?"

| ita call | Wanii**tiani**? | Why are you calling me? |
|---|---|---|
| lia cry | Wali**liani**? | Why are you crying? What are you crying for? |

6. The reflexive **-ji-** used with the Prepositional form expresses "of oneself, by oneself".

| poa get well | Kidonda kimeji**polea**. | The sore has healed of itself. |
|---|---|---|

¹ Note use of A- of relationship. Cf. p. 145.

| | | |
|---|---|---|
| **pata**<br>get | Watu wali**ji**patia ishi-<br>rini. | The people by them-<br>selves (i.e. without<br>counting other things)<br>numbered twenty. |
| **ondoka**<br>get up | Waka**ji**ondokea. | And they took them-<br>selves off. |

## EXERCISE 52b

Translate:

| | |
|---|---|
| **nunua** | buy |
| **pika** | cook |
| **fungua** | open |
| **kata** | cut |
| **lia** | cry |
| **tenda** | do |
| **tafuta** | search for |
| **ona** | feel, see |
| **amba** | say |
| **taka** | want |
| **ruka** | fly |
| **tengeneza** | prepare |
| **jongea** | draw near |
| **salimu** | greet |
| **omba** | pray |
| **shuka** | alight |
| **imba** | sing |
| **tia moto** | put fire to |
| **ku-wa** | to be |
| **ku-la** | to eat |
| **kimbia** | run away |

1. Ninunulie kisu.
2. Unampikia nani?
3. Mfungulie Bwana mlango.
4. Mkatie fimbo ndefu.
5. Mtoto analiliani?
6. Nimesikia uliyomtendea mtoto wetu.
7. Nenda katika mwitu ulio kari-bu, ukanitafutie ndege.
8. Hawakumwonea huruma.
9. Hamisi amekwambia nini?
10. Unakitakia nini kisu hiki?
11. Yule ndege alirukia upesi juu ya mti.
12. Kisha akamtengenezea kitanda laini cha majani.
13. Alimjongelea akamhurumia.
14. Nisalimie Bwana.
15. Nitakuombea salama.
16. Karibu na pahali pa kushukia palikuwa na jiwe.
17. Watakusifu na kukuimbia nyi-mbo.
18. Walitutilia moto mji wetu.
19. (a) Niwie radhi. (b) Niwelee ra-dhi.
20. Ki wapi chumba cha kulia?
21. Amani akamkimbilia baba yake.

| jenga | build | 22. Walijijengea nyumba na kujili-mia mashamba. |
| hama | remove from | 23. Watu walihamia katika vijiji vingine. |
| anguka | fall down | 24. Alimwangukia miguuni pake. |
| ita | call | 25. Wawaitiani? |
| taka | want | 26. Unamtakiani mtoto huyu?. |
| pata | get, amount to | 27. Watoto walijipatia zaidi ya mia. |
| sema | say | 28. Hajui asemalo, ajisemea tu. |
| shona | sew | 29. Ni nani aliyekushonea koti hili? |

## Exercise 52c

Translate:

1. The child is crying for his mother.
2. We have brought you some firewood.
3. Find me a good axe.
4. Which road did he go by?
5. Hamisi will carry your load for you.
6. My brother will receive my wages for me.
7. For whom are you waiting?
8. Greet your brothers for us.
9. Mend this chair for me, please.
10. Ali has built a house for his parents.
11. Do not reply for your companion.
12. These women are cooking for their husbands.
13. He prayed for my safety.
14. Has the bird flown right away?
15. These bananas are rotten, throw them away.
16. To which station is this train going?
17. I want a place to sleep in.
18. Give me some soap for washing these clothes.
19. These stones are no use for building a house.
20. What are they wanting our hoes for?

## THE PASSIVE FORM

Subject to the meaning of the root itself, and common usage, most Swahili verbs may be put into the Passive, either in the simple form or in one or more of the derived forms.

| *Simple form* | | | *Derived forms* | |
|---|---|---|---|---|
| **piga** | beat | **pigwa** | **pigia** | **pigiwa** |
| | | | **pigilia** | **pigiliwa** |
| | | | **pigisha** | **pigishwa** |
| | | | **piganisha** | **piganishwa** |

Variations in the form of the passive suffix are as follows:

| Verbs ending in one vowel | | -WA |
|---|---|---|
| **kata** | cut | **katwa** |
| Verbs ending in -AA or -IA | | -(LI)WA |
| **tia** | put | **tiwa, tiliwa** |
| **twaa** | take | **twaliwa** |
| Verbs ending in -UA | | -LIWA |
| **chukua** | carry | **chukuliwa** |
| Verbs ending in -EA | | -(LE)WA |
| **pokea** | receive | **pokewa, pokelewa** |
| Verbs ending in -OA | | -LEWA |
| **ondoa** | take away | **ondolewa** |
| Monosyllabic verbs | | -IWA, -EWA |
| **la** | eat | **liwa** |
| **pa** | give | **pewa** |
| Verbs of Arabic origin ending in -I or -U | | -IWA |
| **badili** | change | **badiliwa** |
| **jibu** | answer | **jibiwa** |
| Verbs of Arabic origin ending in -E | | -EWA |
| **samehe** | forgive | **samehewa** |
| Verbs of Arabic origin ending in -AU add | | -LIWA |
| **dharau** | despise | **dharauliwa** |

Note that the agent of a Passive verb is preceded by NA.
Alipigwa **na** baba yake.      He was beaten by his father.

### EXERCISE 53a

Give the simple passive forms of the first twelve verbs in Exercise 52a.

### EXERCISE 53b

Translate:

1. The witch was stoned.
2. This coat was made (sewn) by an Indian tailor.

3. This food was cooked by Ali the European's cook.
4. Their words were scorned by all who heard them.
5. When were these oranges bought?
6. Where is the sick man who was brought here?
7. He has been called three times.
8. All the stones have been removed.
9. When was this house built?
10. When were these potatoes cooked?
11. Our donkey is dead, he was buried yesterday.
12. Has the lamp been taken away?
13. The debts have not yet been paid.
14. Has the blanket been folded nicely?
15. Have the Bwana's shirts been ironed?
16. Have the chickens been fed?
17. All their oranges have been eaten.
18. When was this lamp trimmed?

## Prepositional Passive

Prepositional verbs may be put into the Passive in just the same way as the simple verb. In both instances the *object* of the Active verb becomes the *subject* of the Passive.

| *Active* | *Passive* |
|---|---|
| Simple: | |
| Hamisi alipika **chakula**. | **Chakula** kilipikwa na Hamisi. |
| Hamisi cooked some food. | The food was cooked by Hamisi. |
| Prepositional: | |
| Hamisi ali**ni**pikia chakula. | **Ni**lipikiwa chakula na Hamisi. |
| Hamisi cooked me some food. | Food was cooked for me by Hamisi *or* I had food cooked for me by Hamisi. (Lit. I was cooked-for food by Hamisi.) |

**Ni** (me), being the object of the Prepositional verb **kupikia** (to cook for), becomes the subject, **ni** (I), of the Prepositional

Passive **kupikiwa** (to be cooked for), and **chakula** (food) stands in the Nominal Construction.

### Aphorism

15. **Aliye kando haangukiwi na mti.** He that stands to one side does not get a tree falling on him. (Lit. He is not fallen upon by a tree.)

Note that the Prepositional passives of verbs ending in two vowels, or of verbs of Arabic origin, are the same in form as the Simple passives.

Prepositional:

**Nilinunuliwa kofia hii.** This hat was bought for me. (Lit. I was bought-for this hat.)

Simple:

**Kofia hii ilinunuliwa na nani?** By whom was this hat bought?[1]

### EXERCISE 54a

Give the simple and the prepositional passive forms of:

| | | | | | |
|---|---|---|---|---|---|
| piga | chagua | sema | inua | pokea | twaa |
| pika | fanya | ondoa | lima | shona | andika |

### EXERCISE 54b

Translate:

| | |
|---|---|
| **iba** | steal |
| **peleka** | send |
| **ongeza** | increase |
| **tunga** | compose (verses) |
| **pika** | cook |
| **tenda** | do, treat |

1. Ameibiwa jembe lake.
2. Wale waliokaa mbali walipelekewa majumbe kwenda kuwaita.
3. Nitaongezewa mshahara lini?
4. Alitungiwa wimbo wa sifa sana.
5. Tulionyeshwa pahali panapopikiwa chakula.
6. Ni vigumu kuonyesha jinsi tulivyotendewa vyema.

[1] In conversation the active construction would be preferred here.

| | | |
|---|---|---|
| **piga kofi** | clap | 7. Nilipotokea nilipigiwa kofi na vifijo vingi. |
| **jenga** | build | 8. Mgonjwa huyu ajengewe kibanda mbali na nyumba za watu. |
| **suka** | plait | 9. Nilisukiwa mikeka hii mitatu, sikuisuka mimi. |
| **fika** | arrive | 10. Tumefikiwa na vijana watatu. |
| **ku-fa** | to die | 11. Mtu huyu amefiwa na baba wake. |
| **fanya** | make | 12. Walifanyiwa karamu nzuri. |

### EXERCISE 54c

Translate:

1. All sorts of things (vitu aina aina) were brought to him.
2. My load was carried for me.
3. Immediately he arrived, food was cooked for him.
4. His letters were read to him.
5. What was said to him?
6. I am tired, I want to have my food brought to me here.
7. A letter will be sent to the chief to-morrow.
8. Let maize be ground for the sick folk.
9. When I arrived, the door was opened for me by a small child.
10. A chair was placed for him near the table.
11. A cup of tea was brought to me (this) morning.
12. Was this work done for you?

## THE STATIVE (OR NEUTER) FORM

The characteristic suffix of Stative verbs is -KA, but the same principles of vowel harmony apply here as in Prepositional and Passive forms.

| Verbs with -A-, -I-, -U- in root | | -IKA |
|---|---|---|
| fanya | do | fanyika |
| pita | pass | pitika |
| vunja | break | vunjika |
| Verbs with -E- or -O- in root | | -EKA |
| sema | say | semeka |
| soma | read | someka |

| | | |
|---|---|---|
| Verbs ending in -AA, -IA, -UA | | -(LI)KA |
| twaa | take | twalika |
| sikia | hear | sikika, sikilika |
| rarua | tear | raruka, rarulika |
| Verbs ending in -EA, -OA | | -(LE)KA |
| tembea | walk about | tembeleka |
| ng'oa | uproot | ng'oleka, ng'oka |
| Causative verbs ending in -SHA or -ZA | | -IKA,-EKA |
| pendeza | please | pendezeka |
| Verbs of Arabic origin ending in -I, -U | | -IKA |
| rudi | return | rudika |
| shutumu | abuse | shutumika |
| Verbs of Arabic origin ending in -E | | -EKA |
| samehe | forgive | sameheka |
| Verbs of Arabic origin ending in -AU add | | -LIKA |
| sahau | forget | sahaulika |

A few Stative verbs are made from noun, adverb or adjective roots (especially in Arabic borrowings):

| | | | |
|---|---|---|---|
| shughuli | business, occupation | shughulika | be busy |
| imara | firm | imarika | be firm |

## Exercise 55a

Give the stative forms of:

| | | | | | |
|---|---|---|---|---|---|
| zima | nena | tosha | amini | funga | tafuna |
| la | badili | fungua | sadiki | fua | jua |

## Uses of the Stative Form

Stative verbs express two different concepts, which need to be distinguished although they are intimately connected.

1. They express *state* without reference to agency. If agency is implied the Passive should be used.

| | | |
|---|---|---|
| vunja<br>break | Kikombe kime**vunjika**. | The cup is broken (no agency, state indicated). |
| | Kikombe kili**vunjwa** na Hamisi. | The cup was broken by Hamisi. |

2. They also express *potentiality*, i.e. whether or not the subject is capable of receiving a given action.

| | | |
|---|---|---|
| **fanya**<br>do | Kazi hii **haifanyiki**. | This work can't be done. |
| | Kazi hii **yafanyika**. | This work is capable of being done, or can be done. |
| **la**<br>eat | Machungwa haya haya-**liki**, bado kuiva. | These oranges are not fit for eating, they are not yet ripe. |
| **vaa**<br>wear | Koti hili haliva**liki**. | This coat is unwearable. |

Sometimes the Stative form, when expressing potentiality, takes the suffix -LIKA.

| | *Stative* | *Potential* |
|---|---|---|
| **pasua**<br>split | Koti langu lime**pasuka**.<br>My coat is split. | Nguo hii haifai, ya**pasu-lika**.<br>This cloth is useless, it tears easily, *or*, it gets easily torn. |

In a few verbs the suffix is -IKANA or -EKANA.

| *Parent form* | | | *Stative* |
|---|---|---|---|
| **pata** | get | **patikana** | be procurable |
| **ona** | see | **onekana** | be visible |
| **weza** | be able | **wezekana** | be possible |
| **jua** | know | **julikana** | be known, knowable |
| **tambua** | discern | **tambulikana** | be discernible |
| **taka** | want | **takikana** | be required |

In some verbs the suffix -KA or -IKA has a transitive function.[1]

| | | | |
|---|---|---|---|
| **tanda** | extend, be spread out | **tandika** | spread out |

Many of these verbs appear to have a positional implication. Cf. **(w)eka** (put in position), Nsenga: **ika**.

| | | | |
|---|---|---|---|
| vaa | put on clothes | vika | provide with clothing |
| simama | stand | simika | set up |
| inama | stoop | inika | tilt |

Note also:

| | |
|---|---|
| anika | spread out clothes, etc., in sun |
| funika | cover |
| bandika | fasten on, stick on |

## EXERCISE 55b

Translate:

1. Kazi kubwa sana hufanyika hapa.
2. Daraja likainuliwa kwa mashine, likainuka pande mbili.
3. Afrika yataka kuinuka, lakini haitapewa wasaa mpaka imeunganika, yaani (that is) kuwa na umoja.
4. Mji ukajengeka ukakaa.
5. Amenifanyia fadhili nyingi: hazinenekani wala kulipika.
6. Neno hili halisahauliki.
7. Nipitishe (take me round) kwa njia iliyopitika, hii haipitiki.
8. Usiwape watu kazi isiyofanyika.
9. Yafaa nini kuweka chakula kisicholika?

## EXERCISE 55c

Translate:

| | | |
|---|---|---|
| rarua | tear | 1. How did your coat get torn? |
| shughuli | business | 2. If you are busy, I will come again to-morrow. |
| sumbua | annoy | 3. He is annoyed at your words. |
| zima | put out | 4. The lamp has gone out. |
| vunja | break | 5. I didn't break this cup, it merely broke. |
| nena | speak | 6. His kindness is indescribable. |
| pima | measure | 7. His patience cannot be measured. |
| nunua | buy | 8. Oranges are not buyable to-day. Why not? They are too dear. |
| funga | shut | 9. I didn't shut the door, it shut of itself. This door won't shut. |

| kata | cut | 10. The string is cut. Who cut it? |
| **eleza** | explain | 11. You say the matter cannot be explained (the matter is unexplainable). |
| | | 12. Matters which cannot be explained annoy me. |
| **fungua** | open | 13. These windows won't open. |
| **shika** | hold | 14. This man is a clever fellow, he can't be got the better of. |
| **sikia** | hear | 15. His voice cannot be heard afar off (kwa mbali). |
| **tafuna** | chew | 16. This meat cannot be chewed, it is too tough. |
| **kula** | to eat | 17. Throw away this food, it is uneatable. |
| **pata** | get | 18. There are no bananas to be had in the market to-day. (To-day bananas are not procurable at the market.) |
| **weza** | be able | 19. This matter is impossible. |
| **ona** | see | 20. The stars which can be seen cannot be counted, they are without number (idadi). |
| **hesabu** | count | |
| **jua** | know | 21. Hamisi is a man who is well known in the town. |

## THE CAUSATIVE FORM

There are many variations in the Causative suffix, which may be accounted for on phonetic grounds. The original suffix in Old Bantu was probably -YA, and this suffix has undergone assimilation with certain end consonants in the verb root in Swahili as in Table on page opposite.

Other consonants are not assimilated, but the suffix is -ISHA or -ESHA according to the rules of vowel harmony.

| imba | sing | **imbisha** | weza | be able | **wezesha** |
| zima | extinguish | **zimisha** | kosa | err | **kosesha** |
| shiba | be sated | **shibisha** | koma | cease | **komesha** |
| funga | fasten | **fungisha** | soma | read | **somesha** |

In a few cases the suffix is -IZA or -EZA.

**fanya**  do          **fanyiza**[1]   **penda**  like     **pendeza**

Verbs of non-Bantu origin likewise take these suffixes.

**rudi**  return        **rudisha**       **samehe**  forgive  **samehesha**

But note:

**sahau**  forget  **sahaulisha**

### SOUND CHANGE WITH -YA

| | | | | | |
|---|---|---|---|---|---|
| **-P- + -YA > -FYA** | | | **-W- + -YA > -VYA** | | |
| **ogopa** | fear | **ogofya** | **lewa** | be drunk | **levya** |
| | | | **nawa** | wash hands | **navya** |
| **-T- + -YA > -SA or -SHA** | | | **-N- + -YA > -NYA** | | |
| **takata** | be clean | **takasa** | **ona** | see | **onya** |
| **pita** | pass | **pisha** | **kana** | deny | **kanya** |
| **pata** | get | **pasha** | **gawana** | share | **gawanya** |
| **-K- + -YA > -SHA** | | | **-L- + -YA > -ZA** | | |
| **ruka** | jump | **rusha** | **lala** | sleep | **laza** |
| **shuka** | descend | **shusha** | | | |
| **anguka** | fall down | **angusha** | Two vowels + -YA > -ZA | | |
| **waka** | burn | **washa** | **jaa** | be full | **jaza** |
| **amka** | wake up | **amsha** | **paa** | ascend | **pa(a)za** |
| **chemka** | boil | **chemsha** | **kataa** | refuse | **kataza** |
| **kumbuka** | remember | **kumbusha** | **ingia** | enter | **ingiza** |
| **kauka** | be dry | **kausha** | **tulia** | be quiet | **tuliza** |
| | | | **kimbia** | run | **kimbiza** |
| | | | **legea** | be loose | **legeza** |
| | | | **elea** | be clear | **eleza** |

Not all verbs in **-p, -t, -k** and **-n** take the suffix **-ya** with assimilation. Many take **-isha**, etc., instead.

| **lipa** | pay | **lipisha** *or* **lipiza** |
|---|---|---|
| **kata** | cut | **katiza** |
| **weka** | place | **wekesha** |
| **nena** | speak | **nenesha** *or* **neneza** |

A few Causative verbs are made from noun, adverb or adjective roots (especially in Arabic borrowings):

**bahati**  luck, chance      **bahatisha**  guess, try one's luck
**tayari**  ready            **tayarisha**  make ready
**sawa**  alike, equal      **sawazisha**  equalize, compare

---

[1] Also **fanza**.

## Uses of the Causative Form

These verbs, as their name implies, express causation, but not always along lines logical to an English way of thinking.

This term as applied to Swahili verbs includes compulsive, permissive, persuasive and helpful causation as well as simple causation.

Madan, in the introduction to his Dictionary, says: "The causal sense includes . . . varieties of causation . . . often needing delicate discrimination and totally different translations."

In short, one may say that a Causative verb indicates the action which "causes" its object to be, to become or to do that which is expressed in the parent form of the verb, which may be either simple or derived.

| Parent forms | | Causative forms | |
|---|---|---|---|
| Simple: | | | |
| jaa | be full | jaza | fill |
| imba | sing | imbisha | let sing, make sing |
| Stative: | | | |
| chemka | boil (intrans.) | chemsha | make boil, boil (trans.) |
| amka | be awake | amsha | awaken |
| Passive: | | | |
| chelewa | be late | chelewesha | delay (trans.) |
| Associative: | | | |
| patana | agree together, be in agreement | patanisha | reconcile |

Examples:

Mtungi ume**jaa**.
    The water-pot is full.
Watoto wana**imba**.
    The children are singing.

Nimeu**jaza** mtungi.
    I have filled the water-pot.
Mwalimu anawa**imbisha** watoto.
    The teacher is giving the children a singing lesson *or* taking them for singing (Lit. causing them to sing).

Maji yame**chemka**.
The water is boiling.

**Chemsha** maji.
Boil some water.

Wame**amka**.
They are awake.

Umewa**amsha**?
Have you awakened them?

Wapagazi wame**chelewa**.
The porters are late.

Usiwa**cheleweshe** wapagazi.
Do not delay the porters.

Wame**patana**.
They are in agreement,
are reconciled.

Kadhi amewa**patanisha** mtu
huyu na nduguye.
The judge has reconciled this
man and his brother.

The various shades of causation, permissive, compulsive,
etc., are intimately connected with the context.

| | | |
|---|---|---|
| **kopa**<br>borrow | Ni**kopeshe** mikate mi-<br>tatu. | Lend me three loaves<br>(allow me to borrow<br>three loaves). |
| **panga**<br>rent | Ameni**pangisha** nyu-<br>mba yake. | He has let his house to<br>me (allowed me to<br>rent his house). |
| **vuka**<br>cross | Ewe baba tu**vushe**. | Do thou, oh father, take<br>us across. |
| **kimbia**<br>run away<br>from | Ng'ombe mkali ali-<br>m**kimbiza** mtoto. | A fierce cow chased the<br>child away (made the<br>child run away). |
| **ingia**<br>enter<br>**keti**<br>sit | Walipofika nyumbani,<br>wanawake wali-<br>**ingizwa** ndani, na<br>waume waliketi-<br>**shwa** barazani. | When they arrived at<br>the house, the women<br>were allowed to enter,<br>but the men folk were<br>made to sit on the<br>verandah. |
| **ugua**<br>be ill | Kumw**uguza** mtu. | To tend a person in sick-<br>ness. |
| **piga chapa**<br>print | Ataki**pigisha** chapa ki-<br>tabu hiki. | He will get (*or* have)<br>this book printed. |

Certain causative forms imply intensive action rather than
causation. See Augmentative forms, p. 243.

| | | |
|---|---|---|
| **toka**<br>come forth | Jiwe hili la**tokeza**<br>mno. | This stone projects too<br>much. |

Sometimes a verb may have two different forms of suffix. When such is the case, the difference in suffix indicates a difference in meaning. In the one form the verb takes an object only, and in the other it requires a further noun or phrase to complete its meaning.

| Simple form | Causative form + object | Causative form + object and noun in nominal construction |
|---|---|---|
| **kuona** to see, feel, realize | **Kumwonya** mtu. To warn someone. | **Kumwonyesha** mtu kitu. To show someone something. |
| **kupita** to pass | **Mpishe** Bwana. Allow the Bwana to pass. | **Mpitishe** Bwana njia ya kukata. Take the Bwana by a short cut. |
| **kuapa** to take an oath | **Kumwapiza** mtu. To call down a curse on someone. | **Kumwapisha** mtu kiapo. To administer an oath to someone. |

## EXERCISE 56a

Translate:

| | |
|---|---|
| **potea** | be lost |
| **fahamu** | understand |
| **tulia** | be quiet |
| **rudi** | return |
| **nenepa** | grow fat, be fat |
| **amka** | awake |

1. Watu hawa hupoteza maisha yao pwani.

2. Bwana Mkubwa alifungua mkutano kwa kuwafahamisha faida za skuli.

3. Aliwatuliza roho zao kwa kuwadanganya akisema, Msilie, nitawarudisha kwenu.

4. Wanyama hawa wa kiulaya hufugwa vizuri, nao wapata malisho yaliyo safi sana ya kuwanenepesha.

5. Watu wakaenda wakamwamsha wakasema, Zimwi amka.

| | | |
|---|---|---|
| **nyoka** | be straight, stretched out | 6. Alinyosha mkono achukue zile panga. |
| **elea** | be clear to | 7. Alimweleza yote. |
| **karibia** | come near | 8. Walikaribishwa vizuri. |
| **enda** | go | 9. Je mtu awezaje kuendesha motakaa bila (without) petroli? |

## EXERCISE 56b

Translate:

| | | |
|---|---|---|
| **legea** | be loose | 1. Loosen this rope. |
| **lala** | lie down | 2. Lay him down gently. |
| **waka** | burn (intrans.) | 3. Light the lamp. |
| **zimika** | go out (of fire, etc.) | 4. The wind has put out the lamp. |
| **anguka** | fall down | 5. He let fall three coconuts. |
| **shtuka** | be startled | 6. You startled me. |
| **lewa** | be drunk | 7. The palm wine has made him drunk. |
| **ruka** | fly | 8. Do not raise the dust when you sweep. |
| **kimbia** | run away | 9. Do not chase the fowls. |
| **amka** | awake | 10. At what time does the Bwana want to be awakened? |
| **uma** | hurt | 11. Am I hurting you? |
| **rudi** | return | 12. Have you returned my book? Have you sent back your book to the Bwana? (Lit. Have you sent back to him Bwana your book?) |
| **sikitika** | be sorry | 13. Did your words make him sorry? |
| **tangulia** | go in front | 14. He made them go on ahead. |
| **pumzika** | rest | 15. Give the horses a rest. |
| **lazimu** | oblige | 16. He compelled me do this work. |

# CHAPTER XXXV

## DERIVATIVE VERBS (continued)

### THE STATIC FORM

THE suffix -MA expresses a stationary condition or one of inactivity. It is generally found suffixed to the simple form of the verb. Sometimes the simple form on which the Static is made is lacking in modern Swahili.

| *Parent forms* | | *Static forms* | |
|---|---|---|---|
| funga | tie, bind, etc. | fungama | be in a fixed position |
| kwaa | stumble, be stopped by sudden obstacle | kwama | become jammed |
| ficha | hide | fichama | be in a state of being hidden |
| lowa | be wet | lowama | be in a soaked condition |
| andaa | put in order, in array | andama | follow in order |
| lala | lie down | lalama | beg for mercy—originally accompanied by prostration |
| ganda | coagulate, become hard | gandama | adhere to |
| unga | join | ungama | be joined |
| ima | (archaic form) | simama | stand |
| ina | (archaic form) | inama | stoop, bend down |

Note also:

| | |
|---|---|
| chutama | squat on haunches |
| zama | be immersed, sink |
| tazama | gaze upon, examine |

Examples:

Mwandame.          Follow after him, i.e. go next to him.

236

| | |
|---|---|
| Maneno yalim**kwama** kooni. | The words stuck in his throat. |
| Na Fisi kwa kuwa alikuwa mnene . . . ali**kwama** nusu ya njia. | And because Hyena was stout . . . he stuck halfway (through). |
| M**tazame**. | Look at him, gaze upon him. |
| Jambo hili hatukuli**tazamia**. | We did not expect such an event. |
| Rangi ime**gandama** na bura-shi. | The paint has stuck to the brush. |

The -MA suffix frequently takes Associative -NA, the two suffixes expressing a state of interdependence or interaction.

| *Static* | | *Static* + *NA* | |
|---|---|---|---|
| **fungama** | be in a fixed position | **fungamana** | be interlaced |
| **ungama** | be joined | **ungamana** | be joined together |
| **andama** | follow in order, succeed | **andamana** | accompany, associate with |
| **shikama** | be in a state of holding | **shikamana** | hold together |
| **fichama** | be in a state of being hidden | **fichamana** | be hidden from |

In fact the suffix -MANA is more frequently employed than -MA.

| | |
|---|---|
| 549. Ushikwapo, **shikamana**; uchwewapo na jua, lala. | When caught hold of, hold on; when thou hast the sun set on thee, (stay and) sleep. |
| Maji yame**gandamana**. | The water is frozen. |
| Mwitu ime**fungamana**. | The forest is impenetrable. |
| Hapana neno lililo**fichamana** na Mwenyiezi Mungu. | There is nothing which is hidden from Almighty God. |

## THE CONTACTIVE (TENACIOUS) FORM

-TA is suffixed for the most part to the simple form of the verb to express contact.[1] The term "Tenacious" is used in the *Standard Swahili-English Dictionary*.

[1] According to Marconness (*Grammar of Central Karanga*) it indicates "a culmination, the final conclusion and settlement of a process".

| Parent forms | | Contactive forms | |
|---|---|---|---|
| kama | squeeze | kamata | take forcible hold of, arrest |
| (kama ng'ombe milk a cow) | | | |
| fumba | shut by bringing things together | fumbata | enclose with hands or arms |
| (fumba macho close the eyes) | | | |
| kumba | press against, shove | kumbata | hold in the hand |
| kokoa | sweep rubbish together | kokota | drag, haul |
| paka | spread, lay on | pakata | take a child or thing on knee, lap or shoulder |
| suka | plait | sokota | twist, twine with fingers |
| okoa | take out pots etc. from fire | okota | pick up with the fingers |

Note also:

| | |
|---|---|
| ambata | adhere to |
| guruta | smooth with a press, mangle clothes |
| (go)gota | strike, rap |

*Examples:*

Mwivi ame**kamatwa**.

The thief has been arrested.

Siku moja Dunduvule akaa-nguka chini chali asiweze kujiondoa. Lakini Kintu alim**wokota** akam**fumbata**.

One day Dunduvule fell down on his back and couldn't right himself. But Kintu picked him up and held him in his hand.

## THE CONVERSIVE FORM

The insertion of the vowel -U- or -O- between a verb root and its suffix, whether **-a, -ka, -sha** or **-za**, conveys the opposite meaning to that expressed in the root. This form is sometimes spoken of as "Reversive", but the wider term Conversive, suggested by the late Frederick Johnson, is used here.

Laws of vowel harmony dictate that the inserted vowel is -U- if the root vowel is -A-, -I-, -U- or -E-, but -O- if the root vowel is -O-.

The form of the Conversive verb may be:

(a) *Simple*, with suffix -UA or -OA.

| Parent forms | | Conversive forms | |
|---|---|---|---|
| **kunja** | fold | **kunjua** | unfold |
| **kunja uso** | frown | **kunjua uso** | smile |
| **ziba** | stop up | **zibua** | unstop |
| **tega** | put in position, entrap | **tegua** | put out of position |
| **tata** | tangle, complicate | **tatua** | unwind, put straight |
| **vaa** | put on clothes | **vua** | take off clothes |
| **fuma** | weave | **fumua** | unpick |
| **cha** | rise (of sun) | **chwa** | set (of sun) |
| **choma** | pierce, prick | **chomoa** | extract |
| **fundika**[1] | tie a knot | **fundua** | untie a knot |
| **inama**[1] | stoop | **inua** | lift up |
| **funika**[1] | cover up | **funua** | uncover |
| **pak(i)a** | load up a vessel | **pakua** | discharge cargo |
| | | **pakua chakula** | dish up food |

(b) *Stative*, with suffix -UKA or -OKA.

| | | | |
|---|---|---|---|
| **lewa** | be drunk | **levuka** | become sober |
| **angika** | hang up, suspend | **anguka** | fall down |
| **bandika** | stick on | **banduka** | come unstuck |
| **tandika** | spread out | **tanduka** | become gathered up |
| Compare with (a): | | **inuka** | be lifted |
| | | **funuka** | be uncovered |
| | | **tatuka** | get torn, split |
| | etc., etc. | | |

(c) *Causative*, with suffix -USHA or -UZA or -OSHA or -OZA.

| | | | |
|---|---|---|---|
| Compare with (b): | | **levusha** | make sober |
| | | **angusha** | let fall, throw down |
| | etc., etc. | | |

[1] Here the original parent form is no longer in use.

*Examples:*

| | |
|---|---|
| Mwambie mpishi **apakue** chakula. | Tell the cook to dish up the food. |
| Chombo kime**pakuliwa**. | The vessel has been unloaded. |
| Mkutano ume**fumukana**. | The crowd has dispersed. |

Compare:

| | |
|---|---|
| Mchawi amem**bandika** Fulani kiapo. | The wizard has put a curse on So-and-so. |
| Mkia wa nyani haum**banduki**. | An ape's tail does not become detached from its owner. (An ape does not change its habits.) |
| Kume**tandika**. | (The sky) is overcast. |
| Mawingu yame**tanduka**. | The clouds have dispersed. |
| Kumeku**cha**. | It has dawned (it is dawn). Dawn is here. |
| Jua limeku**chwa**. | The sun has set. |

Certain conversive forms imply intense action. See Augmentative forms, p. 243.

**nyaka** catch                    **nyakua** snatch

## THE INCEPTIVE FORM

The suffix -PA occurs in a few verbs to indicate a state entered upon.

| | |
|---|---|
| **ogo-pa** fear | cf. **w-oga** cowardice, **mw-oga** a coward |
| **nene-pa** get fat (persons) | cf. **-nene** thick, stout; **u-nene** thickness |

## THE ASSOCIATIVE FORM

The term "Associative" is used instead of the more generally accepted term "Reciprocal" as found in the *Standard Swahili-English Dictionary*, for in addition to reciprocity -NA expresses other aspects of association such as concerted action, interaction and interdependence (and in some cases disassociation). The force of -NA largely depends upon the

---

[1] Here the original parent form is no longer in use.

preceding suffix and the meaning of the root itself. Generally speaking, -NA suffixed to the Simple, Prepositional or Causative forms expresses reciprocity or concerted action, but suffixed to the Static or Contactive forms implies interaction and interdependence.

| *Parent forms* | | *Associative forms* | |
|---|---|---|---|
| Simple: | | | |
| **piga** | hit, strike | **pigana** | fight |
| **jua** | know | **juana** | be mutually acquainted |
| Prepositional: | | | |
| **imbia** | sing to | **imbiana** | sing to one another |
| **ngojea** | wait for | **ngojeana** | wait for one another |
| Causative: | | | |
| **pendeza** | please | **pendezana** | please one another |
| Static: | | | |
| **shikama** | be in a state of holding | **shikamana** | be in a state of holding together |
| Contactive: | | | |
| **ambata** | adhere to | **ambatana** | adhere together |
| Conversive: | | | |
| **fumuka** | come undone (of weaving, etc.) | **fumukana** | disperse |

*Examples:*

Watu hu**hitalifiana** sana katika maana ya neno hili "ustaarabu".

People differ widely in their interpretation of this word "civilization".

Adabu ni kitu kipatikanacho sana kwa malezi na kwa ku**suhubiana** na marafiki wema.

Correct behaviour is acquired through one's upbringing and through associating with good companions.

Mtu huyu alikuwa na mkewe, waka**sikilizana** sana, na tabia zao wali**juana** vyema.

This man had a wife, they got on well together, and each one knew the other's particular disposition.

I

Vile vile wazee wa vijiji hawata**shirikiana** naye katika mahudhurio, bali wata**shirikiana** naye katika mchezo wa mpira tu.

In like manner the village elders will not co-operate with him in the matter of school attendance, but merely co-operate in matters concerning football.

Huambukizika kwa ku**gusana** mtu mgonjwa na mtu mzima.

Infection takes place through a sick person coming in contact with a healthy person.

Wakarudi waki**ambiana**, Huyu ameshinda wenziwe kwa ujuha.

They returned saying to one another, "This person was a greater simpleton than his companions".

When a noun or pronoun different from the subject follows an Associative Verb, it is preceded by NA.

| | |
|---|---|
| Wali**pigana na** maadui. | They fought with the enemy. |
| Cf. Wali**pigana**. | They fought each other. |
| Ali**kutana na**mi njiani. | He met me on the road. |

## EXERCISE 57

Translate:

| | | |
|---|---|---|
| **kuta** | come across | 1. Wale askari walikwenda "machi" hata kati ya uwanda wakakutana sawa sawa. |
| **apa** | swear | 2. Alizidi kumpenda hata wakaapiana kiapo cha urafiki. |
| **fuata** | follow | 3. Mimi nilifuatana na Bwana X nikakutana na Bwana Z. |
| **songa** | press | 4. Watu wengi wamesongana barabarani. |
| **andama** | follow in order | 5. "Procession" ni maendeleo ya kuandamana. |
| **hukumu** | judge | 6. Machezo mengi yalikuwa ya kuhukumiana. |
| **tenga** | part | 7. Walistaajabu kuona Nurdin apenda kutengana naye. |
| **chagua** | choose | 8. Hao watu waliambiwa watachaguana, mama aende na mwanawe, mtu na mkewe. |

| amkia | greet | 9. Baada ya kuamkiana, alimwa-mbia. . . . |
| gomba | oppose, scold | 10. Hapana kugombana wala kusu-kumana. |
| sukuma | shove | |
| funza | teach | 11. Walifunzana kiume. |
| (mpaka | a boundary) | 12. Shamba lao lapakana na njia. |
| jua | know | 13. Sijuani nao vyema. |
| jua | know | 14. Mtu mbaya ajulikanaye vitendo vyake huuawa vile vile. |
| karibu | draw near | 15. Walipokaribiana wakaona. . . . |
| lala | lie, sleep | 16. Waliona kila pembe imejaa watu-mwa waliolaliana. |
| epua | remove | 17. Tukitaka kuepukana na sifa mba-ya. . . . |

## AUGMENTATIVE AND SUBTRACTIVE FORMS

Just as nouns may be given augmentative or subtractive meanings by means of prefixes, so also may verbs be given an augmentative implication by means of suffixes, and a subtractive meaning by reduplication of the stem.

### Augmentative

The term "Augmentative" includes various degrees of thoroughness and intensiveness, also continuousness and persistence. These ideas are not mutually exclusive, but are frequently complementary.

The suffixes employed are identical in form with certain of the Conversive, Causative and Prepositional suffixes already discussed.

-UA, -OA

| epa | dodge | epua | remove |
| kama | squeeze, especially in milking | kamua | wring, squeeze out |
| chunga | sift | chungua | look carefully into |
| songa | press | songoa | wring |

-SHA, -ZA

| nya | drop like rain | nyesha | fall in torrents |
| nyamaa | be quiet | nyamaza | be quite quiet |

| | | | |
|---|---|---|---|
| jibu | answer | jibisha | answer in detail |
| lipa | pay | lipiza kisasi | pay back, i.e. take revenge |
| chomoa | draw out, extract | chomoza | burst through |
| sikia | hear | sikiza | listen |
| telea | descend | teleza | slide, slip |

### -LIA, -LEA

| | | | |
|---|---|---|---|
| ua | kill | ulia | kill off |
| faa | be of use | falia | be of great use |
| ingia | enter | ingilia | interrupt |
| vaa | put on clothes | valia | dress up |
| potea | be lost | potelea | be lost completely |

The suffixes -ILIA, -ELEA should be noted. Sometimes they represent a form termed Double Prepositional in the *Standard Swahili-English Dictionary*, e.g. **shikilia** < **shika**. When so used these suffixes—sometimes with the addition of -ZA—express continuance of the action and persistence in carrying it out.

### -ILIA, -ELEA

| | | | |
|---|---|---|---|
| shika | hold | shikilia | hold on, insist, hold on tightly |
| piga | strike | pigilia | pound down a stone floor |
| fika | arrive | fikilia | get right there |
| kata | cut | katilia | cut right off |
| shinda | press | shindilia | ram down |
| enda | go | endelea | progress |
| penda | like | pendelea | favour |
| acha | let be | achilia | remit |

### -ILIZA, -ELEZA

| | | | |
|---|---|---|---|
| pata | get | patiliza | visit upon one |
| tosha | suffice | tosheleza | be sufficient, satisfy |
| — | — | omboleza | bewail, lament |

It is difficult to bring these forms under rules, for the method of conveying an augmentative implication varies according to the basic meaning of the root and the form of the verb to which the suffix is added. Thus **sikiza** (listen), which is already an intensive form of **sikia** (hear), may be still further augmented to **sikiliza** (listen attentively).

*Examples:*

| | |
|---|---|
| **Iepue** kandarinya motoni. | Take the kettle off the fire. |
| Jana mvua ili**nyesha** sa-na. | Yesterday the rain came down in torrents. |
| **Nyamazeni** watoto. | Be quiet, children. |
| Ali**jibisha** hotuba kwa maneno mazuri sana. | He fully replied to the address in well-chosen phrases. |
| Sikumw**igiza**. | I didn't mimic him. |
| Nili**chunguza** sana . . . ni-kaona . . . | I inquired very carefully into the matter and I found . . . |
| Nifanyeje hata nikaji**lipiza** kisasi? | What can I do to get my revenge? |
| Jua lime**chomoza**. | The sun has burst through. |
| **Sikizeni** ninyi nyote mlio-po. | Listen all ye who are present. |
| Ali**shikilia** ya kuwa ni mgonjwa. | He insisted that he was an invalid. |
| Haya m**shikilie**. | Here, hold onto him tight. |
| Watu wana**pigilia** sakafu. | People are pounding down the stone floor. |
| Hasara iliwa**fikilia**. | Loss overtook them. |
| Vigingi hivi vi**shindilie** vizuri. | Hammer down these pegs well. |
| Siku hizi nchi yetu inae-**ndelea** vizuri. | Our country is making progress at the present time. |
| Zi**tupilie** mbali. | Throw them right away. |
| Pwanali ali**chelea** wasije wakatoroka. | Pwanali was in a perpetual state of fear lest they should decamp. |
| Kama angaliwa**ingilia**, wa-ngalisahau yote waliyotaka kusema. | Had he interrupted them, they would have forgotten all they were about to say. |
| Je, Kadhi amekwisha ku-**sikiliza** kesi? | Has the Judge finished listening to the case? |
| **Endeleza** kazi hii. | Get a move on with this work (lit. make this work progress). |

Watu hawa wana**ombole-zeani**? — Why are these people wailing?

Mfalme alipeleka askari wake wa**peleleze** nchi. — The King sent his soldiers to spy out the country.

## Subtractive

By duplicating the stem of a verb a lessening of force is indicated. See reduplication, p. 316.

Alimpigapiga tu. — He only hit him gently.

Mtoto huyu alialia mchana kuchwa. — This child whimpers the whole day through.

Kulewalewa. — To sway, stagger, reel.

# CHAPTER XXXVI

## VERBS AND THEIR TENSES (Section VII)

### COMPOUND TENSES

In the tenses already discussed three important facts emerge:

Some tenses refer to Time, past or future, e.g. -LI-, -TA-.

Some tenses refer to some Aspect of time, action or state, or to some condition or supposition, e.g. -KI-, -KA-.

Some tenses may have either of the above functions according to context, e.g. -A-, -NA-, -ME-.

The following reference table makes this clear:

| *Time Prefixes* | | *Aspect Prefixes* | |
|---|---|---|---|
| -A- | Present Indefinite | -A- | Indefinite time |
| -NA- | Present Definite | -NA- | Definite point in time |
| -ME- | Immediate Past | -ME- | Action completed, State entered upon |
| -TA- | Future | | |
| -LI- | Past | HU- | Recurrent or habitual action |
| | | -KA- | Connective, subsequent action |
| | | -KI- | Action going on, Condition |
| | | -SIPO- | Negative of -KI- |
| | | -NGE- and -NGALI- | |
| | | | Suppositional condition |
| | | -NGA- and -JAPO- | |
| | | | Concession |

Compound tenses are numerous, and are based on the Primary tenses, combined with various verbs used in an auxiliary capacity, such as **kuwa, kwisha, kuja, kwenda**. The subject prefix is usually required before both auxiliary and main verb. Nilikuwa **nikisoma**. (I was reading.)

The most important Compound tenses are based on auxiliary **kuwa** and are of three kinds:

A. Time in relation to Aspect.
B. Aspect in relation to Aspect.
C. Aspect in relation to Time.

REFERENCE TABLE

A. COMPOUND TENSES—TIME + ASPECT

| | Past -LI- | Future -TA- | Specific time including Present -NA- |
|---|---|---|---|
| Action taking place at a specific time -NA- | -LIKUWA -NA-<br>-LIKUWA HA-....I | -TAKUWA -NA-<br>-TAKUWA HA-....I | -NAKUWA -NA-<br>-NAKUWA HA-....I |
| Continuous or repetitive action -KI- | -LIKUWA -KI-<br>HA- -KUWA -KI- | -TAKUWA -KI-<br>HA- -TAKUWA -KI- | -NAKUWA -KI- |
| Completion of action, State -ME- | -LIKUWA -ME-<br>HA- -KUWA -ME- | -TAKUWA -ME-<br>HA- -TAKUWA -ME- | -NAKUWA -ME- |

### A. TIME IN RELATION TO ASPECT

-NA-, -LI- and -TA- in the auxiliary combine with -NA-, -KI- or -ME- in the main verb according to whether reference is made to a particular period, to a process or to a state. The compound tenses thus formed cannot always be differentiated in English. The difference in Swahili should be noted, for it exemplifies the preciseness of a Bantu language. The choice is dependent upon context, for in a Bantu language the verb must be in harmony with the context to a finer degree than in English.

A study of the sentences below makes it clear that:

-NA- in the main verb is used in reference to a particular time *which is indicated in the context* by such expressions as **wakati huo, hapo,** the relative of time, etc.;

-KI- in the main verb is used to express a series of occasions or continuous action;

-ME- in the main verb is used to express completion of the action, or state.

In both affirmative and negative tenses the auxiliary carries the Time particle and the main verb carries the Aspect particle, *but the place of the negative varies.* The auxiliary is negatived when combined with -ME- and -KI- tenses. This is not so with the negative counterpart of -NA- tenses; here the auxiliary remains in the affirmative, followed by the simple negative form of the main verb.

| | | |
|---|---|---|
| Alikuwa⎫ | He was⎫ | |
| **Hakuwa**⎭ amelala. | *He was not*⎭ asleep. | |
| Alikuwa⎫ | He used⎫ to read a great | |
| **Hakuwa**⎭ akisoma sana. | *He used not*⎭ deal. | |
| Wakati huo ali-⎰ anasoma. | At that time he ⎰ reading. | |
| kuwa ⎱ **hasomi.** | was ⎱ *not reading.* | |

### Primary and Compound tenses in Past Time, -LI-

| *Affirmative* | *Negative* |
|---|---|
| -li- | ha--ku- |
| -likuwa -na- | -likuwa ha- . . . . -i |
| -likuwa -ki- | ha--kuwa -ki- |
| -likuwa -me- | ha--kuwa-me- |

I*

Wageni **waliondoka** jana.

The guests left yesterday.

**Tulipokuwa tunatazama** ndani ya kanisa kubwa, alitujia mtu mmoja akatuuliza . . .

While we were looking round the cathedral, someone came and asked us . . .

Tokea Kismayu hata hapa **tulikuwa tunatumia** fedha za Kitaliani.

From Kismayu until this point we were using Italian currency.

Hapo majahazi **yalipokuwa yanatoka** bandari, kulisikilizana kelele.

Just as the dhows were leaving the harbour, a noise was heard.

**Tulipokuwa tunatelemka** relini Kampala, kikundi cha Masiki kilitukaribia, kikatuomba lazima tucheze nao.

While we were alighting from the train at Kampala, a company of Sikhs approached us, and begged us to play (a match) with them.

Alikuwa na mbwa **aliyekuwa akienda** naye kuwinda.

He had a dog which used to go hunting with him.

Mwarabu mmoja **tuliyekuwa tukijuana** naye.

A certain Arab whom we used to know.

Kulikuwa na joka kuu, **lililokuwa likishuka** mjini kila siku.

There was once a huge snake, which used to go down to the town every day.

Ng'ombe wangu waliniibia, **nilipokuwa nimelala**.

They robbed me of my cow while I was asleep.

**Alikuwa amebeba** vitu chungu.

He was loaded up with a pile of things.

Sultani **alikuwa amefuatana** na mkwewe.

The Sultan was accompanied by his son-in-law.

Tumbako yake ilianguka, **alipokuwa amepiga** magoti, akiomba msamaha mbele ya Bwana wake.

His tobacco dropped down while he was kneeling before his master, begging forgiveness.

Wageni **hawakuondoka** jana.

The strangers did not leave yesterday.

Nilipomwona, **alikuwa hasomi**.

When I saw him, he was not reading.

| | |
|---|---|
| **Hakuwa akifanya** bidii. | He used not to make any effort. |
| Zamani **hawakuwa wakipatana** vizuri. | Formerly they used not to get on well together. |
| **Hakuwa ameandamana** na mkwewe. | He was not accompanied by his son-in-law. |

Note the following rare use of HU-, found in an article by a Pemba writer:

| | |
|---|---|
| Mchwa, **ilivyokuwa hughasi** kila mtu na kumharibia vipando na vitu vinginevyo, imetubidi . . . | As white ants have always troubled man by destroying his sowings and other things, it behoves us . . . |

## Primary and Compound Tenses in Future Time, -TA-

| *Affirmative* | *Negative* |
|---|---|
| -ta- | ha--ta- |
| -takuwa -na- | -takuwa ha- . . . -i |
| -takuwa -ki- | ha--takuwa -ki- |
| -takuwa -me- | ha--takuwa -me- |

| | |
|---|---|
| Wageni **wataondoka** lini? | When will the guests leave? |
| Kama mama za watoto wameelimishwa, wataelimisha watoto wao nyumbani, kabla ya kwenda chuoni, na elimu wakati ule **itakuwa inaanza** nyumbani siyo chuoni. | If the mothers of the children have been educated, they will educate their children in the home, before they start their school life, and their education will then begin in the home and not at school. |
| Mwaka ujao **tutakuwa tukikaa** katika nyumba yetu mpya. | Next year we shall be living in our new house. |
| Usipokuja mapema, **nitakuwa nimelala**. | Unless you come early, I shall be asleep. |
| **Atakuwa ameandamana** na wafuasi wake wengi. | He will be accompanied by many of his adherents. |
| Wasiposimamiwa, **hawatakuwa wakifanya** kazi usiku kucha. | Unless they are supervised, they won't keep on working all night. |

## Primary and Compound Tenses in reference to a Specific Time including Present Time, -NA-

| Affirmative | Negative |
|---|---|
| -na- | ha- . . . -i |
| -nakuwa -na- | -nakuwa ha- . . . -i |
| -nakuwa -ki- | |
| -nakuwa -me- | |

**Anafanya** nini? **Anasoma** barua.

What is he doing? He is reading a letter.

Yule tajiri, alipoona Abunuwas **anafitini**, akasema . . .

The rich man, when he saw Abunuwas was making trouble, said . . .

Kitoto cha kuku **kinapoku-wa kinakua**, kinajitengeneza kuwa mama wa kutaga mayai, na ukijitahidi katika wakati huo wa uchanga wake **anapokuwa anajitengeneza** basi, atakuwa mama mzuri, mzazi wa mayai mengi.

While a chicken is growing, it is preparing itself to become a good layer, so if you take pains during this period of immaturity while it is preparing itself, it will become a good mother and a good layer.

Nendeni . . . mkawaimbie nzige usiku kucha, **wanapokuwa wakipumzika** chini.

Go and sing to the locusts throughout the night while they are resting on the ground.

Nini maana yake ya kuumbwa sisi wanadamu? Swali hili hunijia sana, **ninapokuwa nimetulia** baada ya kughasika kwa jambo ambalo halipo katika nguvu zangu kulizuia au kulibadilisha.

For what reason have we human beings been created? This question constantly occurs to me, when I have calmed down after worrying about a matter which it is not in my power to prevent or to alter.

**Anasoma?** .La, **hasomi**.

Is he reading? No, he isn't reading.

Njoo wakati **anapokuwa ha-somi.**

Come at a time when he is not (engaged in) reading.

# CHAPTER XXXVII

## VERBS AND THEIR TENSES (Section VIII)

### COMPOUND TENSES (continued)

#### B. ASPECT IN RELATION TO ASPECT

*(For reference table, see folder opposite this page.)*

In this chapter the auxiliary KUWA is discussed with the *Aspect* prefixes -ME-, -KA-, HU-, -KI-, -NGE-, -NGALI-, -NGA- and -JAPO-, in combination again with -NA-, -KI- and -ME- in the main verb.

These compound tenses fall into five groups:

-ME- tenses, which express state.

-KA- tenses, which express subsequent action or state, a connective idea—"and", "so".

HU- tenses, which express a recurring action or state, or habituality, a "generally" or "used to" idea.

-KI-, -NGE- and -NGALI- tenses, which express a condition or supposition, an "if", "should" or "unless" idea.

-NGA- and -JAPO- tenses, which express concession, a "though" idea.

The addition of a second Aspect tense brings out some detail which the simple form alone does not express. Compare:

| | |
|---|---|
| **Akija.** | If he comes. |
| Akiwa **anakuja.** | If is he now coming, i.e. on the way. |

Note that the noun subject frequently stands between the two verbs.

| | |
|---|---|
| Hata siku moja **akawa** Abunawas **anataka** kununua punda, na fedha hana. | Now one day Abunawas wanted to buy a donkey, but he had no money. |

In many of these compound tenses the first subject prefix is replaced by the Impersonal Prefix I-; this practically gives the auxiliary the status of a conjunction.

| | |
|---|---|
| Ikawa amechoka. | And then he became tired. |
| Ikiwa amechoka. | If he is tired. |

253

| | |
|---|---|
| Ingalikuwa amechoka. | If he had been tired. |
| Ingawa amechoka. | Although he is tired. |
| Ijapokuwa amechoka. | Although he may be tired. |

## -ME- Tenses

| *Affirmative* | *Negative* |
|---|---|
| **-me-** | **ha--ku-** |
| **-mekuwa -na-** | **-mekuwa ha- . . . -i** |
| **-mekuwa -ki-** | |

| | |
|---|---|
| **Amekwenda** zake? | Has he gone off? |
| **Hakufa, amelala** tu. | He is not dead, he is merely asleep. |
| Alipoona **amelala**, akaondoka. | When he saw he was asleep, he went away. |
| Tangu siku hiyo watu wengi **wamekuwa wakilitafuta** shimo hilo, lakini hapana aliyepata kuliona. | From that day onwards many people have been seeking for this pit, but no one has ever succeeded in finding it. |
| Amekitia chumvi chakula sana, hata **kimekuwa hakiliki.** | He has salted the food so much, it has become uneatable. (A figure of speech to describe exaggeration.) |

## -KA- Tenses

| *Affirmative* | *Negative* |
|---|---|
| **-ka-** | **-si- . . . -e** |
| **-kawa -na-** | **-kawa ha- . . . -i** |
| **-kawa -ki-** | |
| **-kawa -me-** | |

| | |
|---|---|
| . . . kwa hivyo tuliacha kupiga makasia, **tukawa tunawaangalia** tu (mamba). | . . . so we left off rowing, and then we just watched them (crocodiles). |
| Kibibi wa Tumbatu alistaajabu kusikia neno lile, **akawa analitamka** na kulitamka tena. | The lady at Tumbatu was surprised at hearing this word, and then began saying it again and again. |
| Mbwa akazidi kumfuatia yule mnyama, na kadhalika Mpobe **akawa akienda.** | The dog continued to follow the animal, and Mpobe likewise kept on going. |

| | |
|---|---|
| Alikimbia hata **akawa amechoka**. | He ran on until at length he became tired. |
| Lakini hatimaye kwa bahati **ikawa** wao **wameshindwa**. | At length by luck it so happened that they were defeated. |

The addition of -NA-, -KI- or -ME- to -KA- brings out the details: They *then* began watching, Mpobe *kept on* going, the tired *state* of the one who was running away.

*Negative Forms.*

It has been stated in the earlier chapter that the negative counterpart of a -KA- tense is a form identical with that of the negative subjunctive.[1]

| | |
|---|---|
| Vijana hao hufikiri kuwa wao wanaweza kufanya lo lote wanalolipenda, na **isiwe** kitu. | These lads consider that they can do whatever they like without it mattering. |

If, however, reference is made to a particular time or to particular circumstances a compound form is used: **-kawa ha- . . . -i.**

| | |
|---|---|
| Bibi huyu alitupikia futari na daku, **tukawa hatutaabiki** kabla ya futari. | This Bibi provided us with *futari*[2] and *daku*[2] so then we were no longer distressed (i.e. hungry) before "futari". |
| . . hata mwisho **akawa hataki** kuonana na mtu ye yote. | . . . until at length he did not want to meet anyone. |

### Aphorisms

| | |
|---|---|
| 222. Likiwika **lisiwike**, kutakucha, twende zetu. | Whether (the cock) crow or no, it will dawn, let us away. |

[1] Mr. E. B. Haddon, Lecturer in Swahili at the University of Cambridge, suggests that this form is the negative of an old Perfect tense ending in -E. See "The Perfect Tense in the Eastern Bantu Languages" (*Uganda Journal*, vol. iv, No. 2). See also "The Archaic Perfect Tense in Old and Modern Swahili", by M. A. Bryan (*Bulletin of the School of Oriental Studies*, vol. ix, No. 1).

[2] The first meal in the evening (**futari**) and the last meal at night (**daku**) during Ramathan.

323. Mtenda jambo **asishe** (asiishe), ni kama asi- yetenda.

The man who does a thing without finishing it is as though he had not done it at all.

## HU- Tenses

| Affirmative | Negative |
|---|---|
| hu- | ha- . . . -i |
| huwa -na- | huwa ha- . . . -i |
| huwa -ki- | |
| huwa -me- | |

The English translation varies with the context. The force of HU- may be expressed by words like "usually", "generally", etc., though sometimes an English Indefinite Present Tense suffices.

Njugu hizi mama zenu **huzi- tumia** sana katika mboga.

Your mothers constantly use these nuts in vegetable dishes.

Njugu hizi mno mno **huliwa** na watoto.

These nuts are consumed by children in great quantities.

Hapo kina mama waendapo mashamba ya mbali, wa- toto **huachwa** mjini wali- nde mji.

When the mothers go to shambas some distance away, the children are usually left behind to look after the village.

Hamisi **husoma** kila siku.

Hamisi reads every day.

Kila nikimwona, **huwa ana- maliza** kazi yake.

Every time I see him, he is always on the point of finishing his work.

**Huwa akija** hapa baadhi ya siku.

He generally comes here on certain days.

Maghala ya chakula **huwa yamejaa** vyakula vya mwaka jana.

The food stores are usually full of last year's food.

**Huwa amelala** saa hii.

He is generally asleep at this hour.

Chiponda na watu wake **hu- wa wamejificha** mwituni, kuwavizia.

Chiponda and his people were usually in hiding in the for- est, ready to waylay them.

Akiumwa, **huwa hataki** taa chumbani.

If he is in pain he never wants a lamp in his room.

Chakula namna hii **huwa ha-kiwatoshi** watoto kama hawa.

Food of this sort does not usually satisfy (*or* never satisfies) children such as these.

Recurrent action in the Past or Future is not expressed by HUWA. The auxiliary takes the time particle and the recurrent concept is expressed by -KI-. See p. 250.

Zamani **tulikuwa tukilima** sana.

At one time we used to cultivate a great deal.

### -KI- Tenses

| *Affirmative* | *Negative* |
|---|---|
| -ki- | -sipo- |
| -kiwa -na- | -kiwa ha- . . . -i |
| -kiwa -ki- | |
| -kiwa -me- | |

The functions of -KI- in a primary tense have already been described. In compound tenses they are similar, but have a wider application:

(i) They may correspond to English Participles, but here they may be either present or past.

Kila dakika tatu au tano ili-tulazimu kusimama kwa kuwa magari hayaendi, ao **tukiwa tumesimamishwa** na polisi.

Every three or five minutes we had to stop because the vehicles (in front) were not moving, or because of being halted by the police.

Na **ikiwa** sisi **tulikuwa tu-mekaribishwa** kwenda ku-tazama chuo cha watoto, Bwana akatupa ruksa kuo-ndoka.

We having been invited to visit a school, the Bwana allowed us to leave (early).

(ii) In its "conditional" function, -KI- actually states a premiss, whether suppositional or real, on which the rest of the sentence depends. Note that in some of the following sentences, the English translation demands a participle.

**Akija**, nipe habari. — If he comes, let me know.

**Akiwa anakuja**, fuatana naye. — If he is coming, go along with him.

**Akiwa ameumia**, mpeleke hospitali. — If he is hurt, take him to hospital.

Matunda **yakiwa yanapatikana** kwa namna hii, hapana shaka bei inapunguka. — Fruit being procurable (*or* If fruit is procurable) in this way, the price is bound to fall.

Fulani **akiwa** mwenyewe **amesafiri** Ulaya, aliweza kuwatoa hofu juu ya habari ya makuli. — Fulani himself, having travelled to England, was able to reassure them concerning the matter of food.

**Yakiwa hayafuati** desturi yo yote ila kushabihiana kwa herufi za mwisho tu, basi makusudio yale hayapatikani tena. — But if they (verses) do not follow any one convention except the rhyming of the last letter, the purpose of them cannot be realized any longer.

Note the occasional use of the Impersonal prefix I- instead of the Personal Prefix:

**Ikiwa** malimaji **yamekwenda** chini bara bara, ardhi itapata faida. — If the cultivation has gone down really deep, the soil will profit.

The Arabic word KAMA may often replace the auxiliary verb.

Watu hawa walitakiwa kutoa ushahidi juu ya watu wao, **kama wanapenda** jambo hili, na sababu zake **wakiwa wanapenda** au **hawapendi**. — These people were required to give evidence concerning their people, whether they approved of this matter, and the reasons for approving it or not approving it.

A close study of the sentences, both here and on p. 138 shows that the two "functions" of -KI-, though treated under two headings according to the English translation, are in Swahili really one and the same.

## -NGE- and -NGALI- Tenses

| *Affirmative* | | *Negative*[1] | |
|---|---|---|---|
| nge- | -ngali- | { -singe-<br>ha--nge- | { -singali-<br>ha--ngali- |
| ngekuwa -na- | -ngalikuwa -na- | -ngekuwa ha- . . . -i | -ngalikuwa ha- . . . -i |
| ngekuwa -ki- | -ngalikuwa -ki- | -singekuwa -ki- | -singalikuwa -ki- |
| ngekuwa -me- | -ngalikuwa -me- | -singekuwa -me- | -singalikuwa -me- |

**Angekuwa** mgonjwa, **asinge-kuja** mjini kwa miguu.

If he were an invalid, he would not come to town on foot.

Laiti **ningalifuata** shauri la-ko, mambo haya yote **ya-singalitokea.**

If only I had followed your advice, these things would not have happened.

Hao Waarabu walijua kwa hakika kama hiyo mano-wari **ingalikuwako, haya-ngalitendeka** haya.

These Arabs knew for certain that if the man-of-war had been there, such things could not have been done.

Kama **hungalikuwa** mwasi, haya yote **yasingalitokea.**

If you had not been disobed-ient, all this would not have happened.

Watoto hao . . . kama **wa-ngalikuwa wakikaa** sana, **hawangaliweza** kupanda kurudi kwao katika Nchi ya Mawingu.

If these children had made a habit of staying too long, they would have been un-able to go up again to their home in Cloudland.

In negative Compound Tenses the *auxiliary* carries the negative particle SI when combined with -KI- and -ME- in the main verb.

Angekuwa mvivu, **asingeku-wa akisoma.**

If he were an idle fellow, he would not be continuing with his studies.

**Asingekuwa amechoka,** ange-rudi sasa hivi.

If he were not tired, he would return at once.

The *main verb* carries the negative particle when reference is made to a particular action.

[1] Note that diversity of opinion exists among educated Africans and Europeans as to the difference in usage between the two negative simple forms. However, the fact that both are used by present-day writers—and sometimes by the same writer at different times—and are heard in current speech suggests that both should be studied. Only the -SI-forms are given in the revised edition of *Steere's Exercises.*

| | |
|---|---|
| Kama mama yake **angekuwa hamkemei**, asingetoroka. | If his mother had not reproved him, he would not have run away. |

Note the use of the Impersonal Prefix I-.

| | |
|---|---|
| **Ingekuwa** watu hao **wakiendelea** kusoma, wangekuwa wenye kufaa wenzi wao. | If these people would continue to study, they would become of use to their fellow men. |
| **Ingekuwa** watu **wameendelea** kupanda vyakula mashambani, badala ya kuacha vipande vingi kujaa magugu na vichaka, **ingekuwa haijambo**. | If people had gone ahead with planting foodstuffs in their plantations, instead of allowing many parts of them to be full of weeds and bushes, it would be all to the good. |
| **Ingekuwa** hao wanaoitwa Reformers **wanafanya** kama hayo yaliyotajwa juu, hapo chama chao kingekuwa cha maana. | If those who are termed Reformers would do according to what has just been stated, their society would then serve some purpose. |

## -NGA- and -JAPO- Tenses

These forms frequently take the Impersonal Prefix I-.

| | |
|---|---|
| Labuda katika hiyo nyumba, huwamo mmoja ambaye **ingawa anakaa** humo humo, hampendi mwenye nyumba ile. | Perhaps in such a house there is a man who, although living there, dislikes the owner of the house. |
| **Ingawa hafanyi** kazi, si mvivu. | Although he does no work, he is not a lazy fellow. |
| **Ijapokuwa ananena** maneno mazuri, mara atakaponipata nyumbani kwake,. ataniuza utumwani. | Although he may be speaking fair words, when he gets me in his house, he will sell me into slavery. |
| 338. Mtu halali karibu na mto, **ujapokuwa umekauka** maji yake. | A man does not sleep near a river (bed), even though its water may be dried up. |

## C. ASPECT IN RELATION TO TIME

Certain Aspect tenses of the auxiliary may be followed by Time and HU- tenses in the main verb.

Kumwona Mfalme Mtukufu si neno dogo, na zaidi ** iki-wa** yeye mwenyewe **alifu-rahi** kutuona.

To see His Majesty is no small matter, especially as he himself was glad to see us.

Watoto **wakiwa hawakuta-zamwa** vizuri zaidi kuliko mtazamo wa kuku wa ki-shamba, basi nguvu zile za kutaga mayai mengi zita-potea na kuharibika.

If the chicks have not been given more care than that given to native fowls, the strength necessary to lay well will be lost and dissi-pated.

**Ikiwa hakwenda**, hawana bu-di kumwambia anajidai Uzungu.

If he did not go, they would undoubtedly tell him that he was claiming to be ac-quainted with European ways.

**Ikiwa tutapoteza** wakati we-tu wote kwa kuuliza ma-swali kama hayo, tutaji-fadhaisha sana.

If we are going to waste all our time in asking questions such as these, we shall give ourselves needless trouble.

**Ikiwa** mtoto **hufikiri** ya mi-chezo wakati wa kusoma, hapana budi ya kuwa ha-tasoma kitu cho chote.

If a child gets into the habit of thinking about games during lesson hours, he surely will not learn any-thing.

**Ingekuwa hawakujifundisha** kuwasha moto, na kulitu-mia jembe, na kwendeleza kalamu, tungekuwa bora sasa kuliko sokwe?

If they had not taught them-selves to make fire, to use the hoe, and to make pro-gress in the art of writing, should we now be any better than a chimpanzee?

Kibanda kilikuwa madhubu-ti sana, **ingawa kiliezekwa** na kuchomelewa kwa ma-jani.

The shed was very strong, even though it was thatched with grass and had been patched up.

## REFERENCE TABLE

### C. COMPOUND TENSES—ASPECT + TIME

| | Conditional Aspect | | Concession Aspect | |
|---|---|---|---|---|
| | **-KI-** | **-NGE-** | **-NGA-** | **-JAPO-** |
| Past **-LI-** | -KIWA -LI-<br>-KIWA HA--KU- | -NGEKUWA HA--KU- | -NGAWA -LI-<br>-NGAWA HA--KU- | -JAPOKUWA -LI-<br>-JAPOKUWA HA--KU- |
| Future **-TA-** | -KIWA -TA- | | | -JAPOKUWA -TA- |
| **HU-** | -KIWA HU- | | | |

| | |
|---|---|
| **Ijapokuwa** upepo **ulivuma** kwa dakika moja tu . . . | Although the wind blew for only a moment . . . |
| **Ijapokuwa** mgonjwa **ataona** maumivu wakati ule, lakini atastarehe baadaye. | Even though the patient will feel pain at the time, he will get relief afterwards. |

Sometimes a shortened form, JAPO, is used.

| | |
|---|---|
| Lazima ahudhurie, **japo hakupata** taarifa. | He must put in an appearance, even though he may not have received any notice. |
| Wanapokuwa wanakula mahali pengine kama hoteli, **japo wakiingia** nzi ishirini ndani ya chakula, hawaachi kula, labda kwa sababu . . . | When they eat elsewhere, say for instance at an hotel, even if twenty flies were to settle on the food, they would not leave off eating, probably because . . . |

# CHAPTER XXXVIII

## VERBS AND THEIR TENSES (Section IX)

## FURTHER COMPOUND FORMS BASED ON KUWA

### 1. NI, SI and the Subject Prefix

IT has been shown in the earlier chapters that predication without a verb is expressed by NI, SI or the Subject Prefix.

All these forms may be expressed in relation to Time or Aspect by the help of KUWA. They are best studied in three sections:

(a) *KUWA combined with NI and SI.*

$\left.\begin{array}{l}\text{-likuwa}\\\text{-takuwa}\\\text{-kiwa}\\\text{-kawa}\end{array}\right\}$ + NI or SI    $\left.\begin{array}{l}\text{huwa}\\\text{-ngekuwa}\\\text{-ngawa}\\\text{-japokuwa}\end{array}\right\}$ + NI or SI

| | |
|---|---|
| Basi kama mtu hakusema la moyoni mwake, **ilikuwa ni** kosa lake mwenyewe. | If anyone did not say all that was in his heart (*or* what he had in mind) to say, it was his own fault. |
| Siku zile **ilikuwa si** desturi kwa mtu kufanya neno kama hilo. | In those days it was not the custom for anyone to do a thing like this. |
| Hao watakufa, **tutakuwa** sisi **ni** wazee badili yao. | They will die, it is we who will be the parents in their stead. |
| Nitakusema[1] vyema kwa mfalme, na hivyo **itakuwa ni** ubora kwako kuliko fedha nyingi. | I will speak a good word for you to the king, and thus it will be more to your advantage than much silver. |
| **Ikiwa ni** za dhahabu, nitachukua zote. | If they are of gold, I will take them all. |

[1] But cf. p. 219.

264

**Ilivyokuwa M— ni** kwao, . . . watu wote anajuana nao. **Ikiwa si** ndugu, ni jamaa, **ikiwa si** jamaa, basi ni rafiki.

Seeing that M— is his native home, everyone knows him. If they are not brothers, they are relatives, and if they are not relatives, they are friends.

Walidhani kuwa labda amepotea mwituni. Tena **ikawa ni** kumwuliza habari za alikokuwa na aliyoyaona.

They thought that possibly he had got lost in the forest. And again there was a questioning of him as to where he had been and what he had seen.

Watu wengi wamejaza bongo zao kwa elimu na maarifa mengi sana, lakini hutokea **wakawa si** wastaarabu, kwani hawafuati waliyoyasoma.

Many people have crammed their brains with knowledge and much information, but they do not result in becoming people of education, for they do not follow what they read.

Na laiti kama **angekuwa ni** mtu mwingine aliyefanya jambo kama hili, wangempiga mawe pale njiani wakamwua.

If it had been anyone else who had done a thing like that, they would have stoned him there in the road and killed him.

(b) *Time tenses of KUWA combined with the Subject Prefix.*

**-likuwa**  
**-takuwa** } + { Subject prefix only.  
Subject prefix and NA.  
Subject prefix and -KO, -PO, -MO.

Generally speaking these compound time forms (especially in the negative) refer to a particular occasion, whereas the simple forms merely make a general statement. Compare:

Walikuwa tayari?

Were they ready?

Ilipofika saa sita wote **walikuwa wa** tayari.

By noon all were ready.

Lakini Kityatya hakuwa na hofu.

But Kityatya had no fear.

| | |
|---|---|
| Alipoamka asubuhi, **alikuwa hana** homa. | When he awoke in the morning, he had no fever. |
| Jee hawakuwako? | Were they not there? |
| Nilipofika, **walikuwa hawako**. | When I arrived, they were not there. |
| Ajiweke tayari kwa wakati wa mbele; akikulia kufanyiwa kila jambo bure, atakuta taabu kuu, **atakapokuwa hana** yale aliyokuwa akitegemea. | Let him get ready for the time ahead; if he comes crying to you to have everything done for him, he will come up against great difficulties, when he has not those things on which he used to depend. |

(c) *Aspect tenses of KUWA combined with the Subject Prefix.*

$$\left.\begin{array}{l} \text{huwa} \\ \text{-kawa} \\ \text{-kiwa} \\ \text{-ngekuwa} \\ \text{-ngalikuwa} \\ \text{-ngawa} \\ \text{-japokuwa} \end{array}\right\} + \left\{\begin{array}{l} \text{Subject prefix only.} \\ \text{Subject prefix and NA.} \\ \text{Subject prefix and -KO, -PO, -MO.} \end{array}\right.$$

| | |
|---|---|
| Kila akirudi kazini, **huwa yu** maji kwa kuchoka. | Every time he returns from work, he is overdone with fatigue. |
| Kila akija, **huwa ana** kitabu akisoma. | Always when he comes, he has a book and is reading it. |
| Ng'ombe zao hawapati malisho mengi. Kwa hiyo hudhofu sana na **huwa hawana** mafuta. | Their cattle do not get much pasturage. Because of this they are generally of poor quality and have no fat. |
| Kila ukisema naye, **huwa hana** la kusema. | Whenever you speak to him, he never has a word to say. |
| Kila akiitwa, **huwa hayuko**. | Whenever he is wanted, he is never there. |

Kulipia rupia kumi na tano kila mwezi si kitu, **ikiwa ipo** nafasi, ili mtoto wake mtu atengenee na aondoke na tabia njema.

To pay out 15 rupees a month is nothing if there is a vacancy, so that a person's child may be trained and leave with a disciplined character.

**Ikiwa ana** joto sana, mfute mwili wake kwa kitambaa cha maji.

If he is very hot, sponge his body with a wet cloth.

**Ikiwa hana** la kusema, haidhuru.

If he has nothing to say, never mind.

**Angawa yu** macho, hataki kuondoka.

Although he is awake, he does not want to get up.

**Ingawa hana** mali, amestarehe.

Although he is not wealthy, he is in comfortable circumstances.

**Ajapokuwa ana** kazi, hakosi kunisaidia.

Although he may be busy, he never fails to help me.

Note how the use of an aspect tense brings out a point which the simple form alone fails to do. This applies especially to **huwa** and **-kawa**.

Mwishoni . . . ukubwa wake **akawa hanao** tena.

In the end . . . he no longer has his high position.

To use the simple form here would merely state the fact, whereas the addition of **akawa** indicates the consequence of what has gone before.

## 2. The Subjunctive in Compound Forms

Compound forms of the Subjunctive are occasionally met with expressing some particular aspect of the verb which the simple form alone does not convey.

To express recurrency, action completed, or present time in the Subjunctive, the main verb (if any) takes -KI-, -ME-, -NA- or -A-, while the *auxiliary* verb is put into the Subjunctive.

Amri ikatoka hapo Kisauni ya kusema watu **wawe wakilala** mapema.

An order went forth at Kisauni saying that people were to go to bed early.

| | |
|---|---|
| Harudi mpaka **awe amewaua** wote. | He would not return until he had killed them all. |
| . . . kwa hivyo naona ni bora kuzitaja, **nisiwe nawanyima** waimbaji "tunu" ya wimbo mpya. | Because of this I feel it best to mention them (i.e. certain tunes), so that I do not deprive singers of the tune of a new song. |
| . . . na kwa siku chache **awe hana** kitu. | . . . so that in a few days he would have nothing. |

To express contingency or supposition, the *main verb* is put into the Subjunctive.

| | |
|---|---|
| **Ingalikuwa** kila picha **ipigwe** kwa mkono, ingalikuwa taabu nyingi sana. | If every picture were to have been made by hand, it would have involved much trouble. |
| **Ikiwa niandike** mambo yote, kitabu lazimu kuwa kikubwa sana kuliko hiki. | If I were to write about everything, the book would have to be very much larger than this. |

NGAA or ANGA, meaning "at least", is probably connected with NGA-WA. Here too the principal verb is in the Subjunctive.

| | |
|---|---|
| Sala nyingi ziliombwa juu ya hao . . . **ngaa waone** kikao cha salama. | Many prayers were offered on their behalf . . . that at least they might find a safe resting-place. |
| Haya, fanya upesi chakula kidogo, **anga nipate** nguvu nipate[1] toka nje. | Now then, get ready quickly a little food, that I may at least get strength enough to go outside. |

In many Bantu languages auxiliary verbs followed by the Subjunctive are used to express some adverbial aspect of the action, such as "almost to do", "just to do", etc. In Swahili these auxiliaries have been replaced by words or phrases, but the Subjunctive form of the verb which follows is generally retained.

[1] For meaning of **pata** see p. 276.

*Ndio kwanza.*

| | |
|---|---|
| Akamkuta mchinja nyama, **ndio kwanza achinje** ng'ombe. | He met a butcher, who had just then slaughtered an ox. |
| Wakajifanya kama watu waliokuwa **ndio kwanza wafike**. | They pretended to be people who had only that minute arrived. |

*Nusura* (Arabic borrowing).

| | |
|---|---|
| Ilikuwa **nusura azame**. | He almost sank. |
| Wewe Mrere sasa hivi **nusura ufe** kwa upanga wa Chaliwali. | You, Mrere, just this very minute almost died by the sword of Chaliwali. |
| . . . akawa **nusura afe** kwa baridi. | . . . and he was almost dead with cold. |

*Tangu.*

| | |
|---|---|
| **Tangu azaliwe**, hakupata[1] kuona mzungu. | From the day of his birth he had never seen a white man. |

*Lazima, sharti*, etc.[2]

| | |
|---|---|
| (Ni) **lazima aende**. | He must go. |

[1] See p. 276.
[2] Or may be followed by the infinitive. **(Ni) lazima kwenda.**

# CHAPTER XXXIX

## VERBS AND THEIR TENSES (Section X)

## THE AUXILIARIES NGALI, KWISHA AND JA

THESE auxiliaries are followed mostly by either the stem or the Infinitive form of the main verb. In addition they themselves may be combined with the auxiliary KUWA.

### The -NGALI[1] or "Still" Tenses

This form of the verb implies an action begun and going on in present, past or future time. Note that the main verb is in the Infinitive in the past and future tenses.

| | | |
|---|---|---|
| Present: | **Angali akisoma.** | He is still reading. |
| Past: | **Alikuwa angali kusoma.** | He was still reading. |
| Future: | **Atakuwa angali kusoma.** | He will be still reading. |

| | | |
|---|---|---|
| Present: | **Angali amelala.** | He is still asleep. |
| Past: | **Alikuwa angali kulala.** | He was still asleep. |
| Future: | **Atakuwa angali kulala.** | He will be still asleep. |

| | |
|---|---|
| Na pindi za mvua hata sasa **zingali zikishuka** kutoka nchi ya mawingu. | Even to the present day rainbows still come down from cloudland. |
| Alimwona yule kifaru **angali akicheka.** | He saw the rhino still laughing. |
| **Alipokuwa angali** mbali, baba yake akamwona. | While he was yet a long way off, his father saw him. |

*Note.* **ngali** is made from the **li** root meaning "to be", and can be used as a main verb.

| | |
|---|---|
| Angali kijana. | He is still a child. |
| Kungali mapema. | It is still early. |

Often the word **bado** replaces the **ngali** form.

| | |
|---|---|
| Alikuwa **bado** kusoma. | He was still reading. |
| **Bado** amelala. | He is still asleep. |

[1] **-kali** in Mombasa Swahili.

Yu **bado** kijana.                  He is still a child.

The -NGALI forms have no negative counterpart.

## The KWISHA ("already") and JA ("not yet") Tenses

| *Present Perfect* | *Past Perfect* | *Future Perfect* |
|---|---|---|
| **-mekwisha+** Infinitive | **-likuwa -mekwisha+** Infinitive | **-takuwa -mekwisha+** Infinitive |
| **Ha- -ja-** | **-likuwa ha--ja-** | **-takuwa ha--ja-** |

## KWISHA

Certain tenses formed on the auxiliary **kwisha** (to finish) followed by the verb stem with or without **ku-**, refer to a state existing, or action completed, before a point in time indicated in the context, whether that time be present, past or future. "Already" often expresses the force of these forms.

Amekwisha kwenda.[1]            He has already gone.
 (before a point in present time)
Alikuwa amekwisha kwenda.   He had already gone.
 (before a point in past time)
Atakuwa amekwisha kwe-     He will have already gone.
 nda.   (before a point in future time)

Alipokwisha sema, akaenda   When he had spoken (i.e. fin-
 zake.                                    ished speaking), he went off.

The **ku-** of the infinitive is often left out by some speakers. It is retained in monosyllabic verbs and **kwenda**.

*Further examples:*

Alipoona kuwa lile joka **lime-**   When he saw that the snake
 **kwisha kulala**, alimwita          was (already) asleep, he
 mwanawe.                                 called his son.

Lakini wakati huo mkutano   But by this time the meeting
 **ulikuwa umekwisha anza**.        had already begun.

Amekwisha ondoka kitambo.   He has already left some time
                                               ago.

Walikuwa wamekwisha ku-   They were already gathered
 **kusanyika** ila Jua.                 together except the Sun.

[1] **Ansha kwenda** is also heard in Mombasa Swahili.

| | |
|---|---|
| Wageni **walipokuwa wamekwisha pokea** zawadi, Jua likatoka kwenda kumtafuta Popo. | When the guests had received their presents, the Sun went out to look for the Bat. |
| Wakati huo **tulikuwa tumekwisha tekwa** nyara kale. | At this time we had already been taken captive long ago. |
| Tulipofika, hema **zilikuwa zimekwisha anza kupigwa**. | When we arrived the tents were already being pitched (Lit. had finished beginning to be set up). |
| Waambie warudi halafu— hapo **utakapokuwa umekwisha kula**. | Tell them to return presently —when you have finished eating. |

This form may also be combined with the HU- forms of the auxiliary and with -KI-.

| | |
|---|---|
| Wakati wa kukopa hufurahi, kwani zile haja zetu **huwa zimeisha**[1] **tekelezeka**, na **zikiisha tekelezeka**, husahau kulipa. | At the time of borrowing we are jubilant, because our needs are met, and once they are met, we often forget to repay. |

## -JA-

The *negative* counterparts of the KWISHA tenses indicate that the action or state has not yet occurred. Here -JA- is found, used as a tense prefix only.

| | |
|---|---|
| Haja(ku)ja. | He has not yet come. |
| Sijakula bado.[2] | I have not eaten yet. |
| Mpaka wakati huu **tulikuwa** bado **hatujaonana** na rafiki zetu. | Up to this time we had not yet met our friends. |
| Wakati ule walikuwa na njaa sana, kwani **walikuwa hawajalishwa** bado. | At that time they were very hungry, as they had not yet been fed. |

See next chapter for KUJA as an auxiliary verb.

[1] A local variation of **zimekwisha**.
[2] The addition of **bado** indicates expectation.

# CHAPTER XL

## VERBS AND THEIR TENSES (Section XI)

### OTHER AUXILIARIES

#### KUJA (to come)

KUJA, used as an auxiliary verb, refers to an action to take place at an implied time in the near or distant future. It is followed by the Future, the Subjunctive or the Infinitive form of the main verb.

*Affirmative*

| | |
|---|---|
| Nawe uwe na fahamu sawa sawa, **uje uwaeleze** wanao. | Now do understand thoroughly, so that (in future days) you may explain matters to your children. |
| Mkiambatana nami kwa kila jambo, **mtakuja kuwa** na cheo kama kile cha Mrere. | If you give me your loyalty in everything (now), later on you will have a position such as Mrere has. |
| Najua tutapata fedha, halafu **tutakuja tutatumia.** | I know we shall get some money, then later on we will use it. |
| Enda ukaombe moto, **tuje tuote**, maana baridi imezidi. | Go and beg some fire, so that we may then warm ourselves, for it has become colder. |
| Basi kafunge mlango kwanza **tuje tule.** | Well, first shut the door, and then let us eat. |

The *negative* form is generally followed by -KA-, and often expresses a "lest" idea.

| | |
|---|---|
| Nikumbushe, **nisije nikasahau**. | Remind me, lest I forget. |
| Aliogopa **asije akashindwa**. | He was afraid lest he should be conquered. |

| | |
|---|---|
| Nenda sasa, usikawie, **usije ukachelewa**. | Go quickly and do not delay, lest you be late. |
| Hakuna lililofunikwa **lisilo-kuja likafunuka** wazi. | There is nothing hid which shall not be revealed. |

The same idea of a point in time to be arrived at, or, negatively, a point not arrived at, is apparent also in those forms based on KUJA, which have been noticed elsewhere.

| | |
|---|---|
| Ha**ja**fika. | He has not yet arrived. |
| Kab(u)la asi**ja**fika *or* asi**je**fika. | Before he arrives. |
| A**ja**pofika. | Even if he should arrive. |

## KWENDA (to go)

As an auxiliary this verb has several meanings:

(i) With the -ME- or -LI- tense it indicates that the action is being carried out at the time indicated in the context. Here it is followed by the Infinitive or the verb stem.

| | |
|---|---|
| Maji **yamekwenda kuletwa**. | Water is just now being fetched. |
| Mwite Hamisi. Hamisi, Bwana, **amekwenda kuitwa**. | Call Hamisi. Hamisi, sir, is now being called. |
| Watumwa wengi **walikwenda fichwa** mbali sana kwa hofu ya Mwingereza. | Many of the slaves were being taken away to some distant place to be hidden for fear of the Englishman. |

(ii) With or without the subject prefix and with the relative -PO of time it indicates "should it happen, if by chance", etc.

| | |
|---|---|
| Na **wendapo** huyazingatii, huwezi kuelewa. | And if it happens that you do not give these (matters) consideration, you cannot be clear (about them). |
| **Endapo** nikienda, itakuwaje? | And supposing I do chance to go, how about it? |
| Na **endapo** katoka mmoja, basi lazima kuja mwingine kushika mahali pake. | Should it happen that one person goes out, it is essential that another should come to take her place. |

(iii) HUENDA followed by a -KA- or -ME- tense expresses "maybe, perhaps".

Akasema **Huenda ikawa** bahati yangu nikapata pembe.

He said "Maybe it will be my luck to get some ivory."

**Huenda** jambo lisilokuwa na faida sasa **likawa** na faida zama zinazokuja.

It may so happen that something which is of no profit now may chance to be of value at some future date.

Msitucheke sana, maana leo ni sisi, na kesho **huenda ikawa** ni siku yenu ya kuteseka.

Don't laugh at us overmuch, for although we are up against it to-day, maybe to-morrow will be your day of trouble.

Aliwaza **huenda** wale wenye nguvu zao **wakanuia** kumwua, na wengine **huenda wakatoroka**.

He thought that perhaps the strong ones were planning to kill him, and others perhaps to run away.

. . . kwani watu husema mengi aghalabu yale wanayoyapenda wenyewe, na **huenda ikawa hawayaamini** yale yaliyofika masikioni mwao.

. . . for people talk a great deal as a rule about what they themselves like, and perhaps do not give credence to hearsay.

## KUWEZA (to be able)

Certain negative tenses of WEZA have a specialized meaning.

Siwezi, huwezi, etc.

I am not well, you are not well, etc.

Nilikuwa siwezi, etc.

I was not well, etc.

Nitakuwa siwezi, etc.

I shall not be well, etc.

(Cf. Sijambo.

I am well.

Nilikuwa sijambo.

I was well.)

**Kujiweza** is frequently used to indicate ability to look after oneself.

Kipofu huyu hajiwezi.

This blind person cannot look after himself.

When used as an auxiliary, this verb assumes a meaning into which potentiality and possibility must be read. The English equivalent varies with the context, but the underlying idea remains constant. Its use can best be learnt from examples. It is followed by the Infinitive.

| | |
|---|---|
| Watoto **hawawezi** kupigwa jambo kama hili. | Children could not possibly be punished for a (small) matter such as this. |
| Mtu **huweza** kustaajabu. | One may well be surprised. |
| Hivi mtu **ataweza** kuelewa jinsi London ilivyo kubwa. | In this way it is possible for one to realize how big (a city) London is. |
| Hana fedha ya **kuweza** kuingilia melini. | He has no money to allow of his taking a passage on the mail steamer. |
| Mtu akijipitia ovyo, **aweza** kupondwa. | If anyone crosses the road without due care, he is liable to be run over. |
| Siku yo yote **waweza** kuwaona po pote. | Any day you can see them anywhere. |

## KUPATA (to get)

As an auxiliary it is followed by the verb stem with or without **ku-**. It implies ability or opportunity to accomplish something.[1] With a negative construction it may mean "never".

| | |
|---|---|
| Ni vizuri mji wetu ukue, adui zetu wakitushambulia, **tupate** washinda. | It is good that our town grows, so that if our enemies attack us, we may get the better of them. |
| Na wenyeji **wakapata** kuelimika kwa kazi za mikono. | The natives had opportunity to become skilled in handicrafts. |
| **Hajapata** kwenda kusafiri bado. | He has not yet had the chance to travel. |

[1] Cf. its use in: Kisu **hakipati**, p. 115. Note also: Mwezi umepatwa. "The moon is eclipsed." The traditional belief is that it is swallowed by a snake.

Kwa bahati njema aliona tunda moja, ambalo **haja-pata** kuliona mtu ye yote katika mji wao.

By good luck he saw a fruit, the like of which no one in their town had ever seen before.

Maneno matupu **hayajapata** kujenga mji.

Words only have never yet built a city.

## KUTAKA (to want) (see p. 36)

As an auxiliary it indicates "to be on the point of". It probably corresponds to an Immediate Future tense which many Bantu languages have in addition to a General Future and/or Far Future. This verb is also followed by the verb stem, with or without **ku-**.

Mtu huyu **ataka** kufa.

This man is at the point of death.

Damu hii iliyotapakaa jaha-zini ni ya nani? Ni ya sa-maki mkubwa, nimemkata **akitaka** kurukia jahazi.

Whose blood is this spattered over the dhow? It is that of a large fish. I cut it as it was about to jump (*or* fly) on to the dhow.

# CHAPTER XLI

## MISCELLANEOUS NOTES ON VERBS

### Uses of the Infinitive Form

I. When two actions are closely associated, and the second is not resultant or subsequent in time to the first, the second verb is put into the Infinitive.

| | |
|---|---|
| Watu walikuwa **wanaingia na kutoka**. | People were coming in and out. |

This construction does not imply that they first entered and then came out, nor that the same people went in and came out.

| | |
|---|---|
| Tulipenda **kusimama na kutazama** umande kama moshi uliojaa mabondeni, na **uliokuwa ukiyeyuka na kupotea** kila jua likizidi kupanda. | We liked to stand and watch the mist which filled the valleys like smoke, melting away and getting lost as the sun got higher and higher. |
| Tulionyeshwa mahali ngozi **zinaposafishwa na kupasuliwa** vipande viwili. | We were shown the place where hides are cleaned and split into two parts. |
| Mbele tuliona kilima **kikishuka na kushuka** mpaka mabondeni mbali huko. | In front of us we saw the mountain sloping away down to the valleys in the far distance. |

Should the construction be in the negative, **wala** must be used instead of **na**.

| | |
|---|---|
| Hakusema **wala** kucheka. | He neither spoke nor laughed. |

II. A verb in the Infinitive *preceding* the finite form of the same verb gives prominence to the idea conveyed by the verb.

A mother was asked if her daughter helped in the housework. Her reply was: "**Kufagia** afagia." (As for sweeping, she sweeps.) There is no emphasis on the mode of sweeping, whether thoroughly or otherwise.

| | |
|---|---|
| Hukusikia jana mbiu ya mgambo aliyotangaza mzee kuku, ya kuwa kuku akiona mdudu . . . awe chakula kwake, **kufa** afe tu pasipo huruma? | Did you not hear the fowl's proclamation yesterday, namely, that should a fowl see an insect, let it be food for him, let it die without mercy? |

III. When the Infinitive form *follows* the main verb, it imparts strong emphasis.[1]

| | |
|---|---|
| Akaanza kumwapiza akasema, Zama **kuzama** we! Zama kuko huko! | And he began to curse him, saying "Drown! Drown just there (where you are)! " |

IV. The Infinitive form of a verb is sometimes used in an impersonal sense.

| | |
|---|---|
| Kwa nini **kufanya** hivi? | Why do this? |

### Negative Forms of the Infinitive

The verb **toa** is used in the negative infinitive. It takes several forms, e.g.:

### kutoafanya, kutofanya, kutokufanya.

| | |
|---|---|
| Wengi huwa na desturi ya **kutokuandika** majina yao halisi katika "article" waziandikazo. | Many people have a custom of not writing their real names in articles which they write. |
| Huko **kutokusikilizana** kwao ndiko kulikofumua vita. | It was their lack of mutual understanding which started the war. |
| Kufika upesi, **kutofika** upesi ni mamoja, bora ni kufuliza kwenda. | Whether we arrive soon or whether we don't, it's all the same, what does matter is to get on with our journey. |

---

[1] These constructions are found in other Bantu languages. See Barlow's *Kikuyu Grammar*, p. 110.

Minazi si aghalabu **kutoku-zaa**.

It is unusual for coconut trees not to bear fruit.

It may also be used in the -KI- tense.

"Akija Hasani, **akitokuja** Huseini." Maana ya "idiom" hii ni kuonyesha kwamba kufanyika na **kutofa-nyika** kwa kitendo hicho ni sawasawa.

"If Hasani comes or if Huseini doesn't come." The point of this idiom is to indicate that whether some particular thing is done or not done it's all the same.

### Active Voice Constructions

Wendapi? Nenda **kukata** nywele.

Where are you off to? I am going for a haircut.

Amekwenda hospital **kuziba** meno au **kung'oa**?

Has he gone to the hospital to have his teeth filled or extracted? (for fillings or extractions?)

### Verbs of Prohibition, Prevention and Denial

Verbs such as **kana**, **zuia**, **kataa**, must be followed by a negative construction.[1]

Aliwakataza wanawe **wasi-toke** nje.

He forbade his sons to go outdoors.

Waarabu walipigiwa marufuku **wasikate** mikoko, wala **wasiteke** maji katika kisima cha Fundi James.

The Arabs were prohibited from cutting mangroves, or drawing water from the well belonging to Fundi James.

Alimzuia **asiende**.

He prevented him from going.

Baba amenikataza **nisisome**.

Father has forbidden me to read.

Leo halitawika jimbi ila utakwisha nikana mara tatu **kutoanijua**.

The cock shall not crow this day before thou shalt thrice deny that thou knowest Me.

[1] This construction is logical from a Bantu standpoint, if it is realized that the verbs **kukana**, **kukataa**, **kukataza** mean "to say 'no'," and that **kuzuia** means "to put an obstacle in the way of".

| | |
|---|---|
| Kuku alia Si mimi!—yaani ajaribu kukataa kuwa yeye **hakuwapo**. | The fowl calls out "Not me!" —that is to say, he tries to deny that he was there. |
| Hakukataza walimu **wasiende** katika mikahawa, bali walikatazwa wanafunzi tu. | He did not forbid teachers to visit cafes, only the pupils were forbidden. |

### Kuingia

Constructions with this verb are logical if its basic meaning is understood, viz. to enter into or pass into a *place* or *state*.

| | |
|---|---|
| Ameingia nyumbani. | He has entered the house. |
| Kisu kimeingia kutu. | The knife has become rusty, i.e. entered into a state of rust. |
| Nchi imeingia vita. | The country has entered upon a state of war. |
| Mji umeingia maradhi. | An epidemic is prevalent in the town, i.e. the town has entered into a state of epidemic. |
| Mji umeingia ndui. | Smallpox has made its appearance in the town. |

### More about KUWA and LI

WA in a Present or timeless tense carries a different implication from that of LI. It occurs in three contexts.

(*a*) With a pronominal relative + **-ote**.

| | | | |
|---|---|---|---|
| Niwaye yote. | Whoever I be. | Tuwao wote. | Whoever we be. |
| Uwaye yote. | Whoever you be. | Muwao wote. | Whoever you be. |
| Awaye yote. | Whoever he be. | Wawao wote. | Whoever they be. |
| Kiwacho chote. | Whatever it be. | Viwavyo vyote. | Whatever they be. |

*Examples:*

| | |
|---|---|
| **Awaye yote**, na aje. | Whoever he is, let him come. |

ĸ*

| | |
|---|---|
| Wakakaa katika hali hii siku nyingi pasipo hitilafu **iwayo yote**. | And they lived in this state for a long time without any difference of opinion arising. |
| 225. **Liwalo lo lote**, na liwe. | Whatever it is that is, be it so. |

(b) With an adverbial relative:

| | | | |
|---|---|---|---|
| Niwapo . . . | Should I be . . . | Tuwapo . . . | Should we be . . . |
| Uwapo . . . | Should you be . . . | Muwapo . . . | Should you be . . . |
| Awapo . . . | Should he be . . . | Wawapo . . . | Should they be . . |
| Kiwapo . . . | Should it be . . . | Viwapo . . . | Should they be . . . |
| | etc. | | etc. |

| | |
|---|---|
| Akasema Nitakuwa rafiki yako siku zote, na kukusaidia **uwapo** na shida. | And he said, I will be your friend for ever, and will help you should you be in difficulties. |

Negative forms are:

| | |
|---|---|
| Nisipo**kuwa** . . . | Unless I be . . . |
| Usipo**kuwa** . . . | Should you not be . . . |
| etc. | etc. |

(c) Without a relative particle. This is seldom heard except in negation.

| | |
|---|---|
| Si**wi**, etc. | I, etc., am not. |
| Haki**wi**, etc. | It, etc., is not. |
| Mtumishi **hawi** mkubwa kuliko bwana wake. | The servant is not greater than his master. |
| Mapenzi **hayawi** mapenzi ila yawe na wivu. | Love is not love except it contain (be with) jealousy. |
| Ninyi **hamwi** kama vile.[1] | Ye are not so. |
| 87. **Hawi** Musa kwa kuchukua fimbo. | He is not a Moses by carrying a rod. |
| 106. Subili **haiwi** tamu. | Aloes do not become sweet. |
| 200. Mchomwa mwiba **hawi** mtembezi. | He that has a thorn pricking him will not be a walker. |

LI forms without a relative are occasionally met with in proverbs. In modern Swahili the Subject Prefix alone suffices. See p. 95.

[1] St. Luke xxii. 25, Mombasa version.

516. Udongo upatize uLI
maji.

Use the clay while it is wet.

364. Mwana-mongwe    aLI
kwao, na mchanga
hangelile.

Were the nobly born one in
his native land, he had
never eaten sand.

(The forms **hangelile** for **hangalikula**, and **ali** for **yu**, attest
the antiquity of this proverb.)

Contrast the definiteness of LI and the indefiniteness of
WA in the following:

Ni-LI-ye.  I who am.

Ni-**wa**-ye yote.  Whoever I may
be.

Ni-LI-po.  When or where
I am.

Ni-**wa**-po.    Should I be.

Nilipokuwa kijana nilinena
kama kijana. . . . Sasa **ni-
lipo** mtu mzima, nimevio-
ndoa vile vya ujana.

When I was a child I spoke as
a child. . . . Now that I am
a man, I have put away
childish things.

**Uwapo** mtaratibu, wamshi-
**nda** mwenye nguvu.

When thou art a man of well-
ordered measures, thou dost
overcome the forceful man.

# CHAPTER XLII

## NOUNS

### FORMATION OF NOUNS FROM VERBS

Words derived from verbs are termed Deverbatives. Noun deverbatives take a prefix and a suffix. The prefixes concerned are the Class Prefixes and their underlying ideas have already been explained. The suffixes are -I, -JI, -U, -O, -E, -A; like the prefixes, each has its own significance except perhaps -A. They should be studied in conjunction with the prefixes in order to understand the exact meaning of each deverbative.

Suffixes **-i** and **-u** cause phonetic change in certain sounds of the verbal stem. Suffixes **-o, -e, -a** and **-ji** do not affect these sounds.

### SUFFIX -I

*Phonetic change brought about by Suffix -I.*

| Verb ending | Noun ending | Verb | | Noun | |
|---|---|---|---|---|---|
| Two vowels | ZI | **okoa** | save | **mwokozi** | Saviour |
| LA | ZI | **lala** | sleep | **malazi** | sleeping arrangements |
| NDA | NZI | **panda** | sow | **mpanzi** | sower |
| KA | { SHI | **pika** | cook | **mpishi** | cook |
| | { SI | **suka** | plait | **msusi** | ladies' hairdresser |
| TA | SI | **fuata** | follow | **mfuasi** | follower |
| MBA | MVI | **gomba** | quarrel | **ugomvi** | quarrel |
| | { WI | **ziba** | stop up | **kiziwi** | deaf person |
| BA | { VI | **iba** | steal | { **mwivi** | thief |
| | { ZI | | | { **mwizi** | |
| WA | VI | **lewa** | be drunk | **mlevi** | drunkard |
| PA | FI | **lipa** | pay | **mlifi** | payer |
| NGA | NZI | **jenga** | build | **mjenzi** | builder |

Other consonants are unaffected.

| | **soma** | read | | **msomi** | reader |

Nor are the above sounds affected in all cases. Compare:

| | **pinda** | bend | | **pindi** | a bend |
| | **kopa** | borrow | | **mkopi** | borrower |
| | **ua** | kill | | **nduli** | killer |

284

*Function.*

M- WA- and KI- VI- deverbatives with -I as suffix indicate the person or thing which does the action.

MA- deverbatives with -I as suffix express the action, the process or method whereby the action is carried out. They also convey a plural concept; this is consistent with the basic meaning of MA-, p. 67. With U- as prefix the action is viewed in the abstract as a whole.

| | *Verb* | | M- WA- | MA- | U- |
|---|---|---|---|---|---|
| lea | bring up, educate | mlezi | a nurse, tutor governess | malezi | ulezi |
| shona | sew | mshoni | a tailor | mashoni | ushoni |
| zika | bury | mzishi | an undertaker | mazishi | uzishi |
| tumika | be employed | mtumishi | a paid servant | matumishi | utumishi |
| linda | guard | mlinzi | a watchman | malinzi | ulinzi |
| | | KI- VI- | | | |
| ongoza | lead | kiongozi | a leader | maongozi | uongozi |
| nyoa | shave | kinyozi | a barber | manyozi | unyozi |

Note also **mboni** (N- Class = pupil of the eye) from **ona** (see).

No English is given to the MA- and U- forms, as it is difficult to give an exact meaning to words standing in isolation. Difference in meaning is exemplified in such words as:

**matumishi** services, acts of service    **utumishi** service

The student should consult the dictionary here and elsewhere in this chapter.

# SUFFIX -JI

This expresses habituality or repetition. It is the corresponding noun suffix of the verb suffix -GA found in many Bantu languages to express repetitive action or state.[1] It occurs mostly in nouns of the M- WA- Classes.

| | | | |
|---|---|---|---|
| **mwindaji** | a professional hunter | **mtazamaji** | a spectator |
| | | **mchezaji** | a member of a sports team |
| **msomaji** | a reader | | |
| **mwombaji** | a professional beggar | **mwimbaji** | a professional singer, chorister |

---

[1] -GA is found in Swahili in verbs such as **koroga** (stir), **taga** (lay eggs), **kanyaga** (tread), etc. See p. 216. But note derived noun **mkorogi** (stirrer, agitator).

Notice the following occurrences of -JI in nouns of other classes:

| | | | |
|---|---|---|---|
| **uwindaji** | hunting | **uombaji** | professional begging |
| (mti) **mtambaaji** | a creeper | | |
| **kinwaji** | beverage | | |

## SUFFIX -U

*Phonetic change brought about by Suffix -U.*

| Verb ending | Noun ending | Verb | | Noun | |
|---|---|---|---|---|---|
| Two vowels | VU | **legea** | be slack | **ulegevu** | slackness |
| KA | FU | **punguka** | diminish | **upungufu** | shortage |

These suffixes are inconsistent and overlap to a considerable extent. Compare:

| | | | |
|---|---|---|---|
| **okoa** | save | **wokovu** *or* **wokofu** | deliverance |
| **choka** | be tired | **mchofu** *or* **mchovu** | one who tires easily |

Similarly suffixes **-ivu** *or* **-ifu** may be used in the formation of nouns from verbs of Arabic origin.

| | | | |
|---|---|---|---|
| **haribu** | destroy | **uharibifu** | destruction |
| **sahau** | forget | **msahaulivu** *or* **msahaulifu** | a forgetful person |

Sound change does not take place in every instance.

**kua**  grow  **ukuu**  greatness

*Function.*

Words with -U as Suffix express the possessor of a state when used with M- WA- prefixes, and the state itself with prefix -U.[1]

| | Verb | M- WA- | | U- |
|---|---|---|---|---|
| **potea** | lose | **mpotevu** | a wasteful person | **upotevu** |
| **tulia** | be quiet | **mtulivu** | gentle quiet person | **utulivu** |
| **tukuka** | be exalted | **mtukufu** | an exalted person | **utukufu** |
| **kunjuka** | be unfolded | **mkunjufu** | a genial amiable man | **ukunjufu** |

[1] There are also some deverbative adjectives ending in -U. See p. 46.

Many nouns with Suffix -U are made from intransitive verbs, whereas those with Suffix -I are mainly derived from transitive verbs.

Some verbs give rise to two nouns, the -U suffix stresses State and -I indicates Activity.

| Verb | | -U of State | | -I of Activity |
|---|---|---|---|---|
| ikia | msikivu | a well-disciplined | msikizi | a hearer, one who |
| ear | | obedient person | msikiaji | attends classes |
| ngalia | mwangalivu | a careful attentive | mwangalizi | a caretaker, |
| ake care | | person | mwangaliaji | guardian |
| osa | mkosevu | a careless person | mkosaji | one who makes |
| rr | | by temperament | | mistakes |

## SUFFIX -O

This suffix has a wide function, which varies according to the prefix with which the suffix is used.

With names of *concretes* -O indicates the instrument which implements the action of the verb. Words of this kind are found mainly in the KI- VI- Classes, but a few also occur in other Classes.

| Verb | | KI- VI- | |
|---|---|---|---|
| tua | alight | kituo | stopping-place |
| funika | cover | kifuniko | lid |
| ziba | stop up | kizibo | stopper |
| vuka | cross | kivuko | ford |
| funga | fasten | kifungo | button |
| pima | measure | kipimo | measure |
| | | U- N- | |
| fungua | unfasten | ufunguo | key |
| fagia | sweep | ufagio | brush |
| pepea | sift | upepeo | winnowing tray |
| | | M- MI- | |
| tega | entrap | mtego | trap |
| shona | sew | mshono | seam |
| | | JI- MA- | |
| ponya | make well | ponyo | remedy |
| sikia | hear | sikio | ear |
| | | N- | |
| unda | construct | nyundo | hammer |

With names of *non-concretes* -O indicates verbal action or

its ultimate results. Words of this kind are mostly found in the M- MI- and JI- MA- Classes. Those in the M- MI- Classes refer to the action as a whole, and many of these words are not used in the plural. Those which are found in the JI- MA- Classes frequently refer to actions which can occur singly, but which normally occur collectively. Words normally found only in the MA- Class express a collective idea of action, or the process by means of which the action is carried out; many of these are made on the -ANA form of the verb. A few words are in the U- and N- Classes. For the various translations of the following nouns see the dictionary.

| *Verbs* | | M- | MI- |
|---|---|---|---|
| sema | say | msemo | |
| isha | finish | mwisho | |
| enda | go | mwendo | |
| gota | knock | mgoto | |
| tetema | tremble | mtetemo | |
| lia | cry | mlio | milio |
| cheza | play | mchezo | michezo |
| | | JI- | MA- |
| nena | speak | neno | maneno |
| piga | strike | pigo | mapigo |
| waza | think | wazo | mawazo |
| funza | teach | funzo | mafunzo |
| tenda | act | tendo | matendo |
| ondolea | remove | | maondoleo |
| onja | taste | | maonjo |
| onya | warn | | maonyo |
| patana | agree | | mapatano |
| jibizana | answer one another | | majibizano |
| kutana | meet together | | makutano |
| | | U- | N- |
| imba | sing | wimbo | nyimbo |
| apa | swear | uapo | nyapo |
| | | N- | N- |
| ota | dream | ndoto | ndoto |
| nguruma | growl | ngurumo | |

Certain words like **maponyo**, **mazuio** can be used in reference to both concretes and abstracts.

## SUFFIX -E

Noun deverbatives ending in -E express passivity or the sufferer of an action, whether the sufferer be animate or inanimate.

| *Verb* | | **M- WA-** | |
|---|---|---|---|
| **shinda** | conquer | **mshinde** | a vanquished one |
| **tuma** | send | **mtume**[1] | a sent one, apostle |
| **pamba** | decorate | **mpambe** | a bedecked one, generally a serving girl |
| **teua** | choose | **mteule** | a chosen one, such as for leadership, etc. |
| | | **KI- VI-** | |
| **toboa** | pierce | **kitobwe** | a hole made by piercing |
| **tona** | fall in drops | **kitone** | a small drop of liquid |
| **peta** | bend | **kipete** | something bent round, a small ring, ferrule, etc. |
| **umba** | create | **kiumbe** | a created thing |
| **zidisha** | multiply | **kizidishe** | multiplicand |
| **ta** | put forth | **kite** | something put forth, a groan, etc. |
| | | **MA-** | |
| **ta** | put forth | **mate** | saliva, etc. |
| **hama** | remove | **mahame** | a place from which people have removed |
| **vunda** | be high (of meat) | **mavunde** | something which has become high |
| **tanda** | spread out | **matande** | something spread out, hence used of a frame or sticks or a line upon which clothes are hung out to dry |
| | | **M- MI-** | |
| **kata** | cut | **mkate** | a loaf (of bread) or a plug of tobacco |

[1] pl. **mitume** with **wa** concords.

| Verb | | N- | |
|------|------|------|------|
| peta | bend | pete | a ring |
| | | U- | |
| shinda | conquer | ushinde | a state of being vanquished |

## SUFFIX -A

Some deverbatives with -A as suffix occur in all classes, and in words such as the following the suffix appears to carry no distinctive meaning.

| Verb | | M-, WA- | |
|------|------|------|------|
| ogopa | fear | mwoga | coward |
| wia | be owed[1] | mwia | creditor |
| wiwa | owe | mwiwa | debtor |
| lima | cultivate | mkulima[2] | cultivator |
| | | MA- | |
| tata | tangle | matata | complications |
| zoea | get used to | mazoea | familiarity |
| nyonyota | drizzle | manyonyota | drizzle |
| teka | plunder | mateka | booty |
| kosa | err | makosa | mistakes |
| | | KI- VI- | |
| chana | separate | kitana[3] | comb |
| pewa[4] | be given | kipawa | gift |
| faa | suit | kifaa | useful thing |
| nywa | drink | kinywa | mouth |
| | | U- | |
| shinda | conquer | ushinda | conquest |
| ogopa | fear | woga | fear |
| ganga | cure | uganga | doctoring |
| | | M- MI- | |
| zinga | go round | mzinga | anything of cylindrical shape |
| | | N- | |
| ja | come | njia | path |
| oa | marry | ndoa | marriage |

[1] See Dictionary under Prepositional form of WA.
[2] The -ku- element is probably from root KUU = great. Cf. **mkufunzi** a skilled apprentice, **mkurugenzi** a leader, pioneer. (**genda** < **enda**.)
[3] t and ch are sometimes interchangeable.
[4] pawa in Mombasa and old Swahili.

Some deverbatives of the M- WA- and KI VI- Classes, which express the doer of the action or impersonal agency, end in -A and are followed by a qualifying noun to particularize the meaning.

| | | | |
|---|---|---|---|
| **shona** | sew | **mshona viatu** | a sewer of shoes, i.e. a shoemaker |
| **panda** | mount | **mpanda farasi** | a horseman |

This happens particularly in the case of verbs which cover a wide variety of meanings.

| | | | |
|---|---|---|---|
| **mpiga pasi** | ironer | **mwuza ng'ombe** | cattle dealer |
| **mpiga kinanda** | pianist, organist | **mwuza watu** | slave trader |
| | | **mwuza samaki** | fishmonger |
| **mpiga chapa** | printer | **mwuza chakula** | grocer |
| **mpiga mbiyu** | town crier | | |
| **mpiga ngoma** | drummer | | |
| **mpiga picha** | photographer | | |
| **mpiga simu** | telegraphist | | |

When there is no likelihood of misunderstanding, the qualifying noun is occasionally omitted.

260. Mgema (tembo) akisifi-   If the winetapper has his
wa tembo, hulitia ma-   toddy praised (in his hear-
ji.   ing), he puts water in it.

A few nouns in the KI- VI- Classes express *impersonal* agency:

| | |
|---|---|
| **kifunga bei** | a deposit on something |
| **kishika kalamu** | a tip on commencing a task of writing |
| **kipa mkono** | a wedding fee |
| **kinyosha mgongo** | a tip after carrying a heavy load—a back-straightener |
| **kiinua mgongo** | (of same import) |
| **kichinja** (*or* **kitinda**) **mimba** | the youngest child |
| **kifungua tumbo** | the firstborn |

Note that nouns ending in -JI may also take a qualifying noun.

**mwangaliaji hostel** the warden of a hostel

The qualifying noun, if used with nouns ending in -I or -U, is generally introduced by the -A of relationship.

| | |
|---|---|
| Mshoni wa viatu. | A shoemaker, a shoe repairer |
| Mkunjufu wa moyo | An open-hearted man |
| Mwongofu wa dini | A convert to religion |

## Aphorisms illustrating the -A Suffix

254. Mchea mwana kulia hulia mwenyewe.
He that fears lest his child cry will cry himself.

258. Mfumbata moshi.
A grasper at smoke.

279. Mla mbuzi hulipa ng'ombe.
The eater of a goat pays a cow.

302. Mpa nyongo si mwenzio.
The giver of the back is not thy companion.

308. Mpiga konde ukutani huumiza mkonowe.
He that smites his fist upon the wall hurts his hand.

317. Mtaka yote hukosa yote.
He that wants all is wont to lose all.

331. Mchimba kisima njiani huingia yeye, mwandani.
The digger of a well in the pathway gets into it himself, friend.

398. Mzika pembe ndiye mzua pembe.
The burier of the ivory is the bringer to light of the ivory.

439. Nyati mwenda-pweke.
A buffalo that goes alone.

As can be seen, this construction often corresponds to a relative phrase in English. See also Aphorisms 311 (p. 73) and 323 (p. 256).

## Nouns formed from Derivative Verbs

There are a great many nouns derived from both simple and derivative verbs, which show a corresponding change in their meaning. This difference in meaning often necessitates the use of an entirely different noun in English, as the following examples indicate:

| Verb | | Noun | |
|---|---|---|---|
| patana | agree | mapatano | agreement |
| patanisha | | mapatanisho | reconciliation |
| zaa | bear | mzazi | parent |
| | | mzao, mazao | offspring |

| zalia | | mzalia | one born at ... |
| zalisha | | mzalisha | midwife |
| tuma | send | mtume | one sent, an apostle |
| tumika | | mtumishi | servant |
| tumwa | | mtumwa | slave |
| la | eat | mla, mlaji | eater |
| lisha | | mlisha | herdsman |
| funga | fasten | kifungo | fastener |
| fungua | | ufunguo | key |
| toa | put out | mtoaji | giver |
| toza | | mtozi | exactor |
| omba | pray | mwombi | suppliant |
| ombea | | mwombezi | interceder |
| enda | go | mwendo | journey |
| endelea | | maendeleo | progress |
| endesha | | mwendesha gari | engine-driver |
| lipa | pay | malipo | payment |
| lipiza | | malipizo | revenge |
| andama | follow in order | mwezi mwanda-mo | the following month |
| andamia | | mwandamizi | successor[1] |
| andamana | | mwandamano | procession |

Note also nouns made from the Associative form of derivative verbs, such as **masikilizano** (mutual respect < **sikilizana** < **sikiliza** < **sikia** (hear).

## Arabic Loan Words

Verbs and verbal nouns of Arabic origin generally show a difference in vowel quality, because they have been adopted direct from the corresponding Arabic forms.

| *Verb* | | *Noun* | |
| safiri | travel | safari | journey |
| hutubu | give an address | hotuba | address |
| subiri | be patient | subira | patience |
| abudu | worship | ibada | worship |

[1] Aph. 47. **Boriti ina mwandamizi wake.** A (fallen) beam has its successor, i.e. It never rains but it pours.

| *Verb* | | *Noun* | |
|--------|--------|--------|--------|
| hasibu | count | hesabu | arithmetic |
| furahi | rejoice | furaha | joy |
| sali | pray | sala | prayer |
| tubu | repent | toba | repentance |
| dhuru | harm | madhara | harm |
| samehe | forgive | msamaha | forgiveness |
| amini | believe | imani | faith |
| sifu | praise | sifa | praise |
| fariji | comfort | faraja | comfort |

On the other hand, however, nouns may be also derived from Arabic verbs in a Bantu manner.

| *Verb* | | *Noun* | |
|--------|--------|--------|--------|
| safiri | travel | msafiri | a traveller |
| samehe | forgive | msameheji | merciful person |
| badili | change | ubadilifu | exchange |
| starehe | be at ease | ustarehevu | tranquillity |

This fact will account for synonyms like the following:

| *Verb* | | *Noun* | |
|--------|--------|--------|--------|
| hasidi husudu | } envy | uhasidi husuda | } envy |
| himidi | praise | himidi hamdu | } praise |
| halifu | oppose | uhalifu halafa | } opposition |
| jalidi | whip, scourge | mjeledi jalada | } whip |

# CHAPTER XLIII

# NOUNS (continued)

## DIMINUTIVES, AUGMENTATIVES AND COLLECTIVES

CERTAIN nouns, by a change of prefix, may express a diminutive, augmentative or collective idea, which sometimes, but not necessarily always, conveys a derogatory implication as well.

### Diminutives

The KI- and VI- prefixes are used to express a diminutive idea, with or without a derogatory implication. The resultant forms are subject to certain phonetic rules:

Disyllabic or polysyllabic roots take KI-, pl. VI-.

| | | | | |
|---|---|---|---|---|
| mtoto | child | kitoto | infant | vitoto |
| mjakazi | female slave | kijakazi | girl slave | vijakazi |
| mtwana | male slave | kitwana | youth of slave class | vitwana |
| mlima | mountain | kilima | hill | vilima |
| mbuzi | goat | kibuzi | little goat | vibuzi |
| njia | road, path | kijia | narrow path | vijia |
| kombe | platter, etc. | kikombe | cup | vikombe |
| pete | ring | kipete | ferrule | vipete |
| uvuli | shade | kivuli | shadow | vivuli |

Where the root is monosyllabic or begins with a vowel, -J(I)- is inserted.

| | | | | |
|---|---|---|---|---|
| mtu | person | kijitu | dwarf, etc. | vijitu |
| mji | town | kijiji | hamlet | vijiji |
| mto | river | kijito | streamlet | vijito |
| kichwa | head | kijichwa | small head | vijichwa |
| jiwe | stone | kijiwe | pebble | vijiwe |
| mwana | son, daughter | kijana | child, youth | vijana |
| mwiko | spade, etc. | kijiko | spoon | vijiko |
| nyoka | snake | kijoka | small snake | vijoka |

-JI- may also be inserted before disyllabic roots to express an additional diminutive idea, generally with a derogatory implication.

| | | | |
|---|---|---|---|
| mtoto | child | kijitoto | a very small infant |
| mbuzi | goat | kijibuzi | a poor specimen of a goat |
| pesa | pice | vijipesa | a few worthless pice |
| duka | shop | kijiduka | an insignificant little shop |

*Examples;*

| | |
|---|---|
| Basi wale ndugu zake waka-tumia sehemu ya mali yao, wakajiwekea **viduka**. | So his brothers used a portion of their wealth, and set up small shops for themselves. |
| Wakaona mali zao zote si kitu, wakaacha **vijiduka** vyao wakahama. | And they saw their wealth become as nothing again, so they left their good-for-nothing little shops and removed elsewhere. |
| Nipe chakula hicho tu—pumba na **kibuzi**. | Give me this food only—some chaff and a small goat. |
| Ananitia aibu kwa ile pumba na kile **kijibuzi**. | He is insulting me with the chaff and that poor specimen of a goat. |
| Ala[1] Bwana! Mbona unajia-ndalia pekeyo! hunibaki-shii hata **kijikiroma** ki-moja? | Sir! Why are you putting them (i.e. coconuts) aside for yourself only! Aren't you leaving even one poor little unripe coconut for me? |

## Augmentatives (Amplicatives)

Nouns may take the prefixes of the JI- Class with plural prefixes MI- or MA- to give them an augmentative or amplicative meaning in regard to size, number or character.

Where the root is monosyllabic or begins with a vowel, the prefix is J(I)- in the singular, and this prefix is retained in the plural.

| | | | | | |
|---|---|---|---|---|---|
| mtu | person | jitu | giant | mijitu and majitu |
| mti | tree | jiti | large tree | mijiti and majiti |

[1] An expression of impatience, annoyance, etc.

| | | | | | |
|---|---|---|---|---|---|
| **mto** | river | **jito** | large river | **mijito** and **majito** |
| **kisu** | knife | **jisu** | large knife | **majisu** |
| **mwana** | child | **jana** | loutish youth | **mijana** and **majana** |
| **nyoka** | snake | **joka** | large snake | **majoka** |
| **nyuni** | bird | **juni** | large bird | **mijuni** |
| **nyumba** | house | **jumba** | large house | **majumba** |
| **nyungu** | cooking-pot | **jungu** | large cooking-pot | **majungu** |

With most disyllabic and polysyllabic roots no prefix is apparent in the singular (compare other words in the JI-Class, pp. 65–6), and the plural prefix is MA-.

| | | | | | |
|---|---|---|---|---|---|
| **mtoto** | child | **toto** | a big fine child | **matoto** |
| **kidude** | a what-you-call-it | **dude** | a big what-you-call-it | **madude** |
| **paka** | cat | **paka** | a big cat | **mapaka** |
| **tanzi** | loop | **tanzi** | a big loop | **matanzi** |
| **chungwa** | orange | **chungwa** | a big variety of orange | **machungwa** |
| **kawa** | dish cover | **kawa** | a large dish cover | **makawa** |

In the last four examples, although no difference appears in the written word, there is considerable difference in the pronunciation of the N- and JI- Class words. In the former the **p**, **t**, **ch** and **k** are aspirated, in the latter there is no aspiration.

In the following examples also, there is a difference in pronunciation, viz. in the N- Class forms the **b**, **d**, **j** and **g** are explosive whereas normal **b**, **d**, **j** and **g** are implosive. (Cf. p. 4.)

| | | | | | |
|---|---|---|---|---|---|
| **mbuzi** | goat | **buzi** | large goat | **mabuzi** |
| **ndege** | bird | **dege** | large bird | **madege** |
| **njia** | road | **jia** | broad path | **majia** |
| **ngoma** | drum | **goma** | large drum | **magoma** |

A few disyllabic nouns take JI- in the singular and retain it in the plural.

| | | | | | |
|---|---|---|---|---|---|
| **kivuli** | shadow | **jivuli** | big shadow | **majivuli** |
| **nguzo** | pillar | **jiguzo** | big pillar | **majiguzo** |

Augmentatives, when used in reference to living beings or animals, are followed by like concords, not by concords of the M- WA- Classes.

| | |
|---|---|
| Lile joka kuu, lililowala watu wengi, limekamatwa. | The big snake, who ate so many people, has been caught. |
| Jana hili. | This ill-mannered child. |

The same rule, however, does not always apply to diminutives. Compare:

| | |
|---|---|
| Kijana huyu. | This child. |
| Kitwana hiki. | This slave lad. |

## Collectives

Some nouns belonging to the U- and the N- Classes have two plural forms, with a corresponding differentiation in meaning. The plural form in N- expresses mere plurality of the singular form; the plural form in MA- expresses collectiveness.

| *Singular* | | *Plural* | | *Collective* |
|---|---|---|---|---|
| unyasi | blade of grass | nyasi | manyasi | weeds, grass in general |
| unyoya | strand of hair or wool | nyoya | manyoya | hair, wool, etc. |
| simba | lion | simba | masimba | a pride of lions |
| fisi | hyena | fisi | mafisi | a pack of hyenas |
| samaki | fish | samaki | masamaki | a shoal of fish |
| rafiki | friend | rafiki | marafiki | a circle of acquaintances |
| baba | father | baba | mababa | forefathers |
| pesa | pice | pesa | mapesa | small change |
| kabila | tribe | kabila | makabila | tribes in general |
| taifa | nation | taifa | mataifa | nations in general |

Note that the MA- as amplicative of size or number and the MA- denoting collectiveness are not mutually exclusive. Context indicates the particular meaning to be read into this prefix.

*Examples.*

| | |
|---|---|
| Afadhali kuvumilia joto kuliko kuliwa na **masimba**. | It is better to put up with great heat than to be eaten by a whole lot of lions. |
| Walitaka kumtosa majini, aliwe na mamba na **masamaki**. | They were about to throw him into the water, to be eaten by crocodiles and big fish. |
| **Mapaka** mengi hayagwii panya. | Too many cats do not catch a rat. |
| Ah, kula **manyamanyama**[1] yako wee! | All right then, eat your old animals! |

Another aspect of collectiveness is apparent in the use of MA- to express the process, method, etc., of action in contrast to the purely abstract idea expressed by U-.

**kugomba** to scold   **ugomvi** quarrelling   **magomvi** quarrels
See p. 67.

## THE NOMINAL CONSTRUCTION

A characteristic of Bantu speech is the frequent use of nouns with no preceding preposition to introduce them. This is termed here the "Nominal Construction", and in recognition of this idiom lies the key to much that would otherwise baffle the student in the understanding of Swahili.

The Nominal Construction occurs in three different contexts:

I. After Intransitive, Neuter and Passive verbs, the noun adds some detail in respect to the action or state expressed by the verb, whether in time, place, manner or reason, etc.

| | |
|---|---|
| Alifika **usiku**. | He arrived at night. |
| Amekwenda **Mombasa**. | He has gone to Mombasa. |
| Mto umekauka **maji**. | The river is dried up (water)- |
| Walivunjwa **viungo vyao**. | Their limbs were broken. (Lit. They were broken (as to) their limbs.) |
| Matanga yalitota **maji**. | The sails were soaked through with water. |

[1] Reduplication to express diversity, See also p. 316.

| | |
|---|---|
| Walikufa **maji**. | They were drowned. (Lit. They died water.) |
| Alitulizwa **moyo**. | His mind was put at ease. |
| Wana heri walio safi **moyo**. | Blessed are the pure in heart. |
| Ameumia **mwili wote**. | He feels pain all over his body. |
| Watoto walipangwa **safu** wawili wawili. | The children were arranged in rows two abreast. |
| 187. Kununua ng'ombe **wayo**. | To buy an ox by his hoof mark. |
| Matanga yalishiba **upepo** hata yakapasuka. | The sails were so full of wind that they split. |
| Nchi yenyewe yaonekana kama isiyopandika **kitu**. | The country itself appears incapable of supporting any vegetation. |
| Walikwenda **kichwa wazi**. | They went bareheaded. |
| Tumekaa **nyumba moja**. | We live in one house. |
| Wazazi wangu walikufa **mfulizo**. | My parents died one after the other in quick succession. |
| Mji mzima uliwashwa **taa**. | The whole town was lit up with lamps. |
| Njoo **saa tano**. | Come at eleven o'clock. |
| Watoto, simameni **msimamo wa kiaskari**. | Children, stand like soldiers. |
| Amekamatwa **utumwa**. | He has been taken away into slavery. |

II. It is met with in sentences with an adverbial subject; here the noun corresponds to the *subject* in the English translation.

| | |
|---|---|
| Humu nyumbani mmelala **watu wengi**. | Many people are asleep in this house. |
| Hazina zenu za akiba ziwekeni mbinguni, pasipoharibika **kitu** kwa nondo wala kutu. | Lay up for yourselves treasure in heaven, where neither moth nor rust doth corrupt. |
| Kwa Fulani kumekufa **mtu**. | Someone has died at So-and-so's house. |
| Kuliwekwa **askari**. | Some soldiers were stationed there. |

III. It occurs with a Transitive verb which already has a direct object, and supplies some further detail in connection with the action of the verb.

| | |
|---|---|
| Amejikata **kidole**. | He has cut his finger (cut himself as to the finger). |
| Atakuponya upesi **mguu wako**. | He will soon cure your leg (cure you as to your leg). |
| Wakatushika **mkono**. | They took us by the hand. |
| Jiwe likampiga na kumvunja **mguu**. | The stone struck him and broke his leg. |
| Hukunisadiki **maneno yangu**. | You did not believe my words. |

In the foregoing sentences the direct object is a *pronoun*, and the noun supplies the detail. Sometimes, however, *two nouns* are used, one of which is the direct object while the other supplies the detail. Word order depends on the relative importance of the two nouns in the mind of the speaker, though the direct object usually comes first, and is frequently emphasized by the use of the Object Prefix.

| | |
|---|---|
| (Zi)jazeni ndoo maji. | Fill the buckets with water (not milk). |
| Zijazeni maji ndoo. | Fill the buckets (not tin cans) with water. |

In both sentences **maji** supplies the detail and is in the Nominal Construction.

Should one of the nouns be qualified by a phrase, etc., this always comes last, otherwise the remaining noun would be too far away from the verb.

| | |
|---|---|
| Ni kama kumpa maji mtu **asiye na kiu**. | It is like giving a man who is not thirsty some water. |
| Zijazeni ndoo maji **ya moto**. | Fill the buckets with hot water. |
| Jazeni maji ndoo **hizi zote mbili**. | Fill both these buckets with water. |

It should also be noted that in constructions where attention is directed to the object of the verb, this may even precede the verb itself.

| | |
|---|---|
| **Ndoo hizi** zijaze maji. | Fill these buckets with water. |

This construction is useful when both nouns are qualified:

| | |
|---|---|
| Ndoo hizi mbili zijaze maji ya moto. | Fill these two buckets with hot water. |

The following sentences exemplify variation in word order:

| | |
|---|---|
| Sungura akakijaza maji kibuyu chake. | The Hare filled his gourd with water. |
| Nenda ukaujaze mtungi huu umande. | Go and fill this water-jar with dew. |
| Alimpa nguo nzuri yule kijana. | He gave the youth handsome clothes. |
| Nimempa Bwana habari. | I have given the Bwana the news. |
| Ni halali kumpa taja kaisari? | Is it lawful to give tribute to Caesar? |
| Aliwatolea watoto hotuba. | He gave the children a talk. |
| Alitokea, akaanza kumshika mkono yule mtumwa wake akimwambia, Twen'zetu, twen'zetu. | He appeared upon the scene, and took hold of his slave by the arm, saying, "Let's be off, let's be off." |
| Askari mmoja akaharaka kwenda kumshika yule mtu mkono. | One of the soldiers hastily went and caught hold of the man's hand.[1] |
| Kwa nini umemkata kichwa huyu ndege? | Why have you cut off the head of this bird? |
| Akamfunga kamba Chura katika mkia wake. | He fastened a rope to the Frog's tail. |
| Akamfungua farasi mzigo wake. | He unfastened the load from his horse. |

[1] Full context indicates the reason, viz. to restrain him from striking a man.

## The Object Prefix

Note the use of the Object Prefix, especially when attention is directed to the person or thing in question.

| | |
|---|---|
| Zikamgeuka sura za uso wake. | The fashion of his countenance was changed (i.e. was changed—him). |
| Akili zikamtoka. | He lost his wits. |
| Macho yalimtoka kwa hofu. | His eyes started out of his head with fear. |
| Akanena, Simjui alipo. | He said, "I do not know where he is." |
| Nilimwona amefurahiwa. | I saw that he was pleased. |

# CHAPTER XLIV

## PRONOUNS (Section V)

### MISCELLANEOUS NOTES

#### Impersonal (or Neuter) Pronouns and Emphatic Demonstratives

REFERENCE TABLE

|                        | Impersonal Forms | | Emphatic Demonstrative Forms | |
|                        | Simple | Reference | Simple | Reference |
|------------------------|--------|-----------|--------|-----------|
| **Noun Class Prefixes** | It, they | It, they, already mentioned | This same one, these same ones | This, these very same one(s) already mentioned |
| M-   | uu   | uo    | uu huu     | uo huo      |
| MI-  | ii   | iyo   | ii hii     | iyo hiyo    |
| KI-  | kiki | kicho | kiki hiki  | kicho hicho |
| VI-  | vivi | vivyo | vivi hivi  | vivyo hivyo |
| JI-  | lili | lilo  | lili hili  | lilo hilo   |
| MA-  | yaya | yayo  | yaya haya  | yayo hayo   |
| N-   | ii   | iyo   | ii hii     | iyo hiyo    |
| N-   | zizi | zizo  | zizi hizi  | zizo hizo   |
| U-   | uu   | uo    | uu huu     | uo huo      |
| KU-  | kuku | kuko  | kuku huku  | kuko huko   |

|                        | It, viz. place, time, manner | It, viz. place, etc. already mentioned | This same place, time, manner | This very same place, time, manner, already mentioned |
|------------------------|------|-------|-----------|-------------|
| **Adverbial Prefixes** | | | | |
| KU-  | kuku | kuko  | kuku huku  | kuko huko   |
| PA-  | papa | papo  | papa hapa  | papo hapo   |
| MU-  | mumu | mumo  | mumu humu  | mumo humo   |
| VI-  | vivi | vivyo | vivi hivi  | vivyo hivyo |

THERE are two sets of Impersonal or Neuter Pronouns, which correspond somewhat to the Self-standing Personal Pronouns **mimi**, **yeye**, etc. The simple form is expressed by reduplicating the concord prefix, e.g. **lili**, **yaya**, etc. The reference form

304

takes the -O of Reference, e.g. **lilo, yayo**. The simple forms are seldom used alone except in such phrases as **lili kwa lili, yaya kwa yaya**. The reference forms have a wider use.

Both forms more frequently occur combined with demonstratives to express emphasis, e.g. **lili hili, lilo hilo, yaya haya, yayo hayo**.

As adverbs they are frequently met with, e.g. **papo, vivyo, mumu humu**, etc.

### Examples

*Impersonal (or Neuter) Forms.*

Tusiandike **yaya** kwa **yaya**.

Don't let us write the same (words) over and over again.

Enyi jamaa, haya mazungu-mzo yetu yakiwa **yayo** kwa **yayo**, humchosha mtu kusikiliza.

Well, friends, if our conversation is merely going over the same subject again and again, it bores one.

Kipimo mpimiacho mtapi-miwa **kicho**.

With what measure ye mete it shall be measured to you again. (Lit. you shall be measured-for the same one.)

224. Lisilo mkoma hujikoma **lilo**.

(The matter) which has no one to end it, ends itself of itself.

460. Penye wimbi, na mila-ngo i **papo**.

Where the breaker is, just there is the entrance (through the reef) too.

241. Mambo ya ngoma nda ngoma, hwishia **papo** ngomani.

Matters concerning the dance belong to the dance, they are wont to finish there at the same dance.

Kwani palipo na akiba yako, na moyo wako u **papo**.

For where your treasure is, there is your heart also. (Lit. your heart it same place.)

Hatimaye ndezi akakimbilia shimoni, na yule mbwa akamfuatia **mumo**.

Eventually the animal ran into a hole, and the dog followed him into it.

L

| | |
|---|---|
| Wakamuandamia **kuko**. | And they followed him there. |
| Nikamwambia Na mimi **vi-vyo**, Bwana, sijui nienda-ko. | And I said to him, "I likewise, sir, do not know where I am going." |
| Enda kafanye **vivyo**. | Go and do thou likewise. |

*Emphatic Demonstrative forms.*

| | |
|---|---|
| Na yeye, katika kuugua kwake, neno lake **lili hili**, Binti Hamadi. | And he, throughout his illness, was always calling out "Binti Hamadi". (Lit. his word the very same.) |
| **Papo hapo** mfalme akamchu-kua Pambazuko mikononi mwake. | There and then the king took Pambazuko into his arms. |
| Wakaanza kuruka juu ya ziwa, na **papo hapo** yule mchawi akawapelekea dhoruba. | They began to fly over the lake, but just then the magician sent down a storm upon them. |
| Basi ikawa mambo **vivyo hivyo**, hata siku moja... | Matters went on in exactly the same way until one day. . . |
| Pana nini hapa? Mwenziwe akamjibu, Kila siku watu hawa hukusanyika hivi wakifanya **vivi hivi**. | "What's going on here?" His companion replied, "Every day these people gather together in this fashion and carry on just like this." |

## Reduplicated Forms of the Simple Demonstratives

These are often met with, apparently carrying much the same meaning as the Emphatic Demonstratives.

| | |
|---|---|
| Wakapelekwa . . . Mabwana kutoa habari ya jambo **hili hili**. | Gentlemen were sent to make known this particular (or this same) matter. |
| Twende tukaanze kwiba kwa baba mdogo, maana na baba yao mdogo kazi yake ni **hii hii**. | "Let us begin stealing from Uncle," for their uncle's profession was the same as theirs. |

| | |
|---|---|
| Maneno **hayo hayo** ndiyo niliyomwambia. | These were the exact words I said to him. |
| Kwa bahati zile nguo zilipelekwa kiwanda **kile kile** cha Fundi wake Fikirini. | By a lucky chance the clothes were sent to that very workshop belonging to Fikirini's master. |
| Muda **ule ule** mke wa Sungura akafungua mlango. | At that exact minute the wife of the Hare opened the door. |
| Walifika bandarini mnamo saa mbili za usiku, wakatiwa majahazini usiku **ule ule**. | They arrived at the harbour about 8 o'clock in the evening, and were put into the dhows that very same night. |
| 297. Mnywa maji kwa mkono, kiu yake i **papale**.[1] | He that drinks water with his hand, his thirst is just where it was. |
| Siku moja tai alileta wana mbuzi wawili mle tunduni . . . wakakua **mle mle** tunduni. | One day the eagle brought two young goats into the nest . . . and they grew up there in the nest. |
| Yule wa pili akamwuliza **vile vile**, Ile salaam si yangu? | In like manner the second one asked him, "Was not the greeting for me?" |

## Contracted Possessive Forms

Names of relatives, etc., often take a contracted form of the possessive. In Swahili they follow no one particular pattern, and contractions which are in vogue in one district are not necessarily acceptable in another.

The following is a list of those heard among Swahili-speaking people, but they do not all conform to the requirements of standardized Swahili. The full forms should therefore be used in written Swahili, except perhaps in the case of **mwenzi**, **mke** and **mume**, where contraction seems to be fairly general.

No contractions are used in the 3rd person plural, except occasionally **wenzao**.

---

[1] This shortened form is characteristic of Mombasa and old Swahili.

| | 1st Sing. | 2nd Sing. | 3rd Sing. | 1st Plur. | 2nd Plur. |
|---|---|---|---|---|---|
| mwenzi | mwenzangu | mwenzio | mwenziwe | mwenzetu | mwenzenu |
| wenzi | wenzangu | wenzio | wenziwe | wenzetu | wenzenu |
| mwana | mwanangu | mwanao | mwanawe | mwenetu[1] | mwenenu |
| wana | wanangu | wanao | wanawe | wenetu[1] | wenenu |
| baba | babaangu | babaako | babaake | babaetu | babaenu |
| | babangu | babako | babaye | | |
| | | | babake | | |
| mama | mamaangu | mamaako | mamaake | mamaetu | mamaenu |
| | mamangu | mamako | mamaye | | |
| | | | mamake | | |
| ndugu | | nduguyo | nduguye | | |
| ndugu | | nduguzo | nduguze | | |
| rafiki | | rafikiyo | rafikiye | | |
| rafiki | | rafikizo | rafikize | | |
| mume | | mumeo | mumewe | | |
| mke | | mkeo | mkewe | | |

Contracted possessive forms other than those with words denoting living people are occasionally met with, especially in proverbs.

329. Mti ukifa **shinale**, na **tanzuze** hukauka. (< shina lake na tanzu zake)

When a tree dies at its root, its boughs dry up also.

290. Mnyonyore hanuki, hupendeza **mauae**. (< maua yake)

The mnyonyore shrub gives forth no perfume, (and yet) its flowers are pleasing.

275. Mkwaju muwi una **tumbiriwe**.

The bad tamarind-tree has its monkey (i.e. birds of a feather).

375. Mwenda-mbizi nchi kavu huuchunua **usowe**.

He who dives on dry land scarifies his face.

Compare also such words as:

**mwishowe** its end, i.e. finally
**hatimaye** its conclusion, i.e. eventually
**mbeleye** its front or sequel, i.e. in the future
**keshoye** its morrow, i.e. on the morrow
**baadaye** afterwards

[1] Note vowel harmony in the stem.

## Further Notes on AMBA

AMBA (say) is the simple form of AMBIA (say to, tell). The verb itself is seldom heard in modern Swahili, except in certain well-defined contexts:

(*a*) in the salutation **Wambaje na hali.** (How are you?)

(*b*) with an object prefix to convey a detrimental implication, in sentences such as **Kumwamba mtu** (to speak against someone).

(*c*) with prefix **ku-** in the conjunctions[1]:—**kwamba** *or* **ya kwamba** (that), **kana kwamba** *or* **kama kwamba** (as if).

The main use of the stem AMBA, however, is to carry the relative particle, **ambacho, ambalo**, etc., and it occurs in several types of sentence:

I. As has been stated before, the only tenses which can combine with the relative particle are **-na-, -li-, -ta-**, together with the negative **-si-** and the form without any time prefix. (See p. 110.) When therefore other tenses such as -ME-, -NGE-, HU-, -JA-, etc., are used, the relative particle is suffixed to AMBA-.

| | |
|---|---|
| Kuna mambo mengi katika nchi hii, **ambayo hujajifunza** bado. | There are many matters in this country which you have not yet learnt about. |
| Nyumba **ambazo zimezungukwa** na milimao. | Houses which are surrounded by lemon trees. |
| Hakuweza kuuona mti **ambao haukuwa** rafiki yake. | He was unable to find a tree which was not his friend. |
| Njiani nilitia sahihi, kwamba Uganda ni nchi ya vilima vya namna **ambayo** kwetu **hupatikana** katika mabuku ya picha tu. | On the way I saw as an actual fact that Uganda is a country of mountains, the like of which at home are only found in picture books. |

II. But very often the AMBA construction is necessary with -NA- etc. tenses in longer sentences, especially those containing qualifying words: here incorporation of the rela-

[1] Cf. verb **ti** (say), and the conjunction formed from it, **kuti** (that), occurring in many Bantu languages.

tive particle with the verb would interfere with the balance of the sentence.

Wanaweza kuchukua masa-
nduku makubwa maku-
bwa, **ambayo** sisi watu
wawili au watatu **hatu-
wezi** kuyainua.

They are able to carry huge
boxes, which two or even
three of us could not lift.

Here the relative particle, when affixed to AMBA, is not only nearer to its antecedent the object, but also allows the noun subject to precede its verb. " . . . **tusiyoweza** sisi watu wawili au watatu kuyainua" would be very heavy Swahili.

III. Sentences in which the relative is *continuative* rather than restrictive also require the AMBA construction.

Wote walimsifu isipokuwa
mtu mmoja tu, **ambaye
alimwambia**. . . .

All praised him except one
man, who told him. . . .

Hapo kale nchi ya Uganda
haikuwa na watu ila mmo-
ja, **ambaye aliitwa** Kintu.

Long ago the country of
Uganda had no inhabitants
except one, who was called
Kintu.

Katika safari zetu, **ambazo
zilikuwa** ndefu, mara nyingi ilitulazimu kustahimili
njaa.

During our journeys, which
were long, often we had to
put up with hunger.

IV. The AMBA construction corresponds to an English relative governed by a preposition—*in which, of which, of whom, to whom,* etc., with appropriate words in the context to define the prepositional relationship.

Nitaweza wapi kusoma vitabu, **ambavyo majina yake**
sijapata kusikia?

How am I able to read books,
the names of which I have
never heard?

Walifika katika bustani,
**ambayo ndani yake** mna
**maua ya** kila rangi.

They came to a garden, in
which were flowers of every
colour.

Ile **nyumba ambayo paa lake**
limeungua.

The house, the roof of which
was scorched.

Yule jumbe **ambaye** tulizu-
ngumza **habari zake**.

The messenger about whom
we were talking.

Mbele kidogo liko ziwa la
Victoria, **ambalo ukubwa
wake** ni kama upeo wa
macho.

A little way in front was Lake
Victoria, the vastness of
which stretched beyond the
limit of one's vision.

V. The AMBA construction is also used with the NI of
Identification.

Tulifika kwenye kinu **ambacho ni** mali ya Muhindi.

We arrived at the mill which
is owned by an Indian.

Alituonyesha vito **ambavyo
ni** vya ajabu.

He showed us jewels which
were wonderful.

Huyo Chaliwali, **ambaye ni**
mwenye safari hii, aliku-
wa mtu mwovu.

This Chaliwali, who owned the
caravan, was an evil man.

VI. Occasions sometimes arise in which the relative is used
both with AMBA and in the verbal form.

Maneno **ambayo** ali**yo**sema
ni haya.

These are the words he said.

Mahali **ambapo** ili**po**funguli-
wa bendera ya Kiingereza.

A place where the British flag
had been unfurled.

#### Further Notes on Concordial Agreement

*Two or more Subjects.*

A verb having as its subjects two or more nouns of different
classes takes **vi-** as its concord, if the nouns are names of concretes. Sometimes the verb agrees with the last-named noun,
especially if it is an abstract noun.

Mkewe akamwuliza, Jinsi
gani Bwana, nguo zako na
farasi **viko** wapi?

His wife asked him, "How
now, Bwana, where are
your clothes and your
horse?"

Tumetendewa heshima ku-
bwa na wema mkubwa,
**usio** na kifani.

We were shown unparalleled
courtesy and kindness.

Naona ama wema huu na hisani hii **hainenekani** wala kupimika.

As for the goodness and kindness (shown us), I feel it can be neither expressed in words nor measured.

*Impersonal Subject.*

Impersonal "it", when not referring to a noun previously mentioned, is translated by **i-**.

**Haifai.** It won't do.

**Imekupasa.** It behoves you.

**Haidhuru.** It doesn't matter.

**Yafaa.** It is proper.

*Omission of Antecedent.*

A few words such as **neno**, **kitu**, **pahali**, are sometimes omitted, and are represented by the relative particle with its appropriate concord.

Such constructions are often preceded by **kila**.

| | | |
|---|---|---|
| Kila asema**lo**. | (**neno**) | Every word he says. |
| Kila asema**po**. | (time) | Every time he speaks. |
| Kila aenda**ko**. | (direction) | Everywhere he goes. |

The -A of relationship has a similar usage.

| | | |
|---|---|---|
| Hana **la** kusema. | (**neno**) | He has nothing to say. |
| Hana **la** zaidi. | (**neno**) | He has nothing more to add. |
| Lete chakula. | (**kitu**) | Bring some food (something to eat). |

Watu wamesongana sana njiani, hapana **pa** kukanyaga.

People were so crowded together on the road, that there was no room to tread.

Mambo haya ya kuumiza yalizidi juu yake kila alipokuwa akiendelea mbele.

The pains increased every time he went forward,

# CHAPTER XLV

## ADVERBS (Section III)

### IDEOPHONES[1]

IDEOPHONES are found in many Bantu languages. Some are common to several languages or dialects, others have a local use only.

Many of these words are onomatopoeic,[2] but not all, for the term ideophone covers a wider field than that of sound imitation.

The majority of ideophones function as adverbs, and some of these give rise to verbs. A few nouns are basically ideophonic.

*Ideophones functioning as Adverbs.*

The following are onomatopoeic:

| | |
|---|---|
| Kuanguka **tifu**! | To fall down in sand. |
| Kuanguka **chubwi**! | To fall down in water. |
| Kuanguka **tapwi**! | To fall down in mud. |
| Kuanguka **pu**! | To fall down as a waterfall. |
| Kuanguka **tang'**! | To fall down as a coin. |
| Kuanguka **kacha**! | To fall down as a branch or twig. |

The following are not onomatopoeic:

| | |
|---|---|
| Kufunga **ndi**. | To fasten securely. |
| Kutega sikio **ndi**. | To listen attentively. |
| Kulowa **chepe chepe**. | To be soaked to the skin. |
| Kujaa **pomoni**. | To be full to the utmost capacity. |
| Kufa **fo-fo-fo** *or* **fooo**. | To be utterly dead. |
| Kunuka **fee** *or* **mff**. | To emit an unpleasant odour. |

---

[1] "A vivid representation of an idea in sound. A word often onomatopoeic which describes a predicate, qualificative or adverb in respect to manner, colour, sound, smell, action, state or intensity." (*Bantu Linguistic Terminology*, p. 118.)

[2] Onomatopoeia: Imitation in word or sound approximating thereto. (*Bantu Linguistic Terminology*, p. 155.)

*Examples*

| | |
|---|---|
| **Kukuru kakara, kukuru kakara,** miezi ilipita katika kutengeneza. | Hustle and haste, hustle and haste, the months passed in making preparation. |
| Basi Bwana, wacha nyembe ziseme **Parakacha parakanja!** | Now, sir, let the razors say "Parakacha parakanja". |
| Mipapayu imejaa **kocho kocho!** | The pawpaw trees were loaded down with fruit. |
| Maarusi wanawake wamepambwa kwa dhahabu **kocho kocho!** kichwani mpaka miguuni. | The ladies in the bridal party were loaded from head to foot with ornaments of gold. |
| Mara akatokea korongo mkubwa akamjia **Njongwa! Njongwa!** | Just then a crane appeared and approached him with long deliberate steps. |
| Tuliwaimbia Wazungu wa manowari hata wakalala **foooo!** | We sang to the Europeans on the man-of-war until they almost fell down dead (with laughter). |
| Na yule nguruwe anachimba chini **ng'! ng'! ng'!** wala haangalii mtu. | The pig dug steadily on, nor did he notice anyone. |
| Tuliufuta mchuzi **fyu!** | We mopped up the gravy. |
| Wakaleta shoka wakamkata mkia **te!** | They brought an axe and cut off his tail "te!" |
| Mtu akatoa kisu akampiga **pa!** | The man took out a knife and stabbed him "pa!" |
| Akazidi kumminya **loo!** tumbo likapasuka **pu!** ndege akafa. | He continued to squeeze him and then his stomach burst "pu!" the bird was dead. |
| Mara ikawa mkia wa Sungura kupiga **pu-pu-pu-pu!** . . . | Thereupon the Rabbit's tail began to twitch "pu-pu-pu-pu!" . . . |
| Ikawa mguu wa Sungura kupiga **pi-pi-pi-pi-!** . . . | Then the Rabbit's foot twitched "pi-pi-pi-pi-!..." |
| Ikawa mkono wa Sungura kupiga **pa-pa-pa-pa-!** | Then the Rabbit's paw twitched "pa-pa-pa-pa!" |

| | |
|---|---|
| Ndege akatelemka **kooo**! | The bird swooped down "kooo!" |
| Ndege akaenda zake **sssh**! | The bird went off with a swish. |
| Inzi akaondoka **z-z-z**! kwenda kumwita Mzee Mamba. | The fly buzzed off to go and call the old crocodile. |
| Shilingi ilitumbukia **chubwi**! majini. | The shilling fell plumb into the water. |
| Nazi ilianguka mchangani **tifu**! | The coconut fell into the sand "tifu!" |
| Alisikia kitagaa kikianguka **kacha**! | He heard a branchlet falling down "kacha!" |
| Aliteleza topeni akaanguka **pwata**! | He slipped in the mud and fell down "pwata!" |

## Ideophones giving rise to Verbs

| | |
|---|---|
| Teketea **teke teke** (*or* **tiki tiki**). | Be burnt to a cinder—often used of food. |
| Mwagika **mwa**. | Rush out—of liquids. |
| Katika **ka-ka-ka**. | Cracking noise made by a tree or branch before falling. |
| Chirika **chiriri**. | Trickle. |
| Bweta **bwe**. | Bark. |
| Bwatika **bwata**. | Drop down with a bang. |
| Gongomelea **ngo-ngo-ngo**. | Drive in a nail. |

**Gugumiza** (stutter) and **mumunya**[1] (mumble) are also obviously ideophonic in origin.

## Ideophonic Nouns

**Ting'a-ting'a** tractor      **Piki-piki** motor-cycle

The following expressions are also probably ideophonic in origin:

kupiga **chafya** (to sneeze)
kupiga **mbeu** (to belch)
kupiga **miayo** (to yawn)

---

[1] Cf. **mumunye** (vegetable marrow).

# CHAPTER XLVI

## FIGURES OF SPEECH

### REDUPLICATION

REDUPLICATION is a characteristic of Bantu languages. It affects syllables, verb stems, words and phrases.

It has four main uses:

I. To express various phases of intensiveness, i.e. to emphasize, to increase or extend the idea contained in the word, to express abundance or diversity.

| | |
|---|---|
| Chungu kikavunjika **vipande vipande**. | The cooking-pot broke into pieces. |
| Maua hayo . . . tena yako ya kila namna **rangi rangi**. | These flowers . . . are of many kinds and of various colours. |
| Waliamrishwa kuogolea **namna namna**. | They were ordered to swim in various styles. |
| Magari ya motakaa **elifu elifu** yalikuwa yakipeleka abiria huko. | Thousands of motor vehicles were conveying passengers there. |

Emphasis is also expressed in the reduplicated demonstrative forms, **hivi hivi**, **vile vile**, **vivi hivi**, **vivyo hivyo** (see p. 304).

II. To lessen or to modify the force of a word.

| | |
|---|---|
| Kiwanja kilikuwa **maji-maji**. | The playing-field was somewhat wet. |
| Mtoto huyu **alia-lia** tu. | This child does nothing but whimper. |
| **Sijambo-jambo.** | I'm not feeling too well. |
| **Kizungu-zungu.** | Giddiness. |

III. To express continuous action, or state.

| | |
|---|---|
| Tulipotoka nje, tulianza **kutanga-tanga** huko na huko. | When we got outside, we began wandering about. |

Msitu na nyika, msitu na nyika, msitu na nyika, akapata mwendo wa siku mbili kwa miguu.

One succession of grass and forest, until he had accomplished two days' journey on foot.

Wakaenda wakaenda msitu na nyika.

They went on and on through forest and grasslands.

IV. To express a distributive idea.

Funga mzigo hii mitatu mitatu.

Fasten these loads in threes.

Wakapata nao vivyo thumuni thumuni.

And they received likewise each man a penny.

Wauzaje machungwa haya?

How do you sell these oranges?

Moja senti tatu, moja senti tatu.

Three cents each.

The reduplication of a syllable often indicates an action made up of a series of actions.

| | |
|---|---|
| kufufua (to revive a fire, etc.) | kupepeta (to sift, winnow) |
| kuzizima (to get quite cold) | kupapasa (to grope about) |
| kutetema (to tremble) | kubabata (to tap—as in metal working) |

## SIMILES

Watoto wakatupwa kama kuni.

The children were thrown down like bundles of firewood.

Aliwachinja kama mbuzi.

He slaughtered them as one slaughters goats.

Usimchokoze, ana ulimi kama upatu wa gungu.

Don't irritate him, he has a tongue like an "upatu wa gungu" (a drum of a particularly insistent tone).

Ama mji huo, humfikirisha mtu yuko nje ya Afrika ya Mashiriki, ulivyokuwa na watu wengi na motakaa kama siafu.

As for this town (Nairobi), it makes one imagine one is outside East Africa, because of its many people and motor-cars as numerous as ants.

| | |
|---|---|
| Watu huwa wengi sana njia-ni kama mchanga. | People abound along this road like sand. |
| . . . kama mwangaza wa jua la mchana. | . . . like the brightness of the morning sun. |
| Ewe mtoto, wacha uchafu, nenda ukajionyesha maji kidogo, umekuwa kama ngamia. | Now then, child, leave off being dirty, go and intro-duce yourself to a little water, you are like a camel for dirt. |
| Maswali yalikuwa yakitole-wa mfano wake kama mi-shale. | Questions were showered on them like arrows. |
| Mtoto huyu mkaidi kama mkia wa nguruwe. | This child is as obstinate as the tail of a pig. |
| Ukienda huko, utamwona Ali yu moto, mkali kama siki ya miaka saba. | If you go there, you will find Ali all "het up", as sharp as seven-year-old vinegar. |
| Tulikaa naye kama watoto na baba yao. | We lived with him as children with their father. |
| Umati wote ule uliokuwako ulitiririka kama nyoka. | The whole crowd which was there trickled away like a snake. |
| Pesa ni kama wali, kila uki-zila, zaisha. | Pice are like rice, every (time) you eat, they come to an end. |

Another aspect of similes may be found in the naming of new or foreign objects.

**ndege** aeroplane          **faru** tank

# CHAPTER XLVII

## TIME, WEIGHTS, MEASURES, CURRENCY

### TIME

THERE is a difference of 6 hours in the Swahili and English systems of reckoning time, thus:

| | |
|---|---|
| Saa moja | 7 a.m. or 7 p.m. |
| Saa mbili | 8 a.m. or 8 p.m. |
| Saa tatu | 9 a.m. or 9 p.m. |
| Saa sita (ya usiku) | 12 midnight |
| Saa sita (ya mchana) | 12 noon |
| Saa kenda | 3 a.m. or 3 p.m. |
| Saa kumi na moja | 5 a.m. or 5 p.m. |
| Saa kumi na mbili | 6 a.m. or 6 p.m. |

The difference between a.m. and p.m. is often indicated by adding words such as alfajiri (dawn), asubuhi (morning), alasiri (early afternoon), jioni (evening), etc.

Arabic numbers are frequently used for 9, 11 and 12, viz. tisa, edashara and thenashara, respectively.

Intervening time between the hours is expressed thus:

| | |
|---|---|
| Saa nane kasa robo | a quarter to two |
| Saa nane u robo | a quarter past two |
| Saa nane u nusu | half-past two |
| Saa nane na dakika kumi | 10 minutes past two |
| Saa nane kasa dakika kumi | 10 minutes to two |
| Saa ngapi? | What is the time? |

| MONTHS OF THE YEAR | DAYS OF THE WEEK |
|---|---|

The Swahili names for their Lunar Months[1] are as follows:

| Januari | Mfunguo Mosi | Jumapili | Sunday |
|---|---|---|---|
| Februari | Mfunguo Pili | Jumatatu | Monday |
| Machi | Mfunguo Tatu | Jumanne | Tuesday |

[1] Since the Swahili year is about 11 days shorter than the solar year, their position in the calendar is constantly changing. They do *not* coincide with English months.

319

| Months of the Year | | Days of the Week | |
|---|---|---|---|
| Aprili | Mfunguo Nne | Jumatano | Wednesday |
| Mei | Mfunguo Tano | Alhamisi | Thursday |
| Juni | Mfunguo Sita | Ijumaa | Friday |
| Julai | Mfunguo Sabaa | Jumamosi | Saturday |
| Agosti | Mfunguo Nane | | |
| Septemba | Mfunguo Tisa *or* | | |
| Oktoba | Rajab(u)    [Kenda | | |
| Novemba | Shaban(i) | | |
| Desemba | Ramadhan(i) | | |

Cardinal numbers are used to express the days of the month:

Mei mwezi kumi na tano    May 15th

## WEIGHTS AND MEASURES, ETC.

| Weight | | Currency | |
|---|---|---|---|
| ratli | 1 lb. | noti | note |
| farasila | 36 lb. | shilingi | shilling, 100 cts. |
| jizla | 10 farasilas | nusushilingi | 50 cts. |
| | | kikumi | 10 cts. |
| *Capacity* | | kitano | 5 cts. |
| pishi | about 6 lb. in weight | senti | cent |
| kisaga | ½ pishi | | *Length* |
| kibaba | ¼ pishi | dhiraa, | |
| | | mkono | cubit |
| | | wari, yadi | yard |
| *Number* | | futi | foot |
| korija | a score | jora | a whole roll of cloth |

### Fractions

⅛ thumuni    ¼ robo    ⅓ theluthi    ½ nusu
¾ is expressed by a whole number less ¼:
1¾  mbili kasa robo

# CHAPTER XLVIII

## SUMMARIES

### 1. INTONATION SUMMARY

| *Tone Pattern I* | *Tone Pattern II* |
|---|---|
| `\` or `⎯` page | `⎯ \` page |
| I. Words in isolation . 13<br>Ia. Statements . . 16<br>    Commands . 26<br>Ib. Questions *with* an inter-<br>    rogative particle 20a, 32, 33<br>Ic. Answers to questions 20a, 23b | Questions *without* an inter-<br>rogative particle . 23a, 23b<br><br>Superimposition of T.P. II<br>on T.P. I . . . 33 |

| *Tone Pattern III* | *Tone Pattern IV* |
|---|---|
| `⎯ ⎯` or `⎯ ·` or `⎯ ⎯` or `⎯ ·` | `⎯ /` or `\ /` or `⎯ _` or `\ _` |
| A "carry on" tone . . 77<br>List of things . . . 78<br>List of actions . . . 135<br>Initial adverbs . . . 78<br>Adverbial subjects . . 129<br>Relative clauses . . 115<br>Conditional clauses . . 138 | An emphatic alternative to<br>III when extra emphasis<br>or antithesis is required . 191 |

| *Tone Pattern in Paren-<br>thesis*<br>(all syllables low level) | *Other emphatic Tone<br>Patterns* |
|---|---|
| Titles . . . . 16, 33,<br>74, 75<br>Reversed word order . 75, 94,<br>129<br>Certain adverbs at end of<br>sentence . . 75<br>Direction of emphasis . 76, 94<br>Occasional use in middle or<br>beginning of sentence . 77 | Alternative to Tone Pat-<br>tern II . . . 193<br>Alternative to Tone Pat-<br>tern Ic . . . 193<br>Alternative to Tone Pat-<br>tern Ic . . . 193<br>Vocative Intonation . . 194 |

## 2. SOUND CHANGES IN CLASS AND CONCORD PREFIXES BEFORE VOWELS

| | | | | | | | |
|---|---|---|---|---|---|---|---|
| wa<br>ma<br>pa | } + i > | { | we<br>me<br>pe | wa<br>ma<br>pa<br>ya | } + a, e, o > | { | wa we w(a)o<br>ma me m(a)o<br>pa pe po<br>ya ye yo |
| ki<br>vi<br>mi | } + i > | { | ki<br>vi<br>mi | ki<br>vi<br>mi | } + a, e, o > | { | cha che cho<br>vya vye vyo<br>mia mie mio<br>mye |
| u<br>m(u)<br>ku<br>n | } before vowel > | { | w-<br>m(w)-<br>k(w)-, ku-<br>ny- | i<br>ji<br>li<br>zi | } before vowel > | { | y-<br>j-<br>l-<br>z- |

These sound changes do not always occur with Object Prefixes, nor with Subject Prefixes immediately before a verb stem.

## 3. SOUND CHANGES WITH CLASS PREFIX N- BEFORE CONSONANTS

| *Unvoiced Consonants and Nasals* | | *Voiced Consonants* |
|---|---|---|
| n- + { | p   > p    (mp in monosyllabic stems)<br>t   > t    (nt in monosyllabic stems)<br>ch > ch   (nch in monosyllabic stems)<br>k   > k<br><br>f   > f<br>s   > s    (ns in monosyllabic stems)<br>sh > sh<br>h   > h<br><br>m   > m<br>n   > n    (nn in monosyllabic stems)<br>ny > ny<br>ng' > ng'<br>ng > ng | n- + {   b > mb<br>d > nd<br>j > nj<br>g > ng<br><br>v > (m)v<br>z > nz<br><br>r > nd<br>l > nd<br>w > mb |

Apparent anomalies like **mboni** (pupil of eye) < **ona** (see), **ndoto** (a dream), < **ota** (dream), are due to a "submerged" **w-** and **l-** respectively in the parent verb stem. Cf. Nsenga **wona** and **lota**.

Note also that **p, t, ch** and **k** are aspirated, and that **mb, nd, nj, ng** are pronounced *explosively* (as opposed to the normal *implosive* pronunciation of **b, d, j** and **g**).

## 4. CONSONANT ASSIMILATION BEFORE NOUN SUFFIX -I AND VERB SUFFIX -YA

| Unvoiced Consonants and Nasals with | | Voiced Consonants with | |
| Suffix -I | Suffix -YA | Suffix -I | Suffix -YA |
|---|---|---|---|
| p > fi | p > fya | b > vi or zi | |
| t > si | t > sa or sha | d > zi | d > za |
| k > shi or si | k > sha or sa | g > zi | g > za |
| n > ni | n > nya | w > vi or zi | w > vya |
| ny > nyi | ny > nza | l > zi | l > za |

Apparent anomalies like **mjuvi** (a know-all), **mjuzi** (a wise man) < **jua** (know), **mlizi** (one who cries) < **lia** (cry), are due to a "submerged" -w- and -l- respectively in the parent verb stem. Cf. Nsenga **ziwa** and **lila**. These "submerged" letters account for the many verbs in Swahili which end in two vowels.

## 5. CONSONANT ASSIMILATION BEFORE SUFFIX -U

| Unvoiced Consonants | Voiced Consonants |
|---|---|
| $\left.\begin{matrix} p \\ k \end{matrix}\right\}$ + u > fu | w + u > vu |

Apparent anomalies like **-tovu** (lacking) < **toa** (lack), **-nyamavu** (quiet) < **nyamaa** (be quiet), are due to a "submerged" -w- and -l- respectively in the parent verb stem.

# 6. USES OF THE -A OF RELATIONSHIP

| 1 | | 2 | | 3 | |
|---|---|---|---|---|---|
| With the P.C. it helps to express an adjectival concept | page | With KU- it helps to express an adverbial or associative concept | page | With N- of Association it expresses a concept either prepositional or conjunctional | page |
| (i) *Possessive concept* | 55 | (i) *"By means of"* | 171 | *Prepositional* | 98, 102, 242 |
| -a Hamisi    Hamisi's | | kwa miguu    on foot | | na Hamisi    with Hamisi | |
| -a-ngu    my, mine | | | | naye    with him | |
| | | (ii) *"By reason of"* | 171 | nacho, etc.    with it | |
| (ii) *Descriptive concept* | 145 | kwa ukaidi    through stubbornness | | na Hamisi    by Hamisi | 223 |
| -a tatu    third | | | | naye    by him | |
| -a mti    wooden | | (iii) *Manner or State* | 172 | nacho, etc.    by it | |
| -a kizungu    European | | kwa haraka    hastily | | | |
| -a mwituni    wild | | | | *Conjunctional* | 102, 242 |
| -a kupendeza    pleasing | | (iv) *Place* | 172 | na Hamisi    also Hamisi | |
| -a kujengea    for building purposes | | kwa Bwana    at Bwana's | | naye    he also | |
| | | | | nacho, etc.    it also | |
| | | (v) *"In respect to"* | 173 | mimi na Hamisi    Hamisi and I | |
| | | mia kwa tano    5% | | mimi naye    he and I | |
| | | wakubwa kwa wadogo    both old and young | | | |

# 7. USES OF THE -O OF REFERENCE

| | 1 After Subj. Prefix | 2 -O -OTE | 3 As Relative particle | 4 After NDI- | 5 After NA- and KWA- | 6 Demonstratives | 7 After -INGINE |
|---|---|---|---|---|---|---|---|
| With pronominal concord[1] <br> li + o > lo <br> zi + o > zo | | p. 61 <br> lo lote <br> zo zote | pp. 110, 112 <br> lipendezalo zipendezazo ambalo ambazo | p. 179 <br> ndilo ndizo | pp. 99, 178, 185 <br> nalo nazo kwalo kwazo | pp. 178, 304 <br> lilo hilo zizo hizo | pp. 178, 185 <br> jinginelo nyinginezo |
| With adverbial formatives of Place, Time, Manner <br> pa + o > po <br> ku + o > ko <br> mu + o > mo <br> vi + o > vyo | p. 18 <br> nipo hapa yuko kule wamo ndani | p. 159 <br> po pote ko kote mo mote vyo vyote | p. 168 <br> asimamapo aendako aketimo apendavyo ambapo, etc. | p. 179 <br> ndipo ndiko ndimo ndivyo | p. 159 <br> napo nako namo navyo | pp. 178, 304 <br> papo hapo kuko huko mumo humo vivyo hivyo | p. 178 <br> penginepo kwingineko mwinginemo vinginevyo |

[1] Only two Classes are exemplified in this table.

## 8. NOUN DEVERBATIVES—pp. 284-94

| | -I | -JI | -U | -O | -E | -A |
|---|---|---|---|---|---|---|
| **M- WA-** | Doer of the action, agent. mwindi | Habitual doer of action. mwindaji | One possessing a state. mtulivu | — | Passive agent, person acted upon. mteule | Doer of action (requires complement). mwinda tembo |
| **M- MI-** | — | — | — | Ultimate result of the action. mwendo | Passive agent, thing acted upon. mkate | — |
| **KI- VI-** | Agent. kiongozi Action. kikohozi | — | — | Instrument which does the action. kifungo | Passive agent, thing acted upon. kipande | Impersonal agent. kifunga bei |
| **(JI-) MA-** | Action itself, process of the action. malezi | — | State (plural idea). maumivu | Ultimate result of the action (often plural). (ma)wazo | Passive agent, thing acted upon. magandegande | — |
| **N-** | — | — | — | Instrument which does the action. nyundo Ultimate result of the action. ndoto | Passive agent, thing acted upon. pete | Instrument. njia |
| **U- (N-)** | Action expressed in the abstract. ulezi | Habitual profession. uwindaji | State. utulivu | Instrument which does the action. ufunguo, pl. funguo | State of being acted upon. utume | — |

## 9. DEMONSTRATIVE AND IMPERSONAL PRONOUNS

Illustrated with:

(a) Concords of the JI- MA- Classes (li-, ya-)

(b) Typical Adverbial Concords (pa-, vi-)

Note that page numbers in brackets indicate that these specific concords do not occur in the illustrations.

|  | *Simple* | | *Emphatic* | |
|---|---|---|---|---|
|  |  | page |  | page |
| Non-proximity | lile | (58), 69 | lile lile<br>li-lile | (306) |
|  | yale | 69 | yale yale<br>ya-yale | (306) |
|  | pale | 127, 160 | pale pale<br>pa-pale | 161<br>307 |
|  | vile | 164 | vile vile<br>vi-vile | 165, 307 |
| Proximity | hili | (59), 69 | hili hili | 306 |
|  | lili | 305 | lili hili | 306 |
|  | haya | 69 | haya haya | (306) |
|  | yaya | 305 | yaya haya | 305 |
|  | hapa | 127, 159 | (hapa hapa) |  |
|  | papa | (305) | papa hapa | 161 |
|  | hivi | 164 | hivi hivi | (306) |
|  | vivi | (305) | vivi hivi | 306 |
| Reference | hilo | 183 | hilo hilo | (307) |
|  | lilo | 305 | lilo hilo | 305 |
|  | hayo | 183 | hayo hayo | 307 |
|  | yayo | 305 | yayo hayo | 305 |
|  | hapo | 184 | (hapo hapo) |  |
|  | papo | 305 | papo hapo | 306 |
|  | hivyo | 184 | hivyo hivyo | (306) |
|  | vivyo | 306 | vivyo hivyo | 306 |

See also Reference Tables on pp. 159 and 304

## 10. APHORISMS

## 11. HOW ADJECTIVAL CONCEPTS ARE EXPRESSED

page

| | | | | |
|---|---|---|---|---|
| 1. | *Simple adjective stems* | 46 | mti **mzuri** | a fine tree |
| 2. | *Loan words* | 49 | maji **safi** | clean water |
| 3. | *Phrases based on the -A of relationship* | 145 | kiti **cha mti** | a wooden chair |
| | | | maneno **ya kiume** | manly words |
| | | | kazi **ya nyumbani** | housework |
| | | | mambo **ya kuchukiza** | displeasing affairs |
| | | | mtoto **wa tatu** | the third child |
| 4. | *Nouns in apposition* | 147 | askari **koti** | uniformed policeman |
| 5. | *Verbs with relative phrasing* | 147 | mtungi **uliojaa** | a full water-jar |
| 6. | *Use of -ENYE+noun (to express state)* | 147 | **mwenye maarifa** | a learned person |

## 12. HOW ADVERBIAL CONCEPTS ARE EXPRESSED

|  | page |  |  |
|---|---|---|---|
| 1. *Simple adverbs of Bantu origin* | 158 | **tu** | merely, only |
| 2. *Loan words mostly of Arabic origin* | 158 | **sana** | very, etc. |
| 3. *Nouns standing in the Nominal Construction* | 299 | **usiku** | by night, at night |
| 4. *Enclitic -NI of Place* | 18 | nyumba**ni** | in or at the house |
| 5. *Adverbial formatives prefixed to various roots:* |  |  |  |
| *KU-, PA-, MU- of time and place* | 159 | **ko**te **ko**te pengine mle | in all directions sometimes there within |
| *VI- of manner* | 163 | **vi**le | thus |
| *KI- of likeness* | 165 | **ki**falme | in regal fashion |
| *U- of state* | 165 | **u**pesi | quickly |
| 6. *Phrases based on the KWA of reason* | 171 | **kwa** ujinga | through stupidity |
| 7. *Ideophones* | 313 | bwatika **bwata** | drop with a bang |
| 8. *Enclitic -TO of thoroughness* | 158 | fanye**to** | do thoroughly |

## 13. PREDICATION WITHOUT A VERB

page

This is expressed by:

I. Copula NI expressed or understood . . . 92
    Ni nyama.           It is an animal.
    Kitabu cha nani hiki?   Whose book is this?

II. Emphatic form NDI- . . . . . 179
    Hamisi ndiye tumtakaye.   It's Hamisi whom we
                     want.

III. Subject Prefix . . . . . . 93
    Yu hai?           Is he alive?
    Ki wapi?         Where is it?

IV. Subject Prefix + ko, po, or mo . . 18, 24, 29
    Yuko nje.         He is outside.

V. Subject Prefix + NA of Association . . . 98
    Ana kiu.          He is thirsty.

# 14. VERBS AND THEIR TENSES

# KEY TO EXERCISES

## EXERCISE 1a (p. 14)

| | | | | |
|---|---|---|---|---|
| **1.** vikapu | **6.** vikombe | **11.** visu | **16.** viazi | **21.** vizibo |
| **2.** vitanda | **7.** viziwi | **12.** vioo | **17.** vyumba | **22.** vitu |
| **3.** vipofu | **8.** vyakula | **13.** vipimo | **18.** viokosi | **23.** vyombo |
| **4.** vitabu | **9.** vidole | **14.** vyeti | **19.** viatu | **24.** viini |
| **5.** viti | **10.** vitoto | **15.** viko | **20.** vijiko | |

## EXERCISE 1b (p. 17)

1. The knife is lost.
2. The looking-glass is broken, Bibi
3. The book is torn.
4. The pipe has fallen down.
5. The shoes are split.
6. The cups are broken.
7. The note is lost.
8. The chairs have fallen down.
9. The spoons are lost.
10. The vessel is broken.
11. The books are spoilt.
12. The potatoes are mature, etc.
13. The things have arrived.
14. The basket is split.
15. The rooms are untidy.
16. The beds are broken.
17. The food is cooked.
18. The shoe is lost.

## EXERCISE 2 (p.20a)

1. Where are the potatoes? They are outside.
2. Where is the cup? It is upstairs.
3. Where are the shoes? They are downstairs.
4. Where is the basket? It is within.
5. Where are the utensils? They are here.
6. Where are the chairs, Bibi? They are over there.
7. Where is the knife? It is on the table.
8. Where is the food? It is in the kitchen.
9. Where are the books, Bwana? They are on the table.
10. Where is the measure? It is at the house.
11. Where are the utensils? They are on the box.
12. Where are the spoons? They are inside the basket.

## EXERCISE 3a (p. 22)

| | | | |
|---|---|---|---|
| **1.** mikono | **9.** michezo | **17.** misumari | **25.** mitego |
| **2.** miili | **10.** mioyo | **18.** michungwa | **26.** miti |
| **3.** mipaka | **11.** mizigo | **19.** mito | **27.** miji |
| **4.** mifereji | **12.** mikeka | **20.** mito | **28.** miavuli |
| **5.** milango | **13.** misikiti | **21.** misumeno | **29.** mishahara |
| **6.** mioto | **14.** miendo | **22.** mioshi | **30.** miaka |
| **7.** miguu | **15.** miezi | **23.** mikebe | |
| **8.** miitu | **16.** milima | **24.** mitambo | |

## Exercise 3b (p.23a)

| | |
|---|---|
| 1. The door is broken. | 9. The nails are finished. |
| 2. The fire has gone out. | 10. The spring is broken. |
| 3. The saws are spoilt. | 11. The umbrella is split. |
| 4. The mats are split. | 12. The tin can has a hole in it. |
| 5. The game has begun. | 13. The trees have dried up. |
| 6. The orange-trees are dead. | 14. The loads are lost. |
| 7. The river is swollen. | 15. The moon is visible. |
| 8. The pillows are torn. | 16. The boundaries have been destroyed. |

## Exercise 4 (p. 25)

1. Is the game finished? It is finished.
2. Are the trees dead? They are dead.
3. Is the chair upstairs? It is not.
4. Are the shoes downstairs? They are not.
5. Is the door broken? It is broken.
6. Is the mat spoilt? It is spoilt.
7. Has the fire gone out? It has gone out.
8. Are there any tin cans, Bibi? There are some, Bibi.
9. Are the spoons in the box? They are (in).
10. Is the umbrella there? It is not there.

## Exercise 5 (p. 26)

1. Cook some potatoes.
2. Don't cook food here.
3. Take away the tea or breakfast things.
4. Don't bring a chair.
5. Bring spoons and knives.
6. Don't remove the saw.
7. Bring (ye) a bed, don't bring chairs.
8. Take (ye) away the knives, don't take away the spoons.
9. Remove the bread (i.e. loaf), don't remove the cups.

## Exercise 6 (p. 28)

| | | | |
|---|---|---|---|
| 1. Waarabu | 9. Wazungu | 16. wanafunzi | 23. Waswahili |
| 2. wana | 10. wazee | 17. wapagazi | 24. waashi |
| 3. watoto | 11. wanyapara | 18. waokozi | 25. wa(a)limu |
| 4. wapishi | 12. wachunga | 19. watumishi | 26. wevi |
| 5. waoga | 13. waume | 20. waimbaji | 27. wanawake |
| 6. wenzi | 14. wana(wa)ume | 21. wagonjwa | 28. wake |
| 7. waumba | 15. wenyewe | 22. wageni | 29 waandikaji |
| 8. walevi | | | |

# KEY TO EXERCISES

## Exercise 7a (p. 30)

1. Are the sick folk asleep? They are asleep.
2. Is the teacher awake? He is awake.
3. Is the European downstairs? He is not.
4. Have the porters arrived? They have arrived.
5. Where are they? They are outside.
6. Has the stranger arrived? He has arrived.
7. Is the elder standing? He is standing.
8. Where is he standing? He is standing over there.
9. Where are the children? They are upstairs asleep.
10. Is the stranger seated? He is seated.
11. Is the old man drunk? He is drunk.
12. Where is he? He is outside.
13. Is the sick person dead? He is dead.

## Exercise 7b (p. 30)

1. Wapagazi wako wapi? Hawako hapa, wako kule, wamekaa kitako.
2. Kiti kiko wapi? Kiko juu, hakiko hapa.
3. Yu wapi mtoto? Yuko juu, amelala.
4. Wagonjwa wako wapi? Wamo ndani, hawako hapa.
5. Mwavuli haupo hapa, uko juu.
6. Walimu hawako hapa, wako nje.
7. Wanawake hawamo ndani, wapo hapa.

## Exercise 8a (p. 33)

1. Where are the children to cultivate? They are to cultivate here.
2. Where are the sick people to sleep? Let them sleep in the house.
3. Is the old man to buy potatoes? Let him buy some.
4. Are we to bring knives? Bring them.
5. Am I to read now? Read.
6. When is the teacher to come? He is to come to-morrow.
7. When are the children to come? They may come the day after to-morrow.
8. Are the Swahili to bring food? Let them bring (it).
9. May the sick man read? He may read.
10. When is the sick man to eat? Let him eat now.
11. Am I not to cook potatoes to-day? Don't cook (any).
12. Don't let the children take away the chairs.
13. The sick man is not to buy a pipe.
14. Don't let us read this morning, let us read this evening.

## Exercise 8b (p. 34)

1. What has the cook cooked? He has cooked some bread.
2. What are the children to cook? They are to cook potatoes.
3. What have the Europeans bought? They have bought books.
4. What is the cook to buy? He is to buy a loaf of bread.

5. What has the teacher taken away?  He has taken away a chair.
6. What shall I take away?  Don't take away anything.
7. What have the women brought?  They have brought potatoes.
8. What has the child eaten?  He has eaten some potatoes.
9. What has the old man brought?  He has brought a pipe.

## EXERCISE 8c (p. 34)

1. Wana(wa)ume wameleta nini?
2. Mpishi amekula nini?
3. Watoto wamepika nini?
4. Wazee wameleta nini?
5. Wagonjwa wamekula nini?
6. Wanawake wamepika nini?
7. Wagonjwa wale nini?
8. Tulete nini?

## EXERCISE 9a (p. 39)

1. Unasoma nini?
2. Ninasoma kitabu.
3. Wapagazi wamefika.
4. Ali amefika?
5. Ali alisoma jana?
6. Wageni walifika jana?
7. Watafika kesho.
8. Wamefika sasa hivi.
9. Ali atasoma kesho.
10. Utafika lini?
11. Nitafika kesho.
12. Wageni walifika lini?
13. Hamisi alifika jana?
14. Alifika jana.
15. Hamisi asoma vizuri.
16. Hamisi atafika kesho?

## EXERCISE 9b (p. 40)

1. Has the Bwana returned?  He has returned.
2. When did he return?  He returned yesterday.
3. What are you doing?  I am writing.
4. What are you writing?  I am writing a book.
5. What do you want?  I want some potatoes.
6. Where are the loads?  They are lost.
7. The children are singing well.
8. Do the children sing well?  They sing well.
9. The women are cultivating the plantation.
10. The cook has gone to the market.

## EXERCISE 9c (p. 40)

1. Wapagazi wamefika?  Wamefika.
2. Wagonjwa wanafanya nini?  Wamelala.
3. Umeondoa nini?  Nimeondoa viti.
4. Unaondoa nini?  Ninaondoa vyombo.
5. Mgonjwa alikufa juzi.
6. Mwataka nini?  Twataka chakula.
7. Amekula nini?  Amekula viazi.
8. Jana alikula nini?  Alikula viazi.
9. Leo mmesoma?  Tumesoma.
10. Ulilima lini?  Nililima juzi.
11. Jana ulikwenda sokoni?  Nilikwenda.

## Exercise 10 (p. 43)

| | | |
|---|---|---|
| 1. Wameuona. | 9. Ulimwona? | 17. Atakiona. |
| 2. Wamewaona. | 10. Ulituona? | 18. Atajiona. |
| 3. Wametuona. | 11. Ulikiona? | 19. Mwaiona? |
| 4. Wamewaona. | 12. Uliniona? | 20. Mwaniona? |
| 5. Wamekuona. | 13. Atawaona. | 21. Mwaviona? |
| 6. Wameviona. | 14. Atatuona. | 22. Tutawaona? |
| 7. Uliwaona? | 15. Atamwona. | 23. Tutakuona? |
| 8. Uliuona? | 16. Ataniona. | 24. Tutamwona? |

## Exercise 11 (p. 49)

| | | |
|---|---|---|
| mtu mpya | milango mipya | vitanda vipya |
| mtu mwema | milango myema | vitanda vyema |
| mtu mwingine | milango mingine | vitanda vingine |
| mtu mbaya | milango mibaya | vitanda vibaya |
| mtu mfupi | milango mifupi | vitanda vifupi |
| mtu mdogo | milango midogo | vitanda vidogo |

## Exercise 12 (p. 52)

| | |
|---|---|
| mtu mmoja | mlango mmoja |
| watu kumi na wawili | milango kumi na miwili |
| watu thelathini na wanane | milango thelathini na minane |
| watu sita | milango sita |
| watu mia na watatu | milango mia na mitatu |

kitanda kimoja
vitanda kumi na viwili
vitanda thelathini na vinane
vitanda sita
vitanda mia na vitatu

## Exercise 13 (p. 53)

1. Wevi werevu wameiba mtego.
2. Miti mirefu kumi imekufa.
3. Jana tulinunua miavuli miwili na viatu vipya.
4. Vikombe vyeupe vitatu vimeingia ufa, visahani vidogo vitano vime-vunjika.
5. Mpishi ataka kisu kipya.
6. Lete mikate midogo minane.
7. Nilete vikombe vingapi? Lete vitano.
8. Nilete vyeupe? La, lete vyekundu.

## EXERCISE 14a (p. 56)

1. Chumba chao.
2. Watoto wake.
3. Mpagazi wangu.
4. Vitu vya watu.
5. Kikapu cha Ali.
6. Kikombe cha nani?
7. Mgeni wetu.
8. Mikono yangu.
9. Kikombe changu kikubwa.
10. Miti yake mirefu.
11. Kisu cha mgeni.
12. Mikate ya wageni.
13. Mpishi wa nani?
14. Moto wako.
15. Mioto yenu.
16. Mji wao.
17. Kiko cha nani?
18. Kiti cha mzee.
19. Visu vyao virefu.
20. Wageni wetu wachache.

## EXERCISE 14b (p. 58)

1. Wageni wake wawili walifika jana.
2. Kikapu chetu kipya kimepasuka.
3. Kiko cha mgeni kimeanguka. Kimevunjika?
4. Miti yenu mitatu imekufa.
5. Vikombe viwili na visahani vyake vimevunjika.
6. Mwenzio ameondoa kikapu changu?
7. Mtoto wake Hamisi alifika jana?
8. Mtoto wa Ali alifika lini?
9. Umewaona wapagazi wetu? Nimewaona.
10. Wamesoma kitabu chako? Wamekisoma.
11. Weka visu peke yake.
12. Alikuja peke yake?
13. (N)endeni zenu.

## EXERCISE 15a (p. 59)

| | | | |
|---|---|---|---|
| Kiko hiki; | kiko kile. | Mwezi huu; | mwezi ule. |
| Mwalimu huyu; | mwalimu yule. | Mlima huu; | mlima ule. |
| Mzigo huu; | mzigo ule. | Kiatu hiki; | kiatu kile. |
| Viko hivi; | viko vile. | Miezi hii; | miezi ile. |
| W(a)alimu hawa; | w(a)alimu wale. | Milima hii; | milima ile. |
| Mizigo hii; | mizigo ile. | Viatu hivi; | viatu vile. |

## EXERCISE 15b (p. 60)

1. Bring the little knife.
2. These new shoes hurt me.
3. Take away those utensils.
4. This knife pleases me.
5. Do these children read well?
6. Is that old man asleep?
7. This door is broken.
8. This cook cooks well.
9. These two trees are dead.
10. Are these potatoes mature?
11. He struck that child.
12. I want this one and that.

## EXERCISE 16a (p. 61)

Mgonjwa yupi?
Mwezi upi?
Kikombe kipi?

Miji ipi?
Wageni wepi?
Viko vipi?

## EXERCISE 16b (p. 61)

1. Ulimwona mtoto yupi? Nilimwona wako.
2. Ulinunua kitabu kipi?
3. Waliona mlima upi?
4. Wanawake walileta viazi vipi?
5. Nilete kipi?
6. Mpishi ataka kikombe kipi?
7. Wamtaka mpagazi yupi?

## EXERCISE 17 (p. 62)

1. Viatu vyote.
2. Vikombe vyo vyote.
3. Miji yote.
4. Kijiko cho chote.
5. Mtoto ye yote.
6. Wagonjwa wote.
7. Viatu vyo vyote.
8. Vikombe vyote.
9. Mji wo wote.
10. Vijiko vyote.
11. Watoto wote.
12. Mgonjwa ye yote.

## EXERCISE 18 (p. 63)

1. Mwiba wenyewe.
2. Visu vyenye vipini virefu.
3. Chumba chenye milango miwili.
4. Kiko chenyewe.
5. Mwezi wenyewe.
6. Kiti chenye miguu mitatu.
7. Wapagazi wenye mizigo.
8. Viatu vyenyewe.

## EXERCISE 19a (p. 67)

1. Are the pineapples ripe? They are ripe.
2. Is the axe in the shed? It is not there, it is lost.
3. Bring some oil. The oil is finished.
4. Put the eggs in the basin.
5. The porters are not to bring water.
6. What has Hamisi brought? He has brought some hoes.
7. The Mabwana are not in the plantation.
8. The boys are in the kitchen.
9. What is the cook to buy? He is to buy some lemons.
10. Is the milk in the storeroom?
11. Where are the ladies? They are in the house.

## EXERCISE 19b (p. 68)

1. Jani jipya; majani mapya.
2. Nanasi jekundu moja; mananasi mekundu mawili.
3. Maji mengi.
4. Jino jeupe kubwa; meno meupe makubwa.
5. Shoka refu; mashoka marefu.
6. Yai bichi; mayai mabichi.
7. Jicho zuri; macho mazuri.
8. Jina jipya; majina mapya.

M

## EXERCISE 19c (p. 69)

1. Has his tooth come out? It has come out.
2. This branch is broken.
3. All the water has dried up.
4. Bring five fresh eggs.
5. Their quarrels have increased.
6. Which hoe do you want? Any one.
7. Do you want this large one? I want it.
8. Are all the boys asleep?
9. Is your master awake?
10. Do you want these oranges? I want them.
11. This milk has boiled over; take care that it does not boil over again.

## EXERCISE 20a (p. 73)

1. Hatutataka kitu.
2. Hutataka kitu?
3. Hutaki kitu?
4. Sitaki kitu.
5. Sitaki kitu.
6. Hakutaka kitu?
7. Hawatataka kitu.
8. Hawakutaka kitu?
9. Hawataki kitu.
10. Hataki kitu.
11. Sikumbuki.
12. Hawakukumbuka.
13. Hatakumbuka.
14. Hukumbuki?
15. Hakumbuki?
16. Hawatakumbuka.
17. Hamkukumbuka?
18. Hatukukumbuka.
19. Twakumbuka.
20. Hatukumbuki.

## EXERCISE 20b (p. 74)

1. Hatukwenda mjini jana.
2. Sitapika kesho.
3. Mtoto hakulia?
4. Moto hauwaki vizuri?
5. Siandiki.
6. Mananasi hayakuoza.
7. Hamkuja jana?
8. Kesho hataleta viazi.
9. Hawatakuja kesho.
10. Mpishi hapiki vizuri.
11. Hatusomi.
12. Hataandika kesho.
13. Mtoto halii.
14. Hatutaki kitu.
15. Hatutakuja kesho.

## EXERCISE 20c (p. 74)

1. Twataka kusoma.
2. Mlinunua viazi?
3. Viazi vimeoza.
4. Jino lilitoka.
5. Mpishi ataka maji.
6. Nitanunua jembe.
7. Hamisi aliondoa vyombo?
8. Watoto wanasoma.
9. Jana nilikula nanasi.
10. Asoma vizuri.
11. Tunalia. Tunakula kitu.
12. (Ni)nakwenda mjini leo.

# KEY TO EXERCISES

## EXERCISE 21 (p. 77)

1. Where has this water come from?
2. Where is your master?
3. When were these oranges brought?
4. When did this stranger arrive?
5. Where are large stones obtainable? They are not to be had, sir.
6. My hoe is lost again.
7. How many eggs do you want? I want two only.
8. Have you brought any other fruit? No, I have not brought any other, I have brought only this.
9. Have you brought the water? I have not brought any, sir; the water is finished.
10. Have you bought any sacks? I have not bought any; they are not obtainable at the shop, except just one only.
11. This hoe is of no use to me, bring another with a long handle.
12. I am not going to-day, I went yesterday.

## EXERCISE 22 (p. 79)

1. To-day I am very tired.
2. The cook says he wants some large potatoes.
3. How many eggs have you bought? Five, sir. I have told the cook not to cook all five of them; he is to cook three only.
4. Yesterday we cultivated, to-morrow we shall play football.
5. Are all the axes there? All of them are there, sir.
6. This tree has borne very much fruit.
7. What have you brought? I have brought three oranges and eight eggs.

## EXERCISE 23 (p. 79)

1. Do you not want these lemons? Yes, I want them.
2. Do you want these lemons? Yes, I want them.
3. Have you used this new hoe? Yes, I have used it.
4. Have you brought the water? No, sir, I have not.
5. Does he not want to sell his potatoes? No, sir, he does not want (to).

## EXERCISE 24 (p. 80)

1. Unapanda nini? Unauza nini? Ninauza mananasi.
2. Hawauzi viazi, wanauza (wauza) mananasi.
3. Kesho hatutataka maziwa.
4. Malimau hayapatikani sokoni leo.
5. Jana yalipatikana?
6. Jana hayakupatikana.
7. Asema hataki msumeno, ataka shoka.
8. Hamisi anafanya nini? Analima.
9. Jana Ali alikwenda sokoni, kesho atakwenda tena.
10. Wanawake wanapika mchele.

11. Mgonjwa anafanya nini? Anasoma kitabu.
12. Asoma vizuri? Hasomi vizuri.
13. Jana ulimwona? La, nimemwona leo, asubuhi na mapema.
14. Majembe yako wapi? Uliyaweka kibandani?
15. Mlima hauonekani leo.
16. Uliyapata? (machungwa)
17. Mmeyaona? (mawe)
18. Watu wanapita.
19. Nitavinunua kesho.
20. Ametusahau?
21. Ulimwona wapi?
22. Utakwenda mjini kesho, au kesho kutwa?
23. Siendi kesho, nilikwenda jana.
24. Hatujaanza kusoma.
25. Ali asema hawezi kuchukua mzigo.
26. Maji yamechemka?
27. Maziwa yanachemka.
28. Mpishi anapika maboga madogo.
29. Hamisi amewasha moto? Siyo, hajarudi.
30. Moto hauwaki vizuri, wataka mafuta kidogo.
31. (Yako) wapi mafuta? Sijui, labuda yamekwisha.
32. Baba yangu yumo nyumbani, hajatoka bado.

## EXERCISE 25 (p. 84)

1. Do you (pl.) want some salt? Yes, we want some.
2. Is the motor-car outside? It isn't there, sir.
3. Is the work finished? It is not yet finished.
4. Bring a hammer. It isn't here, perhaps it is lost.
5. What are the sick people drinking? They are drinking tea.
6. Don't let them drink tea, they are to drink milk only.
7. What are the skilled workmen doing? They are repairing a bridge.
8. Are the workmen not to come again? Yes, they are to come.
9. Has the bell sounded? It sounded some time ago.
10. Tell the boy to light the lamp.
11. Hamisi, put out the lamp. The lamp has gone out, Bibi.
12. Why has this lamp gone out? Because it needs oil.

## EXERCISE 26 (p. 85)

| | | | |
|---|---|---|---|
| njia pana | njia mbili | njia nyeupe | njia ngumu |
| njia mpya | njia tatu | njia mbaya | njia nane |
| njia ndefu | njia nzuri | njia fupi | njia nyembamba |

## EXERCISE 27a (p. 86)

1. Let us go to the market. What do you want to buy at the market?
I want to buy a kettle because ours has a hole in it, and leaks.

2. Take this letter to Bwana Ali. Am I to wait for an answer, sir? No, don't wait for an answer.

3. Let us set out on our journey to-morrow at daybreak. What am I to take? You will need a tent, a table, blankets, mosquito net, a bucket and a basin.

4. Send a man to buy a fowl, tell him to bring potatoes, milk and vegetables.

5. Is meat to be had in the market? To-day it is to be had; yesterday it was not procurable. It isn't to be had every day.

6. These two plates are broken and this one is cracked.

7. The soup is smoky.

8. This saw is rusty.

9. Where can I buy a good gun?

10. Where are you going? I am going to fetch my watch, it is upstairs in my room. It isn't upstairs, it's here on the table.

11. I feel thirsty, I want some tea. This tea has become cold. I am hungry, bring some food.

12. The children want to know what clothes are they to sew? Let them sew these two.

13. Which hat do you want? Any one will do for me. Do you like this one? I like it.

14. Where is the owner of that motor-car?

## EXERCISE 27b (p. 87)

1. Watoto wanacheza? Hawachezi, wamekaa kitako.
2. Wanawake wanashona nini? Wanashona nguo.
3. Walishona jana? La, jana hawakushona, walifua nguo.
4. Je, Ali amepiga pasi nguo? Bado, asema makaa yamekwisha.
5. Kwa nini mtoto analia? Asema hataki kusoma.
6. Kwa nini hataki kusoma? Asema kichwa chamwuma.
7. Mgonjwa ataka chakula, ana njaa.
8. Leo sipiki, nitapika kesho.
9. Taa haiwaki vizuri, imezimika, yataka mafuta. Mafuta, Bibi, yamekwisha.
10. Mpishi yuko jikoni? Hayuko Bibi. Amekwenda sokoni kununua mayai. Amerudi? Bado, Bibi.
11. Bibi, mpishi amerudi, hakupata mayai, asema leo hayapatikani.
12. Yuko wapi Hamisi? Yuko chini anafagia chumbani.

## EXERCISE 28a (p. 91)

1. Kongoni hawa watatu.
2. Ng'ombe zako wakali.
3. Kondoo huyu mzuri.
4. Majoka matano.
5. Baba zao. (Mababa zao.)
6. Ng'ombe wetu mwekundu.
7. Ndugu yako mrefu.

## EXERCISE 28b (p. 91)

1. Mbwa zako wawili wanapigana.
2. Mabaharia wote walirudi jana.
3. Rafiki zako hawakai hapa.
4. Wake zao walifika jana.
5. Bwana wako atafika lini?
6. Mbuzi zako wako wapi? Wanalisha kilimani.
7. Ndugu yangu mdogo hayuko. Amekwenda sokoni.
8. Sesota lile joka kuu limekufa.
9. Kitoto hiki kimelala.

## EXERCISE 29a (p. 95)

1. Where is my book? Which book? The new one.
2. Whose book is this? It belongs to Hamisi.
3. Our book is lost. Have you seen it?
4. Bring a book. Which one am I to bring, sir? Bring any one. This, sir, is a nice one.

1. Liko wapi shoka langu? Shoka lipi? Lile jipya.
2. Shoka la nani hili? Ni lake Hamisi.
3. Shoka letu limepotea. Umeliona?
4. Lete shoka. Nilete lipi Bwana? Lete lo lote. Hili, Bwana (ni) zuri.

1. Uko wapi mwavuli wangu? Mwavuli upi? Ule mpya.
2. Mwavuli wa nani huu? Ni wake Hamisi.
3. Mwavuli wetu umepotea. Umeuona?
4. Lete mwavuli. Nilete upi Bwana? Lete wo wote. Huu, Bwana, (ni) mzuri.

1. This umbrella is split, bring another.
2. Where is the other one, sir? It is upstairs.
3. Here it is, sir. I have brought (it).
4. This is not mine; mine is a good one, this is a poor one.

1. Kikapu hiki kimepasuka, lete kingine.
2. Kile kingine kiko wapi Bwana? Kiko juu.
3. Hiki hapa Bwana, nimekileta.
4. Hiki si changu, changu (ni) kizuri, hiki (ni) kibaya.

1. Ngoma hii imepasuka, lete ngine (nyingine).
2. Ile ngine iko wapi, Bwana? Iko juu.
3. Hii hapa Bwana, nimeileta.
4. Hii si yangu, yangu (ni) nzuri, hii (ni) mbaya.

1. Where are your children? They are upstairs, two of them are writing, and one is reading.
2. Have you seen our cook? I have seen him, he is in the kitchen (he is) cooking. That one is not our cook.
3. My cook has left. I want another. There is a man outside, he says he is a cook. Which man? The short one.

## EXERCISE 29b (p. 96)

1. Viti viko juu.
2. Kofia ya nani hii?
3. Kofia yako ipi?
4. Miti hii (ni) yangu.
5. Watoto wa macho.
6. Hawako juu.
7. U tayari?
8. Ni mnyama.
9. U mvivu? Wewe mvivu?
10. Kisu hiki (ni) kizuri.
11. Watu hawa (ni) Waswahili?
12. Sisi tu wavivu.
13. Visu vyangu (ni) vichache, vyako (ni) vingi.
14. M tayari? Ninyi tayari?
15. Chumba ki tupu.
16. Kazi hii rahisi.
17. Vikombe vi safi.
18. Wa hai? (nyoka)
19. Wapagazi wako nje.
20. Viatu hivi si vyangu.
21. Vijiko vimo kabatini.
22. Bwana yuko?
23. Hayumo nyumbani.
24. Simba ni mnyama mkali.

## EXERCISE 30a (p. 101)

(a) Nyundo ninayo.  Parafujo tunazo.
Misumari unayo?  Shoka mnalo?
Msumeno anao.  Uzi wanao?

(b) 1. Nyundo sina, anayo Ali.
2. Hatuna matunda, lakini Ali anayo.
3. Ali hana kitabu, wala mimi sina.

## EXERCISE 30b (p. 101)

1. Paka wetu ana miguu mikubwa.
2. Kila mpagazi anao mzigo wake.
3. Mpishi ana watoto wawili.
4. Una vidole vingapi?
5. Ndege wote wana mabawa.
6. Tembo hana ulimi.
7. Hatuna fedha.
8. Una senti ngapi?
9. Ana pete mbili nzuri.
10. Watoto hawa wana nini?
11. Paka ana njaa?
12. Taa haipo mezani, labuda anayo Bwana.
13. Vitabu vyangu unavyo? Ndiyo Bwana, hivi hapa.

## EXERCISE 30c (p. 102)

1. He asked them, Have you anything to eat? and they said, We have not.
2. He said to the Sultan, The thieves have proved too much for me, they have taken away the goat and the honey as well. And the Sultan said, I have the honey.
3. I want the master, for I have a letter for him here.
4. He met his wife, she was in a state of grief. And he asked her, What is the matter, Bibi?
5. Who has the goat?

## EXERCISE 31 (p. 103)

1. Lete taa na fimbo yangu.
2. Wataka mchele, chai na sukari.
3. Wataka na ndizi pia?
4. Enda na kikapu sokoni.
5. Juma na Muhamadi wanalima.
6. Sitaki kwenda peke yangu. Basi enda na Ali.
7. Njoo nami.
8. Enda nao.
9. Wamesimama karibu na mlango.
10. Nimenunua machungwa na malimau.

## EXERCISE 32a (p. 107)

| | | | | |
|---|---|---|---|---|
| nyapo | panga | pepo | nyoya (*also* ma-) | tepe |
| kuta | nyanda | nyimbo | nyuta | nyufa |
| nyuma | nyua | kucha | nyavu | nyayo |
| mbavu | tambi | fito | pande | teo |

## EXERCISE 32b (p. 107)

1. Is the razor on the table? It is not there, it is in the box.
2. Have the women brought the building-sticks? They have brought them.
   Where are they? They are outside. Are they to bring more to-morrow, sir? No, they are not to bring any more.
3. Is the fork in the box? It is not, it is on the table.
4. Where are the keys? They are downstairs.
   No, they are not down, they are upstairs.
5. I don't like porridge, don't cook any more.
6. What has the Swahili brought? He has brought some swords.
7. The ladies do not want cooked rice.
8. The wall is cracked.
9. Cook rice, porridge and potatoes.
10. Are the swords in the shed? They are not there, sir.
11. Take away the planks, they are no longer of any use.
12. The women want a winnowing tray.
13. The wind is blowing, it is raising the dust.
14. Is a fork procurable in the market? Yes, Bibi, it is procurable.
15. Are the children singing songs? No, they are merely making a noise.
16. Is the wick finished? It is not finished.
17. Hamisi is at the door, he has sweeping-brushes for sale.
18. The keys are lost, they are not in the box.
19. Yesterday I brought some firewood, am I to bring more to-morrow? Don't bring any more.
20. Is Hamisi to bring firewood to-morrow? He is not to bring any to-morrow, perhaps the day after to-morrow.

## EXERCISE 33 (p. 108)

Wembe mgumu;  nyembe ngumu.    Wembe mweusi;  nyembe nyeusi.
Wembe mfupi;   nyembe fupi.     Wembe mdogo;   nyembe ndogo.
Wembe mbovu;   nyembe mbovu.                    nyembe nne.

## EXERCISE 34a (p. 109)

1. Uko wapi wembe wangu?  Wembe upi?  Ule mpya.
2. Wembe wa nani huu?  Ni wake Hamisi.
3. Wembe wetu umepotea.  Umeuona?
4. Lete wembe.  Nilete upi Bwana?  Lete wo wote.  Huu Bwana, mzuri.

<br>

1. Wembe huu umeharibika; lete mwingine.
2. Ule mwingine uko wapi, Bwana?  Uko juu.
3. Huu hapa Bwana, nimeuleta.
4. Huu si wangu.  Ule wangu mzuri, huu mbaya.

## EXERCISE 34b (p. 109)

1. These two lamps need new wicks.
2. The wick of your lamp is very short, shall I buy a new one?
3. These planks are very long, they are of no use whatever.
4. The porters say they want three swords and two sweeping-brushes. Very well, give them to them.
5. This is not my key.  Mine is a small one; this is long and thin.
6. This porridge is nice, it is just what I want.

## EXERCISE 35a (p. 116)

1. Have the strangers who came yesterday returned?  They have returned.
2. Those of you who want work, stand on one side; those who don't want work, go back.
3. Do not keep a useless tin can.  If it is useless, throw it away.
4. The cuttings which have been well watered have taken root, and are flourishing, but those which have not been looked after are all dead.
5. The bed which has come back from being repaired is broken.
6. Put these small potatoes apart from these large ones which will be required for the evening meal.
7. What's the use of a bell which won't ring?
8. Where are the sacks?  Which ones, sir?  Those which I bought yesterday.
9. Put back the soap which has not been used.
10. The ink which was spilt yesterday is not easily rubbed off.
11. Is the lad to whom you are teaching Swahili intelligent?
12. The strangers whom I saw yesterday, where are they living?
13. Hamisi has opened the door which I shut.

M*

14. The loaves which the cook cooked are not to be eaten till to-morrow.
15. Is the knife which you borrowed from Sefu a good one?
16. The knives I bought yesterday are poor ones: they won't cut.
17. The nice soap you gave me is finished.
18. Have those letters which I put on the table been posted?

## Exercise 35b (p. 116)

1. Watoto waliókimbia wamerudi wote.
2. Kisu kilichopotea kimeonekana.
3. Yule mgonjwa aliyefika jana amerudi leo.
4. Weko wapi maboi waliotaka kazi?
5. Miti iliyopandwa mwaka jana inasitawi.
6. Vile viazi vilivyopikwa jana tumevila vyote.
7. Lete majembe yaliyotumiwa jana.
8. Sukari uliyoinunua jana inekwisha?
9. Watu wachukuao mizigo huitwa Wapagazi.
10. Twataka watu walimao vizuri.
11. Chafaa nini kisu ambacho hakipati?
12. Sitaki jembe lisilofaa kitu.
13. Ile sabuni niliyokupa, imekwisha?
14. Wageni uliowaona jana wanakaa Mombasa.
15. Mlango ulioufunga, umefunguka.
16. Mikate yote niliyoipika imeliwa.
17. Yako wapi magunia aliyoyaleta Hamisi?
18. Nimeziondoa sahani zisizotakikana kwa chakula cha jioni.

## Exercise 36a (p. 121)

1. Call Hamisi and tell him to go to market at once.
2. I am here, Bibi; what am I to buy?
3. Buy bread, sugar and fish.
4. How many loaves shall I buy? Buy only one.
5. Fill the kettle with water.
6. Tell the cook to dish up the food.
7. When is he to dish up, Bibi?
8. Tell him to dish up at 12 o'clock and not to be late.
9. The boy is not to bring any water now.
10. Why isn't he to bring any?
11. Now then, go back.
12. Don't make a noise.
13. Ring the bell; ring it loudly.
14. Call your friends.
15. What are we to tell them?
16. Tell them to come to-morrow early in the morning.
17. Am I to close the door? No, don't close it.
18. Cheer up (pl.).
19. Are the children to go away? Don't let them go yet.

20. Come here (pl.).
21. Bwana says, Do not cook any potatoes to-day.
22. Now then, be off with you.
23. Get up, it is past the time.
24. Don't speak in a slovenly way, speak nicely.
25. He who smokes tobacco must use a pipe.
26. It is the custom here that everyone who wants medicine must bring a bottle.

## EXERCISE 36b (p. 122)

1. Nguo hizi zina taka nyingi, usikose kuzifua.
2. Zikunje kwa uangalifu.
3. Andika meza, usikunje-kunje nguo.
4. Ijaze taa mafuta.
5. Mwambie aje mapema.
6. Kandarinya hii ijaze maji.
7. Barua hii ipeleke kwa Bwana.
8. Usichelewe njiani.
9. Nunua samaki, nyama na mayai.
10. Mwambie leo asipike kitu.
11. Chemsha mayai mabichi mawili.
12. Usitupe chakula.
13. Mwambie Ali afanye chai.
14. Mpe Hamisi taa.
15. Funga dirisha.
16. Hesabu mizigo.
17. Waambie wapagazi wasichelewe.
18. Mwite karani, mwambie aondoe kalamu hii.
19. Peleka barua hizi posta.
20. Nipe bahasha ndefu.

## EXERCISE 37a (p. 130)

1. Some soldiers have been stationed in the town.
2. The house is whitewashed inside.
3. It has been cultivated here.
4. Some sick folk have died in the village over there *or* there have been some deaths, etc.
5. Some people are standing on the mountain *or* there are some people etc.
6. The house is full of people.
7. There is nothing in the well.
8. There is nothing in the market to-day.
9. There are people in the plantation.
10. Are there snakes in the forest? There are.
11. Are there shops in the town? There are none.
12. Are there any shops within the town? There are none.
13. There is a snake down below.

14. Isn't there anything on the table? There isn't.
15. There is nothing here in front of the box.
16. There is nothing in the box.
17. Are there any strangers here?
18. There are trees over there.
19. There is a river here.
20. There are books in the box.

## Exercise 37b (p. 131)

1. Sandukuni mna kitu?
2. Hapa hapana kitu.
3. Pana taa nyuma ya sanduku.
4. Kule kuna nyumba?
5. Huku hakuna miji.
6. Hapa hapana kisima.
7. Huku juu hakuna kitu.
8. Hapa pana watu?
9. Mwituni mna maua.
10. Humu mwituni hamna watu.
11. Humu mwituni hamna wanyama.
12. Nyumbani mna kuni?
13. Nje kuna kuni nyingi.
14. Kuna machungwa sokoni?
15. Hapana maji hapa.
16. Humu jikoni hamna vyombo.
17. Bakulini mna sukari?
18. Pana nyoka chini ya mti.

## Exercise 37c (p. 132)

1. Is the cook there? He is not about, he has gone to market.
2. Is there fish at the market? There is none to-day.
3. Is the soap upstairs? It is not upstairs, there is nothing upstairs.
4. Is the rice on the table? No, there is nothing on the table.
5. Is there any oil? Yes, it is in the store.
6. The oil is not in the store, there is nothing in the store.
7. Bring some water. There is no water, Bibi; there is none in the well, it has dried up.
8. Is there any sugar in the basin? No, it is finished.

## Exercise 37d (p. 132)

1. Kuni ziko? Ziko. Hakuna.
2. Kuni ziko nje? Haziko nje, zimo kibandani.
3. Sokoni kuna kuni? Hakuna.
4. Mtu yuko? Yuko mtu.
5. Hamisi yuko nje? Hayuko nje, yuko juu.
6. Hapa pana wagonjwa? Hapana. Wako hospitali.
7. Wagonjwa wako? Hawako.

## Exercise 38a (p. 137)

One day they went for a walk to a certain place and came across some guinea-fowl eggs. The hare said, Let us snare this guinea-fowl. The *cheche* said, Very well. The hare went off and made a snare and set it. The guinea-fowl came along and was snared, and they carried him off to the house. The hare said to the *cheche*, Friend, roast this guinea-fowl, I am a little tired. I want to take a nap. The *cheche* replied, Very well.

2. The *cheche* said, A man came here, and fastened me up, and beat me soundly, and then made his way off.

3. Now one day the *cheche* said to the hare, Let us go and play *kiumbizi* to-day. The hare said, All right, but first I want to go home and see my relatives.

4. That night he went out and the police arrested him. And he said, Don't take me to prison, take me home first that I may eat some food, then later on take me to prison.

5. Let us go to our mother again, and ask her about our father's work.

6. The Sultan said to Fikirini, Go inside and greet your mother.

7. My husband, let us go inside and then let me tell you about the calamity which has befallen me.

8. And I said to my wife, Go and shut the door. My wife said to me, You go and shut it.

9. I have been told to go and search for a bird with wings of gold.

10. Thereupon the Sultan started off to follow the thief, and he searched for him without finding him.

11. And they stayed until evening without receiving even a drop of coffee.

12. The cat went out to search for the elephant, and he found him and said to him, I desire friendship. The elephant did not refuse and said to him, Very well.

13. The cock heard his words, but said nothing, and merely sat quiet.

14. He came across his wife in a dejected state. And he asked her, Bibi, what is the matter with you? The lady did not reply.

15. Along the road the Sultan said to his vizier, Did you understand the words? He said, No, I did not understand them. And he said, You, a vizier of full rank, and you do not understand those words?

## EXERCISE 38b (p. 140)

1. The cock sat quiet, listening intently up to the end of their conversation.

2. The poor man went off crying.

3. And there appeared a tall genie and stood near him and said to him, Human being, whether you wish or no, you are dead. (If you desire it you are dead, and if you do not desire it you are dead.)

4. If you hear people conversing, well, they are asleep, and if you hear that they are quiet, well, they are awake.

5. The hunter, observing it was merely a cat, replied, All right, let us go along to my home.

6. During their conversation the cock said to the hare, My friend, at night do you generally hear me talking? The hare replied, I have never yet heard you speaking, not even once, except that towards morning I hear you say *Kucha kucheree*.

7. Unless you remove this misfortune you will die, you or your husband.

8. Very well, I am prepared to give you your portion (fee), but what about it if my child does not get well?

## EXERCISE 38c (p. 141)

1. Ukitafuta, utakiona.
2. Asipokuja mapema, hatamaliza kazi yake.
3. Usipoangalia, utaharibu kitabu chako.
4. Kama hujui, utaambiwa.
5. Tuliwaona wapagazi wakicheza mpira.
6. Mti ukianguka, rudi mara moja.
7. Ukimwona mnyapara, mwambie kesho aje nyumbani kwangu.
8. Zikipatikana ndizi, zinunue.
9. Usiponiambia, siwezi kukusaidia.
10. Kama hawarudi, sitawalipa.
11. Kesho isipokunya mvua, maua yote yatakufa.
12. Wasipochukua mizigo, hawatalipwa mshahara.
13. Niliwaona wakilima.
14. Tuliwaona wakirudi kutoka mji.
15. Ukitazama, utawaona wanyama wakikimbia.
16. Askari wakimwona yule mwivi, watamkamata.

## EXERCISE 39a (p. 143)

1. Umempa Hamisi senti za mayai haya?
2. Ndizi hizi utazila lini?
3. Tule lini ndizi hizi?
4. Jana mgonjwa hakunywa dawa yake.
5. Mwambie ainywe kesho.
6. Yuko wapi yule paka aliyemla panya?
7. Mti huu ulikufa lini?
8. Haukufa, u hai.
9. Kesho nitakupa mshahara wako.
10. Mtoto wa mbwa asinywe maziwa yote.
11. Fedha niliyompa haitoshi.
12. Jua linakuchwa, twende zetu.
13. Simchi.
14. Mti huu ukifa, nitapanda mwingine.

## EXERCISE 39b (p. 144)

1. Mizigo imekuwa tayari kitambo.
2. Mizigo ilikuwa tayari jana.
3. Mizigo itakuwa tayari saa sita ya mchana.
4. Mizigo ikiwa tayari, nitaondoka alasiri.
5. Haitakuwa tayari mpaka kesho.
6. Mizigo iwe tayari kesho asubuhi na mapema.
7. Mizigo ilikuwa wapi?
8. Jana ilikuwapo pale mlangoni.
9. Mizigo yako itakuwa tayari lini?
10. Uko wapi mzigo wa mpishi?
11. Uko nje karibu na mnazi.
12. Mzigo mmoja haupo.

## Exercise 40 (p. 148)

1. Nguo za kifalme
2. Maji ya moto
3. Kazi ya moto
4. Mshahara wa kawaida
5. Pete za thamani
6. Desturi za kizungu
7. Maneno ya kiswahili
8. Watu wa kiungwana
9. Watoto wa kishenzi
10. Watoto wa kiume
11. Walimu wa kike
12. Vyumba vya juu
13. Kazi ya chini
14. Wanyama wa mwituni
15. Kazi za nyumbani
16. Vyombo vya jikoni
17. Kazi ya jikoni
18. Maua ya kondeni
19. Mazao ya shambani
20. Mkono wa kuume
21. Mikono ya kushoto
22. Supu ya maji-maji
23. Samaki wa baharini
24. Maji ya baharini
25. Maji ya chumvi
26. Viti vya kutosha
27. Chumba chenye madirisha mengi
28. Kosa la tano
29. Ndege wa thenashara
30. Mtoto wa nne
31. Taa ya tatu
32. Mpagazi wa edashara
33. Mlango wa pili
34. Ukurasa wa kwanza
35. Nyama ya baridi
36. Watoto werevu
37. Pete ya dhahabu
38. Ukurasa wa mwisho
39. Mtu mwenye haki (wa haki)
40. Michezo ya kitoto
41. Habari za kweli
42. Mahali pa juu
43. Blanketi ya chini
44. Samaki wa mtoni
45. Chakula cha kutosha
46. Kazi ipendezayo
47. Vikombe vilivyojaa
48. Maneno yaliyosikilika
49. Mwaka ujao
50. Mwaka jana

## Exercise 41a (p. 155)

1. Where can I buy a hat?
2. What are you saying? What does he say?
3. How much is the fare?
4. Where is the owner?
5. What are you selling here?
6. What is the usual price?
7. How do you sell these oranges?
8. What house is that?
9. How long a journey is it to Maweni?
10. What are these fine trees?
11. Who are these people who are working here?
12. Which is the road that goes to the town?
13. How long will it take to get there?
14. What will you buy in the market?
15. How many shillings have you spent?
16. Where is the padlock?
17. What is the matter with you? What is the matter with you (in health)?
18. How are you to-day?
19. Since when have you been ill?
20. How long does it take to get to the other side?
21. How many porters are wanted?
22. What shall I take with me?
23. What is the weight of each load?
24. Whose load is this?

25. What is this rope for?
26. How many people are there at Tanga?
27. What house is that with the clock?
28. How long is this lake? What is its width?
29. When will the rain cease?
30. When will it rain?
31. How long will it be before the food is ready?
32. Why are you wanting work?

33. How is it you are needing more soap?
34. Where has this water come from?
35. What food is there in the kitchen?
36. Why did you not cook some potatoes?
37. When will the train leave?
38. Where do we get our tickets?
39. How can we improve school attendance?
40. What is your name?

## EXERCISE 41b (p. 156)

1. Nani mtu huyu?
2. Nguo za nani hizi?
3. Nani aliyevunja kikombe hiki?
4. Nani amevunja kikombe hiki?
5. Wauza nini hapa?
6. Wauzaje mikeka hii?
7. Mmoja kiasi gani?
8. Jumla kiasi gani?
9. Nini bei ya kawaida?
10. Kelele gani ile?
11. Mnyama gani huyu?
12. Matunda gani haya?
13. Wataka mshahara gani?
14. Wataka wapagazi wangapi?
15. Iko mizigo mingapi nyumbani?
16. Jina lake nani, mtoto huyu?

17. Leo yapatikana nyama gani sokoni?
18. Ratli moja, kiasi gani?
19. Umenunua matunda mangapi?
20. Leo ninunue mayai mangapi?
21. Wanawake hawa wanachukua nini?
22. Vitu hivi vyatoka wapi? (vyatokapi?)
23. Ni vya nini?
24. Ipi taa yako?
25. Tuendee njia ipi?
26. Kwa nini hukwenda jana?
27. Mbona hukufanya kazi jana?
28. Wafanyaje?

## EXERCISE 42a (p. 162)

1. He returned to his island in the lake.
2. They are in their room.
3. They arrived at the buffalo's house.
4. The child is not at school: he has gone home.
5. Where there is smoke, there is sure to be fire.
6. A place with trees does not lack shade.
7. His arrow does not fall on an empty spot.
8. They wore nothing on their heads.
9. In another place the footprints were not visible.
10. Amani got down to look round about.
11. Where is your home?
12. Put down the loads there in the shade.
13. They left and went in another direction.
14. And he took the bag of silver and went and put it on the veranda belonging to Abunawas.

15. He inquired about the Europeans and was told, No, there are none here.
16. And he said to him, Do you know where your home is? And he said, How should I know it seeing that I am in a pit.
17. He said to him, Sir, are there any thieves in this town?
18. The Sultan issued a proclamation that after 10 o'clock there would be no permission to walk about.
19. Meanwhile Kedhab carried away all the clothes and made his way off.
20. We sat until at length a donkey came into the house. And then a dog came right into the house and came to the table.

## EXERCISE 42b (p. 163)

1. Hamna kitu ndani.
2. Mahali penye watoto hapakosi kelele.
3. Alichukua mizigo mabegani mwake.
4. Hapa petu.
5. Amevaa useja shingoni mwake.
6. Wamekwenda kwingine.
7. Waliingia nyumbani mwao?
8. Amerudi mjini kwake?
9. Wamesimama mlangoni pa nyumba yangu.
10. Unakwenda nyumbani kwao?
11. Weka barua pale.
12. Pengine nasahau, pengine nakumbuka.
13. Vikombe vimo humu kabatini.

## EXERCISE 43a (p. 166)

1. He has given me the money just the same as before.
2. Why have you done thus?
3. These insects are anything but nice if handled carelessly.
4. Don't do your work just anyhow.
5. Our king does not drink water just anyhow.
6. When he did this, he did it stealthily.
7. Go quickly.
8. They taught each other in manly fashion.
9. Don't hang the picture askew.
10. The fowls are fed like this twice a day.
11. They greeted me in Swahili fashion.
12. This man was born blind.
13. This child limps (walks lame).
14. He will know by degrees.
15. They are sitting down.
16. Don't lie on your face.
17. The genie said, If you do not believe, wait and let me show you. And he got into the bottle and said, I sat like this.

### EXERCISE 43b (p. 167)

1. Hamisi afanya kazi yake vizuri.
2. Alisema hivi.
3. Fanya (kama) hivi.
4. Waliimba hivi.
5. Jaribu vingine.
6. Walituamkia kizungu.
7. Asema kifalme.
8. Watu hawa hulima ovyo.
9. Najuaje?
10. Enda kafanye vivyo. (vile vile)
11. Fanya vivi hivi.
12. Alisema kitoto.
13. Tenda kiume.

### EXERCISE 44 (p. 171)

1. Wembley is the place where the Exhibition was held.
2. Here where we live is a lovely spot; I have not yet seen a place to surpass it.
3. When the porters return, give them some food.
4. We do not know where they live.
5. It was a poor place where we lived formerly, for there was little water there.
6. The rabbit went along until he arrived at the market, where he met a butcher.
7. How well this man sings!
8. I will do what I can to help you.
9. It appears to me that this work is finished.
10. In whatever direction he looked he saw nothing.
11. Ali did not find the goat at the place where he went, so he returned to where the honey was, but found neither the honey nor the poor man.
12. The peasant told him all about it from the beginning, how he came and how he had spoken.
13. From that day forward the dog began to follow the scent of the cat and to find out where she had passed.
14. Long ago Kalungu was a grief-stricken spot.
15. Hemedi replied, Ah, sir, I do not know where I am going. Then Hemedi asked Fikirini, And what about you, where are you going? And he said, I also, sir, do not know where I am going.
16. When I spoke to him, he did not answer me.

### EXERCISE 45a (p. 174)

1. He took him away out of pity.
2. The witch was killed by stoning.
3. The water went by with a rush.
4. The beehive has broken the branch with its weight of honey.
5. In this canal you will encounter vessels both large and small.
6. These walls are termed breakwaters in English.
7. This firewood cannot be split except with an axe.
8. Translate into English.
9. Our chief ordered the dance to be continued for many days.

10. All the plants have dried up with the fierce sun, even the weeds, grass and thorns as well.
11. Cut the root with a hoe.
12. The people of this country fight with bows and arrows.
13. Take this letter to the master.
14. Come to me to-morrow at twelve.
15. All the women have returned to their homes.
16. Kintu and Nambi lived happily together and had many children, both girls and boys.
17. Do your work carefully.
18. Carry these things carefully.
19. From whom have these bananas come?
20. He is living at his brother's (house).

## EXERCISE 45b (p. 175)

Long ago knowledge of how to follow a thing by scent was possessed by the cat. . . . And the dog realized that the cat had a splendid method of getting food, because other (animals) had to find it by sight, whereas the cat found it by smell. So the dog went to the cat and said, Teach me also this art. The cat replied, Very well. And the dog lived with the cat. After some time had elapsed, and the dog knew the work, he went to his instructor the cat and begged permission to leave.

## EXERCISE 46 (p. 180)

1. I am your son, father, not this (person).
2. It is the offspring of those who were taken captive, who alone are able to tell of the misfortunes which befell their parents.
3. My husband is not here; it is he who manages the money affairs.
4. Take this and give it to the Sultan, and tell him it is the thunderbolt sword.
5. There is but one way of removing this doubt, and that is by examination.
6. And they realized that it was their father who had carried off the sheep.
7. It is these people who have wronged me. I cannot accuse one who has not wronged me.

## EXERCISE 47a (p. 183)

1. It was their lack of mutual understanding which started the war.
2. It is evident that Kintu will have no millet, and so my fowls will die of hunger.
3. He had some children, and the custom of these children was . . .
4. Long ago the hen and the cock were not town creatures but forest creatures.
5. From that time onwards the snake and the millipede have never agreed.

6. My child, I want you to pretend to be dumb. The child agreed. His mother took him off to the doctor and said to him, I have brought you a pupil. And he asked her, Is this child dumb? She replied, Dumb from birth. He said to her, You realize that this is exactly what I desire.

7. Instead of imprisoning them, he gave them presents, and allowed them to depart; nevertheless he did not want to let the children go home.

8. Do you hear some things making a noise? The Sultan replied, I hear. Abunawas replied, They are workmen constructing a stone floor, and the things making a noise are hammers and nails.

## EXERCISE 47b (p. 184)

1. And he got up and went to his brothers, and explained everything to them. And his brothers asked, Brother, of what tribe is this woman? The youth did not mention the woman's name, he said, I just picked her up along the road, and this sword, I came across it, and this bird is what my father is longing for. . . .

His brothers were asked by their father, What is the name of this woman? They replied, We don't know her, we picked her up along the road, together with her sword.

2. Abunawas took twelve of his rupees and gave them to the poor man. He said to him, I give you these rupees, go and pay your debt. In the morning they all assembled before the Sultan. The poor man said that he had come to pay the money. Abunawas asked the poor man, Have you the twelve rupees? He replied, I have. Then Abunawas took the pieces of silver and held them, and called to the rich man to take his money. When he was about to receive them, Abunawas said to him, Wait! And he threw them down. And he said to him, Here, take the sound of these rupees, because the poor man did not eat the food, he merely ate its smell.

## EXERCISE 48 (p. 189)

1. If you had arrived yesterday you would have heard all the news.
2. If you had told me at the time that you do not like travelling, I would not have ordered you to go.
3. If you had searched diligently for the knife, it would have been found.
4. Had I heard anything, I should have told you.
5. If I had bungled my work, I should have been dismissed.
6. If you had gone at once to meet him, he would have paid you, and you would not have returned empty-handed.
7. If I had known, I would not have given him my cents.
8. Had you acknowledged your fault, probably the Bwana would have forgiven you.
9. If he had come yesterday, I should have seen him.
10. If you would but eat a little, you would not feel hungry.
11. If you were to do this work, you would gain by it.
12. If he had not been a thief, he would not have gone off with everything.

## EXERCISE 49 (p. 199)

1. Bring a knife and a cup; bring a spoon as well.
2. This drum won't sound because it is split.
3. The harbour itself is not convenient for disembarkation because it is rocky.
4. We must drive him off because he will destroy our happiness.
5. The rope has cut the stone because it passes over it every day.
6. We were told to keep our eyes "skinned", because we should be passing the place where there were crocodiles and hippos.
7. He flew on ahead for the purpose of showing him the way.
8. We were told that a crocodile makes no sound, except when emerging from its egg.
9. One day the rat went to lay a complaint before the cat because he had (lately) become judge.
10. He went to see if there was any water.
11. The flag was lowered as he had promised.
12. He said that according to Islamic law . . .
13. I have no doubt but what many readers will look forward to hearing news of our journey.
14. Had it not been for these dates, they would have died of hunger.
15. We had to be taken round the workyards by motor, because there were so many of them.
16. In addition to this, food was very expensive.

## EXERCISE 50a (p. 203)

1. Hamisi is Ali's junior. Hamisi is younger than Ali.
2. Juma's brother is the more intelligent, but this boy surpasses them both.
3. Talking is not taking action, it is best to see for oneself.
4. This child is more liked than his companions.
5. His condition is better than that of his friend.
6. Their town is a very small one, in addition its houses are much smaller than ours.
7. The main streets of Paris are famous because they are broader than the main streets of other countries.
8. Among forest animals there is not one who is more cunning than the rabbit.
9. Better to lose one's eyes than to lose heart.
10. It is nicer to go by motor-car than by rail.
11. Yesterday we worked hard, to-day we have worked still harder.
12. Hamisi is stronger than Ali.

## EXERCISE 50b (p. 204)

1. Ali ni mrefu kuliko Juma.
2. Yupi mrefu, Juma au Ali? Ali ndiye mrefu.
3. Mbwa ni mkubwa kuliko paka.
4. Mti huu ndio ulio mrefu sana.

5. Tembo awashinda wanyama wote kwa nguvu.
6. Kazi iliyo bora ndiyo hii.
7. Mtoto wangu ni mrefu sawa na wako, ila apata miaka zaidi.

## EXERCISE 51a (p. 209)

1. He returned to where his friend was.
2. All the little islands in the great lake are not in my kingdom.
3. The king gave him many presents and numberless cattle.
4. Presently you will see which is best.
5. Greetings, Uncle! Here in Paradise I am well, and all the kinsmen who are here are well.
6. The captain of the man-o'-war knew that all who were on board (the dhow) were slaves.
7. Well, said he, so there are a lot of fools about, and I thought my wife was the only one! There are fools even among the mighty. And they went to a distant place where there were no people.
8. All (the slaves) had one particular brand, that is to say, six marks, three on each buttock. This was the brand of Mwinyi Rashidi's slaves.
9. Mrere, one of the slaves who had been sold by M——, was in this group.
10. On hearing this, all of us who were there, left.
11. He chose to go into the rustic district of the Wahadimu, because ignorant folk lived there, who didn't know how to read.
12. Just then Hemedi came out from where he was, and pushing people aside, entered the room where his mother was.
13. But when the ox reached the stable where the donkey was, he did not mention anything about work.
14. When he died, his parents and the people who were there asked, What was the meaning of the words they (the deceased man and his wife) said?
15. All this time the lion was somewhere along the road.
16. The rat said, True, this is a trap for rats, but it is also a trap which affects both those for whom it is intended, and those who are not concerned with it.
17. Discontentment is widespread, because the attendance at school is not going ahead as it should.
18. Had Abunuwas been here, he would have told us the meaning of this hand.
19. In that I am not white, you do not consider me a human being, or what?

## EXERCISE 51b (p. 211)

1. Nyundo niliyo nayo;  niliyokuwa nayo;  nitakayokuwa nayo.
2. Misumari uliyo nayo;  uliyokuwa nayo;  utakayokuwa nayo.
3. Msumeno alio nao;  aliokuwa nao;  atakaokuwa nao.
4. Parafujo tulizo nazo;  tulizokuwa nazo;  tutakazokuwa nazo.
5. Shoka mlilo nalo;  mlilokuwa nalo;  mtakalokuwa nalo.
6. Uzi walio nao;  waliokuwa nao;  watakaokuwa nao.

## EXERCISE 51c (p. 212)

1. This is the agreement they had with them.
2. If anyone tells you that I like the plight I am in, don't believe him.
3. We had better make our dwelling here, and found our town, the people with us suffice.
4. The cock, seeing how matters had turned out, had no choice but to return to his home.
5. The ox said, To-day I was not given any work, I was just tethered where there was grass, and I kept on eating.
6. Eventually he lost everything that he had.
7. Every good tree beareth good fruit and an evil tree beareth evil fruit.
8. To him that hath shall be given, and from him that hath not shall be taken away even that which he hath.
9. Because of the doubt which assailed him, he said nothing.
10. Along the road they enjoyed no pleasant conversation, because the Sultan was annoyed.
11. There was a man and his wife, both of whom possessed no means, their whole wealth consisted of a sheep and a cock.
12. God rewarded his faith, and He took his shell (the turtle's) and covered him with it, putting his head and feet inside.

## EXERCISE 52a (p. 218)

| (a) | jibia | letea | ponyea | ingilia | elezea | fungia |
| | fungulia | jongelea | pasulia | dhania | zuilia | tubia |
| (b) | nyoa | kaa | nunua | piga | enda | vuka |
| | chagua | sokota | inua | fasiri | fumbua | shuhudu |

## EXERCISE 52b (p. 221)

1. Buy a knife for me.
2. Who are you cooking for?
3. Open the door for the Bwana.
4. Cut him a long stick.
5. What is the child crying for?
6. I have heard how you treated our child.
7. Go to the nearby forest and find a bird for me.
8. They showed him no mercy.
9. What did Hamisi say to you?
10. What are you wanting this knife for?
11. The bird flew quickly on to the tree.
12. Then he prepared for him a soft bed of leaves.
13. He drew near to him and had pity on him.
14. Give my kind regards to the Bwana.
15. I will pray for your safety.
16. Near to the place for alighting there was a stone.
17. They will praise you and sing songs about you.

18. They set fire to our town.
19. Excuse me, i.e. be content to me.
20. Where is the dining-room?
21. Amani ran towards her father.
22. They built houses for themselves and cultivated plantations for their own benefit.
23. People moved to other villages.
24. He fell down at his feet.
25. Why are you calling them?
26. What are you wanting this child for?
27. The children alone numbered more than a hundred.
28. He doesn't know what he says, he speaks for himself only.
29. Who made this coat for you?

## EXERCISE 52c (p. 222)

1. Mtoto anamlilia mama wake.
2. Tumekuletea kuni.
3. Nitafutie shoka zuri.
4. Aliendea njia ipi?
5. Hamisi atakuchukulia mzigo wako.
6. Ndugu yangu atanipokelea mshahara wangu.
7. Unamngojea nani?
8. Tusalimie ndugu zako.
9. Unitengenezee kiti hiki.
10. Ali amewajengea wazazi wake nyumba.
11. Usimjibie mwenzio.
12. Wanawake hawa wanawapikia waume wao chakula.
13. Aliniombea salama.
14. Ndege amerukia mbali?
15. Ndizi hizi (ni) mbovu, zitupilie mbali.
16. Gari hii inaendea stesheni ipi?
17. Nataka (pahali) pa kulalia.
18. Nipe sabuni ya kufulia nguo hizi.
19. Mawe haya hayafai ya kujengea nyumba.
20. Majembe yetu wanayatakiani?

## EXERCISE 53a (p. 223)

| jibiwa | letwa | ponywa | ingiliwa | elezwa | fungwa |
| funguliwa | jongelewa | pasuliwa | dhaniwa | zuiliwa | tubiwa |

## EXERCISE 53b (p. 223)

1. Mchawi alipigwa mawe.
2. Koti hili lilishonwa na fundi wa kihindi.
3. Chakula hiki kilipikwa na Ali, mpishi wa Bwana Mzungu.
4. Maneno yao yalidharauliwa na wote walioyasikia.
5. Machungwa haya yalinunuliwa lini?

6. Yuko wapi yule mgonjwa aliyeletwa hapa?
7. Ameitwa mara tatu.
8. Mawe yote yameondolewa.
9. Nyumba hii ilijengwa lini?
10. Viazi hivi vilipikwa lini?
11. Punda wetu amekufa, alizikwa jana.
12. Taa imeondolewa?
13. Madeni hayajalipwa bado.
14. Blanketi limekunjwa vizuri?
15. Shati za Bwana zimepigwa pasi?
16. Je, kuku wamelishwa?
17. Machungwa yao yameliwa yote.
18. Taa hii ilisafishwa lini?

## EXERCISE 54a (p. 225)

| | | | |
|---|---|---|---|
| pigwa, | pigiwa | pikwa, | pikiwa |
| chaguliwa, | chaguliwa | fanywa, | fanyiwa |
| semwa, | semewa | ondolewa, | ondolewa |
| inuliwa, | inuliwa | limwa, | limiwa |
| pokelewa, pokewa, } pokelewa | | shonwa, | shonewa |
| | | andikwa, | andikiwa |
| twaliwa, | twaliwa | | |

## EXERCISE 54b (p. 225)

1. His hoe has been stolen from him.
2. Messengers were sent to call those who lived afar off.
3. When will I get an increase in wages?
4. A song of praise was composed in his honour.
5. We were shown where the cooking was done.
6. It is hard to explain how well we were treated.
7. When I appeared I was given a great clapping and cheering.
8. Let a hut be built for this sick man away from people's houses.
9. These three mats were plaited for me, I did not plait them myself.
10. We have been visited by three young people.
11. This man has been bereaved of his father.
12. A fine feast was made for them.

## EXERCISE 54c (p. 226)

1. Aliletewa vitu aina aina.
2. Nilichukuliwa mzigo wangu.
3. Alipofika tu, akapikiwa chakula.
4. Alisomewa barua zake.
5. Aliambiwa nini?
6. Nimechoka, nataka kuletewa chakula hapa.
7. Kesho jumbe atapelekewa barua.
8. Wagonjwa wasagiwe mahindi.

9. Nilipofika, nilifunguliwa mlango na mtoto mdogo.
10. Aliwekewa kiti karibu na meza.
11. Asubuhi nililetewa kikombe cha chai.
12. Umefanyiwa kazi hii?

## EXERCISE 55a (p. 227)

zimika { neneka     tosheka     aminika     fungika     tafunika
       { nenekana

lika     badilika     funguka     sadikika     fulika     { julika
                                              { julikana

## EXERCISE 55b (p. 229)

1. Much work takes place here.
2. The bridge was raised by machinery, it was raised on both sides.
3. Africa desires to rise, but it will have no chance to rise until it has become united, that is to say, has unity.
4. The town was built and grew up.
5. He has conferred many favours on me: they cannot be expressed in words, neither can they be repaid.
6. This matter is unforgettable.
7. Take me round by a road which is passable; this is impassable.
8. Don't give people work which is impossible.
9. What is the use of keeping food which is uneatable?

## EXERCISE 55c (p. 229)

1. Koti lako jinsi gani limeraruka?
2. Kama umeshughulika, nitarudi kesho.
3. Amesumbuka kwa maneno yako.
4. Taa imezimika.
5. Sikuvunja kikombe hiki, kimevunjika tu.
6. Hisani yake hainenekani.
7. Subira yake haipimiki.
8. Machungwa hayanunuliki leo. Kwa nini? Ni ghali mno.
9. Sikufunga mlango, umefungika tu. Mlango huu haufungiki.
10. Uzi umekatika. (Ni) nani ameukata?
11. Wasema jambo hilo halielezeki.
12. Mambo yasiyoelezeka, yanisumbua.
13. Madirisha haya hayafunguki.
14. Mtu huyu mwerevu sana, hashikiki.
15. Sauti yake haisikiliki kwa mbali.
16. Nyama hii haitafuniki, ni ngumu mno.
17. Katupilie chakula hiki, hakiliki.
18. Leo ndizi hazipatikani sokoni.
19. Jambo hili haliwezekani.
20. Nyota zilizoonekana hazihesabiki, hazina idadi.
21. Hamisi ni mtu aliyojulikana mjini.

## EXERCISE 56a (p. 234)

1. These people spend their life on the seashore.
2. The *Bwana Mkubwa* opened the proceedings by making clear to them the advantages of schooling.
3. He quieted them by deceiving them, saying, Don't (ye) cry, I will send you home again.
4. These English animals are well looked after. and get very clean grazing grounds to help them get fat.
5. The people went and awakened him saying, *Zimwi*, wake up.
6. He stretched out his hand that he might take the swords.
7. He explained everything to him.
8. They were welcomed in fine style.
9. How can anyone drive a motor-car without petrol?

## EXERCISE 56b (p. 235)

1. Legeza kamba hii.
2. Mlaze pole pole.
3. Washa taa.
4. Upepo umezimisha taa.
5. Aliangusha nazi tatu.
6. Ulinishtusha.
7. Tembo limemlevya.
8. Ufagiapo usirushe mavumbi.
9. Usikimbilize kuku.
10. Bwana ataka kuamshwa saa ngapi?
11. Ninakuumiza?
12. Umerudisha kitabu changu? Umemrudishia Bwana kitabu chako?
13. Je, maneno yako yalimsikitisha?
14. Aliwatanguliza mbele.
15. Wapumzishe farasi.
16. Alinilazimisha kazi hii.

## EXERCISE 57 (p. 242)

1. The soldiers marched until they met exactly in the middle of the parade ground.
2. His love for him was so great that they swore an oath of friendship.
3. I accompanied Bwana X and met Bwana Z.
4. People were crowded together on the highroad.
5. A procession is a following of one another in order.
6. Many of the games were those of passing judgment on one another.
7. They marvelled to see that Nurdin was willing to part with her.
8. These people were told that they would do the choosing among themselves, a mother could go with her son, a man with his wife.
9. After they had exchanged greetings, he said to him . . .
10. There is no quarrelling or jostling of one another.
11. They taught one another in manly style.
12. Their plantation borders on the road.
13. I am not well acquainted with them.
14. A bad man, who is notorious for his evil deeds, is killed in like manner.
15. When they got near to one another they saw . . .
16. They found every corner full of slaves lying huddled up together.
17. If we wish to avoid getting a bad reputation . . .

# VOCABULARY

ONLY the nouns and verbs in the lists and in the exercises are given here. Many of the words have more meanings than the one given; frequent reference to the standard dictionaries is therefore advisable.

In the Swahili–English section, nouns are listed under their respective Class Prefixes. In the English–Swahili section, nouns for which no plural prefix is given, either do not change in the plural, or have no plural form. Plurals of (L)U- Class nouns are given in full, also a few plurals which might cause difficulty. In a few cases, where nouns have an alternate plural form, both forms are given.

Verbs are listed under their stem form. For other parts of speech, see text:

|  |  |  | page |
|---|---|---|---|
| Adjectives | . . . | . | 48–9, 148 |
| Adverbs . | . . . | . | 175–7 |
| Prepositions | . . . | . | 195–6 |
| Conjunctions | . . . | . | 197–9 |

## NOUNS. SWAHILI–ENGLISH

### M- Wa-

| | |
|---|---|
| mchawi | witchdoctor |
| mchunga | herdsman |
| mdeni | debtor |
| mganga | medicine man |
| mgeni | stranger |
| mgonjwa | sick person, invalid |
| mjinga | simpleton |
| mjomba | uncle, nephew |
| mke | wife |
| mkulima | farmer, peasant, cultivator |
| mlevi | drunkard |
| mnyama | animal |
| mnyapara | headman |
| mpagazi | porter, carrier |
| mpishi | cook |
| msimamizi | overseer |
| mtoto | child |
| mtumishi | servant |
| mtumwa | slave |
| mume | husband |
| muumba | creator |
| mwalimu | teacher |

| | |
|---|---|
| mwana | child, son, daughter |
| mwanafunzi | pupil, disciple |
| mwanahewa | airman |
| mwanamaji | sailor |
| mwanamke | woman |
| mwanamume | man |
| mwandikaji | writer |
| Mwarabu | Arab |
| mwashi | stonemason |
| mwenyewe | owner |
| mwenzi | companion |
| mwimbaji | singer |
| mwinda ⎫ mwindaji ⎭ | hunter |
| mwivi ⎫ mwizi ⎭ | thief |
| mzalia | offspring |
| mzee | elder, old person |
| Mzungu | European |

### M- Mi-

| | |
|---|---|
| mche | shoot (of a tree) |
| mchele | rice (husked) |
| mchezo | game |

| | | | |
|---|---|---|---|
| mfereji | drain, ditch | kibanda | shed |
| mguu | foot, leg | kiboko | hippopotamus |
| mji | town, village | kidole | finger |
| mkebe | tin container | kifaru | rhinoceros |
| mkeka | mat | kifijo | shout of joy, applause |
| mkono | hand, arm | | |
| mkuki | spear | kiini | kernel |
| mkutano | meeting | kijana | young person, child |
| mlango | door, doorway | kijiko | spoon |
| mlima | mountain | kikapu | basket |
| moshi | smoke | kiko | pipe |
| moto | fire, heat | kikombe | cup |
| moyo | heart | kilima | hill |
| mpaka | boundary | kiokosi | reward for picking up something |
| msiba | calamity | | |
| mshahara | monthly wage | kioo | looking-glass |
| mshale | arrow | kipimo | measure |
| msumari | nail | kipini | handle |
| msumeno | saw | kisahani | saucer |
| mtama | millet | kisiwa | island |
| mtambo | metal spring | kisu | knife |
| mtego | trap | kitabu | book |
| mtihani | examination | kitendo | action, deed |
| mto | pillow | kiti | chair |
| mto | river | kitoto | infant, baby |
| mwaka | year | kitu | thing |
| mwanzo | beginning | kiwanda | workshop, workyard |
| mwavuli | umbrella | | |
| mwendo | journey | kiwete | lame person |
| mwezi | moon, month | kizalia | offspring |
| mwiba | thorn | kizibo | stopper |
| mwili | body | kiziwi | deaf person |
| mwisho | end | | |
| mwitu | thick bush or scrub | **Ji- Ma-** | |
| mzigo | burden, load | baba | father, parent |
| mzinga | cannon, beehive | baharia | sailor |
| | | banda | workshop |
| **Ki- Vi-** | | bibi | lady, madam, miss, mistress of household |
| chakula | food | | |
| chakula cha jioni | evening meal | | |
| | | boga | pumpkin |
| chandalua | mosquito net | boi | houseboy |
| cheti | note, ticket | bubu | dumb person |
| chombo | implement, utensil | bwana | master, sir, Mr. |
| chumba | room | chungwa | orange |
| kiapo | oath | duka | shop |
| kiatu | shoe | embe | mango |
| kiazi | sweet potato | fundi | skilled workman |

| | | | |
|---|---|---|---|
| fungu | portion | sharti | obligation, stipulation, binding contract |
| ghala | storehouse, godown | | |
| gugu | weed | | |
| gunia | sack | shati | shirt |
| jambo | affair | shina | root |
| jembe | hoe | shoka | axe |
| jicho | eye | sikio | ear |
| jiko | kitchen, fireplace | soko | market |
| jino | tooth | tajiri | merchant |
| jogoo | cock | tako | buttock |
| joka | huge snake | tawi | branch |
| jongoo | millipede | teka | prisoner of war |
| juha | simpleton | tunda | fruit |
| kaa | ember | umbu | sister |
| kadhi | judge | yai | egg |
| kosa | mistake | ziwa | lake |
| koti | coat | | |
| kundi | flock | **N- N-** | |
| limau | lemon | | |
| maarifa | knowledge | aina | kind, sort |
| machezo | sport, game | ahadi | promise |
| maendeleo | progress | alama | sign, mark |
| mafuta | oil, grease, fat | alfajiri | dawn, daybreak |
| magomvi | quarrels | akili | ability, intellect |
| mahudhurio | attendance at school, etc. | asali | honey, syrup |
| | | askari | soldier, policeman |
| | | baba | father |
| maisha | life, continuance | babu | grandfather |
| maji | water | bahasha | envelope |
| majivu | ashes | bakshishi | gratuity, tip |
| majonzi | grief | bakuli | basin |
| mali | wealth | bandari | harbour |
| malisho | feeding, pasture | barabara | highroad |
| manukato | perfume | barua | letter |
| manung'uniko | discontent, grumbling | bei | price |
| | | bendera | flag |
| mate | saliva | bunduki | gun |
| mauti | death | chupa | bottle |
| mavumbi | dust | daraja | bridge, rank |
| mazao | crops | dawa | medicine |
| maziwa | milk | debe | tin container for petrol, etc. |
| mazungumzo | conversation | | |
| nanasi | pineapple | desturi | custom |
| neno | word | fadhili | favour |
| pigo | blow | faida | profit |
| seremala | carpenter | fimbo | stick |
| shaka | doubt | furaha | joy |
| shamba | plantation, estate | gari | any vehicle on wheels |
| shangazi | aunt, father's sister | | |

| | | | |
|---|---|---|---|
| gereza | prison | ng'ombe | ox, cow, cattle |
| giza | darkness | ngurumo | rumbling sound, growl |
| hali | state, condition | | |
| harufu | smell, odour | njaa | hunger |
| hema | tent | njia | path, road |
| (k)heri | happiness | nta | beeswax |
| hisani | kindness | nyama | meat, flesh |
| huruma | pity, mercy | nyumba | house |
| idadi | computation, large number | nyundo | hammer |
| | | parafujo | screw |
| jamaa | family | pembe | horn |
| jinsi | sort, kind | pesa | pice |
| kadiri | amount, extent | pete | ring |
| kahawa | coffee | picha | picture |
| kamba | rope | radhi | contentment, pardon |
| kandarinya | kettle | | |
| karamu | feast | radi | clap of thunder |
| kazi | work | rafiki | friend |
| kelele | noise, uproar | ratli | pound (in weight) |
| kengele | bell | saa | clock, watch, hour |
| kufuli | padlock | sabuni | soap |
| kuku | chicken, fowl | safari | journey |
| maana | cause, meaning, import | sahani | plate |
| | | sakafu | cement floor (or roof) |
| maisha | continuance, life | | |
| ma(a)kuli | victuals, food | salaam | greetings |
| mali | property, riches | sanduku | box, case, chest |
| mashini | machine | senti | cent |
| mashua | boat | sharti | binding contract, by-law, obligation |
| masikini | poor man | | |
| mbega | seed | | |
| mboga | vegetable | sheria | law |
| mbu | mosquito | sifa | renown |
| meza | table | siku | day |
| milki | kingdom, dominion | siri | secret |
| motakaa | motor-car | supu | soup |
| mvi | grey hair | tende | date |
| mvua | rain | tik(i)ti | ticket |
| namna | kind, sort, pattern | tumbako | tobacco |
| nauli | fare | wasaa | opportunity |
| nazi | coconut | zawadi | present |
| ncha | tip, point | zimwi | goblin |
| nchi | country | | |
| ndizi | banana | **Names of Animals** | |
| ndoo | pail, bucket | cheche | small animal like mongoose |
| ndugu | brother | | |
| ng'ambo | the farther side | chui | leopard |
| ngoma | drum, dance | chura | frog |

| | | | |
|---|---|---|---|
| farasi | horse | ufunguo | key |
| fisi | hyena | uji | gruel |
| kanga | guinea-fowl | ukucha | finger-nail |
| kondoo | sheep | ukuni | piece of firewood |
| kongoni | hartebeest | ukuta | wall |
| mamba | crocodile | ulimi | tongue |
| mbuzi | goat | uma | fork |
| mbwa | dog | uombi | supplication, begging |
| ndege | bird | | |
| ndovu | elephant | unyoya | single feather |
| nyani | baboon | unywele | single hair |
| nyoka | snake | upana | width |
| nyumbu | mule | upande | side |
| paka | cat | upanga | sword |
| panya | rat | upepo | wind |
| punda | donkey | urafiki | friendship |
| punda milia | zebra | ushanga | single bead |
| samaki | fish | usiku | night |
| simba | lion | uso | face |
| sungura | hare | uta | bow |
| tembo | elephant | utambi | wick |
| twiga | giraffe | utaratibu | arrangement, order, method |

### U- (N-)

| | | | |
|---|---|---|---|
| ua | enclosure, fence | uteo | winnowing tray |
| uangalifu | attention | utepe | tape, chevron |
| uapo | oath | utoto | childhood |
| ubao | plank, form | uvuli | shade |
| ubavu | rib | uvumbi | dust |
| ubaya | badness, wickedness | uwati | pole supporting roof |
| | | uwanda | open space |
| uchache | scarcity | uwezo | might, authority, power |
| udevu | single hair of beard | | |
| udongo | clay | uwongo | falsehood |
| ufa | crack | uzee | old age |
| ufagio | sweeping-brush | uzuri | beauty |
| ufalme | kingdom | wali | cooked rice |
| ufito | thin piece of stick | wembe | razor |
| | | wimbo | song |

## VERBS.  SWAHILI–ENGLISH

### A

| | | | |
|---|---|---|---|
| | | angalia | take care, look at |
| ambia | tell | angaliwa | be looked at |
| ambiwa | be told | angika | hang up |
| amka | awake | anguka | fall down |
| amkia | greet | anza | begin |
| amuru | order | apa | swear a formal oath |
| andama | follow in order | azima | borrow or lend |
| andika | write | | |

## B

| | |
|---|---|
| bandika | fasten on |

## C

| | |
|---|---|
| cha | fear |
| cha | rise (of sun) |
| chafuka | be untidy |
| chagua | choose |
| chelewa | delay, be late |
| chemka | boil (intr.) |
| chemsha | boil (tr.) |
| cheza | play |
| cheza mpira | play football |
| choka | be tired |
| choma | pierce |
| choma moto | apply fire |
| chukua | carry, carry off |
| chunga | tend cattle, etc. |
| chwa | set (of sun) |

## D

| | |
|---|---|
| danganya | deceive |
| dharau | scorn |

## E

| | |
|---|---|
| elea | make clear |
| eleza | explain |
| enda | go |
| enda tembea | go for a walk |
| endelea | progress |
| enea | spread (intr.) |
| epa | step aside |

## F

| | |
|---|---|
| fa | die |
| faa | be of use |
| fagia | sweep |
| fahamu | understand |
| fanya | do, make, etc. |
| fasiri | translate |
| ficha | hide |
| fika | arrive |
| fua nguo | wash clothes |
| fuata | follow |
| fuma | weave, knit |
| fumba | close by bringing together |
| fumua | unpick, unravel |

N

| | |
|---|---|
| fundisha | teach |
| funga | bind, fasten, shut |
| funga safari | pack up for a journey |
| fungua | unfasten, open |
| funguka | become undone |
| funika | cover |
| funza | teach |
| funzana | teach one another |

## G

| | |
|---|---|
| ganda | congeal |
| gawana | divide up between people |

## H

| | |
|---|---|
| hama | remove from |
| hamia | remove to |
| haribu | spoil, destroy |
| haribika | be spoilt, etc. |
| hasibu | count, reckon |
| hesabu | count, reckon |
| hitaji | be in need of |
| hukumu | judge |
| hurumia | have pity on |

## I

| | |
|---|---|
| iba | steal |
| iga | imitate, copy, mimic |
| imba | sing |
| inama | stoop, bend down |
| ingia | enter |
| ingia kutu | become rusty |
| ingia moshi | become smoked |
| ingia ufa | become cracked |
| inua | lift up |
| ita | call |
| itwa | be called |
| isha | finish (intr.) |
| ishi | live |
| iva | ripen, mature |

## J

| | |
|---|---|
| ja | come |
| jaa | be full |
| jaribu | try |

| | |
|---|---|
| jenga | build |
| jibu | answer |
| jongea | move on |
| jua | know |

**K**

| | |
|---|---|
| kaa | live, stay, remain |
| kaa kitako | sit down |
| kaa kimya | remain silent |
| kama | squeeze |
| kana | deny |
| kanyaga | tread |
| kata | cut |
| kataa | refuse |
| kauka | dry up |
| kimbia | run away |
| kokota | drag |
| koma | come to an end |
| kopa | borrow |
| kosa | make a mistake |
| kua | grow |
| kumbuka | remember |
| kunja | fold |
| kunja uso | frown |
| kuta | come across |
| kutana | meet together |
| kwaa | stumble |

**L**

| | |
|---|---|
| la | eat |
| lala | lie down, sleep |
| lazimu | compel |
| legea | be loose |
| leta | bring |
| lewa | be drunk |
| lia | cry, emit a sound |
| lima | cultivate |
| lipa | pay, pay back |
| lipwa | be paid |
| lisha | feed |
| lishwa | be fed |
| liwa | be eaten |

**M**

| | |
|---|---|
| maliza | finish (tr.) |
| mwaga | pour out |
| mwagika | be spilt |

**N**

| | |
|---|---|
| naswa | be caught (in a trap) |
| nenepa | become fat |
| ngoja | wait |
| nuka | smell (intr.) |
| nunua | buy |
| nusa | smell (tr.) |
| nya | fall like rain |
| nyamaza | be silent |
| nyoka | be straight |
| nywa | drink |

**O**

| | |
|---|---|
| okoa | save |
| okota | pick up |
| omba | pray |
| omba ruksa | ask permission |
| ona | see |
| ondoa | remove |
| onekana | be visible |
| ongeza | increase |
| onyesha | show |
| oza | rot |

**P**

| | |
|---|---|
| pa | give |
| paa | ascend |
| pak(a)a | spread on |
| paka rangi | paint |
| pakia | load up a vessel |
| pakua | unload a vessel |
| pakua chakula | dish up food |
| pakwa cho-kaa | be whitewashed |
| panda | ascend |
| panda | plant |
| pasua | split |
| pasuka | be split |
| pata | get |
| patikana | be procurable |
| peleka | send, convey |
| penda | love, like |
| pendeza | please |
| piga | beat, strike, hit |
| piga chapa | print |
| piga kinanda | play a musical instrument |
| piga pasi | iron clothes |

| | |
|---|---|
| pigana | fight |
| pika | cook |
| pima | measure |
| pisha | allow to pass |
| pita | pass |
| poa moto | get cool |
| pokea | receive |
| pona | get well |
| ponya | cure |
| pumzika | rest, take a holiday |

**R**

| | |
|---|---|
| rejea | return |
| rejesha | send back |
| rudi | return |
| rudisha | send back |
| ruhusu | give permission |
| ruka | fly, jump |
| rusha | raise, make fly |

**S**

| | |
|---|---|
| saga | grind |
| sahau | forget |
| saidia | help |
| salimu | greet |
| sema | say |
| shiba | be satisfied |
| shika njia | set out on a journey |
| shinda | conquer |
| shona | sew |
| shtaki | accuse |
| shughulika | be busy |
| shuka | descend |
| shusha | lower |
| sifu | praise |
| sikia | hear |
| sikia kiu | feel thirsty |
| sikia njaa | feel hungry |
| sikiliza | listen attentively |
| sikitika | be sorry |
| simama | stand |
| simulia | talk about |
| singizia | allege as excuse |
| sitawi | flourish |
| soma | read |
| somesha | teach |
| songana | be pressed together |
| sukuma | push |

| | |
|---|---|
| sumbua | annoy |
| staajabu | wonder |

**T**

| | |
|---|---|
| tafuna | chew |
| tafuta | search |
| taka | want, desire |
| takata | become clean |
| takikana | be required |
| takiwa | be required |
| tambua | discern |
| tandika | spread out |
| tangulia | go before |
| taraji | hope, expect |
| tata | tangle |
| tazama | gaze upon |
| tega | set a trap |
| tema mate | expectorate |
| tenda | do, perform |
| tenga | separate |
| tengeneza | put right |
| tengenezwa | be repaired |
| tia | put |
| tiwa | be put |
| toboka | be pierced |
| toka | come out |
| tulia | be quiet |
| tuma | send |
| tumia | employ, use |
| tumiwa | be used for |
| tunga | put in order |
| tupa | throw |
| twaa | take to oneself |
| twika | place a load on head |

**U**

| | |
|---|---|
| ua | kill |
| uawa | be killed |
| ugua | be sick, ail |
| uliza | ask |
| ulizwa | be asked |
| uma | hurt (intr.), sting, bite |
| umiza | hurt (tr.) |
| unga | join together |
| uza | sell |
| uzwa | be sold |

## V

| | |
|---|---|
| vaa | put on clothes, dress |
| vua | take off clothes |
| vuja | leak |
| vuka | cross |
| vuma | roar, blow hard |
| vunja | break |
| vunjika | be broken |
| vuta | pull |

## W

| | |
|---|---|
| wa | be |
| waka | burn (intr.) |
| washa | light (a fire, etc.) |

| | |
|---|---|
| weka | place, put away |
| weza | be able |
| winda | hunt |

## Z

| | |
|---|---|
| zaa | bear fruit, etc. |
| zaliwa | be born |
| ziba | stop up |
| zidi | increase (intr.) |
| zidisha | increase (tr.) |
| zika | bury |
| zima | put out (fire, etc.) |
| zimika | go out (of fire, etc.) |
| zoea | be used to |
| zungumza | converse |

# NOUNS. ENGLISH–SWAHILI

## A

| | |
|---|---|
| ability | akili |
| action | kitendo (vi-) |
| advice | shauri (ma-) |
| airman | mwanahewa (wa-) |
| amount | kiasi (vi-) |
| | jumla |
| animal | mnyama (wa-) |
| applause | kifijo (vi-) |
| Arab | Mwarabu (wa-) |
| arm | mkono (mi-) |
| arrangement | utaratibu |
| arrow | mshale (mi-) |
| attendance | mahudhurio |
| attention | uangalizi |
| aunt (father's sister) | shangazi (ma-) |
| authority | uwezo |
| axe | shoka (ma-) |

## B

| | |
|---|---|
| baboon | nyani |
| baby | kitoto (vi-) |
| badness | ubaya |
| banana | ndizi |
| basket | kikapu (vi-) |
| bead | ushanga (shanga, also ma-) |
| beauty | uzuri |

| | |
|---|---|
| beehive | mzinga (mi-) |
| beeswax | nta |
| beginning | mwanzo |
| bell | kengele |
| bird | ndege |
| blind person | kipofu (vi-) |
| blow | pigo (ma-) |
| body | mwili (mi-) |
| book | kitabu (vi-) |
| | chuo (vy-) |
| bottle | chupa (chupa, also ma-) |
| boundary | mpaka (mi-) |
| bow | uta (nyuta) |
| box | sanduku (sanduku, also ma-) |
| branch | tawi (ma-) |
| bridge | daraja |
| brother | ndugu |
| brush (sweeping) | ufagio (fagio) |
| bucket | ndoo |
| burden | mzigo (mi-) |
| bush, thick | msitu (mi-) |
| buttock | tako (ma-) |

## C

| | |
|---|---|
| calamity | msiba (mi-) |
| cannon | mzinga (mi-) |
| captive in war | teka (ma-) |
| carpenter | seremala (ma-) |

| | | | |
|---|---|---|---|
| carrier | mpagazi (wa-) | daybreak | alfajiri |
| case (law) | shauri (ma-) | deaf person | kiziwi (vi-) |
| | kesi | death | mauti |
| cat | paka | debtor | mdeni (wa-) |
| cattle | ng'ombe | disciple | mwanafunzi |
| cause | sababu | | (wa-) |
| cent | senti | discontent | manung'uniko |
| chair | kiti (vi-) | ditch | mfereji (mi-) |
| charcoal | makaa | dog | mbwa |
| chevron | utepe (tepe) | dominion | milki |
| chicken | kuku | donkey | punda |
| child | mtoto (wa-) | door, doorway | mlango (mi-) |
| | mwana (wana) | doubt | shaka (ma-) |
| | kijana (vi-) | drum | ngoma |
| childhood | utoto | drunkard | mlevi (wa-) |
| clay | udongo | dust | uvumbi (vumbi, |
| clerk | karani (ma-) | | *also* ma-) |
| clock | saa | | |
| coat | koti (ma-) | **E** | |
| cock | jogoo (ma-) | | |
| coconut | nazi | ear | sikio (ma-) |
| coffee | kahawa | egg | yai (ma-) |
| companion | mwenzi (wenzi) | elder | mzee (wa-) |
| company | kundi (ma-) | elephant | tembo |
| | jamaa | | ndovu |
| condition | sharti (ma-) | ember | kaa (ma-) |
| contract | sharti (ma-) | enclosure | ua (nyua) |
| conversation | mazungumzo | end | mwisho (mi-) |
| cook | mpishi (wa-) | envelope | bahasha |
| counsel | shauri (ma-) | estate | shamba (ma-) |
| country | nchi | European | Mzungu (wa-) |
| cow | ng'ombe | examination | mtihani (mi-) |
| crack | ufa (nyufa) | extent | eneo (maeneo) |
| craftsman | fundi (ma-) | eye | jicho (macho) |
| Creator | Muumba (wa-) | | |
| crocodile | mamba | **F** | |
| crops | mazao | face | uso (nyuso) |
| cultivator | mkulima (wa-) | falsehood | uwongo |
| cup | kikombe (vi-) | family | jamaa |
| custom | desturi | fare | nauli |
| | | farmer | mkulima (wa-) |
| **D** | | farther side | ng'ambo |
| | | fat | mafuta |
| dance | ngoma | father | baba (baba, *also* |
| darkness | giza | | ma-) |
| date (fruit) | tende | feather | unyoya (nyoya, |
| daughter | binti | | *also* manyoya) |
| dawn | alfajiri | fence | ua (nyua) |
| day | siku | finger | kidole (vi-) |

| | | | |
|---|---|---|---|
| fire | moto (mi-) | hippo | kiboko (vi-) |
| firewood | ukuni (kuni) | hoe | jembe (ma-) |
| fish | samaki | honey | asali |
| flag | bendera | horn (of cattle) | pembe |
| flesh | nyama | horn (motor) | honi |
| flock | kundi (ma-) | horse | farasi |
| food | chakula (vy-) | hour | saa |
| fool | mjinga (wa-) | house | nyumba |
| | mpumbavu (wa-) | houseboy | boi (ma-) |
| foot | mguu (mi-) | hunger | njaa |
| fork | uma (nyuma) | hunter | mwinda (wa-) |
| form | ubao (mbao) | | mwindaji (wa-) |
| fowl | kuku | husband | mume (wa-) |
| friend | rafiki | hyena | fisi |
| friendship | urafiki | | |
| frog | chura (vy-) | **I** | |
| fruit | tunda (ma-) | implement | chombo (vy-) |
| | | Indian | M(u)hindi (wa-) |
| **G** | | infant | kitoto (vi-) |
| game | mchezo (mi-, *also* | intellect | akili |
| | ma-) | invalid | mgonjwa (wa-) |
| giraffe | twiga | island | kisiwa (vi-) |
| goat | mbuzi | | |
| grandfather | babu | **J** | |
| gratuity | bakshishi | journey | mwendo (mi-) |
| grease | mafuta | | safari |
| greetings | salaam | joy | furaha |
| grief | majonzi | judge | kadhi (ma-) |
| gruel | uji | | |
| guest | mgeni (wa-) | **K** | |
| guinea-fowl | kanga | kernel | kiini (vi-) |
| gun | bunduki | kettle | kandarinya |
| | | key | ufunguo (funguo) |
| **H** | | kind | jinsi |
| hair (of head) | unywele (nywele) | | namna |
| hair (grey) | mvi | kindness | hisani |
| hammer | nyundo | kingdom | ufalme |
| hand | mkono (mi-) | kitchen | jiko |
| handle | kipini (vi-) | knife | kisu (vi-) |
| harbour | bandari | knowledge | maarifa |
| hare | sungura | | |
| hartebeest | kongoni | **L** | |
| headman | mnyapara (wa-) | lady | bibi (ma-) |
| heart | moyo (mi-) | | mwanamke (wa- |
| heat | moto | | nawake) |
| herd | kundi (ma-) | lake | ziwa (ma-) |
| herdsman | mchungaji (wa-) | lame person | kiwete (vi-) |
| highroad | barabara | law | sheria |

| | | | |
|---|---|---|---|
| leg | mguu (mi-) | **mountain** | mlima (mi-) |
| lemon | limau (ma-) | **mule** | nyumbu |
| leopard | chui | | |
| letter | barua | **N** | |
| life | maisha | | |
| lightning | umeme | nail | msumari (mi-) |
| lion | simba | nail (finger) | ukucha (kucha) |
| load | mzigo (mi-) | name | jina (ma-) |
| looking-glass | kioo (vi-) | night | usiku |
| luck | bahati | note | cheti (vy-) |
| luckless person | masikini | number (large) | idadi |

**M**

**O**

| | | | |
|---|---|---|---|
| machine | mashini | oath | kiapo (vi-) |
| Madam | Bibi (ma-) | obligation | lazima |
| man | mwanamume | odour | harufu |
| | (wanawaume) | offspring | kizalia (vi-) |
| mango | embe (ma-) | | mzalia (wa-) |
| mark | alama | oil | mafuta |
| | dalili | old age | uzee |
| market | soko (ma-) | old person | mzee (wa-) |
| mason | mwashi (wa-) | open space | uwanda (nyanda) |
| master | bwana (ma-) | opportunity | wasaa |
| mat | mkeka (mi-) | orange | chungwa (chu- |
| meaning | maana | | ngwa, also ma-) |
| measure | kipimo (vi-) | order | taratibu |
| meat | nyama | overseer | msimamizi (wa-) |
| medicine | dawa | ox | ng'ombe |
| medicine man | mganga (wa-) | | |
| merchant | tajiri (ma-) | **P** | |
| mercy | huruma | padlock | kufuli |
| method | namna | pail | ndoo |
| | jinsi | parent | mzazi (wa-) |
| | utaratibu | path | njia |
| might | uwezo | pattern | namna |
| | nguvu | | kielezo (vi-) |
| milk | maziwa | peasant | mkulima (wa-) |
| millet | mtama | pen | kalamu |
| mistake | kosa (ma-) | perfume | manukato |
| Mister | Bwana | pice | pesa |
| mistress of | bibi (ma-) | picture | picha |
| household | mwana (ma-) | pillow | mto (mi-) |
| month | mwezi (mi-) | pineapple | nanasi (ma-) |
| moon | mwezi (mi-) | pipe | kiko (vi-) |
| mosquito | mbu | pity | huruma |
| mosquito net | chandalua (vy-) | plan | shauri (ma-) |
| mother | mama | plank | ubao (mbao) |
| motor-car | motakaa | plantation | shamba (ma-) |
| | | plate | sahani |

| | | | |
|---|---|---|---|
| point | ncha | screw | parafujo |
| policeman | askari | scrub (bush) | msitu (mi-) |
| poor man | masikini | secret | siri |
| porter | mpagazi (wa-) | seed | mbegu |
| | mchukuzi (wa-) | servant | mtumishi (wa-) |
| portion | fungu (ma-) | shade | uvuli |
| pound (lb.) | ratli | shed | kibanda (vi-) |
| power | uwezo | | banda (ma-) |
| | nguvu | sheep | kondoo |
| present | zawadi | shoe | kiatu (vi-) |
| price | bei | shop | duka (ma-) |
| prison | gereza | sick person | mgonjwa (wa-) |
| | kifungoni | side | kando |
| progress | maendeleo | sign | dalili |
| promise | ahadi | simpleton | mjinga (wa-) |
| prophet | nabii (ma-) | | juha (ma-) |
| pumpkin | boga (ma-) | singer | mwimbaji (wa-) |
| pupil | mwanafunzi(wa-) | Sir | Bwana (ma-) |
| | | sister | umbu (ma-) |

**Q**

| | | | |
|---|---|---|---|
| quarrels | magomvi | skilled workman | fundi (ma-) |
| | | smell | harufu |

**R**

| | | | |
|---|---|---|---|
| | | smoke | moshi (mi-) |
| | | snake | nyoka |
| rain | mvua | soap | sabuni |
| rat | panya | soldier | askari |
| renown | sifa | son | mwana (wa-) |
| reward for pick-<br>ing up some-<br>thing | kiokosi (vi-) | sort | namna |
| | | | jinsi |
| | | soup | supu |
| rhino | kifaru (vi-) | spear | mkuki (mi-) |
| rib | ubavu (mbavu) | spoon | kijiko (vi-) |
| rice (husked) | mchele | sport | machezo |
| rice (cooked) | wali | spring (metal) | mtambo (mi-) |
| ring | pete | state | hali |
| river | mto (mi-) | stick | fimbo |
| road | njia | stipulation | sharti |
| root | mzizi (mi-) | stopper | kizibo (vi-) |
| | shina (ma-) | stranger | mgeni (wa-) |
| rope | kamba | sweet potato | kiazi (vi-) |
| rumbling sound | ngurumo | sword | upanga (panga) |
| | | syrup | asali |

**S**

| | | | |
|---|---|---|---|
| sailor | baharia (ma-) | | **T** |
| | mwanamaji (wa-) | table | meza |
| saliva | mate | tailor | mshoni |
| saucer | kisahani (vi-) | tea | chai |
| saw | msumeno (mi-) | teacher | mwalimu (wa·) |
| scent | manukato | tent | hema |

| | | | |
|---|---|---|---|
| thief | mwivi (wevi) | watch (time) | saa |
| thing | kitu (vi-) | wall | ukuta (kuta) |
| thorn | mwiba (mi-) | water | maji |
| ticket | tikti | weed | gugu (ma-) |
| | cheti (vy-) | wick | utambi (tambi) |
| tin (petrol) | debe | wickedness | ubaya |
| tin can | mkebe | width | upana |
| tip (gratuity) | bakshishi | wife | mke (wa-) |
| tobacco | tumbako | wind | upepo (pepo) |
| tongue | ulimi (ndimi) | window | dirisha (ma-) |
| tooth | jino (meno) | witchdoctor | mchawi (wa-) |
| town | mji (mi-) | withe (building-stick) | ufito (fito) |
| trap | mtego (mi-) | word | neno (ma-) |
| tray (winnowing) | uteo (teo) | work | kazi |
| | | workshop | kiwanda (vi-) |
| **U** | | | banda (ma-) |
| umbrella | mwavuli (mi-) | woman | mwanamke (wa-nawake) |
| utensil | chombo (vy-) | | |
| | | writer | mwandikaji (wa-) |
| **V** | | | |
| vegetable | mboga | **Y** | |
| vehicle | gari (ma-) | | |
| village | mji (mi-) | year | mwaka (mi-) |
| | kijiji (vi-) | | |
| | | **Z** | |
| **W** | | | |
| wage | mshahara (mi-) | zebra | punda milia |

## VERBS. ENGLISH–SWAHILI

| **A** | | **B** | |
|---|---|---|---|
| able, be | weza | be | wa |
| accuse | shtaki | bear fruit | zaa |
| ail | ugua | beat | piga |
| allege as excuse | singiza | begin | anza |
| annoy | sumbua | bend down | inama |
| answer | jibu | bind | funga |
| apply fire | choma moto | boil (tr.) | chemsha |
| arrive | fika | boil (intr.) | chemka |
| ascend | paa | born, be | zaliwa |
| | panda | borrow | azima |
| ask | uliza | | kopa |
| asked, be | ulizwa | break | vunja |
| ask permission | omba ruhusa | broken, be | vunjika |
| awake | amka | build | jenga |
| awaken | amsha | burn (tr.) | choma |
| N* | | burn (intr.) | waka |

| | | | |
|---|---|---|---|
| bury | zika | drink | nywa |
| busy, be | shughulika | drunk, be | lewa |
| buy | nunua | dry up | kauka |

**C**

**E**

| | | | |
|---|---|---|---|
| call | ita | eat | la |
| called, be | itwa | eaten, be | liwa |
| carry | chukua | emit a sound | lia |
| chew | tafuna | employ | tuma |
| choose | chagua | enter | ingia |
| clear, be | elea | expect | taraji |
| clear, make | eleza | | tumaini |
| come | ja | expectorate | tema mate |
| come across | kuta | explain | eleza |
| come out | toka | | |
| come to an end | koma | **F** | |
| compel | lazimu | fall down | anguka |
| congeal | ganda | fall (like rain) | nya |
| conquer | shinda | fasten | funga |
| converse | zungumza | fasten on | bandika |
| convey | peleka | fat, get (persons) | nenepa |
| cook | pika | feed | lisha |
| cool, get | poa moto | fed, be | lishwa |
| copy | iga | fight | pigana |
| cover | funika | fill | jaza |
| count | hesabu | finish (tr.) | maliza |
| | hasibu | finish (intr.) | isha |
| cracked, become | ingia ufa | flourish | sitawi |
| cross | vuka | fly | ruka |
| cry | lia | fold | kunja |
| cure | ponya | follow | fuata |
| curse | apa | follow after | fuatia |
| cut | kata | follow in order | andama |
| | | forget | sahau |
| **D** | | frown | kunja uso |
| decay | oza | full, be | jaa |
| delay | chelewa | | |
| deny | kana | **G** | |
| descend | shuka | gaze upon | tazama |
| desire | taka | get fat | nenepa |
| destroy | haribu | give | pa |
| destroyed, be | haribika | give permission | ruhusa |
| die | fa | go | enda |
| discern | tambua | go before | tangulia |
| dish up food | pakua | go for a walk | enda (ku) tembea |
| divide between | gawana | go out (of fire, light, etc.) | zimika |
| do | fanya | | |
| drag | kokota | greet | amkia |

| | | | |
|---|---|---|---|
| grind | saga | loose, be | legea |
| grow | kua | love | penda |
| | | lower | shusha |

**H**

**M**

| | | | |
|---|---|---|---|
| hang up | angika | | |
| hear | sikia | make | fanya |
| help | saidia | make mistake | kosa |
| herd | chunga | mature | iva |
| hide | ficha | measure | pima |
| hit | piga | meet with | kuta |
| hope | taraji | meet together | kutana |
| | tumaini | mimic | iga |
| hungry, feel | sikia njaa | move on | jongea |
| (feel thirsty | sikia kiu) | | |
| hunt | winda | **N** | |
| hurt | uma | need | hitaji |
| | umiza | | |

**I**

**O**

| | | | |
|---|---|---|---|
| increase (tr.) | zidisha | open | fungua |
| increase (intr.) | zidi | order | amuru |
| imitate | iga | | |
| iron clothes | piga pasi | **P** | |

**J**

| | | | |
|---|---|---|---|
| | | pack up for a | funga safari |
| | | journey | |
| join | unga | paint | paka rangi |
| jump | ruka | pass | pita |
| | | pass, allow to | pisha |
| **K** | | pay | lipa |
| | | paid, be | lipwa |
| kill | ua | perform | tenda |
| killed, be | uawa | pick up | okota |
| knit | fuma | pierce | toboa |
| know | jua | | choma |
| | | pierced, be | toboka |
| **L** | | place | weka |
| late, be | chelewa | place on head | twika |
| lend | kopesha, azima | plant | panda |
| lie down | lala | play | cheza |
| lift up | inua | play football | cheza mpira |
| light (fire or | washa | play piano | piga kinanda |
| lamp) | | please | pendeza |
| like | penda | pour out | mwaga |
| listen | sikiza | print | piga chapa |
| listen attentively | sikiliza | procurable, be | patikana |
| live | ishi | progress | endelea |
| load up | pakia | pull | vuta |
| look at | angalia | push | sukuma |
| looked at, be | angaliwa | put | tia |

| | | | |
|---|---|---|---|
| put, be | tiwa | smell (tr.) | nusa |
| put away | weka | smell (intr.) | nuka |
| put in order | panga | smoked, become | ingia moshi |
| put in place | weka | sold, be | uzwa |
| put on clothes | vaa | sorry, be | sikitika |
| put out (fire or lamp) | zima | spilt, be | mwagika |
| | | spit | tema mate |
| | | split | pasua |
| **Q** | | split, be | pasuka |
| quarrel | gombana | spoil | haribu |
| | | spoilt, be | haribika |
| **R** | | spread (intr.) | enea |
| read | soma | spread on | paka |
| receive | pokea | squeeze | kama |
| reckon | hesabu | stand | simama |
| | hasibu | stay | kaa |
| refuse | kataa | steal | iba |
| remain | kaa | step aside | epa |
| remember | kumbuka | sting | uma |
| remove | ondoa | stone | piga mawe |
| remove from | hama | stoop | inama |
| remove to | hamia | stop up | ziba |
| required, be | takikana | straight, become | nyoka |
| | takiwa | strike | piga |
| rest | pumzika | stumble | kwaa |
| return | rudi, rejea | swear a formal oath | apa kiapo |
| ripen | iva | | |
| rise (of sun) | cha | sweep | fagia |
| rusty, become | ingia kutu | | |
| | | **T** | |
| **S** | | take a holiday | pumzika |
| satiated, be | shiba | take care | angalia |
| save | okoa | take off, take away | ondoa |
| say | sema | | |
| scorn | dharau | take to oneself | twaa |
| search for | tafuta | talk about | simulia |
| see | ona | tangle | tata |
| sell | uza | teach | funza |
| send | peleka | | fundisha |
| send back | rudisha | teach one another | funzana |
| set trap | tega | | |
| set (of sun) | chwa | tell | ambia |
| sew | shona | told, be | ambiwa |
| shut | funga | thirsty, be | sikia kiu |
| silent, remain | kaa kimya | throw | tupa |
| sing | imba | tired, be | choka |
| sit down | kaa kitako | translate | fasiri |
| sleep | lala | trapped, be | naswa |

| | | | |
|---|---|---|---|
| tread | kanyaga | **used, be** | tumiwa |
| trim | tengeneza | | tumika |
| try | jaribu | | |

**V**

**U**

| | | | |
|---|---|---|---|
| | | **visible, be** | onekana |
| understand | fahamu | | |
| undone, become | funguka | **W** | |
| undress | vua | **wait** | ngoja |
| unfasten | fungua | **want** | taka |
| unload | pakua | **wash clothes** | fua nguo |
| unpick | fumua | **well, get** | pona |
| untidy, be | chafuka | **whitewashed, be** | pakwa chokaa |
| use | tumia | **wonder** | staajabu |
| use, be of | faa | **write** | andika |

# ADDITIONAL PASSAGES FOR READING AND TRANSLATION

The first five passages are elementary exercises on concordial agreement. The remaining seven, dealing with everyday Swahili life, give the student the opportunity for free translation of colloquial speech. A dictionary is necessary here, for no key is given, nor do all the words appear in the vocabulary.

## I

A. Hamisi!
B. Sa!
A. Lete vikombe na visahani na vijiko na visu.
B. Nilete vikombe vingapi Bwana?
A. Lete vikombe vitatu, visahani viwili na vijiko vine.
B. Nilete vikombe namna gani?
A. Lete vikubwa viwili na kimoja kidogo.
B. Vile vikubwa vyeupe vimevunjika Bwana.
A. Vimevunjika vyote?
B. Vyote Bwana.
A. Basi lete vingine.
B. Nilete vile vyekundu?
A. Vilete.
B. Hivi hapa Bwana, nimevileta.
A. Kwa nini umeleta visu navyo si vyangu?
B. Kweli Bwana si vyako, labuda ni vya Bwana Mgeni.
A. Basi usilete vitu vya watu.  Haifai.  Nenda kalete vile vyangu.
B. Vyema Bwana.
A. Lete na kiti.
B. Kiti kipi Bwana?  Hiki?
A. La, si hiki, lete kile cha juu.

Bwana amemwambia Hamisi alete nini?
Bwana amemwambia Hamisi alete vikombe, visahani, vijiko na visu.

Hamisi ameambiwa alete vikombe namna gani?
Vikombe vikubwa na vidogo.
Vikombe vikubwa vingapi?
Vikombe vikubwa viwili na kidogo kimoja.
Vikombe vyeupe vikubwa vimevunjika vingapi?
Vyote vimevunjika.
Hamisi ameambiwa alete vikombe vingine namna gani?
Ameambiwa alete vikombe vyekundu.
Kwa nini Hamisi asilete vile visu?
Kwa sababu si vya Bwana. Vya watu.
Ameambiwa alete na nini tena?
Ameambiwa alete na kiti.
Kiti kipi?
Kiti cha juu.

## II

A. Mchukuzi! Njoo uchukue mizigo hii.
B. Vyema; naona kama mizigo ya mgeni hii.
A. Ndiyo, mwenyewe amefika sasa hivi kutoka Ulaya.
B. Mizigo hii ni yote?
A. La, si yote, mingine iko kule.
B. Wapi?
A. Pale karibu na mlango.
B. Niilete yote?
A. Huwezi kuileta yote mara moja, kwa sababu mingi mizito
   na mingine mikubwa.
B. Mizigo yenyewe mingi sana?
A. Si haba, lakini huwezi kuichukua mmoja mmoja, uta-
   kawia sana, bora utafute wenzio.
B. Wenzangu tayari.
A. Vizuri kaeni tayari, mningoje, msiondoke bila ya amri
   yangu.
B. Vyema.

Mchukuzi anaitiwa nini?
Anaitiwa kuchukua mizigo.
Mchukuzi anaona mizigo ile ya nani?

Anaona kama mizigo ile ya mgeni.

Mwenye mizigo amefika lini kutoka Ulaya?

Amefika sasa hivi.

Mizigo mingine iko wapi?

Mingine iko kule.

Kule wapi?

Pale karibu na mlango.

Mchukuzi ailete yote?

Hawezi kuileta yote mara moja.

Kwa nini?

Kwa sababu mingi mizito, na mingine mikubwa.

Mizigo yenyewe haba?

Si haba wala si mingi sana.

Kwa nini mchukuzi hawezi kuichukua mmoja mmoja?

Kwa sababu atakawia sana.

Basi bora afanye nini?

Bora atafute wenziwe.

Wachukuzi wasiondoke mpaka lini?

Mpaka wapate amri.

## III

A. Ulinunua vitu gani jana Bwana Ali?

B. Nilinunua majembe na mashoka na magunia.

A. Jembe lako la mwaka jana liko wapi?

B. Limeibiwa zamani.

A. Yako wapi mashoka yako?

B. Yako ndani ya pakacha karibu na matofali.

A. Umeyanunua kwa kiasi gani?

B. Nimeyapata rahisi sana.

A. Utaniuzia shoka moja na jembe moja, hili dogo?

B. La, siwezi, mashoka yangu machache sana, nami nayataka yote kwa kazi.

A. Majembe yepi ya kuchimbia mashimo?

B. Majembe haya mapana.

A. Haya majembe madogo ya nini?

B. Ya kupalilia makonde.

A. Magunia je, ya nini wakati huu?

B. Nimeyanunua mapema yasije kupanda bei.

Bwana Ali alinunua vitu gani jana?
Alinunua majembe na mashoka na magunia.
Jembe lake la mwaka jana liko wapi?
Limeibiwa zamani.
Mashoka yake yako wapi?
Yamo ndani ya pakacha, karibu na matofali.
Aliyanunua kwa kiasi gani?
Aliyapata kwa bei rahisi sana.
Kwa nini hataki kuuza mashoka au majembe yake?
Kwa sababu mashoka yake machache sana, naye anayahi-
    tajia yote kwa kazi.
Majembe yepi ya kuchimbia mashimo?
Majembe yale mapana.
Nini kazi ya madogo?
Kupalilia makonde.
Kwa nini alinunua magunia wakati ule?
Kwa sababu aliogopa yasije kupanda bei.


# IV

Karibu Bwana, kila kitu tayari. Tazama nazi nzuri hizi;
    zimefika sasa hivi kutoka shamba. Nyanya zile zitampe-
    ndeza Bibi, sina shaka, kwa sababu za leo, tena kubwa.
Nimezipanga mbali na za jana. Embe[1] hazikufika bado.
Nataraji kuzipata alasiri. Nimekuwekea ndizi—fahari ya
    ndizi. Ukiziona utazitamani. Zitazame Bwana. Wazio-
    naje? Utastaajabu Bwana, ukisikia nyumba zinazoagiza
    vitu kwangu. Kila utakacho kwangu tayari, toka kuku,
    nyama ya mbuzi na ng'ombe, hata mbata na karafuu.
Ndugu zangu vile vile wa tayari kwa vitu kama ngozi za
    simba, za chui, pembe za tembo, hata zana za kuvulia na
    kuwindia, kama vile bunduki, risasi, na ndoana.


Mwenye duka anamtaka Bwana atazame vitu gani?
Anamtaka atazame nazi na nyanya.
Nazi hizi zimetoka wapi?
Zimetoka shamba.
Zimefika lini?

[1] Also in the JI- MA- Classe.

Zimefika sasa hivi.

Kwa nini nyanya hizi zitampendeza Bibi?

Kwa sababu ni kubwa.

Mwenye duka amezipanga mbali na nini?

Amezipanga mbali na zile za jana.

Mwenye duka anazisifu sifa gani ndizi zake?

Anasema ndizi hizi ni fahari ya ndizi.

Maana yake nini "fahari ya ndizi"?

Ubora wake haupitiki.

Nyumba ngapi huagiza vitu dukani?

Nyumba nyingi.

Tena duka hili huuza vitu gani?

Vitu kama kuku, nyama ya mbuzi, na ya ng'ombe, hata m-
bata na karafuu.

Je, hawa nduguze nao huuza vitu gani?

Kila kitu toka zana za kuvulia hata zana za kuwindia.

## V

A. Yule Mzungu mgeni aliyefika usiku amepoteza miwani
karibu na hapa.

B. Miwani namna gani?

A. Nyeusi ya jua. Asema kuwa atakayeiona atampa shilingi
kumi kiokosi chake.

B. Miwani hii lazima iwe ghali sana.

A. Ndiyo, anasema kuwa aliinunua katika duka maarufu
huko Ulaya.

B. Duka hilo linauza vitu kama hivi tu, yaani miwani tu?

A. Sijui, watu wakishughulika hawana wasaa wa kuuliza
mengi. Lakini najua maduka ya Ulaya yanauza vitu
vingi toka vidogo hata vikubwa, kama vile ndoana za
wavuvi, mavazi ya watoto, ya wanawake na waume,
wakubwa na wadogo.

B. Miwani hii imo ndani ya kisanduku chake?

A. La, mkakasi wake anao mwenyewe.

Huyu mgeni alifika lini?

Alifika usiku.

Amepoteza nini?

Amepoteza miwani yake.

Miwani namna gani?

Miwani nyeusi ya jua.

Amesema nini juu ya hiyo miwani yake?

Amesema atampa mtu atakayeiona kiokosi chake.

Kiokosi chenyewe kiasi gani?

Shilingi kumi.

Miwani hii alinunua wapi?

Aliinunua katika duka maarufu Ulaya.

Huko Ulaya vitu gani huuzwa katika maduka?

Vitu vya kila namna toka kitu kilicho kidogo sana hata viku-
    bwa sana.

Kama nini?

Mavazi ya watoto na ya watu wazima, ya wanawake na ya
    wanaume, hata vitu vilivyo vidogo sana, kama ndoana za
    wavuvi.

Miwani yake huyo Mzungu imo ndani ya kisanduku?

La, kisanduku chake anacho mwenyewe.


# VI

## STESHENI

A. Afisi ya habari i wapi?

B. Ile kule, Bwana.

A. Nataka kujua habari kidogo za reli za bara zitakazoo-
    ndoka kesho asubuhi baina ya saa 2 na saa 9, kwa
    hisani yako.

B. Vyema Bwana. Unataka kujua habari za reli za mizigo
    au za wasafiri?

A. Za wasafiri.

B. Ziko mbili, moja itaondoka saa 3 bara bara, na moja saa
    8 u nus.

A. Ahsante sana. Tikti hukatwa wapi?

B. Dirisha lile, Bwana, pale waliposimama watu.

A. Ahsante.

A. Nataka tikti fasklas kwenda Bara.

B. Tayari Bwana.

A. Mizigo yangu iko nje ndani ya lori.
B. Ukisema na wachukuzi wataitia ghalani mpaka kesho, wakati wa safari.
A. Reli nitakayoipanda, itaondoka wapi?
B. Upande huu uliosimama, nambari moja.
A. Ahsante sana.

*Siku ya pili yake.*

B. Reli utakayopanda ni hii Bwana.
A. Vyema, toeni mizigo yangu muipakie upesi, sitaki kuchelewa nikaachwa nyuma. Taratibu na mzigo huu, una vitu vya kuvunjika. Sasa bara bara, ujira wenu huu. Stuedi anaitwaje humu?
B. Bonyeza kengele hii.
A. Stuedi, nataka chai.
C. Vyema Bwana, utakunywa hapa katika chumba chako au katika restaurant?
A. Bora uniletee hapa mara hii. Chakula cha usiku saa ngapi?
C. Utasikia kengele hapa, kila kikiwa chakula tayari, stuedi hupita akiliza kengele kuarifu wote watakao kula.
A. Vitu gani vinapatikana kununuliwa relini?
C. Karibu kila kipatikanacho mjini, toka vyakula mpaka vinywaji.
A. Mnatoa bei ya vitu vyenu?
C. Naam, ukija katika restaurant utajua kila utakachokila, la, hutaki, hata mimi naweza kukuletea orodha ya vitu na bei zake.

# VII

## KORTINI

A. Juma bin Hasan!
B. Naam!
A. Kamata msahafu huu. Sasa sema "Wallahi nitasema kweli".
B. Wallahi nitasema kweli.

A. Umeshitakiwa kuwa jana umelewa, na mnamo saa kumi na mbili ya jioni ulifanya ghasia, ukaudhi watu na mwishowe ukampiga askari. Unakiri makosa yako au hukiri?

B. Nitakiri niliyoyafanya, nitakataa nisiyoyafanya. Kulewa sikatai, kweli nililewa, lakini mengine uliyoyataja, 'a'a hasha! sikuyafanya miye.

A. Eleza yote uliyoyafanya.

B. Unasikia Bwana wangu, jana adhuhuri Mungu aliniruzuku mtumwa wake, neema nisiyoyataraji. Mdeni wangu aliyenikopa milele hata nikakata tamaa, alinitokea ghafla akanilipa mali yangu yote. Nilimshukuru Mola, nami nikakumbuka wanaonidai, nikafunga safari kwenda walipa. Huko nilikumbana na maafriti, na maafriti hawa walinialika ulevi. Niliporudi ulevini, nilisimama njiani, naimba. Mara huyu bwana askari akaniamuru ninyamaze. Kuimba haramu? Basi nilikataa kunyamaza, na nilipokataa, mara, Bwana wangu, huyu alinitia pingu na kunichukua stesheni.

A. Nadhani unasema uwongo wewe.

B. Bwana wangu we, nitasemaje uwongo nami nimekula kiapo?

A. Mashahidi wanasema kuwa ulisimama kati ya njia ukazungusha fimbo yako na kupigana na kivuli chako, hata watu wasiweze kupita kwa hofu ya kupigwa.

B. Mashahidi wale wote waongo, Bwana, kwa sababu nao vile vile wote walilewa jana. Kwa mintaraf ya kupigana na kivuli changu, mimi ni mtu wa heshima, Bwana, si paka au mwenda wazimu.

A. Unatozwa fain ya shilingi kumi au siku nne jela.

B. Hewallah Bwana wangu, sisi ndio wa kutii amri yako. Faini nimeikubali.

## VIII

## SKULINI

Watoto. Subalkheri, Bwana.

Mw. Subalkheri. Kaeni. Ubao umefutwa vibaya leo; mki-
futa kwa kitambaa cha maji, futeni vizuri, ubao usi-
we kama umepakwa chokaa. Toeni mabuku yenu ya
kwandikia, na kalamu mweke tayari. Mtoto mmoja
ende akalete ramani ya Afrika, chumba cha pili.

Wa. Chumba cha pili kitupu Bwana, watoto wanacheza drill
uwanjani.

Mw. Haidhuru, ingia uitungue ramani—juu yangu.

Wa. Ati, kweli Bwana, kengele ya mwisho, leo italia mapema?

Mw. Ndiyo, kwa sababu hedmasta anataka kusema na skuli
nzima, kabla ya watoto hawajatawanyika kwenda
makwao. Anataka kuwaambia habari za mtihani na
za kugawiwa zawadi.

Wa. Zawadi ngapi zitatolewa mwaka huu Bwana?

Mw. Kama desturi, za masomo, za mahudhurio, za adabu,
za mashindano ya mpira, na kukimbia, kuogelea na
za kazi ya bustani.

Wa. Nini habari za insha tulizoandika, ambazo tuliambiwa
zina zawadi?

Mw. Kweli hata hizi, siku hiyo hiyo mtayasikia haya yote
leo adhuhuri. Itakapolia kengele tu, monita, wapange
watoto nje ya chumba uwapeleke uwanjani kwa ni-
dhamu njema. Sitaki kusikia mtoto mmoja kuzu-
ngumza. Atakayesema andika jina lake katika buku
la kufunga uniletee nitie saini. Chaki ziko wapi?

Wa. Watoto wanazichukua Bwana, wanazificha mifukoni
na kuchorea milango ya watu.

Mw. Hamjui imekatazwa kufanya hivi? Ukimwona mtoto,
mlete kwangu. Nimefurahi kuwa wiki hii tena tuta-
pata zawadi ya mahudhurio. Tukiendelea namna hii
kila mwaka tutashinda.

## IX

## KAMBI YA WASKAUTI

Ali.  Ee amka baba! ulale kama umekufa!

Juma.  Wacha wenzio walale Bwana, niamke usiku wote huu
hata hakujapambazuka!

A.  Utaona wapi kuwa kumekucha nawe umejifunika
gubi gubi?

J.  Kwani kipenga kimelia?

A.  Leo yaje! Wenzio wote wamekwisha amka isipokuwa
wewe tu.

J.  Ah, taabu gani hii! umeniamsha ndio kwanza napata
usingizi mzuri, kucha sikulala uzuri.

A.  Kwa nini? Mbu?

J.  Ah! usingizi umenipaa tu.

A.  Eh, mtoto wacha uwongo wee. Aliyekuwa akikoroma
nalipokuwa nashika zamu, nani?

J.  Basi mtu kupotelewa na usingizi dakika mbili tatu
ndio kulala?

A.  Nazijua dakika zako mbili tatu wee. Ukiachiliwa una-
weza kulala moja kwa moja mpaka uote mvi.
Amka baba!

J.  Usinivutie blangeti yangu saa! Likichanika jee?

A.  Ntalishona, amka.

J.  Nirushie viatu vyangu basi. Sasa mswaki wangu uko
wapi? Kibanda hiki mtu haweki kitu, kila uwekacho
kinatupwa.

A.  Ule pale umeupachika paani.

J.  Nipachulie yakhe, kwa hisani yako.

A.  Ama uvivu wako umezidi kiasi. Utaondoka mwenyewe uupachue.

J.  Haya Bwana, mle wewe hafi nawe.

A.  Potelea mbali! Sasa utaniweka mpaka saa ngapi?
Tazama wenzetu wale wamerudi pwani. Watu wote
watakwisha kupiga mswaki, wakoge, sisi bado hata
kibandani, hatukutoka, tunapachua miswaki tu.

J.  Haya Bwana, twen' zetu, suruwali ya kuogea iko wapi?

# X

## OFISINI

Bwana. Boi!

Hamisi. Yesso.

Bw. Hukusafisha ofisi vizuri leo. Meza yangu ina vumbi jingi, na pete za watoto wa meza nyeusi, kama hazi-kuguswa, licha ya kusafishwa. Nakumbuka jana nali-kwambia ubadilishe nibu tena upeleke mto ule wa kiti uliotoboka ukashonwe, nawe hukufanya lolote. Kwa nini?

H. Niwie radhi sana Bwana, kwa sababu leo nimechelewa katika ofisi, kwa sababu watoto nyumbani wanaumwa.

Bw. M-m, leo haidhuru, lakini jaribu usifanye haya mara nyingine. Chukua barua hizi, peleka kwa karani. Hizi peleka kwa Bwana Mkubwa wa Polisi, ungojee majibu. Hii moja inakwenda ofisi ya Zaraa; haina majibu. Hii katika bahasha kubwa ni muhimu sana. Ipeleke posta uipimishe, tena uitie rejista ya meli ya kuruka. Inakwenda Ulaya. Tazama usiondoke posta bila ya risiti. Kabla hujaondoka, nunua tikti ya shilingi tano—nusu ya senti kumi kumi, na nusu ya senti tano tano.

H. Vyema Bwana.

Bw. Tena, kabla hujaondoka, mwambie karani mdogo alete vitu aje kuisafisha taipu.

H. Amekwisha isafisha Bwana. Jana alibakia ofisi ulipoo-ndoka, akamaliza kazi zake zote. Karatasi vile vile nilizipokea mimi, nikazitia kwenye mtoto wa meza wa chini kabisa, mkono wa kushoto.

Bw. Nzuri.

H. Boi mkubwa amesema kuwa mfereji mmoja umehari-bika, umelegea na maji, unamiminika tu.

Bw. Mwambie karani apige simu P.W. kwa fundi wa mife-reji, amwambie kuwa mimi nataka kusema naye. Kweli nini habari ya panka yangu ya mezani? Ime-rudi kutengenezwa au bado?

H.   Ililetwa moja jana asubuhi, lakini si yako, basi tuliire-
     jesha huko huko.
Bw.  Basi pitia ofisi ya taa uihimize.


## XI

## HOSPITALI

A. Jee Mzee Fundi, unaonaje hali yako leo?
B. Sijambo sana leo. Ninatumia dawa nzuri alizonipa daktari, moja ya kupakaa, na moja ya kunywa. Hasa hii
   ya kupakaa ni ajabu. Huipakaa pakaa kifua kizima cha
   mbele na cha nyuma, halafu nikajifunika guo zito nika-
   lala. Nikiamka, uzito na maumivu ya kifua yote yame-
   pungua.
A. Ama mimi, nami nashukuru kwa upande wangu; kidonda
   changu kilichonitaabisha dahari, kabla ya kuja hospitali, lakini toka kupata malhamu hii ninayoitumia sasa,
   kidonda kinakauka kama kidoa. Mtazame yule kijana aliyefungwa matambaa ya shingo. Unamwona?
   Kijana yule alikuwa heshi kuvimba shingo kwa ndani
   na kutoka usaha. Kumeza mate, masikini alikuwa hawezi, licha ya kula. Lakini tangu aliponukizwa dawa,
   madaktari wakayaondosha maribi yao huko shingoni
   mwake, taabu zote zimempungua. Alilazwa hospitali
   siku chache tu, halafu akapewa ruhusa. Sasa mzima.
   Amebakia kusukutua dawa tu nyumbani, na kutaza-
   mwa na daktari kila wiki mara moja. Leo njiani nali-
   kutana na mtu mmoja, mwele wa meno. Tukafuatana
   pamoja mpaka hapo, halafu tukapoteana. Sijui kenda
   wapi.
B. Ala! Hujui kuwa upande wa meno ni mbali. Tangu ku-
   panuka hospitali yetu, magonjwa yamegawiwa-gawiwa
   mbali mbali. Ama kung'olewa meno, siku hizi ni miu-
   jiza. Mtu hutiwa dawa ya kufa ganzi asihisi hata kidogo, anasitukia jino ng'ong'! tasani.
A. Naam, nimesikia. Huyu mtu aliyefuatana nami anataka
   kuziba pango za meno matatu, yasije yakaoza kabisa.
B. Naam, ajabu. Alhamdulillahi!

## XII

### MJINI

A. Nataka mtu wa kunitembeza mjini.

B. Mimi tayari, Bwana. Nitakutembeza mji mzima, uone kila ukitakacho.

A. Vyema, twende zetu, lakini kwa miguu, sitaki motakaa. Mnara ule wa nini?

B. Wa msikiti Bwana. Tukizunguka njia ile tutapita mlangoni, na ukiwa unapenda naweza kupata ruhusa ya kuingia ndani.

A. La, si sasa, labuda wakati wa kurudi. Yule mtu amechukua nini?

B. Yule ni mzegazega, kazi yake ni kuteka maji kisimani au ferejini na kuyauza majumbani. Lile gongo analoliweka begani kuchukulia madebe linaitwa "maarasi".

A. Maduka haya makubwa na mazuri sana.

B. Kweli Bwana, maduka ya matajiri haya, na wenyewe aghlabu ni Maselani au Madrasi, au Wahindi, nayo yanauza mazulia, hariri, vito vya kila namna, vitu vya pembe, mpingo na vingi vinginevyo.

A. Nani wale watu wawili?

B. Yule aliyevaa koti refu na winda ni Baniani, na yule aliyevaa kilemba na kanzu na jambia kiunoni ni Mwarabu.

A. Mtu huyu anataka nini?

B. Anataka uingie katika riksho yake uzungukie mjini.

A. Mwambie sitaki. Tazama mtu yule anapigia nini upatu?

B. Anataka kunadi jambo.

A. Anasemaje?

B. Ananadi mkutano wa Jumuiya moja leo usiku.

A. Unamwona mtu yule? Amechukua dele juu ya seredani ya moto, na mkono wa pili anagonga vikombe.

B. Yule ni mwuza kahawa.

A. Duka lile lina vitu vingi sana?

B. Naam, Bwana, maduka yetu mengi yanauza vitu namna kwa namna, matunda, mchele, viungo, nguo na vinginevyo.

# GENERAL INDEX

# STUDENT'S NOTES